W9-CZZ-546

# A Grammar for Biblical Hebrew

*Revised Edition*

*C. L. Seow*

*Abingdon Press*
*Nashville*

A Grammar for Biblical Hebrew, Revised Edition



Library of Congress Cataloging-in-Publication Data

Seow, C. L. (Choon-Leong)
A Grammar for Biblical Hebrew / C. L. Seow. – Rev. ed.
p. cm.
ISBN 0-687-15786-2 (cloth : alk. paper)
1. Hebrew language – Grammar. I. Title.
PJ4567.S424 1995
492.4'82421 – dc20 95-31784
CIP

Composition by Kelby Bowers, Compublishing, Cincinnati, Ohio.
United States of America.
This book is printed on acid-free paper.

99 00 01 02 03 04 05 — 10 9 8 7 6

# Contents

## Excursus F



## XV



## XVI



## XVII



## XVIII



## XIX



## XX

## XXIX



## XXX



## Appendix

# Preface

The purpose of the book is to teach Biblical Hebrew grammar through a combination of deductive and inductive methods. The general outline of the book is deductive; elements of grammar are presented systematically. Yet the approach adopted is inductive, inasmuch as it utilizes biblical texts in the examples and in the exercises. The student encounters a biblical text as early as in Lesson II and, by the end of the book, will have read something from every book of the Hebrew Bible, including several full chapters of prose and poetry.

A salient feature of the second edition of this grammar is its emphasis on the use of the Hebrew-English dictionary. In order to prepare for this task, some of the early lessons discuss in some detail the idiosyncrasies of the so-called "weak radicals," consonants that are susceptible to changes in certain environments. A thorough understanding of these radicals will make it much easier to learn the large number of forms that appear to be irregular; otherwise, these forms will simply have to be learned by rote. The purpose of the historical reconstructions of various forms, then, is not academic but pedagogical: it is to equip the student to work independently with the lexical tools as quickly as possible. Moreover, following Lesson V, there is an excursus on the use of the Hebrew-English dictionary, where the rules learned in Lessons IV and V are reviewed inductively. From this point on in the book, the student is expected and required to use the dictionary constantly. There is, therefore, no Hebrew-English glossary provided; the student is encouraged to use the dictionary whenever there is a need, for only through constant practice will one become comfortable with this important tool.

The major reading markers are introduced in Excursus B, following Lesson VI. Biblical texts cited after that excursus will include the markers. With the guidance of an instructor, the student should learn to read the texts out loud, discerning the meaningful units in each case. The instructor may, of course, want to supplement the information provided in this grammar, or emphasize certain of the markers.

The texts used to illustrate various grammatical points have been carefully chosen. In most instances, the vocabulary and forms in the examples should be familar to the student, thus giving one the opportunity to review. On the other hand, it is not necessary to know all the words in order to get the point illustrated by the example. In each case, the student should pay attention to the issue at hand, focusing on any italicized word or words in the illustration.

The emphasis from the beginning to the end of this book is on reading actual biblical texts. The student encounters Biblical Hebrew with all its peculiarities. One will not, therefore, have to move later on from the artificial language of an introductory textbook to the "real world" of the Hebrew Bible. Thus, this textbook endeavors to introduce the student not only to the grammar, but to the language of the Hebrew Bible. Ideally the student should have a teacher who serves as a knowledgeable guide and commentator, who points to the pitfalls and promises of reading the Bible in Hebrew.

This book is written primarily for my students. I write it to pass on the love and knowledge of Hebrew imparted to me by my teachers, particularly Professor Thomas O. Lambdin, whose influence on me is evident at every turn. In the writing of this edition, I am grateful for the many helpful suggestions and words of encouragement sent to me by colleagues who have used the first edition. In particular, I want to thank Gordon J. Hamilton, F. W. Dobbs-Allsopp, Richard E. Whitaker, Gerald Bilkes, and Leslie Traylor, all of whom read through some version of the manuscript and helped saved me from many errors. Richard Whitaker and Gregory Glover spent countless hours helping me sort through seemingly insurmountable computer problems. Jeffrey Rogers went beyond the call of duty and friendship in his editorial work. I remain, of course, solely responsible for the content of this book and whatever failings there remains. Finally I must also acknowledge the contribution of my wife, Lai-King, without whose support and understanding this book would never have been completed.

# Abbreviations

| | |
|---|---|
| abs. | absolute state |
| BDB | Brown, Driver, Briggs, *Lexicon* (see Excursus A) |
| *BHS* | *Biblia Hebraica Stuttgartensia* (see Excursus F) |
| C | consonant |
| Chron | Chronicles |
| cp | common plural |
| consec. | consecutive |
| cs | common singular |
| cs. | construct state |
| Dan | Daniel |
| Deut | Deuteronomy |
| du. | dual |
| Eccl | Ecclesiastes |
| Esth | Esther |
| Exod | Exodus |
| Ezek | Ezekiel |
| Ezr | Ezra |
| fd | feminine dual |
| fp, fp. | feminine plural |
| fs, fs. | feminine singular |
| Gen | Genesis |
| GKC | Gesenius-Kautzsch-Cowley, *Grammar* (see Excursus D) |
| Hab | Habakkuk |
| Hag | Haggai |
| Hi. | Hiphil |
| Hisht. | Hishtaphel |
| Hith. | Hithpael |
| Ho. | Hophal |
| Hos | Hosea |
| impf. | imperfect |

| | |
|---|---|
| impv. | imperative |
| inf. | infinitive |
| Isa | Isaiah |
| Jer | Jeremiah |
| Josh | Joshua |
| Judg | Judges |
| juss. | jussive |
| Kgs | Kings |
| Lam | Lamentations |
| Lev | Leviticus |
| Mal | Malachi |
| Mic | Micah |
| md | masculine dual |
| mp, mp. | masculine plural |
| ms, ms. | masculine singular |
| MT | Massoretic Text |
| Nah | Nahum |
| Neh | Nehemiah |
| Ni. | Niphal |
| Num | Numbers |
| Obad | Obadiah |
| perf. | perfect |
| Pi. | Piel |
| pl. | plural |
| Prov | Proverbs |
| Ps | Psalms |
| ptc. | participle |
| Pu. | Pual |
| Sam | Samuel |
| sfx. | suffix |
| sg. | singular |
| translit. | transliteration |
| v | verse |
| Zech | Zechariah |
| Zeph | Zephaniah |

# Lesson I

## 1. The Alphabet

The Hebrew alphabet consists only of consonants.

| *Sign* | *Name* | *Translit.* | *Classical pronunciation* | *Modern pronunciation*[1] |
|---|---|---|---|---|
| א | *ʾā́lep̄* | ʾ | see Note i below | |
| בּ | *bêṯ* | b | **b**, as in "**b**an" | |
| ב | | ḇ | **v**, as in "**v**an" | |
| גּ | *gîmel* | g | **g**, as in "**g**od" | |
| ג | | ḡ | **g**, as in "do**g**" | **g**, as in "**g**od" |
| דּ | *dā́leṯ* | d | **d**, as in "**d**ay" | |
| ד | | ḏ | **th**, as in "**th**ey" | **d**, as in "**d**ay" |
| ה | *hē* | h | **h**, as in "**h**ay" | |
| ו | *wāw* | w | **w**, as in "**w**ay" | **v**, as in "**v**an" |
| ז | *záyin* | z | **z**, as in "**Z**ion" | |
| ח | *ḥêṯ* | ḥ | **ch**, as in "Ba**ch**" | |
| ט | *ṭêṯ* | ṭ | **t**, as in "s**t**op" | **t**, as in "**t**ank" |
| י | *yôḏ* | y | **y**, as in "**y**et" | |
| כּ | *kap̄* | k | **k**, as in "**k**ing" | |
| כ ך | | ḵ | **ch**, as in "Ba**ch**" | |
| ל | *lā́meḏ* | l | **l**, as in "**l**ake" | |
| מ ם | *mêm* | m | **m**, as in "**m**oth" | |
| נ ן | *nûn* | n | **n**, as in "**n**eck" | |
| ס | *sā́meḵ* | s | **s**, as in "**s**ack" | |
| ע | *ʿáyin* | ʿ | see Note ii below | |
| פּ | *pe(h)* | p | **p**, as in "**p**at" | |
| פ ף | | p̄ | **f**, as in "**f**at" | |
| צ ץ | *ṣā́ḏe(h)* | ṣ | **ts**, as in "be**ts**" | |
| ק | *qôp̄* | q | **q**, as in "pla**q**ue" | **k**, as in "**k**ing" |
| ר | *rêš* | r | **r**, as in "**r**ash" | |
| שׂ | *śîn* | ś | **s**, as in "**s**een" | |
| שׁ | *šîn* | š | **sh**, as in "**sh**een" | |
| תּ | *tāw* | t | **t**, as in "**t**ank" | |
| ת | | ṯ | **th**, as in "**th**ank" | **t**, as in "**t**ank" |

1. Only pronunciations that differ from the classical are given.

*Notes:*

i. **א** is produced by a momentary stoppage of breath in the throat; it may be compared with the silent *h* in English (e.g., *an heir*).

ii. **ע** is like **א**, but has a slightly rougher sound. Most students of Hebrew do not distinguish **ע** from **א** in pronunciation, but one must take care never to confuse the two in spelling.

## 2. The Writing

**a.** Most of the letters fit within an imaginary square frame. Compare the relative sizes and shapes of the letters.

א ב ג ד ה ו ז ח ט י כ [ך] ל מ [ם] נ [ן] ס ע פ [ף] צ [ץ] ק ר שׂ שׁ ת

**b.** Hebrew is written from right to left, but the characters are represented in transliteration from left to right.

ישׂראל *yśrʾl*    יצחק *yṣḥq*    נחמיה *nḥmyh*

**c.** When a *kap̄*, *mêm*, *nûn*, *pe*(*h*), or *ṣā́ḏē*(*h*) occurs at the end of a word, it always takes the final form (ך, ם, ן, ף, ץ); when it occurs independently, or at the beginning or in the middle of a word, it has the "medial" form (כ, מ, נ, פ, צ). In transliteration, however, no distinction is made between medial and final forms.

כלך *klḵ*    מים *mym*    נתן *nṯn*    ציץ *ṣyṣ*

**d.** There are several letters that are easily confused with one another. One must take care to distinguish them both in reading and in writing.

| | | |
|---|---|---|
| ב b | כ ḵ | פ p̄ |
| ג ḡ | נ n | |
| ד ḏ | ר r | ך ḵ |
| ה h | ח ḥ | ת t |
| ו w | ז z | ן n |

| | |
|---|---|
| ך ḵ | ן n |
| ם m | ס s |
| צ ṣ | ע ʿ |
| שׂ ś | שׁ š |

## 3. The *Dāḡēš*

The *dāḡēš* is a dot put within a consonant, usually to indicate one of two things.

**a.** The consonant is a stop (articulated with a momentary stoppage of air, as in English *b* and *p*), not a spirant (articulated with the friction of air through the lips, as in English *v* and *f*). This rule applies only to the six consonants to be discussed in I.4 below.

**b.** The consonant is doubled (e.g., מּ = *mm*, נּ = *nn*, שּׁ = *šš*).

*Note*: When a *dāḡēš* indicates only a stop (as in a.), it is called *weak* (*dāḡēš lene*); when it indicates doubling (as in b.), it is called *strong* (*dāḡēš forte*).

## 4. The *Bĕḡaḏkĕp̄aṯ* Letters

**a.** The consonants *bêṯ*, *gîmel*, *dāleṯ*, *kap̄*, *pe*(*h*), and *tāw*, known as the *bĕḡaḏkĕp̄aṯ* letters, were originally each capable of two pronunciations: they could be stops or spirants. (As indicated in the chart in I.1, however, Modern Hebrew makes a distinction in pronunciation between the stops and the spirants only in *bêṯ*, *kap̄*, and *pe*[*h*].)

**Stops vs. Spirants**

| Stops | | | | Spirants | | | |
|---|---|---|---|---|---|---|---|
| *Voiced* | | *Unvoiced* | | *Voiced* | | *Unvoiced* | |
| בּ | b | | | ב | ḇ | | |
| גּ | g | | | ג | ḡ | | |
| דּ | d | | | ד | ḏ | | |
| | | כּ | k | | | כ, ך | ḵ |
| | | פּ | p | | | פ, ף | p̄ |
| | | תּ | t | | | ת | ṯ |

*Note*: A voiced consonant is one pronounced with a vibration of the vocal chords.

**b.** Only stops may be doubled; spirants are never doubled. Thus, ב may represent either *b* or *bb*, but never *ḇḇ*.

**c.** Since *bĕgadkĕpat* letters may be doubled when they are stops, a *dāgēš* within such a consonant may be weak (indicating only a stop, but not doubling) or strong (indicating a doubled stop). The rules for distinguishing the strong *dāgēš* from the weak will be given in II.8.

*Note*: A *dāgēš* within a non-*bĕgadkĕpat* letter is always strong.

## Exercise 1

**a.** Recite the alphabet from beginning to end and write it out in its proper order, including the final forms in parentheses.

**b.** Write the following in Hebrew:

| | | |
|---|---|---|
| 1. *yśrʾl* | 6. *np̄tly* | 11. *ṭwḇyhw* |
| 2. *yʿqḇ* | 7. *nṯn* | 12. *mlʾḵy* |
| 3. *mlkyṣḏq* | 8. *byṯ lḥm* | 13. *yḥzqʾl* |
| 4. *yrḇʿm* | 9. *ʾsp̄* | 14. *ḥgy* |
| 5. *ʾstr* | 10. *ʿmwṣ* | 15. *dwḏ* |

**c.** Transliterate the following:

| | | |
|---|---|---|
| 1. ירושלם | 6. שׁמואל | 11. זכריה |
| 2. אברהם | 7. אחימלך | 12. שׁמעון |
| 3. שׂרה | 8. ציון | 13. בּנימין |
| 4. יצחק | 9. צפון | 14. רבקה |
| 5. רחל | 10. חברון | 15. לבנון |

# Lesson II

## 1. Syllables

Each Hebrew word may have one syllable or more.

**a.** Every syllable begins with one, and only one, consonant. Hence, with only one exception (the conjunction *û*), a syllable cannot begin with a vowel: thus, *Pé/reṣ* (not *Pér/eṣ*).

**b.** Every syllable has one, and only one, vowel.

**c.** A syllable may end in a vowel or a consonant. When it ends in a vowel, it is said to be *open* (e.g., *Pé-*); when it ends in a consonant, it is said to be *closed* (e.g., *-reṣ*).

**d.** A syllable may be stressed (accented) or unstressed (unaccented).

## 2. The Simple Vowels

**a.** There are three classes of vowels in Hebrew: *a*, *i*, and *u*. In each class there are vowels that are short and vowels that are long. Short vowels have no special mark in transliteration; long vowels are marked by a horizontal stroke above the letter, known as a *macron*.

**b.** The following is a summary of the simple vowels. To indicate the relative position of the vowel points, we show them with the letter בּ. Our concern is with the vowels only, so בּ is not represented in transliteration.

## Long and Short Vowels

| *Class* | *Sign* | *Translit.* | *Name* | *Pronunciation* |
|---|---|---|---|---|
| a | בַ | a | *páṯaḥ* | a, as in “car” |
| | בָ | ā | *qā́meṣ* | a, as in “car” |
| | בֶ | e | *sĕḡōl* | e, as in “met” |
| i | בֵ | ē | *ṣērê* | e, as in “they” |
| | בִ | i / ī | *ḥī́req* | i, as in “unique” |
| | בָ | o | *qā́meṣ ḥāṭûp̄* | o, as in “loft” |
| u | בֻ | u / ū | *qibbûṣ* | u, as in “rule” |
| | בֹ | ō | *ḥṓlem* | o, as in “role” |

*Notes*:

i. The vowel sign is usually placed under the consonant and pronounced after it: אָדָם *ʾāḏām*, עֵנָב *ʿēnāḇ*.

ii. The *ḥṓlem* is the only vowel point that is placed above the consonant it follows – at the top left hand corner of that consonant: שֹׁפֵט *šōpēṭ*, קָטֹן *qāṭōn*.

iii. The *ḥṓlem* may be confused with the supralinear dot of the letters שׁ and שׂ. Indeed, in some printed texts a *ḥṓlem* immediately after שׁ may merge with the dot at the top left corner of that letter, so that only one dot appears. A *ḥṓlem* immediately before שׂ may also merge with the dot that marks that consonant.

יֹשֵׁב = יֹשֵׁב *yōšēḇ*     שֹׂנֵא = שֹׂנֵא *śōnēʾ*

iv. *Ḥī́req* and *qibbûṣ* may be short or long. The short is more common. One should assume that the vowel is short unless it is in an open syllable (e.g., דָּנִיאֵל *dā/nī/ʾēl*, תֻּבַל *tū/ḇal*) or if it is stressed (e.g., דָּוִד *dā/wiḏ*, עַמֻּד *ʿam/mūḏ*).

v. The rules for distinguishing between *qā́meṣ* (*ā*) and *qā́meṣ ḥāṭûp̄* (*o*) will be given later (see 9, below).

vi. A vowel that follows a final Kap̄ or Nûn will ordinarily appear to the left of that consonant: e.g., פָּנֶיךָ *pā/nê/ḵā*, תָּבֹאנָה *tā/ḇōʾ/nā*.

## 3. The *Matres Lectionis*

**a.** The alphabetic signs ה, ו, and י, in addition to their normal use as consonants, frequently function as markers of long vowels. When the signs are used this way, they are *not* consonants. Therefore, they are called *matres lectionis*, "mothers of reading" (singular: *mater lectionis*).

**b.** The following is a summary of long vowels marked by *matres*. Again, we show them with the letter בּ, but we are concerned here only with the vowels; the בּ is not represented in transliteration.

### Long Vowels with *Matres*

| *Class* | י*–mater* | ו*–mater* | ה*–mater* |
|---|---|---|---|
| a | | | בָּה ā(h) |
| i | בִּי î<br>בֶּי ê<br>בֵּי ê | | <br>בֶּה e(h)<br>בֵּה ē(h) |
| u | | בּוֹ ô<br>בּוּ û | בֹּה ō(h) |

*Notes*:

i. ו and י may be used as *matres* in the middle or at the end of a word, but ה may be a *mater* only at the end of a word.

ii. Vowels with *matres* are known by the names of the vowel plus the vowel marker: *ḥī́req-yōḏ* (ִי), *ḥṓlem-wāw* (וֹ), and so forth. Only וּ (*û*) has a distinctive name, *šū́req*.

iii. Some scholars transliterate all *matres* with the circumflex (ˆ). But this makes it difficult for the student to know if *ê* in any situation stands for ֶי, ֵי, ֶה, or ֵה, or if *ô* represents וֹ or הֹ. We will, therefore, transliterate the ה*-mater* as *h*, but keep it in parentheses to indicate that it is not to be taken as an actual consonant; all the other *matres* will be transliterated with the circumflex (*î*, *ê*, *ô*, etc.).

iv. Since ה at the end of a word may be taken as a *mater* or as an actual consonant, a dot (called the *mappîq*) is usually put in the ה when it is a consonant.

סוּסָהּ *sûsāh* (her horse)   סוּסָה *sûsā(h)* (mare)

## 4. Full and Defective Spellings

Long vowels in certain words are always or usually written with *matres*; but in other instances, long vowels are either rarely (or never) marked in this way. With experience one learns to expect the *mater* in certain words. When a word is written with a *mater*, it is said to have *full* spelling; when it is written without a *mater* (where one is expected), it is said to be *defective*. There is no distinction in meaning between the full spelling and the defective spelling.

| *Full* | *Defective* |
|---|---|
| דָּוִיד *dāwîd* | דָּוִד *dāwīd* (David) |
| כּוֹכָב *kôkāb* | כֹּכָב *kōkāb* (star) |
| שׁוּעָל *šûʿāl* | שֻׁעָל *šūʿāl* (fox) |

## 5. Stress

Every Hebrew word has a primary stress. In this book, primary stress on individual words (when indicated) is indicated by the sign ˂ over the stressed syllable of the word in Hebrew script; but in transliteration, stress is represented by ´: עֶ֫בֶד *ʿébed*.

**a.** The primary stress of an independent word usually falls on the ultima (last syllable). Less frequently, it falls on the penultima (next-to-last syllable). Since the ultima usually receives the stress, it will not be marked in this grammar; only syllables other than the ultima will be marked for stress.

דָּוִד *dā/wīḏ* (stress on ultima)

עֶ֫בֶד *ᶜéḇeḏ* (stress on penultima)

**b.** The stressed syllable is said to be *tonic*; the syllable immediately before the stress is *pretonic*, and the syllable before the pretonic syllable is *propretonic*.

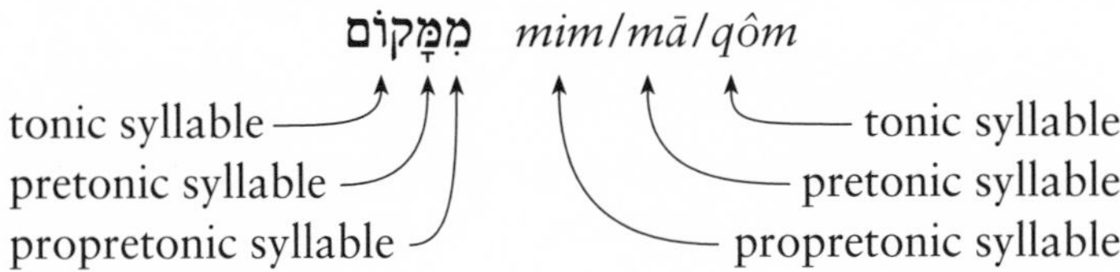


## 6. The *Šĕwā*ᵓ

The *šĕwā*ᵓ is the sign ְ placed under a consonant to indicate either a half vowel or no vowel at all. When it represents a half vowel, it is said to be *vocal*; when it represents nothing, it is said to be *silent*. The vocal *šĕwā*ᵓ sounds like the first vowel in the English word "careen." It is represented by *ĕ* in transliteration (e.g., בְּרִית *bĕrîṯ*). The silent *šĕwā*ᵓ has no phonetic value, and so is not represented in transliteration. It simply indicates the close of a syllable; it is present under every consonant that closes a syllable, except at the end of a word: יִשְׂרָאֵל *yiśrā*ᵓ*ēl*; עֶ֫בֶד *ᶜéḇeḏ*.

**a.** The ְ in a word is *vocal* in the following situations.

**i.** It is at the beginning of a word.

שְׁמוּאֵל *šĕmû*ᵓ*ēl* מְלָכִים *mĕlāḵîm*

**ii.** It is the second of two ְ in immediate succession.

יִשְׁמְרוּ *yišmĕrû* מִזְבְּחִי *mizbĕḥî*

**iii.** It comes immediately after a consonant with a strong *dāgēš*.

דִּבְּרוּ *dibbĕrû* הַכְּלִי *hakkĕlî*

**iv.** It comes immediately after a long vowel.

שֹׁפְטִים *šōpĕṭîm* יֵלְכוּ *yēlĕḵû*

**b.** The ְ in a word is *silent* in the following situations.

**i.** It is at the end of a word, even if it is the second of two ְ immediate succession.

תֵּשְׁתְּ *tēšt* יָלַדְתְּ *yāladt*

*Note*: The *šĕwāʾ* in the final position is actually quite exceptional.[1] It occurs only in the rare instance when a word ends in two consonants.

**ii.** It is the first of two ְ in immediate succession.

יִשְׁמְרוּ *yišmĕrû* מִזְבְּחִי *mizbĕḥî*

**iii.** It comes immediately after a short unstressed vowel.[2]

מַלְאָךְ *malʾāḵ* מֶרְכָּבָה *merkāḇā(h)*

**iv.** It comes immediately after a stressed syllable.

לֵ֫כְנָה *lḗḵnā(h)* נֶ֫גְבָּה *négbāh*

## 7. The Composite *Šĕwāʾ*'s

**a.** The consonants א, ה, ח, and ע are called *gutturals* because they are generally pronounced in the throat (Latin *guttur*). Due to the way they sound, gutturals do not take the simple vocal *šĕwāʾ*. Instead, they prefer one of the *composite šĕwāʾ*'s.[3]

**b.** Like the majority of vowels, composite *šĕwāʾ*'s appear under the consonants. The consonant ח is used below as a reminder that composite *šĕwāʾ*'s usually appear under gutturals.

1. With very few exceptions, the final consonant of a word does not receive the silent *šĕwāʾ*. Final Kap̄ (except for ךְ-), however, is normally written as ךְ, e. g., מַלְאָךְ, מֶ֫לֶךְ.

2. Under the first of two *identical* consonants, however, the ְ is always vocal: הַלְלוּ *halĕlû* (not *hallû*).

3. This does not mean that composite *šĕwāʾ*'s occur only with gutturals; occasionally they may also occur with other consonants.

| *Sign* | *Translit.* | *Name* | *Pronunciation* |
|---|---|---|---|
| חֲ | *ă* | *ḥấṭep̄-páṯaḥ* | same as *páṯaḥ* |
| חֱ | *ĕ* | *ḥấṭep̄-sĕḡôl* | same as *sĕḡôl* |
| חֳ | *ŏ* | *ḥấṭep̄-qấmeṣ* | same as *qấmeṣ-ḥāṭûp̄* |

**c.** Although a silent ְ may occasionally appear with a guttural (e.g., מַעְיָן *spring*), a composite *šĕwāʾ* is far more common (e.g., יַעֲקֹב *Jacob*). The composite *šĕwāʾ* is always pronounced, but rule 6.b.iii above suggests that we are to take the composite *šĕwāʾ* after a short unstressed vowel as closing the syllable and, for the purpose of syllable division, technically silent. Thus, owing to the nature of gutturals, יַעֲקֹב is pronounced with an additional ă sound, but we should analyze the word as having two syllables.

*yaᶜ(ă)/qōḇ*, not *ya/ᶜă/qōḇ*

*Note*: In this book, the technically silent composite *šĕwāʾ* will be indicated in parentheses.

**d.** Infrequently, a composite *šĕwāʾ* may also appear with a non-guttural consonant – especially Rêš – instead of a simple vocal *šĕwāʾ*.

בָּרֲכוּ *bārăḵû* (instead of בָּרְכוּ *bārĕḵû*)

## 8. Stops vs. Spirants

In addition to the rules given in I.4, note the following.

**a.** If a *bĕgaḏkĕp̄aṯ* letter is in the initial position of a word, it will be a stop (e.g., כֹּהֵן *kōhēn*), unless the preceding word ends in a vowel (e.g., לִפְנֵי כֹהֵן *lip̄nê ḵōhēn*).

**b.** If a *bĕgaḏkĕp̄aṯ* letter is in the final position of a word, it will ordinarily be a spirant (טוֹב *ṭôḇ*), except in the rare instance when it is doubled (אַתְּ *ʾatt*).

**c.** If a *bĕgaḏkĕp̄aṯ* letter is immediately preceded by a vowel, it will be a spirant (לֵבָב *lēḇāḇ*), unless it is doubled (לִבּוֹ *libbô*).

**d.** If a *bĕgaḏkĕp̄aṯ* letter is immediately preceded by a consonant, it will normally (but not always) be a stop (מִשְׁכָּן *miškān*).

## 9. The *Qā́meṣ Ḥāṭûp̄*

As already mentioned in 2.b.v above, ָ may be either *qā́meṣ* (*ā*) or *qā́meṣ ḥāṭûp̄* (*o*).

**a.** In a closed, unaccented syllable, ָ is almost always *o*.

**b.** Before ֳ, the ָ sign is always *o*.

**c.** If the small vertical stroke called the *mé̱teg* (bridle) appears with the ָ, the vowel is always *ā*.

| | |
|---|---|
| שָׁמְרָה *šomrā*(*h*) keep! | שָֽׁמְרָה *šāmĕrā*(*h*) she kept |
| חָכְמָה *ḥok̲mā*(*h*) wisdom | חָֽכְמָה *ḥāk̲ĕmā*(*h*) she is wise |
| בָּאֳהָלִים *boʾ*(*ŏ*)*hālîm* in tents | בָּֽאָרֶץ *bāʾáreṣ* on the earth |

## 10. The Furtive *Páṯaḥ*

When a word ends in הּ, ח, or ע, an additional *páṯaḥ* appears under the guttural, if the word does not already end in an *a*-class vowel. This *furtive páṯaḥ* is pronounced before the final guttural, although it is written under that guttural, and in most editions of the Hebrew Bible, slightly to the right of center: רוּחַ (wind, spirit). In transliteration, the furtive *páṯaḥ* is most frequently indicated by a raised letter *a*, but in this book it will be indicated by the letter *a* in parentheses *before* the guttural.

| | |
|---|---|
| גָּבוֹהַּ *gāḇô*(*a*)*h* tall | רוּחַ *rû*(*a*)*ḥ* spirit, wind |

The furtive *páṭaḥ* is not considered a vowel, not counted as a syllable, and not stressed; it is understood that the stress is on the vowel before the furtive *páṭaḥ*. Thus, גָּבוֹהַּ is considered to have two syllables, while רוּחַ has one.

## 11. The Quiescent ʾÁlep̄

Whenever א closes a syllable it is not vocalized, even though the Hebrew character is written in the text. The silent *šĕwāʾ* never appears under the א in such a case. In transliteration we represent this *quiescent ʾālep̄* in parentheses: לֵאלֹהִים *lē(ʾ)lōhîm* (to/for God).

## 12. Syllabification

Given the rules learned so far, one may conclude that the following combinations (where C represents any consonant and v represents any vowel) are theoretically possible.

| | *Unstressed* | *Stressed* |
|---|---|---|
| *Open* | Cv̆ | |
| | [Cv] | Cv́ |
| | Cv̄ / Cv̂ | Cv̄́ / Cv̂́ |
| *Closed* | CvC | Cv́C |
| | [Cv̄C / Cv̂C] | Cv̄́C / Cv̂́C |

*Notes*:

i. The parentheses in the chart above indicate that Cv unstressed and Cv̄C/ Cv̂C unstressed syllables are in fact exceptional. For now the student should assume that they are unacceptable or must be explained in some way.

ii. The conjunction וּ (û) is an exception to the rules inasmuch as it is not preceded by a consonant (see 1.b).

וּשְׁמוּאֵל *û/šĕ/mû/ʾēl* (and Samuel)

Study the following examples carefully, paying attention to the proper division of syllables.

| | | | | | |
|---|---|---|---|---|---|
| דָּבָר | *dā/ḇār* | מֶרְחָק | *mer/ḥāq* | מְדַבֵּר | *mĕ/ḏab/bēr* |
| מֶ֫לֶךְ | *mé/leḵ* | אָכְלָה | *ʾoḵ/lā(h)* | כְּרֻבִים | *kĕ/rū/ḇîm* |
| שֹׁפֵט | *šō/p̄ēṭ* | מִשְׁכָּן | *miš/kān* | מְלָכִים | *mĕ/lā/ḵîm* |
| עָנְיִי | *ʿon/yî* | יִשְׂרָאֵל | *yiś/rā/ʾēl* | בֵּאלֹהִים | *bē(ʾ)/lō/hîm* |
| תּוֹרָה | *tô/rā(h)* | נָעֳמִי | *noʿ(ŏ)/mî* | מְשַׁלֵּחַ | *mĕ/šal/lē(a)ḥ* |
| פִּ֫יהוּ | *pî́/hû* | וַיְהִי | *way/hî* | מַחֲנֶה | *maḥ(ă)/ne(h)* |

*Note*: When a strong *dāḡēš* is found within a word, that *dāḡēš* indicates a syllable division.

## Vocabulary

*Nouns*

אָדָם human, humanity, people, person, Adam (the first human)

אֲדָמָה ground, land, soil

בְּרִית covenant, treaty, alliance

גּוֹי nation

דָּבָר word, thing, affair, matter

דַּ֫עַת knowledge

זָהָב gold

חֹ֫דֶשׁ new moon, month. *Adjective*: חָדָשׁ new

חָכְמָה wisdom. *Adjective*: חָכָם wise

כֹּהֵן priest

כֶּ֫סֶף silver, money

מֶ֫לֶךְ king. מַמְלָכָה kingdom. מַלְכוּת kingship, reign. *Verb*: מָלַךְ to reign, rule

נָבִיא prophet

עֶ֫בֶד servant, slave. עֲבוֹדָה service, work. *Verb*: עָבַד to serve, work, till, worship

עוֹלָם eternity, perpetuity

צֶ֫דֶק (also צְדָקָה) righteousness. *Adjective*: צַדִּיק righteous

קֹ֫דֶשׁ holiness, sanctuary (holy place). *Adjective*: קָדוֹשׁ holy

קוֹל voice, sound, thundering

## Exercise 2

**a.** Write the following in Hebrew:

1. *ʾiššā(h)*
2. *ḥokmā(h)*
3. *šēmôt*
4. *tĕhillîm*
5. *gābô(a)h*
6. *ʾîšāh*
7. *yĕhûdā(h)*
8. *ʾah(ă)rōn*
9. *liwyātān*
10. *śĕdē(h)*
11. *mizbē(a)ḥ*
12. *maʾ(ă)kāl*
13. *kĕrūbîm*
14. *malʾākî*
15. *boʿ(ŏ)nî*

**b.** Transliterate and translate the following:

1. אֲדָמָה
2. חָדָשׁ
3. בְּרִית
4. עוֹלָם
5. כֶּ֫סֶף
6. נָבִיא
7. כֹּהֵן
8. חֹ֫דֶשׁ
9. דָּבָר
10. קוֹל
11. זָהָב
12. גּוֹי

**c.** Transliterate the following passage. Divide the words into syllables and read the passage out loud. Then pick out the words (including proper names) that you recognize, and translate them.

מִשְׁלֵי שְׁלֹמֹה בֶן־דָּוִד[4] מֶ֫לֶךְ יִשְׂרָאֵל

לָדַ֫עַת חָכְמָה וּמוּסָר לְהָבִין אִמְרֵי בִינָה

לָקַ֫חַת מוּסַר הַשְׂכֵּל צֶ֫דֶק וּמִשְׁפָּט וּמֵישָׁרִים

לָתֵת לִפְתָאִים עָרְמָה לְנַ֫עַר דַּ֫עַת וּמְזִמָּה (Prov 1:1–4)

---

4. The horizontal stroke (called a *maqqēp̄*) simply means that the two words are read together – pronounced as if they constituted one word.

# Lesson III

## 1. The Noun: Gender and Number

Hebrew nouns may be masculine or feminine in gender; and they may be singular, dual, or plural in number. Except for the masculine singular (ms) form, the gender and number of each noun are generally marked by distinctive endings.

| | *Masculine* | *Feminine* |
|---|---|---|
| *Singular* | no ending | ָה– or ת– |
| *Dual* | ַ֫יִם– | ַ֫יִם– |
| *Plural* | ִים– | וֹת– |

**a.** Masculine singular (ms) nouns have no special endings.

סוּס horse מֶ֫לֶךְ king

**b.** Feminine singular (fs) nouns have either ָה– or ת– endings.

**i.** Feminine nouns with the ָה– ending are always stressed on the ultima.

סוּסָה mare מַלְכָּה queen

**ii.** Feminine nouns with וּת– or ִית– endings are also stressed on the ultima.

בְּרִית covenant אַלְמָנוּת widowhood

**iii.** Feminine nouns with the ֶת– ending are stressed on the penultima.

קְטֹ֫רֶת incense מִשְׁמֶ֫רֶת obligation

**iv.** Feminine nouns with the ַת– ending may be monosyllabic, or, if they have more than one syllable, stressed on the penultima.

בַּת daughter דַּ֫עַת knowledge

**v.** Some feminine nouns are not marked as feminine. These are irregular and will be noted as such in the Vocabulary.

אֵם mother אֶ֫רֶץ earth, land

*Note*: Parts of the body that come in pairs are almost always feminine (e.g., רֶ֫גֶל foot; יָד hand).

**c.** Masculine plural (mp) nouns are normally marked by the ending ִים–.

| | | | |
|---|---|---|---|
| *ms* | סוּס horse | *mp* | סוּסִים horses |

**d.** Feminine plural (fp) nouns are normally marked by the ending וֹת–. The וֹת– ending takes the place of the fs ending.

| | | | |
|---|---|---|---|
| *fs* | תּוֹרָה law | *fp* | תּוֹרוֹת laws |
| *fs* | מִשְׁמֶ֫רֶת obligation | *fp* | מִשְׁמָרוֹת obligations |

Feminine nouns which are unmarked for gender in the singular are usually marked for gender in the plural.

| | | | |
|---|---|---|---|
| *fs* | אֶ֫רֶץ land | *fp* | אֲרָצוֹת lands |
| *fs* | יָד hand | *fp* | יָדוֹת hands |

**e.** The dual (md; fd) is marked by the ending ַ֫יִם– (from original **–aym*).[1]

| | | | |
|---|---|---|---|
| *ms* | יוֹם a day | *md* | יוֹמַ֫יִם two days |

Before the dual ending, the feminine ending ָה– changes to ָת–, and certain internal vowel changes may take place (see 2.a below).

1. An asterisk (*) before a form indicates that the form is hypothetical – it is reconstructed from what we know of the history of the language.

| | |
|---|---|
| *fs* שָׁנָה a year | *fd* שְׁנָתַ֫יִם two years |

Not every noun has the dual form. Indeed, the dual is restricted to the following.

**i.** Nouns that come in natural pairs.

יָדַ֫יִם two hands　　　רַגְלַ֫יִם two feet

**ii.** Certain expressions of time.

יוֹמַ֫יִם two days　　　פַּעֲמַ֫יִם twice

**iii.** Measures of two.

שְׁנַ֫יִם two　　　מָאתַ֫יִם two hundred

A few nouns that have no clear relation to the dual number are, nevertheless, marked as duals.

מַ֫יִם water　　　שָׁמַ֫יִם heaven

This is true of many geographical names.

יְרוּשָׁלַ֫ם[2] Jerusalem　　　מִצְרַ֫יִם Egypt

**f.** Some singular nouns may be used collectively.

עוֹף bird *or* birds　　　בְּהֵמָה beast *or* beasts

**g.** A few nouns may be plural in form but have singular meanings.

אֱלֹהִים god / God *or* gods　　　אֲדוֹנִים lord *or* lords

## 2. Changes in Nouns with Endings

The addition of an ending may cause certain changes in the form of the noun.

**a.** Vowel Reduction

The addition of an ending and the resultant shift of the stress

---

2. The name is attested five times as יְרוּשָׁלַ֫יִם, but most often it appears as יְרוּשָׁלַ֫ם, (see Excursus F.2).

from the old ultima to the new one (the ending), may cause certain vowels to be reduced to a *šĕwāʾ*.

**i.** In the propretonic open syllable, *ā* ( ָ ) or *ē* ( ֵ ) reduces to *šĕwāʾ*.

| | | | |
|---|---|---|---|
| נָבִיא | prophet | נְבִיאָה | prophetess |
| | | נְבִיאִים | prophets |
| לֵבָב | heart | לְבָבוֹת | hearts |

Gutturals, of course, prefer the composite *šĕwāʾ*, usually *ă* ( ֲ ).

| | | | |
|---|---|---|---|
| חָכָם | wise man | חֲכָמִים | wise men |
| עֵנָב | grape | עֲנָבִים | grapes |

**ii.** If there is no reduction in the propretonic syllable, *ē* ( ֵ ) in a pretonic open syllable is reduced to *šĕwāʾ*.

| | | | |
|---|---|---|---|
| שֹׁפֵט | judge | שֹׁפְטִים | judges |
| מוֹעֵד | assembly | מוֹעֲדִים | assemblies |

*Note*: *ā* ( ָ ) in a pretonic position is not reduced; only *ē* ( ֵ ) is reduced.

| | | | |
|---|---|---|---|
| מִשְׁפָּט | judgment | מִשְׁפָּטִים | judgments |

**b.** Contraction

**i.** *áyi* contracts to *ê*

| | | | |
|---|---|---|---|
| זַ֫יִת | olive | זֵיתִים | olives |
| אַ֫יִל | ram | אֵילִים | rams |

**ii.** *ā́we* contracts to *ô*

| | | | |
|---|---|---|---|
| אָ֫וֶן | trouble | אוֹנִים | troubles |
| מָ֫וֶת | death | מוֹתִים | deaths |

**c.** Nouns with Final ֶה –

Final ֶה is removed before the mp, fs, or fp ending.

| | | | |
|---|---|---|---|
| חֹזֶה | seer | חֹזִים | seers |
| רֹעֶה | shepherd | רֹעִים | shepherds |

## Vocabulary

*Nouns*:

אֹ֫זֶן (fs; fd: אָזְנַ֫יִם) ear

אֵל god, God, (the god) El

אֱלֹהִים God, gods

אֵם (fs; fp: אִמּוֹת) mother

אֶ֫רֶץ (fs; fp: אֲרָצוֹת) land, earth, country

דָּם blood

דֶּ֫רֶךְ (ms or fs) way, road

חֶ֫רֶב (fs; fp: חֲרָבוֹת) sword

יָד (fs) hand, power

לֵב/לֵבָב (ms; irreg. mp: לְבָבוֹת; לִבּוֹת) heart, mind

מַ֫יִם (always dual) water

מִשְׁפָּט judgment, justice, right, custom. שֹׁפֵט judge.
*Verb*: שָׁפַט to judge

נֶ֫פֶשׁ (fs; fp: נְפָשׁוֹת) self, person (traditionally, "soul"), breath, will

עַ֫יִן (fs) eye, spring

פֶּה mouth

פָּנִים (always plural) face, presence. *Verb*: פָּנָה to face, turn

רֶ֫גֶל (fs; fd: רַגְלַ֫יִם) foot

שָׁמַ֫יִם (always dual) heaven, sky

## Exercise 3

**a.** Give the plural of the following:

1. שִׁיר (song)
2. תּוֹרָה (law)
3. אָדוֹן (lord)
4. כּוֹכָב (star)
5. יָד (hand)
6. אֵל (god)
7. לֵבָב (heart)
8. חָגָב (locust)
9. כֹּהֵן (priest)
10. עֵנָב (grape)
11. זַיִת (olive)
12. אֹיֵב (enemy)
13. צַדִּיק (righteous)
14. הֵיכָל (palace)
15. מַלְאָךְ (messenger)
16. מִלְחָמָה (battle)
17. מִשְׁפָּחָה (family)
18. מִנְחָה (offering)

**b.** Write the following in Hebrew:

1. face
2. (two) hands
3. kingdoms
4. (two) ears
5. prophets
6. heaven
7. priests
8. mothers
9. nations
10. (two) eyes
11. judgments
12. judges

**c.** Read the following passage out loud. Then pick out the words that you recognize and translate them. (*Note*: וְ prefixed to a word means "and.")

עֵינַיִם רָמוֹת לְשׁוֹן שָׁקֶר וְיָדַיִם שֹׁפְכוֹת דָם־נָקִי
לֵב חֹרֵשׁ מַחְשְׁבוֹת אָוֶן רַגְלַיִם מְמַהֲרוֹת לָרוּץ לָרָעָה

(Prov 6:17–18)

# Lesson IV

## 1. Hebrew Roots and Patterns

Every Hebrew word is theoretically characterized by (a) its *root*, usually comprised of three consonants called "radicals," and (b) by its *pattern*, the combination of the radicals with various vowels, prefixes, and/or suffixes, if any.

**a.** Roots

Consider the following forms.

מָלַךְ he reigned

יִמְלֹךְ he reigns, he will reign

מֹלֵךְ reigning, one who reigns

מֶ֫לֶךְ king

מַלְכָּה queen

מַלְכוּת kingship, reign

מַמְלָכָה kingdom, sovereignty

The common element in all these words is the appearance of the consonants *mlk*. Hence scholars say that *mlk* is the *root* of these words, and they theorize that this root has something to do with reigning. Since words having the same root tend to fall within the same semantic range, it is convenient to classify them accordingly.

**b.** Word Patterns

To facilitate discussion of word patterns, it is customary to use a model root, *qṭl*. Although not widely attested in the Bible, this particular root is chosen because its radicals are less susceptible to changes than some others. In discussions of roots on the *qṭl* model, then, *q* stands for the first radical of any root, *ṭ* for the second, and *l* for the third. If the second and third radicals are identical, the root is said to be *qll*.

| | *Pattern* | *Meaning* |
|---|---|---|
| מָלַךְ | qāṭal | he reigned |
| יִמְלֹךְ | yiqṭōl | he reigns, he will reign |
| מֹלֵךְ | qōṭēl | reigning, one who reigns |
| מֶ֫לֶךְ | qéṭel | king |
| מְלָכִים | qĕṭālîm | kings |
| מַלְכָּה | qaṭlā(h) | queen |
| מַלְכוּת | qaṭlûṯ | kingship, reign |
| מַמְלָכָה | maqṭālā(h) | kingdom |

This system allows us to make generalizations about word patterns. For instance, *qāṭal* and *yiqṭōl* are verb patterns indicating different aspects of a verb, the *qōṭēl* pattern indicates a participle, the form with the *-ûṯ* ending indicates an abstract noun, and so forth.

c. Root Types

Roots having the same kinds of radicals tend to behave the same way. It is helpful, therefore, to classify roots according to their types. To do this, it is convenient to refer to the first radical as *I*, the second radical as *II*, and the third radical as *III*. Consider, for example, the following classification of roots.

| *I-Nûn* | *I-ʾÁlep̄* | *II-Wāw* | *II-Yōḏ* | *III-Hē* | *III-ʾÁlep̄* |
|---|---|---|---|---|---|
| נתן | אסף | קום | בין | בנה | מצא |
| נפל | אהב | כון | שׂיר | גלה | ברא |
| נצר | אמר | נוח | גיל | שׁתה | טמא |
| נגד | אמן | מול | ליץ | היה | מלא |

Roots like קלל and סבב are said to be “geminate” (Latin *geminus* “twin”) or “II = III” because their second and third radicals are alike.

In summary, a word may be described in terms of its root, pattern, or root type. Examples:

| *Word* | *Root* | *Pattern* | *Root type* |
|---|---|---|---|
| מָלַךְ | מלך | qāṭal | Strong |
| נֹתֵן | נתן | qōṭēl | I-Nûn |
| מִלֵּא | מלא | qiṭṭēl | III-ᵓÁlep̄ |
| אָמֵן | אמן | qāṭēl | I-ᵓÁlep̄ |
| דַּיָּן | דין | qaṭṭāl | II-Yōḏ |
| אֵם | אמם | qēl | Geminate |

## 2. Weak Radicals

Word patterns can sometimes be problematic because some radicals are more susceptible to change than others. Such radicals are said to be *weak*, and a root with such a radical is called a *weak root*. By the same token, a root with two weak radicals is regarded as *doubly weak*. It is common to treat the nouns and verbs with these radicals as irregular. But then the number of “irregularities” in Hebrew becomes enormous, and the task of memorizing the forms daunting. The weak radicals are, in fact, not difficult to understand, once their idiosyncracies are isolated. A good grasp now of how these radicals behave will greatly facilitate learning Hebrew forms later on.

[From time to time it will be necessary to show how a particular form developed from a hypothetical earlier form (marked by an asterisk, *). The sign < indicates development *from*, whereas the sign > indicates development *to* (e. g., *ragláyim* < **raglaym* means *ragláyim* is developed from an hypothetical earlier form, *raglaym*).]

**a.** Gutturals

**i.** Gutturals cannot be doubled by the *dāḡēš*. When the normal word pattern calls for doubling at the position where the guttural stands, one of the following obtains.

**α.** *Compensatory lengthening* of the vowel immediately preceding the guttural, as follows.

**i.** *a* ( ַ ) > *ā* ( ָ )

qaṭṭēl pattern: **ma*ʾʾ*ēn* > *māʾēn* (מָאֵן)

**ii.** *i* ( ִ ) > *ē* ( ֵ )

qiṭṭēl pattern: **bi*ʾʾ*ēr* > *bēʾēr* (בֵּאֵר)

**iii.** *u* ( ֻ ) > *ō* ( ֹ )

quṭṭal pattern: **ṭuhhar* > *ṭōhar* (טֹהַר)

*Note*: ר behaves like a guttural insofar as it, too, cannot ordinarily be doubled by the *dāḡēš*.

qaṭṭāl pattern: **parrāš* > *pārāš* (פָּרָשׁ)

qiṭṭēl pattern: **ḥirrēš* > *ḥērēš* (חֵרֵשׁ)

quṭṭal pattern: **burrak* > *bōrak̲* (בֹּרַךְ)

**β.** *Virtual doubling* of the guttural. In this case, there is no marker of doubling; one simply has to know that doubling is expected.

אַחִים = **ʾaḥḥîm*     הַהֵיכָל = **hahhêk̲āl*

In both these examples, the first syllable should be closed, not open (i.e., not *ʾa/ḥîm*, and not *ha/hê/k̲āl*), because Cv unaccented syllables are "unacceptable" (II.12).

**ii.** Gutturals never take the simple *vocal šĕwāʾ*; they prefer a composite *šĕwāʾ*.

| | *Strong root* | *With guttural* |
|---|---|---|
| qĕṭālîm pattern: | מְלָכִים | עֲבָדִים |
| qōṭĕlîm pattern: | שֹׁפְטִים | פֹּעֲלִים |

**iii.** Gutturals prefer *a*-class vowels (compare II.11).

| | | |
|---|---|---|
| mĕqaṭṭēl pattern: | מְדַבֵּר | מְשַׁלַּח |
| qĕṭōl pattern: | שְׁמֹר | שְׁלַח |

*Note*: For reasons that will become apparent later, roots that have ה, ח, or ע as the third radical are usually grouped together as "III-Guttural" roots. Even though א is a guttural, "III-ʾÁlep̄" roots are treated separately. See Excursus C on the classification of root types.

**b.** *Nûn*

As a rule, a Nûn standing immediately before another consonant (i.e., without an intervening vowel) will be assimilated into the following radical.

**mantān* > *mattān* (מַתָּן; *maqṭāl* pattern)

**yinpōl* > *yippōl* (יִפֹּל; *yiqṭōl* pattern)

If the consonant that follows the Nûn happens to be a guttural or Rêš, compensatory lengthening or virtual doubling occurs in accordance with 2.a.i above.

**minʾéreṣ* > *mēʾéreṣ* (מֵאֶרֶץ; see 2.a.i.α)

**minḥûṣ* > *miḥûṣ* (מִחוּץ; see 2.a.i.β)

c. *Wāw* and *Yōḏ*

**i.** With very few exceptions,[1] *w* cannot stand at the beginning of a word. Words that may appear in some other Semitic lan-

1. Notably the conjunction ו (and) and the noun וָו (nail).

guages with initial *w* typically appear in Hebrew with initial *y*. In the dictionaries, therefore, original I-Wāw roots are listed as I-Yōḏ.

**ii.** When the *w* of a root is in a non-initial position, it normally remains unchanged.

הִתְוַדַּע from ידע (originally **wdᶜ*)

הִתְוַכַּח from יכח (originally **wkḥ*)

In these forms, original I-Wāw roots are easily recognized as such – when one is able to isolate the prefixes (see Lesson XXVIII). But since initial *w* does become *y*, the root will still be listed in the dictionaries as if it were initial *y*.

**iii.** Originally it was not uncommon to have the diphthong **aw* (the vowel *-a* + the radical *w*). But in Biblical Hebrew original **aw* is usually treated in two ways.

**α.** The original diphthong **aw* becomes *ā́we* when stressed.

**máwt* > *mā́weṯ* (מָ֫וֶת) death

**táwk* > *tā́weḵ* (תָּ֫וֶךְ) midst

The ו in each of these cases is treated as a consonant.

**β.** The original diphthong **aw* becomes *ô* when unstressed.

*mā́weṯ* (מָ֫וֶת) death but *môṯî* (מוֹתִי) my death

*tā́weḵ* (תָּ֫וֶךְ) midst but *tôḵî* (תּוֹכִי) my midst

The ו in *môṯî* and *tôḵî* is a *mater.*

*Note*: We have already learned in III.2.b.ii that the plural of אָ֫וֶן and מָ֫וֶת are אוֹנִים and מוֹתִים, respectively. We see now that the contraction of *ā́we* (< **aw*) to *ô* is according to rules.

**iv.** Originally it was not uncommon to have the diphthong **ay* (the vowel *-a* + the radical *y*). But in Biblical Hebrew original **ay* is usually treated in two ways.

**α.** The diphthong **ay* becomes *-áyi-* when stressed.

**ʿáyn* > *ʿáyin* (עַ֫יִן) eye

**ʾáyl* > *ʾáyil* (אַ֫יִל) ram

The י in each of these cases is treated as a consonant.

**β.** The diphthong **ay* becomes *ê* when unstressed.

*ʿáyin* (עַ֫יִן) eye but *ʿênô* (עֵינוֹ) his eye

*ʾáyil* (אַ֫יִל) ram but *ʾêlô* (אֵילוֹ) his ram

The י in *ʿênô* and *ʾêlô* is a *mater.*

*Note*: We have already learned in III.2.b.i that the plural of אַ֫יִל and זַ֫יִת are אֵילִים and זֵיתִים, respectively. Similarly, the dual of עַ֫יִן is עֵינַ֫יִם. We see now that the contraction of *áyi* (< **ay*) to *ê* is according to rules.

**v.** In other instances where ו or י is the second radical, the ו or י may appear as a *mater* (*ô*, *û*, *î*, *ê*). As a general rule, II-*Wāw* roots have *-ô-* or *-û-*, while II-*Yōḏ* roots have *-î-* or *-ê-*; but since II-Wāw and II-Yōḏ roots were not always distinguished, this can only be a rule of thumb.

| *Root* | *Noun* | |
|---|---|---|
| אור | אוֹר | light |
| בוז | בּוּז | contempt |
| שׁיר | שִׁיר | song |
| חיק / חוק | חֵיק | bosom |

Some nouns of this type may take the feminine ending.

| *Root* | *Noun* | |
|---|---|---|
| קום | קוֹמָה | height |
| סוף | סוּפָה | storm-wind |

**vi.** Some nouns with II-Wāw/ Yōḏ roots show only two consonants. The middle weak radical is, thus, not evident.

| *Root* | *Noun* | |
|---|---|---|
| נור | נֵר | lamp |
| עוב | עָב | cloud |
| קום | קָמָה | standing grain |
| אול | אֵלָה | mighty tree |

**vii.** Many words that originally had Wāw or Yōḏ as the third radical appear with a final Hē. In the standard dictionaries and grammars, such roots (original III-Wāw/ Yōḏ) are classified as III-Hē.

*Note*: Ironically, roots that originally had Hē as the third radical – genuine III-הּ – are classified not as III-Hē, as one might expect, but as III-Guttural (see above, section 2.a.iii.Note). In other words, the label "III-Hē Roots" refers to roots that are really III-Wāw/ Yōḏ, but not to those that are really III-הּ!

**α.** III-Hē ms nouns frequently end in ֶה–. Indeed, one may assume that any noun ending in ֶה– is III-Hē (i.e., original III-Wāw or III-Yōḏ).

| *Root* | *Noun* | |
|---|---|---|
| שׂדה | שָׂדֶה | field |
| חזה | חֹזֶה | seer |

As we have seen in III.2.c, feminine forms of such nouns take the fs ending, ָה–, instead of the ms, ֶה–. In fact, any ending may be added directly to the first two radicals, after the final weak radical is dropped.

| *Root* | *Noun* | |
|---|---|---|
| שׁנה | שָׁנָה | year |
| זנה | זְנוּת | harlotry/prostitution |
| שׁבה | שְׁבִית | captivity |

**β.** A few nouns retain the original III-Wāw/Yōḏ. These are, nevertheless, listed under the hypothetical III-ה in the dictionaries.

| *Root* | *Noun* | |
|---|---|---|
| ענה | עָנָו | poor, afflicted |
| ענה | עֳנִי | affliction |
| פרה | פְּרִי | fruit |

**γ.** A few monosyllabic nouns with ָ or ֵ are classified as III-Hē: אָב father, אָח brother, עֵץ tree, רֵעַ friend.

*Note*: Since II-Wāw and II-Yōḏ nouns may also have forms like these (see 2.c.vi above), one will simply have to check the dictionary to know which is correct – at least in the judgment of the lexicographers.

**viii.** A few nouns related to original I-Wāw roots show only two consonants (apart from the endings) because the first radical has been lost.

| *Root* | *Noun* | |
|---|---|---|
| יעד | עֵדָה | congregation |
| ישׁן | שֵׁנָה | sleep |

## 3. Nouns with Prefixes

Some nouns patterns require a prefix, usually מ–, ת–, or א–.

**a.** Nouns with מ– prefix

i. *ma-*

| *Root* | *Noun* | |
|---|---|---|
| לאך | מַלְאָךְ | messenger |
| רפא | מַרְפֵּא | health |

Nouns with weak radicals behave according to the rules given above.

| *Root* | *Noun* | | *Rules* | |
|---|---|---|---|---|
| נתן | מַתָּן | (**mantān* > *mattān*) | 2.b | gift |
| ישׁב | מוֹשָׁב | (**mawšāb* > *môšāḇ*) | 2.c.iii.β | residence |
| יקשׁ | מוֹקֵשׁ | (**mawqēš* > *môqēš*) | 2.c.iii.β | trap |
| ישׁר | מֵישָׁרִים | (**maysārîm* > *mêšārîm*) | 2.c.iv.β | equity |
| נטה | מַטֶּה | (**manṭe[h]* > *maṭṭe[h]*) | 2.b, c.vii.α | staff |

Nouns with II-Wāw/ Yōḏ take the –מָ prefix, instead of –מַ; but the addition of an ending will cause the shift from –מָ > –מְ, according to the rules for vowel reduction in III.2.a.i.

| *Root* | *Noun* | *Rules* | |
|---|---|---|---|
| קום | מָקוֹם | 2.c.v | place |
| הום | מְהוּמָה | 2.c.v; III.2.a.i | confusion |
| דין | מְדִינָה | 2.c.v; III.2.a.i | province |

**ii.** *mi-* or *me-*

| *Root* | *Noun* | |
|---|---|---|
| שׁפט | מִשְׁפָּט | judgment |
| רכב | מֶרְכָּבָה | chariot |

Nouns with weak radicals behave according to rules.

| *Root* | *Noun* | | *Rules* | |
|---|---|---|---|---|
| שׁתה | מִשְׁתֶּה | | 2.c.vii.α | banquet |
| נטה | מִטָּה | (**minṭā*[*h*] > *miṭṭā*[*h*]) | 2.b, c.vii.α | bed |

**b.** Nouns with –תּ Prefix.

**i.** *ta-*

| *Root* | *Noun* | |
|---|---|---|
| רדם | תַּרְדֵּמָה | deep sleep |

Nouns with weak radicals behave according to the rules given.

| *Root* | *Noun* | | *Rules* | |
|---|---|---|---|---|
| אוה | תַּאֲוָה | | 2.a.ii, c.vii.α | desire |
| ישב | תּוֹשָׁב | (**tawšāḇ* > *tôšāḇ*) | 2.c.iii.β | alien |
| ילד | תּוֹלֵדוֹת | (**tawlēḏôṯ* > *tôlēḏôṯ*) | 2.c.iii.β | generations |
| ימן | תֵּימָן | (**taymān* > *têmān*) | 2.c.iv.β | south |

Nouns with II-Wāw or II-Yōḏ may take the –תָּ prefix, instead of –תַּ; but the addition of an ending will cause the reduction of the vowel from –תָּ > –תְּ, according to III.2.a.i.

| *Root* | *Noun* | *Rule* | |
|---|---|---|---|
| בוא | תְּבוּאָה | 2.c.v | yield |
| שׁוב | תְּשׁוּבָה | 2.c.v | return |
| בין | תְּבוּנָה | 2.c.v | aptitude |

**ii.** *ti-*

| *Root* | *Noun* | *Rule* | |
|---|---|---|---|
| פאר | תִּפְאֶרֶת | | glory |
| קוה | תִּקְוָה | 2.c.vii.α | hope |

**c.** Nouns with א Prefix.

| *Root* | *Noun* | | *Rule* | |
|---|---|---|---|---|
| רבע | אַרְבַּע | | | four |
| יתן | אֵיתָן | (**ʾaytān* > *ʾêṯān*) | 2.c.iv.β | everflowing |

The details in this lesson may seem pedantic to the student, but they are included here because they are foundational for understanding many of the peculiarities of Hebrew forms. A thorough understanding of the materials in this lesson, therefore, will save one much trouble later on. It may be difficult to remember all the rules at this point, but we shall be returning time and again to them. The rules will make more and more sense as we apply them repeatedly.

## Weak Radicals: A Summary

Gutturals and Rêš cannot be doubled

Gutturals prefer composite *šĕwāʾ*'s

Gutturals prefer *a*-class vowels

Nûn before a strong consonant is assimilated

Initial **w* > *y*

Original **aw* > *ā́we* (stressed) or *ô* (unstressed)

Original **ay* > *áyi* (stressed) or *ê* (unstressed)

## Vocabulary

*Nouns*:

אֶ֫בֶן (fs; fp: אֲבָנִים) stone

אָדוֹן lord, master, sir. The plural אֲדוֹנִים, like אֱלֹהִים, frequently has the singular meaning.

אוֹר (fs; mp: אוֹרִים) light

אַ֫יִל ram

אֱנוֹשׁ humanity, a human

| | |
|---|---|
| הֵיכָל[2] | palace, temple |
| חַ֫יִל | (irreg. mp: חֲיָלִים) valor, power, army, wealth |
| חֶ֫סֶד | devotion, loyalty, faithfulness, proper act |
| חֹ֫שֶׁךְ | darkness |
| לֶ֫חֶם | bread, food |
| מַלְאָךְ | messenger, angel |
| מִלְחָמָה | battle, war |
| מָקוֹם | (mp: מְקוֹמוֹת) place |
| סוּס | horse, stallion |
| עָוֺן | (mp: עֲוֺנוֹת) guilt, iniquity |
| עוֹלָה | burnt offering. *Verb*: עָלָה to go up, ascend |
| פְּרִי | fruit |
| רוּחַ | (fs) spirit, wind, breath |

## Exercise 4

**a.** Match the words below with the following patterns: (a) qāṭēl, (b) qōṭēl, (c) qiṭṭēl, (d) qaṭṭāl, (e) qāṭōl, (f) miqṭāl.

| | | | | | |
|---|---|---|---|---|---|
| 1. כֹּהֵן priest | 7. כָּבֵד heavy | 13. מִשְׁכָּן tabernacle |
| 2. גַּנָּב thief | 8. עִוֵּר blind | 14. שֹׁפֵט judge |
| 3. זָקֵן old | 9. מַלָּח sailor | 15. מִדְבָּר desert |
| 4. פִּסֵּחַ lame | 10. רָעֵב hungry | 16. רָחוֹק far |
| 5. גָּדוֹל great | 11. שֹׁטֵר officer | 17. מִקְדָּשׁ sanctuary |
| 6. דַּיָּג fisherman | 12. קָדוֹשׁ holy | 18. אִלֵּם mute |

2. Since this is a loanword derived ultimately from Sumerian, a non-Semitic language, the dictionaries simply list it as it is spelled (not by root).

**b.** Give the probable roots of the following, according to where they would be found in the dictionary (e.g. מוֹשָׁב – ישב; פְּרִי – פרה).

| | | |
|---|---|---|
| 1. כּוֹס | 7. מוֹרָא | 13. קַיִץ |
| 2. מִבְצָר | 8. בִּינָה | 14. מַצָּב |
| 3. מָכוֹן | 9. חֲצִי | 15. אֶזְרָח |
| 4. קָנֶה | 10. מוֹעֵד | 16. תְּרוּמָה |
| 5. מַשָּׂא | 11. אוֹר | 17. תּוֹדָה |
| 6. עֶרְוָה | 12. צֵידָה | 18. רֵעֶה |

**c.** Translate the following into Hebrew:

| | | |
|---|---|---|
| 1. words | 6. eyes (pl.) | 11. messengers |
| 2. spirits | 7. iniquities | 12. burnt offerings |
| 3. rams | 8. battles | 13. (two) hands |
| 4. lights | 9. masters | 14. hands (pl.) |
| 5. stones | 10. palaces | 15. places |

**d.** Read out loud the following passage. Then pick out the words that you recognize and translate them.

וֵאלֹהֵינוּ בַשָּׁמָיִם כֹּל אֲשֶׁר־חָפֵץ עָשָׂה
עֲצַבֵּיהֶם כֶּסֶף וְזָהָב מַעֲשֵׂה יְדֵי אָדָם
פֶּה־לָהֶם וְלֹא יְדַבֵּרוּ עֵינַיִם לָהֶם וְלֹא יִרְאוּ
אָזְנַיִם לָהֶם וְלֹא יִשְׁמָעוּ אַף לָהֶם וְלֹא יְרִיחוּן (Ps 115:3–6)

# Lesson V

## 1. Geminate Nouns

Geminate nouns are those with identical second and third radicals (i.e., *qll*). In some cases, the fact that there are two identical radicals does not pose any problem. For instance, the root of the noun לֵבָב (heart) is obviously לבב. More often than not, however, only two of the three radicals are graphically represented, as in לֵב (heart), the root of which is also לבב.

Most geminate nouns with endings are not difficult to recognize, even when the third radical is not actually repeated, because the gemination is ordinarily indicated by a strong *dāḡēš* (indicating doubling). Thus the plural לִבּוֹת is almost as easily identified as being related to the root לבב as the form לְבָבוֹת. It is in the singular forms that one encounters difficulties because Biblical Hebrew does not like to have a strong *dāḡēš* at the end of a word (see II.6.b.i, note).

Study the following types of geminate nouns.

**a.** *a*-type (**qall*)

| *Root* | *Singular* | *Plural* |
|---|---|---|
| עמם | עַם people | עַמִּים peoples |
| שׂקק | שַׂק sack | שַׂקִּים sacks |

When the radical to be doubled is a guttural or Rêš, the rules in IV.2.a.i apply (compensatory lengthening, virtual doubling).

| *Root* | *Singular* | *Plural* |
|---|---|---|
| שׂרר | שַׂר prince | שָׂרִים princes |
| פחח | פַּח trap | פַּחִים traps |

A few **qall* nouns are originally **qanl* (see IV.2.b).

*ʾ*anp* > *ʾ*app* > ʾ*ap̄* (אַף) nose

**b.** *i*-type (**qill*)

| *Root* | *Singular* | *Plural* |
|---|---|---|
| חצץ | חֵץ arrow | חִצִּים arrows |
| אמם | אֵם mother | אִמּוֹת mothers |

*Notes*:

i. In addition to the loss of gemination in the ms, the original *i*-vowel lengthens to *ē*. But when gemination is marked by a *dāgēš*, the *i*-vowel is retained. Thus we have the singular אֵם (not *אִם), but the plural is אִמּוֹת.

ii. A few **qill* nouns are originally **qinl* (see IV.2.b).

*ᶜ*inz* > *ᶜ*izz* > ᶜ*ēz* (עֵז) she-goat

**c.** *u*-type (**qull*)

| *Root* | *Singular* | *Plural* |
|---|---|---|
| חקק | חֹק statute | חֻקִּים statutes |
| דבב | דֹּב bear | דֻּבִּים bears |

*Note*: In addition to the loss of gemination in the ms, the original *u*-vowel lengthens to *ō*. But when gemination is marked by a *dāgēš*, the *u*-vowel is retained. Thus we have the singular חֹק (not *חֻק), but the plural is חֻקִּים.

**d.** Prefixed geminate nouns

Nouns with geminate roots may have prefixes, as in IV.3.

| *Root* | *Singular* | *Plural* |
|---|---|---|
| סלל | מְסִלָּה highway | מְסִלּוֹת highways |
| פלל | תְּפִלָּה prayer | תְּפִלּוֹת prayers |

## 2. Segolate Nouns

Segolate nouns are those that appear as disyllabic, with stress on the penultima, and with different second and third radicals. Originally, however, these were monosyllabic nouns in three different vowel classes. The vowel classes are evident, for instance, in the first syllable in the forms with suffixed pronouns (which we will learn in XII.2.c). Study the following examples.

| *Noun* | *With Suffix* | *Pattern* |
|---|---|---|
| רֶ֫גֶל foot | רַגְלִי my foot | qaṭlî |
| עֶ֫בֶד servant | עַבְדִּי my servant | qaṭlî |
| בֶּ֫רֶךְ knee | בִּרְכִּי my knee | qiṭlî |
| נֵ֫דֶר vow | נִדְרִי my vow | qiṭlî |
| אֹ֫זֶן ear | אָזְנִי my ear | qoṭlî (quṭlî) |
| אֹ֫רַח path | אָרְחִי my path | qoṭlî (quṭlî) |

It appears, then, that there are three classes of segolates, corresponding to the three vowel classes (see II.2): **qaṭl*; **qiṭl*; **qoṭl* (**quṭl*). This helps explain something that we have simply accepted as an irregularity so far: why the dual of רֶ֫גֶל (foot) is רַגְלַ֫יִם while the dual of אֹ֫זֶן (ear) is אָזְנַ֫יִם. Indeed, the three classes are also evident in the dual forms of segolates.

| *Singular* | | *Dual* | | *Class* |
|---|---|---|---|---|
| רֶ֫גֶל | foot | רַגְלַ֫יִם | two feet | *qatḷ |
| בֶּ֫רֶךְ | knee | בִּרְכַּ֫יִם | two knees | *qitḷ |
| אֹ֫זֶן | ear | אָזְנַ֫יִם | two ears | *qotḷ (*qutḷ) |

The three types are clearly distinguishable, not only in the dual and the suffixed forms (see XII.2.c), but in some other forms of the segolate nouns, as well (XI.2.j). Through a complicated process, which need not concern us now, the unsuffixed singular segolates have become so dominated by *sĕḡôl*'s (hence the term *segolate*) and/or *pátaḥ*'s that it is not always easy to tell the three classes apart. Fortunately, there are a few clues: nouns of the *qṓṭel* pattern (חֹ֫דֶשׁ, קֹ֫דֶשׁ, אֹ֫זֶן) are all **qoṭl* (**quṭl*), whereas those of the *qḗṭel* pattern (סֵ֫פֶר, נֵ֫דֶר, עֵ֫דֶר) are all **qiṭl*. As for nouns of the *qéṭel* pattern, one must check the dictionary for the dual, suffixed, and other forms to see what the original vowel might be. Regardless of their original vowels, the plurals of segolate nouns always have the pattern *qĕṭālîm* or *qĕṭālôṯ*.

**a.** **qaṭl*

| | | | |
|---|---|---|---|
| מֶ֫לֶךְ | king | מְלָכִים | kings |
| עֶ֫בֶד | servant | עֲבָדִים | servants |
| נֶ֫פֶשׁ | self | נְפָשׁוֹת | selves |
| אֶ֫רֶץ | land | אֲרָצוֹת | lands |

*Note*: The singular of this type is normally *qéṭel*, but the presence of a guttural may draw a *pátaḥ* in the second syllable (e.g., זֶ֫רַע seed, בֶּ֫טַח trust) or in both syllables (e.g., נַ֫עַר lad; בַּ֫עַל lord).

**b.** **qiṭl*

| | | | |
|---|---|---|---|
| קֶ֫בֶר | grave | קְבָרִים | graves |
| נֵ֫דֶר | vow | נְדָרִים | vows |
| עֵ֫דֶר | herd | עֲדָרִים | herds |

*Note*: The singular of this type may be either *qḗṭel* or *qéṭel*, but the presence of a guttural may draw a *páṯaḥ* in the second syllable (e.g., שֵׁ֫מַע report).

**c.** **qoṭl* (originally **quṭl*)

| | | | |
|---|---|---|---|
| בֹּ֫קֶר | morning | בְּקָרִים | mornings |
| חֹ֫דֶשׁ | new moon | חֳדָשִׁים | new moons |
| אֹ֫הֶל | tent | אֳהָלִים | tents |

*Notes*:

i. The singular of this type is *qṓṭel*, but the presence of a guttural may draw a *páṯaḥ* in the second syllable (אֹ֫רַח path).

ii. The plural is usually *qŏṭālîm/qŏṭālôṯ*, but the *qĕṭālîm/qĕṭālôṯ* type is also attested. It is clear, then, that the plurals of segolates are formed the same way. Apart from the *qŏṭālîm/qŏṭālôṯ* plurals (always from **qoṭl* segolates), it is quite impossible to distinguish the various classes from the plural forms alone.

### Summary: Segolates

| *Type* | *Singular* | *Dual* | *Plural* |
|---|---|---|---|
| *qaṭl | qéṭel | qaṭláyim | qĕṭālîm<br>qĕṭālôṯ |
| *qiṭl | qḗṭel / qéṭel | qiṭláyim | qĕṭālîm<br>qĕṭālôṯ |
| *qoṭl<br>(*quṭl) | qṓṭel | qoṭláyim | qŏṭālîm / qĕṭālîm<br>qŏṭālôṯ / qĕṭālôṯ |

## 3. Irregular Plurals

Some plural nouns look substantially different from the singular. The following are some of the most important.

| | | | |
|---|---|---|---|
| אָב | father | אָבוֹת | fathers |
| אָח | brother | אַחִים | brothers |
| אִישׁ | man | אֲנָשִׁים | men |
| אִשָּׁה | woman | נָשִׁים | women |
| בַּ֫יִת | house | בָּתִּים | houses |
| בֵּן | son | בָּנִים | sons |
| בַּת | daughter | בָּנוֹת | daughters |
| יוֹם | day | יָמִים | days |
| עִיר | city | עָרִים | cities |
| רֹאשׁ | head | רָאשִׁים | heads |

## Vocabulary

*Nouns*:

אָב (irreg. mp: אָבוֹת) father

אֹ֫הֶל tent

אָח (irreg. mp: אַחִים) brother

אָחוֹת (irreg. fp: אֲחָיוֹת) sister

אִישׁ (irreg. mp: אֲנָשִׁים) man, husband. The expected plural אִישִׁים is rarely attested

אִשָּׁה[1] (irreg. fp: נָשִׁים) woman, wife

בַּ֫יִת (ms; irreg. mp: בָּתִּים *bāttîm*[2]) house

בֵּן (irreg. mp: בָּנִים) son, grandson (also figurative meaning: member; one of a category)

בַּת (irreg. fp: בָּנוֹת) daughter

הַר mountain

יוֹם (irreg. mp: יָמִים) day. *Adverb*: יוֹמָם daily, by day

יָם (mp. יַמִּים suggests that the ms יָם an irreg. **qall* noun) sea

כְּלִי (irreg. mp: כֵּלִים) vessel, instrument, weapon

מַעֲשֶׂה deed. *Verb*: עָשָׂה to do, make, perform

עִיר (fs; irreg. fp: עָרִים) city

עַם (mp: עַמִּים) people

רֹאשׁ (irreg. mp: רָאשִׁים) head, top, chief. רִאשׁוֹן the first, former. רֵאשִׁית first, beginning

שַׂר commander, ruler, prince

---

1. Note the doubling of שׁ. This suggests that the root is אנשׁ, with the assimilation of נ.

2. This is an exception to the rule given in II.12, that a long vowel in a closed unaccented syllable (i.e., C$\bar{v}$C) is "unacceptable."

## Exercise 5

**a.** Give the plural of the following geminate nouns, and translate those that you recognize:

| | | |
|---|---|---|
| 1. פַּר | 6. שַׂר | 11. הַר |
| 2. תֹּף | 7. חֹק | 12. אַמָּה |
| 3. צַר | 8. פִּנָּה | 13. כַּר |
| 4. קֵן | 9. חֵץ | 14. עַם |
| 5. סֻכָּה | 10. דֹּב | 15. תֹּם |

**b.** Give the plural of the following:

| | | |
|---|---|---|
| 1. מֶ֫לֶךְ | 8. עֶ֫בֶד | 15. דֶּ֫רֶךְ |
| 2. בֵּן | 9. קֹ֫דֶשׁ | 16. בַּ֫יִת |
| 3. אָח | 10. נֶ֫פֶשׁ | 17. אֶ֫רֶץ |
| 4. עִיר | 11. יָם | 18. מַעֲשֶׂה |
| 5. בַּת | 12. רֹאשׁ | 19. חֹ֫דֶשׁ |
| 6. יוֹם | 13. אִישׁ | 20. אִשָּׁה |
| 7. אָב | 14. כְּלִי | 21. אֹ֫הֶל |

**c.** Read the following passage out loud. Then pick out the words including proper names, that you recognize.

זִכְרוּ תּוֹרַת מֹשֶׁה עַבְדִּי אֲשֶׁר צִוִּ֫יתִי אוֹתוֹ
בְחֹרֵב עַל־כָּל־יִשְׂרָאֵל חֻקִּים וּמִשְׁפָּטִים
הִנֵּה אָנֹכִי שֹׁלֵחַ לָכֶם אֵת אֵלִיָּה הַנָּבִיא
לִפְנֵי בּוֹא יוֹם יְהוָה[3] הַגָּדוֹל וְהַנּוֹרָא
וְהֵשִׁיב לֵב־אָבוֹת עַל־בָּנִים וְלֵב בָּנִים עַל־אֲבוֹתָם
פֶּן־אָבוֹא וְהִכֵּיתִי אֶת־הָאָ֫רֶץ חֵ֫רֶם (Mal 3:22–24)

3. Pronounced as *ʾăḏōnāy*. See Vocabulary in Lesson VI.

# Excursus A
# Introduction to the Dictionary

## 1. BDB

For most of this century, the standard English language lexicon of Biblical Hebrew has been *A Hebrew and English Lexicon of the Old Testament*, edited by Francis Brown, S. R. Driver, and Charles A. Briggs (Oxford: Clarendon, 1907). It is popularly known as BDB, after the initials of the editors. Based on a German lexicon from the nineteenth century, this reference work is now outdated. Yet, for most students who read only English, there is still no substitute that is both adequate and easily affordable.

For the beginning student, BDB is difficult to use primarily because it is not arranged alphabetically, but according to roots. For instance, the noun מִזְבֵּחַ (altars) is not listed as it is spelled, but after the verb זָבַח and the noun זֶ֫בַח; one simply has to know that the root is זבח and that –מ is merely a noun prefix. Yet it is not just a matter of removing the prefixes and suffixes; one must often also take into consideration the morphological changes that take place because of weak radicals. In other words, it is necessary to know the idiosyncracies of the weak radicals even to use the dictionary!

The examples below illustrate how one goes about finding nouns in BDB. The student should follow the commentary on each form with this dictionary at hand.

מַלְאָכִים: This is fairly easy. Since –מ is a common noun prefix, and ִים – is the mp ending, one may discount them both to arrive at the root לאך on p. 521 col. i, at the bottom of the column. If, however, one did not know the root and looked, instead, under the noun מַלְאָךְ itself (on p. 571 col. ii), one will see מַלְאָךְ and related nouns listed, with the remark "v. לאך." This means that one should look (*v.* = *vid.* "look") under the root לאך. So one begins with p. 521 col. i.

The verb does not occur in Hebrew, so no examples are cited. There are cognates in other Semitic languages, however, and the dictionary duly lists them. After this information, at the top of col. ii, one finds the noun מַלְאָךְ. The subscript "214" after the noun indicates the number of times the word occurs in all its forms. The noun is identified as masculine (n.m.) and briefly defined. Then the various forms are given: construct (see Lesson X), forms with suffixes (see Lesson XI), the plural, and so forth. The treatment of this noun continues through most of the column, and there is a wealth of information here. One learns that the word is used of messengers in general (1.), angels as the messengers of God (2.), and of the theophanic angel (3.); the word may refer to a prophet or "the herald of the advent" (1,b), or to a priest (1,c); the word occurs in parallelism (indicated by the sign ||) with מֵלִיץ "interpreter" (1,d) and with רוּחוֹת "winds" (1,e), and so on. In order to properly understand the usage of a word, therefore, one should look not only at the brief definition at the beginning of the entry, but also consider all the details presented.

Two related nouns, מְלָאכָה and מַלְאָכוּת, as well as a proper name, מַלְאָכִי (Malachi, etymologically "my messenger"), follow the entry on מַלְאָךְ. The parentheses of [מַלְאָכוּת] indicate that this precise form (without any suffixes or vowel changes) does not occur; the form is reconstructed. The sign † appearing before [מַלְאָכוּת] and before the personal name מַלְאָכִי indicates that all the passages are cited in each case. One may also note that meaning 3 of מַלְאָךְ (p. 521, col. ii) has the sign † before it, indicating that all passages with *that particular meaning* are cited.

מַפֶּ֫לֶת: Eliminating the final ת— as a marker of the feminine, one conjectures that the —מ is a prefix and that the *dāgēš* indicates an assimilated *nûn* in accordance with IV.2.b. The root cannot be פפל (i.e., a *qql* type) because roots of this type, which are extremely rare in Hebrew, never show gemination by the *dāgēš*. So one looks under the root נפל. The verb is listed first (on p. 656). Discussion of the various verb forms continues to the bottom of col. i on p. 658. Then there are several nouns listed: נֵ֫פֶל, [מַפָּל], נְפִילִים, מַפֶּ֫לֶת, מַפֵּלָה, מַפָּלָה. All the passages are cited in each case, as the sign † before each noun indicates. Again, if one had conjectured incorrectly that the root is *מפל, and so looked on p. 592 col. i (twelfth line from the bottom), one will be referred to the root.

מוֹשָׁב: There are only two possibilities here: either the וֹ is a *mater*, thus only a marker of a long ō-vowel, or the –מ is a prefix and the root is ישב (from **wšb*). The root *מושב does not exist in Hebrew (see BDB p. 602). One must conclude that –מ is a noun prefix. So one assumes that the form is *môšāḇ* < **mawšāb* (IV.2.c.iii.β). Since original initial *w* generally becomes *y* in Hebrew (IV.2.c.i), however, one must look for the noun under the root ישב on p. 442. Again, the verb is listed first (pp. 442–3), followed by several nouns. The noun מוֹשָׁב appears on p. 444 col. i. The sign † indicates that all passages are cited, and the reference to "2K2,19" in superscript after n.m. indicates where this precise form – without any other prefixes, suffixes, or further vowel changes – is found.

מְקֹמֹת: One may conjecture right away that the word is a defectively spelled form of מְקוֹמוֹת. If one discounts the plural ending וֹת– and the –מ as a noun prefix, one is left with the probable root קום. This noun is found on p. 879.

מֵישָׁרִים: Discounting the mp ending ִים –, one is left with the form מֵישָׁר–. If the י is a *mater*, the root is *משׁר. If the י is not a *mater*, the root is ישר < *ושר. The form is *mêšār* < **mayšār* (IV.2.c.iv.β). One looks, therefore, under ישר on p. 448. After the verb, an adjective, and other forms, one finds the noun [מֵישָׁר] on p. 449, col. ii. The word is in parentheses because that precise form is not attested (although it is the form that one expects); one is told that the noun always appears in the plural.

תִּלְבֹּ֫שֶׁת: This is relatively uncomplicated. The final ת– must be a feminine ending. Since –תּ is also a common noun prefix, the root must be לבשׁ. The noun appears on p. 528 col. ii, after the verb and some other nouns. The sign † and only one citation indicate that this word occurs only once in the Bible.

תַּפּוּחַ: There is no root *תפח, so the root must be נפח; the ־תּ must be a prefix and וּ a *mater.* One may assume the development **tanpû(a)ḥ > tappû(a)ḥ*, in accordance with IV.2.b, 3.b.i. On p. 656 col. i, one sees תַּפּוּחַ and its defective form תַּפֻּחַ listed three times. The first ("I. תַּפּוּחַ") is identified as a common noun (n.[m.]). The parentheses indicate that there is no clear evidence from the contexts that the noun is masculine, but the gender is conjectured to be masculine (presumably because the form is unmarked for gender, and the plural is masculine in form). The second listing ("II. תַּפֻּחַ") is a proper noun, a masculine personal name (n.pr.m.). The third ("III. תַּפּוּחַ") is also a proper noun, the name of a location (n.pr.loc.).

מִקְנֶה: This form is not difficult. The final ֶה– suggests a III-Hē root (IV.2.c.vii.α). The ־מ must be a prefix. The root is קנה. It turns out that there are, according to BDB, two roots קנה. The noun מִקְנֶה appears after "I קנה" (meaning "get, acquire").

מִצְוָה: The ָה– ending is obviously a marker of the feminine. The root is, therefore, either צוה (see III.2.c; IV.2.c.vii.α) or *מצו. If the latter were correct, one should look under מצה (IV.2.c.vii). But there is no such noun associated with the root מצה (p. 594). Thus, the ־מ must be a prefix. The root is צוה.

תּוֹדָה: This form is a bit tricky. Theoretically, the root may be *תדה (with ו as *mater*), *תוד (with the fs ending), or *ודה – i.e., **tawdā(h) > tôḏā(h)* (see IV.3.b.i, 2.c.iii.β, 2.c.vii.α). Since neither *תדה nor *תוד is attested, the third possibility must be correct. One should look under the root ידה, but one knows from this noun that the root is "original I-Wāw."

תַּבְנִית: Since ִית– is the fs ending (III.1.b.ii), the root is either *תבן or בנה (IV.2.c.vii.α, 3.b.i). The latter is correct. The root is בנה.

מַטּוֹת: The final וֹת– is probably the fp ending. Theoretically the root may be מטט, but no such root is found. The most likely alternative is that the –מ is a prefix and the first radical is an assimilated נ. The root begins –נט; the most likely third radical is ה. One conjectures that the word is fp of מַטָּה; look under the root נטה on p. 641. מַטָּה is indeed attested, but only as an adverb; no fp is attested for that. The next entry in BDB is מַטֶּה, whose plural is מַטּוֹת, an irregular plural (we expect מַטֶּה – *מַטִּים). This is the correct form.

אַפַּיִם: Setting aside the dual ending, one conjectures that the root is אפף, and that this is a *qall*-noun. But no such noun is listed under אפף. One then assumes **ʾanpáyim* > *ʾappáyim*. The root is, in fact, אנף. The singular noun, therefore, is *ʾap̄* (< **ʾapp* < **ʾanp*). This is a noun that has secondarily become *qall* – through the assimilation of *n* (V.1.a; IV.2.b).

עִזִּים: Setting aside the mp ending, one conjectures that the root is עזז, and that this is a *qill* noun. But no such noun is listed under עזז. One then assumes **ʿinzîm* > *ʿizzîm*. The root is, in fact, ענז. The singular noun, therefore, is *ʿēz* (< **ʿizz* < **ʿinz*). This is a noun that has secondarily become *qill* – through the assimilation of *n* (V.1.b.2; IV.4.b).

חִטָּה: Setting aside the fs ending, one conjectures that the root is חטט, but no such noun is found under that root. Hence one looks under the root חנט, where one finds the noun. If one looks directly under חִטָּה, one is also referred to the correct root: *v. sub* חנט ("look under חנט").

בַּת: Judging by the form, one should expect this to be a *qall*-noun (see V.1.a). Under the root בתת we find the noun בַּת, which is regularly taken as masculine, but apparently is regarded as feminine in Isa 5:10. The plural of this noun is בַּתִּים, we are told. One should also note that the noun is listed as "II. בַּת," although there is no other noun בַּת subsumed under this root. At the end of the entry, however, one is directed to the other בַּת: I. בַּת *v. sub* בֵּן ("I. בַּת look under בֵּן"). So it is that on p. 123 col. i, after the lengthy entry on בֵּן and other related nouns, we find "I. בַּת." Here the editors of BDB tell us that בַּת is "= *בַּנְתְּ fr. בן." That is, they conjecture that **bant* > **batt* > *bat̲*. The plural of this noun, in contrast to "II. בַּת," is בָּנוֹת.

עֵצָה: After setting aside the fs ending, one is left with –עֵצ, which suggests יעץ (IV.2.c.viii), עצה (IV.2.c.vii.γ), or עיץ/עוץ (IV.2.c.vi). Under יעץ one finds "I. עֵצָה" (p. 420 col. i) and is told that this noun is "= (יְ)עֵצָה". Here the editors of BDB are explaining that the initial radical has dropped out (see IV.2.c.viii). Since no other noun עֵצָה is listed under this root, and since we know that this is just "I. עֵצָה", we will have to look elsewhere also. In this case, the editors do not tell us where else to look, as they sometimes do. We have to rely simply on what we know about weak radicals. And so we try the root עצה (pp. 781–82). As it turns out, עצה is listed as a root four different times, but only under "II. עצה" do we find the noun "II. עֵצָה." The word occurs only once in the Bible, as indicated by the sign † and single citation (Jer 6:6). Although the editors identify the word as a collective noun (n.f.coll.), they are not certain about the text cited, proposing instead to read עֵצָהּ "its tree" (עֵץ) instead of the unique form עֵצָה; and they cite textual witnesses that support this proposal. At the end of the entry one is referred to I. עֵצָה. This would seem to suggest that there is no other noun, besides these two. Indeed, when looks under עוץ and עיץ, the other possibilities, no such noun is found.

עֵדָה: The root may be עדה, יעד, or עוד/עיד. Under עדה one finds two listings of the root (see pp. 723–26), but no noun עֵדָה. On p. 726 col. i, however, one finds a reference: "I. עֵדָה *v.* יעד. II. III. עֵדָה *v.* עוד." This means that there are three nouns עֵדָה, one listed under יעד, and two under עוד. Under יעד, then, one finds the entry for "I. עֵדָה" (p. 417 col i) and at the end of that entry, one is also referred to the other two nouns: "II. III. עֵדָה *v.* עוד."

The student should now be able to locate most Hebrew nouns in BDB. In order to become more comfortable with this important tool, however, one must constantly use it. Hence, if one encounters a Hebrew word that one has forgotten, or if one wonders about the possible range of meaning of any Hebrew word, one should not hesitate to use the dictionary. For more elusive forms, the student may consult Bruce Einspahr's *Index to Brown, Driver and Briggs Hebrew Lexicon* (Chicago: Moody, 1976).

## 2. Other Dictionaries

While there are several Hebrew-English dictionary projects currently under way, BDB remains the only full reference work available to students who read only English. There is an abridged dictionary produced by William L. Holladay, entitled *A Concise Hebrew and Aramaic Lexicon of the Old Testament* (Grand Rapids: Eerdmans, 1971). This is a useful volume for rapid reading. It is easier to use than BDB, inasmuch as the words are listed precisely as they are spelled. The advantages of grouping words by roots, however, are lost. The noun תּוֹרָה ("direction, instruction, law," for instance, is listed after תּוֹר ("turtle-dove") and before תּוֹשָׁב ("alien"). One is not alerted in such a dictionary to the possible semantic relationship of תּוֹרָה with other words from the root ירה (see BDB, pp. 434–46).

## Additional Exercise

Give the roots of the following with the help of a dictionary:

| | | |
|---|---|---|
| 1. תְּשׁוּבָה | 11. מֵיתָר | 21. מוֹלֶ֫דֶת |
| 2. מִרְעֶה | 12. תְּהִלָּה | 22. תּוֹלֵדוֹת |
| 3. מַסַּע | 13. קִינָה | 23. מֶמְשָׁלָה |
| 4. מִזְמֹר | 14. מַגֵּפָה | 24. מַעֲשִׂים |
| 5. אֵיתָנִים | 15. גַּאֲוָה | 25. מַחֲשָׁבָה |
| 6. שָׂפָה | 16. מוֹרֶה | 26. מַרְאֶה |
| 7. מַבָּט | 17. חֲנִית | 27. מְנוֹרָה |
| 8. דֹּב | 18. שְׁפִי | 28. שָׂרָה |
| 9. מַכָּה | 19. גֵּרִים | 29. עֵת |
| 10. מֵאָה | 20. צָרִים | 30. פָּרָה |

# Lesson VI

## 1. The Definite Article

The definite article does not appear in independent form; it is always prefixed to the word it determines.

**a.** The normal form is הַ + the strong *dāgēš* in the next consonant.

| | | | |
|---|---|---|---|
| מֶ֫לֶךְ | a king | הַמֶּ֫לֶךְ | *the* king |
| בַּ֫יִת | a house | הַבַּ֫יִת | *the* house |

*Note*: There is no indefinite article in Hebrew. Thus, מֶ֫לֶךְ means either "king" or "*a* king."

**b.** Gutturals (א, ה, ח, ע) and ר do not normally take the *dāgēš* (IV.2.a.i). Hence, we get the following.

**i.** Compensatory lengthening before א, ע, ר.

| | | | |
|---|---|---|---|
| אִישׁ | a man | הָאִישׁ | the man |
| עִיר | a city | הָעִיר | the city |
| רֹאשׁ | a head | הָרֹאשׁ | the head |

**ii.** Virtual doubling before ה and ח.

| | | | |
|---|---|---|---|
| הֵיכָל | a palace | הַהֵיכָל | the palace |
| חֹ֫דֶשׁ | a new moon | הַחֹ֫דֶשׁ | the new moon |

**iii.** Before unaccented הָ and עָ, and accented or unaccented חָ, the definite article is הֶ with virtual doubling. This rule takes precedence over the previous two.

| | | | |
|---|---|---|---|
| הָמוֹן | an uproar | הֶהָמוֹן | the uproar |
| עָוֺן | iniquity | הֶעָוֺן | the iniquity |
| חָזוֹן | a vision | הֶחָזוֹן | the vision |

**c.** A few words are vocalized a little differently when they take the definite article.

| | | | |
|---|---|---|---|
| אֲרוֹן | an ark | הָאָרוֹן | the ark |
| אֶ֫רֶץ | a land | הָאָ֫רֶץ | the land |
| גַּן | a garden | הַגָּן | the garden |
| הַר | a mountain | הָהָר | the mountain |
| חַג | a festival | הֶחָג | the festival |
| עַם | a people | הָעָם | the people |
| פַּר | a bull | הַפָּר | the bull |

The definite article may also rarely be used to indicate a vocative. Thus, הַמֶּ֫לֶךְ may mean "the king" or "O King!"

## 2. The Prefixed Prepositions

The prepositions בְּ (in, by, with), כְּ (like, as, according to), and לְ (to, toward, for) do not occur independently.

**a.** Before a noun without a definite article, the preposition is simply prefixed.

| | | | |
|---|---|---|---|
| עִיר | a city | בְּעִיר | in a city |
| דָּוִד | David | כְּדָוִד | like David |
| מֶ֫לֶךְ | a king | לְמֶ֫לֶךְ | for a king |

**b.** Before a noun with the definite article, the ה of the definite article ordinarily disappears, the preposition assumes the vowel of the definite article, and any doubling of the following radical is retained.

| | | Rule |
|---|---|---|
| לַמֶּ֫לֶךְ < לְ + הַמֶּ֫לֶךְ* | for the king | I.a |
| לָאִישׁ < לְ + הָאִישׁ* | for the man | I.b.i |
| בַּהֵיכָל < בְּ + הַהֵיכָל* | in the palace | I.b.ii |
| בֶּהָרִים < בְּ + הֶהָרִים* | in the mountains | I.b.iii |
| בָּאָ֫רֶץ < בְּ + הָאָ֫רֶץ* | in the land | I.c |

## 3. The Rule of *Šĕwāʾ*

A sequence of two vocal *šĕwāʾ*'s is not permitted. Thus, if two vocal *šĕwāʾ*'s come together, certain vowel changes take place.

**a.** In a sequence of two simple vocal *šĕwāʾ*'s, the first becomes *i*, and the second becomes silent.

בִּגְבוּל < בְּ + גְּבוּל* (*bigḇûl*) in a territory

בִּמְלָכִים < בְּ + מְלָכִים* (*bimlāḵîm*) among kings

In addition, if the second *šĕwāʾ* stands under a *yōḏ*, the first becomes *i*, and the second disappears.

בִּיהוּדָה < בִּיְהוּדָה* < בְּ + יְהוּדָה* (*bîhûḏā*[*h*]) in Judah

**b.** If a simple vocal *šĕwāʾ* is followed immediately by a composite *šĕwāʾ*, the former becomes the corresponding short vowel of the composite *šĕwāʾ*, and the latter closes the syllable (see II.7.c).

בַּחֲלוֹם < בְּ + חֲלוֹם* (*baḥ*[*ă*]*lôm*) in a dream

בֶּאֱמֶת < בְּ + אֱמֶת* (*beʾ*[*ĕ*]*meṯ*) in truth

בָּאֳהָלִים < בְּ + אֳהָלִים* (*boʾ*[*ŏ*]*hālîm*) in tents

In the case of **אֱלֹהִים**, however, the *ʾālep̄* is quiescent (II.11) and the simple vocal *šĕwāʾ* gives way to a *ṣērê*.

בֵּאלֹהִים < בְּ + אֱלֹהִים* in God

## 4. Other Prepositions

**a.** Some prepositions stand independently, e.g., אַחַר (after, behind), לִפְנֵי (before), תַּחַת (under, instead of), נֶגֶד (in front of).

אַחַר הַמַּבּוּל after the flood    לִפְנֵי הָאָרוֹן before the ark

תַּחַת הָעֵץ under the tree    נֶגֶד הָעָם in front of the people

**b.** Some prepositions are typically linked to the following word by means of a connector known as the *maqqēp̄*, e.g., ־אֶל (to, unto), ־עַל (on, upon, concerning, beside), ־עַד (as far as, until).

אֶל־הָעִיר to the city    עַל־הָאָרוֹן upon the ark

## 5. The Preposition מִן

The preposition מִן (from, because of, some of) occurs in the following forms.

**a.** It may be linked to the following word by the *maqqēp̄*.

מִן־הָאָרֶץ from the land

**b.** It may be treated as a prefixed preposition. If so, the נ behaves according to rules (see IV.2.b).

**i.** It is ordinarily assimilated into the following consonant.

מִמֶּלֶךְ < מִנְמֶּלֶךְ* from a king

**ii.** Before gutturals and ר, the preposition is usually מֵ (with compensatory lengthening) and, rarely, מִ (with virtual doubling).

| | | *Rule* |
|---|---|---|
| מֵעִיר < מִנְעִיר* | from a city | compensatory lengthening |
| מֵהַר < מִנְהַר* | from a mountain | compensatory lengthening |
| מִחוּץ < מִנְחוּץ* | from outside | virtual doubling |

*Note*: This rule also applies when מִן is prefixed to a noun with the definite article. In contrast to the prefixed prepositions בְּ, כְּ, and לְ (see 2.b above), however, the definite article is retained.

| | |
|---|---|
| מֵהָאָ֫רֶץ < מִנְהָאָ֫רֶץ* | from the land |
| מֵהָאֲנָשִׁים < מִנְהָאֲנָשִׁים* | some of the men |

## 6. The Conjunction ו

The conjunction וְ (and, but) never occurs in independent form. It is always prefixed and appears in the following forms.

**a.** Before most consonants it is וְ.

| | | | |
|---|---|---|---|
| דָּבָר | a word | וְדָבָר | and a word |
| עֶ֫בֶד | a servant | וְעֶ֫בֶד | and a servant |
| הָעֶ֫בֶד | the servant | וְהָעֶ֫בֶד | and the servant |

**b.** Before the labials ב, מ, and פ it is וּ.

| | | | |
|---|---|---|---|
| בַּ֫יִת | a house | וּבַ֫יִת | and a house |
| מֶ֫לֶךְ | a king | וּמֶ֫לֶךְ | and a king |
| פֶּ֫תַח | a door | וּפֶ֫תַח | and a door |

**c.** Before most consonants with a simple vocal *šĕwāʾ* it is וּ.

| | | | |
|---|---|---|---|
| דְּבָרִים | words | וּדְבָרִים | and words |
| שְׁמוּאֵל | Samuel | וּשְׁמוּאֵל | and Samuel |

**d.** Before a composite *šĕwāʾ* it takes the corresponding short vowel of the composite *šĕwāʾ*.

| | | | |
|---|---|---|---|
| חֲמוֹר | a he-ass | וַחֲמוֹר | and a he-ass |
| אֱמֶת | truth | וֶאֱמֶת | and truth |
| חֳלִי | sickness | וָחֳלִי | and sickness |

In the case of אֱלֹהִים, however, the *ʾālep̄* is quiescent (II.11) and the simple vocal *šĕwāʾ* gives way to a *ṣērê*.

וֵאלֹהִים < וְ + אֱלֹהִים* and God

## 7. Loss of the Strong *Dāḡēš*

The consonants ו, י, ל, מ, נ, and ק, and the sibilants (ס, צ, שׂ, and שׁ) frequently lose the strong *dāḡēš* when they are followed by a *šĕwāʾ*. The precise rules for retaining or omitting the *dāḡēš* need not concern us now; at this stage one needs only to know that the *dāḡēš* may disappear.

הַיְאֹר < הַיְּאֹר* (*hayʾōr*) the Nile

הַמְרַגְּלִים < הַמְּרַגְּלִים* (*hamraggĕlîm*) the spies

This rule explains the form of the preposition מִן when it is prefixed to nouns beginning with יְ.

מִיהוּדָה < מִיְהוּדָה* < מִיְּהוּדָה* < מִנְיְהוּדָה* from Judah

## 8. The Verbless Clause

A nominal or adverbial clause may be formed simply by juxtaposition of subject and predicate. No verb "to be" is required in such sentences. In such a clause, tense can only be inferred from context. Without context, the student should simply translate with the English present tense.

יְהוָה מֶלֶךְ YHWH *is* king

יְהוָה קָדוֹשׁ YHWH *is* holy

אֱלֹהִים בַּשָּׁמָיִם God *is* in the heavens

*Note*: In each of the above examples, the words may occur in reverse order without any change in meaning.

## Vocabulary

*Prepositions*:

אַחֲרֵי / אַחַר after, behind. *Adverb*: אַחֲרֵי כֵן / אַחַר כֵּן afterward

אֶל־ unto, into, to, toward

בְּ in, with, by, among, through, as

בֵּין between. Note the idiom: Y וּבֵין X בֵּין and, less frequently, Y לְבֵין X בֵּין "between X and Y"

כְּ like, as, about, according to. Note the idiom: Y כְּ ... X כְּ "X and Y alike"

לְ to, for, in regard to, with reference to

לִפְנֵי before (also עַל־פְּנֵי before, on the surface of; מִפְּנֵי, מִלִּפְנֵי from the presence of, because of)

מִן־ from, away from, out of, some of, because of

נֶגֶד in front of

עַד־ as far as, until

עַל־ upon, on, over, concerning, beside, against. It should be noted that אֶל־ and עַל־ are frequently confused with one another

תַּחַת under, beneath, instead of, in place of

*Note*: Sometimes two prepositions may be combined for emphasis. This is particularly frequent with the preposition מִן, e.g., מִתַּחַת under, מֵעַל above.

*Nouns*:

אֲרוֹן ark (of the covenant), chest

חַטָּאת (fp: חַטָּאוֹת) sin, sin offering. *Adjective*: חַטָּא sinful. *Verb*: חָטָא to sin; X לְ חָטָא to sin against X)

יהוה YHWH (the name of Israel's God). In the Hebrew Bible, the vowels of the word אֲדֹנָי "my Lord" are superimposed on the four consonants (thus, יְהֹוָה or יְהוָה). When the consonantal text has אדני יהוה "my lord YHWH," the text is pointed with the vowels for אֲדֹנָי אֱלֹהִים "my lord, God" (i.e., אֲדֹנָי יֱהֹוִה), thus preventing one from saying *ʾăḏōnāy ʾăḏōnāy*. When an inseparable preposition, or the conjunction וְ is prefixed to יהוה, the vowel under the prefix is *a* (ַ), precisely what one would expect with אֲדֹנָי, according to 6.d in this lesson: וַאדֹנָי "and my lord", thus, וַיהוָה "and YHWH."

לַ֫יְלָה (ms; irreg. mp: לֵילוֹת) night. *Note*: הַלַּ֫יְלָה may mean "tonight" (by the same token, הַיּוֹם may mean "today")

*Proper Names*:

| | | | |
|---|---|---|---|
| דָּוִד | David | יִשְׂרָאֵל | Israel |
| יְהוּדָה | Judah | מֹשֶׁה | Moses |
| יְרוּשָׁלַ֫םִ | Jerusalem | מִצְרַ֫יִם | Egypt |

## Exercise 6

**a.** Write the following in Hebrew:

1. the night
2. the city
3. the cities
4. the father
5. the palace
6. the sin offering
7. the people
8. the earth
9. the rams
10. the iniquities
11. the mountains
12. the heads
13. the swords
14. the vessels
15. the women

**b.** Write the following in Hebrew:

1. after the wind
2. from the land
3. and in the cities
4. in a covenant
5. in tents
6. like God
7. instead of David the king
8. a prophet to the nations
9. in the day and in the night
10. between the darkness and the light
11. from heaven to (עַד־) earth
12. some of the men

**c.** Translate the following into English:

1. הַכֶּסֶף וְהַזָּהָב
2. שָׂרִים וַעֲבָדִים
3. פָּנִים אֶל־פָּנִים
4. נֶגֶד הָהָר
5. כָּעָם כַּכֹּהֵן
6. מֵחַיִל אֶל־חָיִל
7. יָד תַּחַת יָד רֶגֶל תַּחַת רֶגֶל
8. מִיּוֹם עַד־לַיְלָה
9. הַמַּיִם מִתַּחַת הַשָּׁמַיִם
10. בִּיהוּדָה וּבִירוּשָׁלַםִ
11. חֹשֶׁךְ לְאוֹר וְאוֹר לְחֹשֶׁךְ
12. בֵּין הַיּוֹם וּבֵין הַלַּיְלָה

**d.** Read the following passage out loud. Then translate the passage with the help of a dictionary and the notes below.

1. בְּרֵאשִׁית בָּרָא אֱלֹהִים אֵת הַשָּׁמַיִם וְאֵת הָאָרֶץ
2. וְהָאָרֶץ הָיְתָה תֹהוּ וָבֹהוּ וְחֹשֶׁךְ עַל־פְּנֵי תְהוֹם וְרוּחַ אֱלֹהִים מְרַחֶפֶת
   עַל־פְּנֵי הַמָּיִם
3. וַיֹּאמֶר אֱלֹהִים יְהִי אוֹר וַיְהִי־אוֹר
4. וַיַּרְא אֱלֹהִים אֶת־הָאוֹר כִּי־טוֹב וַיַּבְדֵּל אֱלֹהִים בֵּין הָאוֹר וּבֵין
   הַחֹשֶׁךְ
5. וַיִּקְרָא אֱלֹהִים ׀ לָאוֹר יוֹם וְלַחֹשֶׁךְ קָרָא לָיְלָה וַיְהִי־עֶרֶב
   וַיְהִי־בֹקֶר יוֹם אֶחָד
6. וַיֹּאמֶר אֱלֹהִים יְהִי רָקִיעַ בְּתוֹךְ הַמָּיִם וִיהִי מַבְדִּיל בֵּין מַיִם לָמָיִם

(Gen 1:1–6)

*Notes*:

[*Note*: In Hebrew prose, the subject of a sentence usually follows the verb.]

v 1: בָּרָא (subject: God) created; אֵת...וְאֵת untranslatable markers of the definite object of the verb (בָּרָא).

v 2: הָיְתָה was; וְרוּחַ אֱלֹהִים and the wind/spirit of God; מְרַחֶפֶת was hovering/swooping.

v 3: וַיֹּאמֶר then (subject) said; יְהִי let there be; וַיְהִי־ and there was.

v 4: וַיַּרְא and (subject) saw; כִּי־טוֹב that it was good; וַיַּבְדֵּל and (subject) made a separation.

v 5: וַיִּקְרָא (subject) called; לָאוֹר (with reference to) the light; קָרָא he called.

v 6: וִיהִי and let there be.

# Excursus B
# Reading Markers and Pausal Forms

As in English, when one reads Hebrew out loud, one must pay attention to the meaningful units in the text and make appropriate pauses along the way. There is a full array of markers in pointed Hebrew texts that help one in reading. These markers were not in the original compositions. Rather, they were secondarily introduced to assist one in public recitation. The most important of these markers are also helpful in the task of translation, inasmuch as they provide a traditional understanding of the meaningful units in the text. Without these additional helps, one has to rely solely on context to know how to break up each sentence – as the student may have noticed in attempting to translate Gen 1:1–6 (Exercise 6.d).

## 1. *Sôp̄ Pāsûq*

There is no marker for the beginning of a verse. At the end of a verse, however, a large colon (:) known as the *sôp̄ pāsûq* (end of verse) appears after the last word.

## 2. Accents

Accents appear in the Hebrew Bible either above or beneath the words. They serve primarily to regulate reading. They are also helpful, however, in marking the position of stress in individual words and the meaningful divisions in each verse. The accents are generally classified either as conjunctive or disjunctive. A conjunctive accent indicates that the word is to be taken with what follows. A disjunctive accent marks a major, intermediate, or minor pause; it may occur at the end of a sentence, clause, or phrase. The disjunctive accents are especially important because they are intended to indicate the end of each logical unit.

There are two systems of accents used. The books of Psalms, Proverbs and Job (called "the Three Books") follow a somewhat different system than the rest of the Bible ("the Twenty-One Books"). Some of the markers are found in both systems, but others occur exclusively in one or the other system. It is not necessary at this stage to learn all the various accents, their peculiarities, and how they are used in each system. It will suffice for us to be able to recognize the following accents as either conjunctive or disjunctive.

| *Disjunctive* | *Conjunctive* |
|---|---|
| XXX sillûq | XXX mûnāḥ |
| XXX ᵓatnāḥ | XXX mĕhuppāḵ |
| XXX sĕḡôltāᵓ | XXX mêrĕḵāᵓ |
| XXX ᶜôle(h) wĕyōrēḏ | XXX ᶜillûy |
| XXX šalšélet | XXX ᵓazlāᵓ |
| XXX zāqēp̄ qāṭōn | XXX dargāᵓ |
| XXX zāqēp̄ gāḏôl | |
| XXX rĕḇî(a)ᶜ | |
| XXX ṭip̄ḥā(h) | |

[Now you should reread Gen 1:1–6 out loud (see Exercise 6.D), this time using your Hebrew Bible and paying attention to the accents. Translate the text again, and observe how the accents assist you in identifying the sense units.]

## 3. *Méṯeḡ*

The *méṯeḡ* (bridle) is a short vertical stroke appearing under a consonant, usually to the left of the vowel. It serves primarily to indicate a secondary stress in a word. In addition, it may call attention to the precise pronunciation of the vowel. There is no need for the student to know all the situations in which the *méṯeḡ* occurs. It is helpful, however, to note the presence of the *méṯeḡ* in the following situations.

**a.** It distinguishes *ā* from *o*.

אָֽכְלָה *ʾāḵĕlā(h)* she ate (not *ʾoḵlā[h]* food)

בָּֽתִּים *bāttîm* houses (not **bottîm*)

**b.** It distinguishes *ī* from *i*.

יִֽרְאוּ *yīrĕʾû* they fear (not *yirʾû* they see)

**c.** It calls attention to an unreduced *ā* or *ē* vowel in a propretonic open syllable (see III.2.a).

אָֽנוֹכִי *ʾānōḵî* I (am)

בֵּֽרֲכַ֫נִי *bērăḵánî* he blessed me

**d.** It calls attention to a short unaccented vowel in an apparently open syllable.

הֶֽעָרִים the cities

## 4. *Maqqēp̄*

The *maqqēp̄* (connector) is a horizontal stroke used to indicate a close link of words. A word so joined to the following becomes proclitic – it becomes so closely dependent on the following word that it loses its stress. When a word becomes proclitic in this way, final *ē* becomes *e* and final *ō* becomes *o*.

אֵת הַשָּׁמַ֫יִם but אֶת־הַשָּׁמַ֫יִם

כֹּל הָאָ֫רֶץ but כָּל־הָאָ֫רֶץ

# 5. Pausal Forms

When a word occurs at a major juncture of a sentence, particularly when at the middle or end of a verse, it is said to be *in pause*. Certain vowel changes in the word may take place. The following are the most common shifts which result in *pausal forms*.

**a.** The *a*-vowel ( ַ ) in a tonic syllable may become *ā* ( ָ ).

| *Normal* | *Pausal* | |
|---|---|---|
| מַ֫יִם | מָ֫יִם | water |
| שַׁ֫עַר | שָׁ֫עַר | gate |
| שָׁפַט | שָׁפָט | he judged |

**b.** The first *e*-vowel ( ֶ ) in a segolate noun may become *ā* ( ָ ).

| *Normal* | *Pausal* | |
|---|---|---|
| עֶ֫בֶד | עָ֫בֶד | servant |
| אֶ֫רֶץ | אָ֫רֶץ | land |

**c.** Words normally stressed on the ultima may have their accent retracted to the penultima.

| *Normal* | *Pausal* | |
|---|---|---|
| אָֽנֹכִי | אָנֹ֫כִי | I (am) |

**d.** A reduced vowel (vocal *šĕwāʾ*) may be reverted to a full vowel.

| *Normal* | *Pausal* | |
|---|---|---|
| יִשְׁמְעוּ | יִשְׁמָ֫עוּ | they will hear |
| יִמָּלְאוּ | יִמָּלֵ֫אוּ | they will be filled |
| יִשְׁפְּטוּ | יִשְׁפֹּ֫טוּ | they will judge |

Noteworthy here, too, are forms like פְּרִי and כְּלִי, where the *šĕwāʾ* becomes a full vowel.

| *Normal* | *Pausal* | |
|---|---|---|
| פְּרִי | פֶּ֫רִי | fruit |
| חֲצִי | חֵ֫צִי | half |
| חֳלִי | חֹ֫לִי | sickness |

*Note*: In addition to the internal changes, prefixed prepositions and the conjunction ו take the *ā*-vowel (instead of the *šĕwāʾ*) before a stressed syllable in a pausal position. This rule applies to monosyllabic nouns, as well as to disyllabic nouns stressed on the penultima.

| | |
|---|---|
| פֶּה לָפֶה | mouth to mouth (2 Kgs 10:21) |
| בֵּין מַ֫יִם לָמָ֫יִם | between the waters and the waters (Gen 1:6) |
| יוֹם וָלַ֫יְלָה | day and night (Gen 8:22) |
| זָהָב וָכָ֫סֶף | gold and silver (Exod 25:3) |

## 6. Conjunctive *Dāḡēš*

Sometimes a strong *dāḡēš* is found not because the form itself requires it, but for smoother reading.

נָֽתְנָה לִּי she gave to me

## 7. *Rāp̄e(h)*

The *rāp̄e(h)* is a short horizontal stroke sometimes placed above a consonant. Its function is the opposite of a *dāḡēš* in that it indicates that a consonant is to be taken as "relaxed" (that's what the name means). In some manuscripts this sign is used consistently to call attention to the absence of a strong *dāḡēš*, a weak *dāḡēš*, or a *mappîq*.

# Lesson VII

## 1. The Inflection of the Adjective

Like the noun, the Hebrew adjective may be inflected for gender and number. The inflection of טוֹב (good) is as follows.

| | | | |
|---|---|---|---|
| *ms* | טוֹב | *mp* | טוֹבִים |
| *fs* | טוֹבָה | *fp* | טוֹבוֹת |

*Note*: Unlike the noun, the dual form of the adjective is unattested. For dual nouns, the plural adjectives are used.

## 2. Adjectival Patterns

The following are the most important adjectival patterns.

**a.** *qāṭōl* (e.g., גָּדוֹל great)

| | | | |
|---|---|---|---|
| *ms* | גָּדוֹל | *mp* | גְּדוֹלִים |
| *fs* | גְּדוֹלָה | *fp* | גְּדוֹלוֹת |

Other examples: קָדוֹשׁ (holy); קָרוֹב (near); רָחוֹק (far).

**b.** *qāṭēl* (e.g., כָּבֵד heavy)

| | | | |
|---|---|---|---|
| *ms* | כָּבֵד | *mp* | כְּבֵדִים |
| *fs* | כְּבֵדָה | *fp* | כְּבֵדוֹת |

Other examples: זָקֵן (old); רָעֵב (hungry); מָלֵא (full).

**c.** *qāṭāl* (e.g., יָשָׁר straight)

| | | | |
|---|---|---|---|
| *ms* | יָשָׁר | *mp* | יְשָׁרִים |
| *fs* | יְשָׁרָה | *fp* | יְשָׁרוֹת |

Other examples: חָזָק (strong); חָכָם (wise); חָדָשׁ (new).

**d.** *qall* (e.g., רַב many, much)

| | | | |
|---|---|---|---|
| *ms* | רַב | *mp* | רַבִּים |
| *fs* | רַבָּה | *fp* | רַבּוֹת |

Other examples: דַּל (poor); עַז (strong); חַי (alive).

*Note*: Adjectives of this pattern behave like *qall* nouns (V.1.a). Thus, when a guttural or Rêš is the geminate radical, there is compensatory lengthening of the first vowel in the forms with endings, e.g., רַע (evil).

| | | | |
|---|---|---|---|
| *ms* | רַע | *mp* | רָעִים |
| *fs* | רָעָה | *fp* | רָעוֹת |

Other examples: מַר (bitter); צַר (narrow).

**e.** *qāṭe(h)* (e.g., קָשֶׁה difficult)

| | | | |
|---|---|---|---|
| *ms* | קָשֶׁה | *mp* | קָשִׁים |
| *fs* | קָשָׁה | *fp* | קָשׁוֹת |

Other examples: יָפֶה (handsome); רָפֶה (slack).

## 3. Uses of the Adjective

The adjective in Hebrew may function as an attribute (e.g., the good man) or a predicate (e.g., the man is good).

**a.** The attributive adjective modifies a noun. In this usage, the adjective agrees with the noun in gender, number, and definiteness. It also comes *after* the noun, not before it as in English.

| | | | |
|---|---|---|---|
| אִישׁ טוֹב | a good man | אִשָּׁה טוֹבָה | a good woman |
| הָאִישׁ הַטּוֹב | the good man | הָאִשָּׁה הַטּוֹבָה | the good woman |
| אֲנָשִׁים טוֹבִים | good men | נָשִׁים טוֹבוֹת | good women |
| הָאֲנָשִׁים הַטּוֹבִים | the good men | הַנָּשִׁים הַטּוֹבוֹת | the good women |

**b.** The predicate adjective describes the state of the noun. In this usage, the adjective agrees with the noun in gender and number, but it never takes the definite article. It may come *before* or *after* the noun. The syntax is that of the verbless clause (VI.8).

| | | | |
|---|---|---|---|
| טוֹב הָאִישׁ | the man is good | טוֹבָה הָאִשָּׁה | the woman is good |
| הָאִישׁ טוֹב | the man is good | הָאִשָּׁה טוֹבָה | the woman is good |

Since the predicate adjective does not take the definite article, there may be some ambiguity when it is used with an indefinite noun: thus, אֲנָשִׁים טוֹבִים may mean either "good men" or "men are good." The precise meaning must be determined from context. In a case like טוֹבִים אֲנָשִׁים, however, it is clear that the adjective is a predicate, since the attributive adjective normally stands *after* the noun (see 3.a above).

**c.** The adjective in Hebrew may be used as a substantive – that is, as a noun.

| | | | |
|---|---|---|---|
| חָכָם | wise = a wise man | הֶחָכָם | the wise = the wise man |

## 4. Agreement of the Adjective

**a.** The adjective agrees with the noun in its actual gender rather than its form.

הָאָרֶץ הַטּוֹבָה the good land (Deut 1:35)

עָרִים גְּדֹלוֹת great cities (1 Kgs 4:13)

**b.** Since there is no dual form of the adjective, the plural form is used instead with the dual noun.

יָדַיִם רָפוֹת slack hands (Isa 35:3)

**c.** Collective nouns (III.1.f) may have adjectives in the plural.

צֹאן רַבּוֹת large flock (Gen 30:43)

**d.** Nouns that are plural in form but refer to a single person (III.1.g) may have the adjective in the singular.

אֲדֹנִים קָשֶׁה a hard master (Isa 19:4)

## 5. Special Uses of מִן

**a.** *Comparative.*

There is no independent word in Hebrew for the English word *than*. Instead, comparison is most commonly expressed by the preposition מִן placed before the noun that is surpassed. The adjective is used with מִן in this way.

מָתוֹק מִדְּבַשׁ *sweeter than* honey (Judg 14:18)

עַז מֵאֲרִי *stronger than* a lion (Judg 14:18)

At times מִן is used to compare a subject's current condition with a desired condition that is unattainable. The adjective is occasionally also used with מִן in this way. In English, one uses the word "too" before the adjective.

קָשֶׁה מֵהָעָם *too* difficult for the people

**b.** *Partitive.*

There is also no word for *some* in Hebrew; instead, the preposition מִן is used to express a portion or a part of something.

מִן־הָעָם *some* of the people (Gen 33:15)

מִן־הַדָּם *some* of the blood (Exod 12:7)

## 6. The Adjective with מְאֹד

The noun מְאֹד (muchness, power) may be used after an adjective or a chain of adjectives as an intensifier. The literal meaning of מְאֹד is still evident in the expression עַד־מְאֹד (to the extreme = very, exceedingly):

וְהַנַּעֲרָה יָפָה עַד־מְאֹד the girl was *exceedingly* beautiful (1 Kgs 1:4)

Most commonly, however, מְאֹד occurs without any preposition and should be translated as "very."

טוֹב מְאֹד *very* good (Gen 1:31)

## 7. Nouns in Apposition

A noun is sometimes clarified by another noun in apposition.

הַנָּהָר פְּרָת the river, Euphrates = the Euphrates river (1 Chron 5:9)

אִישׁ מִצְרִי a man, an Egyptian = an Egyptian man (Exod 2:11)

## Vocabulary

*Adjectives*:

אַחֵר (irreg. fs: אַחֶ֫רֶת; fp: אֲחֵרוֹת) another, other

גָּדוֹל great, big, large

זָקֵן old (as a noun: elder [of a city])

חָזָק strong, powerful. *Verb*: to be strong, prevail

חַי alive, living. Substantive in both genders, "living animal." *Noun*: חַיִּים life

טוֹב good, beautiful

יָפֶה handsome, beautiful

יָקָר precious, valuable, rare

יָשָׁר straight, just, upright. *Nouns*: יֹ֫שֶׁר uprightness, straightness. יְשָׁרָה uprightness

כָּבֵד heavy, severe, important. *Verb*: כָּבֵד to be important; to be heavy, weighty. *Noun*: כָּבוֹד glory, honor

קָטֹן (also קָטָן; fs: קְטַנָּה; mp: קְטַנִּים) small, insignificant

רַב many, much, abundant, mighty. *Noun*: רֹב abundance

רַע bad, evil, ugly. *Noun*: רָעָה evil, harm

רָעֵב hungry. *Noun*: רָעָב famine, hunger. *Verb*: רָעֵב to be hungry

רָשָׁע wicked, criminal

*Proper Names*:

אַבְרָהָם Abraham

יַעֲקֹב Jacob

## Exercise 7

**a.** Translate the following into Hebrew:

1. a holy nation
2. a new king
3. a little city
4. an evil spirit
5. great wisdom
6. many cities
7. precious stones
8. famine in the city
9. the matter is very good
10. the king is very old
11. the criminal matter
12. the righteous and the wicked alike

**b.** Translate the following into English:

1. לְאִישׁ אַחֵר
2. אֱלֹהִים חַיִּים
3. אֶל־אֶרֶץ אַחֶרֶת
4. עַם גָּדוֹל וָרָב
5. לֶחֶם לָרְעֵבִים
6. כַּצַּדִּיק כָּרָשָׁע
7. וְהָרָעָב כָּבֵד בָּאָרֶץ
8. הָאִישׁ מֹשֶׁה גָּדוֹל מְאֹד
9. טוֹב מִבָּנִים וּמִבָּנוֹת
10. הַשָּׁמַיִם הַחֲדָשִׁים וְהָאָרֶץ הַחֲדָשָׁה
11. גּוֹיִם רַבִּים וּמְלָכִים גְּדוֹלִים
12. הַטּוֹבוֹת טוֹבוֹת מְאֹד וְהָרָעוֹת רָעוֹת מְאֹד

**c.** Read Gen 1:14–19 out loud and translate the passage with the help of a dictionary and the following notes.

*Notes*:

v 14: וַיֹּאמֶר (subject) said; יְהִי there be; מְאֹרֹת (defective spelling for מְאוֹרוֹת); בִּרְקִיעַ the expanse of; לְהַבְדִּיל to separate; וְהָיוּ so that they shall be; לְאֹתֹת for signs; וּלְמוֹעֲדִים and for seasons; וְשָׁנִים irreg. fp. of שָׁנָה.

v 15: לְהָאִיר to shine; וַיְהִי־כֵן and it was so.

v 16: וַיַּעַשׂ and (subject) made; אֶת־שְׁנֵי the two (אֶת־ is an untranslatable marker of the definite object); לְמֶמְשֶׁלֶת for dominion of.

v 17: וַיִּתֵּן אֹתָם and (subject) put them.

v 18: וְלִמְשֹׁל and to dominate (object indicated by the preposition ב); וַיַּרְא and (subject) saw; כִּי־טוֹב that it was good.

v 19: וַיְהִי it was.

# Lesson VIII

## 1. The Verbal Patterns

There are seven major verbal patterns in Hebrew. Each pattern has certain distinctive features, such as an *n* prefix (e.g., נִקְטַל), *h* prefix (e.g., הִקְטִיל), doubling of the second radical (e.g., קִטֵּל), and so forth. These distinctive verbal patterns are variously called "conjugations," "stems," or in Hebrew, *binyānîm*, "structures."

The first verbal pattern is the most unencumbered. Therefore, it has traditionally been called *Qal* (light); the others are named according to their typical formation, based on a model root **פעל** (to do, make).

The following are the seven major verbal patterns in Hebrew.

| *Pattern* | *Traditional name* |
|---|---|
| qāṭal | Qal (קַל) |
| niqṭal | Niphal (נִפְעַל) |
| qiṭṭēl | Piel (פִּעֵל)[1] |
| quṭṭal | Pual (פֻּעַל)[1] |
| hiqṭîl | Hiphil (הִפְעִיל) |
| hoqṭal | Hophal (הָפְעַל) |
| hitqaṭṭēl | Hithpael (הִתְפַּעֵל)[1] |

The characteristics and meaning of each verbal pattern will be clarified in due course.

## 2. The Inflection of the Participle

Like the noun and the adjective, the participle is inflected for gender (masculine or feminine) and number (singular and plural).

1. The guttural **ע** is virtually doubled (see IV.2.a.i.β).

| | | | |
|---|---|---|---|
| *ms* | – | *mp* | ִים- |
| *fs* | ֶת- | *fp* | וֹת- |

*Notes*:

i. As in the adjective, there is no dual form; the appropriate plural form is used instead.

ii. The alternative fs ending ָה- is attested rarely.

## 3. The Qal Active Participle

**a.** Normal Pattern

The Qal active participle is based on the *qōṭēl* pattern. The forms of the Qal active participle of שָׁמַר (to keep, observe), then, are as follows.

| | | | |
|---|---|---|---|
| *ms* | שֹׁמֵר | *mp* | שֹׁמְרִים |
| *fs* | שֹׁמֶ֫רֶת | *fp* | שֹׁמְרוֹת |

*Note*: The Qal active participles of verbs with strong radicals, I-Guttural, I-Nûn, I-Yōḏ, and Geminate roots are all inflected normally.

**b.** II-Guttural Roots

Since gutturals do not take the simple vocal *šĕwāʾ*, a composite *šĕwāʾ* is found wherever one expects a vocal *šĕwāʾ*. The forms of the Qal active participle of the verb שָׁאַל (to ask), then, are as follows.

| | | | |
|---|---|---|---|
| *ms* | שֹׁאֵל | *mp* | שֹׁאֲלִים |
| *fs* | שֹׁאֶ֫לֶת | *fp* | שֹׁאֲלוֹת |

**c.** III-Guttural Roots

As we have already learned, final הּ, ח, and ע tend to add the *furtive pátaḥ* and prefer *a*-class vowels (II.10). The forms of the Qal active participle of שָׁמַע (to hear), then, are as follows.

| | | | |
|---|---|---|---|
| *ms* | שֹׁמֵעַ | *mp* | שֹׁמְעִים |
| *fs* | שֹׁמַ֫עַת | *fp* | שֹׁמְעוֹת |

**d.** III-ʾÁlep̄ Roots

Since א tends to be quiescent whenever it closes a syllable (II.11), the fs participle of such verbs will be vocalized slightly differently from the normal form. The forms of the Qal active participle of מָצָא (to find), then, are as follows.

| | | | |
|---|---|---|---|
| *ms* | מֹצֵא | *mp* | מֹצְאִים |
| *fs* | מֹצֵאת | *fp* | מֹצְאוֹת |

**e.** III-Hē Roots

The forms of the Qal active participle of גָּלָה (to uncover) are as follows.

| | | | |
|---|---|---|---|
| *ms* | גֹּלֶה | *mp* | גֹּלִים |
| *fs* | גֹּלָה | *fp* | גֹּלוֹת |

*Note*: An alternate fs like בֹּכִיָּה (crying) is attested.

**f.** II-Wāw / Yōḏ Roots

Verbs with Wāw / Yōḏ as the second radical normally preserve only the first and last consonants. There is no distinction made between II-Wāw and II-Yōḏ types. The forms of the Qal active participle of בּוֹא (come, enter), then, are as follows.

| | | | |
|---|---|---|---|
| *ms* | בָּא | *mp* | בָּאִים |
| *fs* | בָּאָה | *fp* | בָּאוֹת |

**Synopsis of Forms of the Qal Active Participle**

| *Root* | *ms* | *mp* | *fs* | *fp* | |
|---|---|---|---|---|---|
| שׁמר | שֹׁמֵר | שֹׁמְרִים | שֹׁמֶ֫רֶת | שֹׁמְרוֹת | keeping |
| שׁאל | שֹׁאֵל | שֹׁאֲלִים | שֹׁאֶ֫לֶת | שֹׁאֲלוֹת | asking |
| שׁמע | שֹׁמֵעַ | שֹׁמְעִים | שֹׁמַ֫עַת | שֹׁמְעוֹת | hearing |
| מצא | מֹצֵא | מֹצְאִים | מֹצֵאת | מֹצְאוֹת | finding |
| גלה | גֹּלֶה | גֹּלִים | גֹּלָה | גֹּלוֹת | uncovering |
| בוא | בָּא | בָּאִים | בָּאָה | בָּאוֹת | coming |

## 4. Uses of the Participle

**a.** The participle is a verbal adjective; it has some characteristics of both the verb and the adjective. When it is construed as a verb, it usually suggests *continuous* occurrence of an activity.

יֹשֵׁב עַל־כִּסֵּא *sitting* upon a throne (Isa 6:1)

עֹלִים וְיֹרְדִים *ascending* and *descending* (Gen 28:12)

Tense is not indicated in the participle; it must be inferred from context. The participle simply represents a state of affair in the present, past, or future.

i. Present

| | |
|---|---|
| אִישׁ זָקֵן עֹלֶה | an old man *is going up* (1 Sam 28:14) |
| דּוֹר הֹלֵךְ וְדוֹר בָּא וְהָאָרֶץ לְעוֹלָם עֹמָדֶת | A generation *comes* and a generation *goes*, but the earth *stands* forever (Eccl 1:4) |

ii. Past

| | |
|---|---|
| יְהוָה קֹרֵא לַנָּעַר | YHWH *was calling* the boy (1 Sam 3:8) |
| וְרִבְקָה אֹהֶבֶת אֶת־יַעֲקֹב | but Rebecca *loved* Jacob (Gen 25:28) |

iii. Future

The participle is often used for the imminent future. Thus, it may be rendered by English "going to ... " or "about to...."

| | |
|---|---|
| אָנֹכִי עֹשֶׂה דָבָר בְּיִשְׂרָאֵל | I am *going to do* something in Israel (1 Sam 3:11) |
| אֲשֶׁר אֲנִי עֹשֶׂה | what I am *about to do* (Gen 18:17) |

In the examples above, the participle is the predicate of the clause. Just like the predicate adjective (VII.3.b), the participle in this usage agrees with the noun in gender and number, but it does not take the definite article. Compare the usage of the adjective and the participle in the following examples.

| *With adjective* | | *With participle* | |
|---|---|---|---|
| הָאִישׁ טוֹב | the man is good | הָאִישׁ עֹמֵד | the man is standing |
| הָאִשָּׁה טוֹבָה | the woman is good | הָאִשָּׁה עֹמֶדֶת | the woman is standing |

*Note*: For simplicity's sake we assume the present tense in our translation. As in other verbless clauses (VI.8), however, the context may require other translations.

**b.** The participle may also be used like an attributive adjective, e.g., לֵב שֹׁמֵעַ a *listening* heart (1 Kgs 3:9); אֵשׁ אֹכְלָה a *consuming* fire (Deut 4:24). When so used, the participle agrees in number, gender, and definiteness with, and always comes *after* the noun it modifies (see VII.3.a). Compare the use of the adjective and participle in the following examples.

| *With adjective* | | *With participle* | |
|---|---|---|---|
| הָאִישׁ הַטּוֹב | the good man | הָאִישׁ הָעֹמֵד | the standing man |
| הָאִשָּׁה הַטּוֹבָה | the good woman | הָאִשָּׁה הָעֹמֶדֶת | the standing woman |

In the phrase הָאִישׁ הָעֹמֵד, the word הָעֹמֵד "the standing (one)" specifies and describes the noun הָאִישׁ. It is not just any man of whom the phrase speaks, but "the man, the standing one." Thus הָעֹמֵד functions as an attributive adjective. The expression "the man, the standing one" may be compared with the adjectival phrase הָאִישׁ הַטּוֹב "the man, the good one." In idiomatic English, one would translate the participle in this case with the relative pronoun "who." The tense is not specified in Hebrew, so the Hebrew הָאִישׁ הָעֹמֵד could mean "the man who stands," "the man who stood," or "the man who will stand." Thus, the participle (with or without the definite article) can function as the equivalent of a relative clause.

| | |
|---|---|
| מֶלֶךְ יוֹשֵׁב | a king who sits (Prov 20:8) |
| הַמֶּלֶךְ הַיּוֹשֵׁב | the king who sits (Jer 29:16) |

**c.** Like the adjective, the participle may be used as a noun.

| | |
|---|---|
| שֹׁמֵר | keeping, one who keeps = keeper |
| אֹהֵב | loving, one who loves = lover, friend |
| בֹּנֶה | building, one who builds = builder |

**d.** In many instances, the participle is used in such a way that some indefinite subject has to be supplied.

קֹרֵא מִשֵּׂעִיר (someone) *calls* from Seir (Isa 21:11)

## 5. The Qal Passive Participle

**a.** Whereas the Qal active participle has the *qōṭēl* pattern, the passive participle has the *qāṭûl* pattern. Compare the following.

Qal Act. Ptc.: כֹּתֵב writing, one who writes

Qal Pass. Ptc.: כָּתוּב being written, what is written

**b.** Whereas the more common fs ending in the active inflection is usually ֶ ת–, it is ָ ה– in the passive.

### Synopsis of Forms of the Qal Passive Participle

| *Root* | *ms* | *mp* | *fs* | *fp* | |
|---|---|---|---|---|---|
| שׁמר | שָׁמוּר | שְׁמוּרִים | שְׁמוּרָה | שְׁמוּרוֹת | kept |
| אסר | אָסוּר | אֲסוּרִים | אֲסוּרָה | אֲסוּרוֹת | bound |
| ידע | יָדוּעַ | יְדוּעִים | יְדוּעָה | יְדוּעוֹת | known |
| קרא | קָרוּא | קְרוּאִים | קְרוּאָה | קְרוּאוֹת | called |
| גלה | גָּלוּי | גְּלוּיִים | גְּלוּיָה | גְּלוּיוֹת | uncovered |

*Notes*:

i. III-Hē (i.e., original III-Wāw/ Yōḏ) verbs have י as the third radical.

ii. II-Wāw/Yōḏ verbs are extremely rare in the passive participle, but note the following.

| *Root* | *Qal passive ptc.* |
|---|---|
| מול | מוּל, מוּלִים circumcised |
| שׂים | שִׂים, שִׂימָה placed |

**c.** Like the active participle, the passive participle is a verbal adjective (see 4 above).

**i.** *attributive*

מִשְׁפָּט כָּתוּב a *written* judgment (Ps 149:9)

**ii.** *predicative*

כָּתוּב בַּסְּפָרִים *it was written* in the letters (1 Kgs 21:11)

**iii.** *substantive*

כַּכָּתוּב בַּתּוֹרָה׃ according to *what is written* in the law (Neh 10:35)

## Vocabulary

*Verbs*:

אָהַב to love. *Noun*: אַהֲבָה love

אָכַל to eat, consume, devour. *Nouns*: אֹכֶל / אָכְלָה food

אָמַר to say

בּוֹא to come, enter

בָּנָה to build

גָּלָה to uncover, go away, go into exile

הָלַךְ to walk, go

יָדַע to know

יָלַד to bear, beget. *Noun*: יֶלֶד boy, child

יָצָא to go out, go forth

יָרַד to go down, descend

יָשַׁב to dwell, sit, remain

כָּתַב to write, record, register

מָצָא to find

נָטָה to stretch out, extend, incline. *Nouns*: מַטֶּה (pl. מַטּוֹת) branch, tribe, staff

נָתַן to give, deliver, set, permit

עָבַר to cross over, pass over, transgress. Xבְּ עָבַר to pass through X

עָמַד to stand, remain, persist

קָרָא to call, proclaim. Xלְ קָרָא to call / summon X, name X, invite X

רָאָה to see. *Noun*: מַרְאֶה sight, appearance

שָׁאַל to ask, inquire

שָׁמַע to hear, listen, obey

שָׁמַר to keep, observe, watch

## Exercise 8

**a.** Parse the following forms – e.g., יֹשֶׁ֫בֶת Qal Act. Ptc. fs of יָשַׁב "to dwell, sit"; גָּלוּי Qal Pass. Ptc. ms of גָּלָה "to uncover."

| | | |
|---|---|---|
| 1. נֹתֵן | 6. אֲהוּבָה | 11. כְּתוּבִים |
| 2. יֹצֵאת | 7. אֹמְרִים | 12. יֹדַ֫עַת |
| 3. עֹלִים | 8. עֹמֶ֫דֶת | 13. עֲשׂוּיָה |
| 4. עֹשֶׂה | 9. נָטוּי | 14. מֹצְאִים |
| 5. בָּאָה | 10. קֹרֵאת | 15. בְּנוּיָה |

**b.** Parse the following forms with the help of a dictionary:

| | | | | | |
|---|---|---|---|---|---|
| 1. | כֹּרְעוֹת | 6. | שָׁב | 11. | אֹפִים |
| 2. | סֹבֵב | 7. | שֹׁדְדִים | 12. | נָס |
| 3. | צָם | 8. | נֹפֶ֫לֶת | 13. | שָׁבִים |
| 4. | אֹפָה | 9. | שֹׁמָה | 14. | רָם |
| 5. | גֹּאֲלִים | 10. | כֹּרֵת | 15. | בֹּכִיָּה |

**c.** Translate the following into Hebrew:

1. the one (fs) who bore
2. the one (ms) stretching out the heavens
3. the ones (mp) who were registered
4. the ones (mp) who resided in Judah
5. with an outstretched hand
6. Jerusalem, built like a city
7. a woman who knows a man
8. another angel was going forth
9. the one (ms) who is recorded for life
10. the vessels that were made

**d.** Translate the following into English:

1. יְהוָ֥ה עֹבֵ֛ר (1 Kgs 19:11)
2. יְהוָ֨ה ׀ אֹ֘הֵ֤ב מִשְׁפָּ֗ט (Ps 37:28)
3. הָעֹבְרִ֣ים בָּאָ֔רֶץ (Ezek 39:15)
4. הָעָ֔ם הַיֹּשֵׁ֖ב בָּאָ֑רֶץ (Num 13:28)
5. אֹ֣זֶן שֹׁ֭מַעַת וְעַ֣יִן רֹאָ֑ה (Prov 20:12)
6. אִֽישׁ־אֹהֵ֣ב חָ֭כְמָה (Prov 29:3)

7. הָעָם֙ הַהֹלְכִ֣ים בַּחֹ֔שֶׁךְ (Isa 9:1)

8. בּוֹנִ֥ים הֵיכָ֖ל לַיהוָ֥ה (Ezr 4:1)

9. רָעָ֣ה יֹצֵ֔את מִגּ֖וֹי אֶל־גּ֑וֹי (Jer 25:32)

10. עֲבָדִ֖ים עַל־סוּסִ֑ים וְשָׂרִ֛ים הֹלְכִ֥ים
כַּעֲבָדִ֖ים עַל־הָאָֽרֶץ (Eccl 10:7)

**e.** Read Ps 146:5–10 out loud and translate vv 6–10 with the help of a dictionary and these notes.

*Notes*: The passage begins in v 5: "How fortunate is the one whose help is the God of Jacob, whose hope is in YHWH his God … "

v 6: וְאֶת־ an untranslatable marker of definite direct object; וְאֶת־כָּל־אֲשֶׁר־בָּ֑ם and all that is in them.

v 7: מַתִּ֥יר one who sets free.

v 9: גֵּרִ֗ים this and the next few nouns should be treated as definite, even though the definite article is not present. The absence of the article in poetic Hebrew is, in fact, quite typical (see Excursus D). יְעוֹדֵ֑ד he supports; וְדֶ֖רֶךְ and the way of; יְעַוֵּֽת he thwarts.

v 10: יִמְלֹ֤ךְ (subject) shall reign; אֱלֹהַ֣יִךְ צִ֭יּוֹן your God, O Zion; הַֽלְלוּ־יָֽהּ praise Yah! (יָֽהּ is a shortened form of the divine name יהוה.)

# Excursus C
# Nomenclature for Verbal Patterns and Root Types

## 1. Verbal Patterns

As noted in Lesson VIII, the basic verbal pattern in Hebrew is called *Qal* (light); the names of the other sets are derived from their patterns according to the root פעל (to do, make). The traditional grammars and dictionaries all follow this convention of using the root פעל, a convention borrowed from Arabic grammar. Unlike Arabic, however, the root פעל in Hebrew is susceptible to changes under certain conditions: the first radical may be spirantized and the second radical resists doubling by *dāgēš*. The root is, therefore, not ideal for paradigms and is, in fact, not regularly so used.

Occasionally scholars also use a set of sigla to designate the various patterns. In this system, the basic verbal pattern (i.e., *Qal*) is called *G* (from the German *Grundstamm* "basic stem"). Other sigla indicate the prefixes, infixes, or doubling (thus *N*, *D*, *H*). The passive patterns corresponding to the main active patterns are designated by the letter *p*: *Gp*, *Dp*, *Hp*. In many ways, this system is more descriptive of the forms than the names that have been assigned. Thus, for instance, the *N* pattern is so called because an *n* is prefixed (as in נִקְטַל) or infixed and assimilated (as in יִקָּטֵל); the *D* pattern has doubling of the second radical in all its forms. The same sigla are used for other Semitic languages, as well, and thus facilitate comparative studies.

Since the standard reference works still use the traditional nomenclature, however, it is necessary for the student to become familiar with it. The following are the names of the main verbal patterns, and their alternative designations and abbreviations in the standard reference works.

| *Name* | *Alternat. spelling* | *Abbreviation* | *Siglum* |
|---|---|---|---|
| Qal | | | G |
| Niphal | Nifal, Nip̄$^{c}$al | Niph.; Nif.; Ni. | N |
| Piel | Pi$^{c}$ēl | Pi. | D |
| Pual | Pu$^{c}$al | Pu. | Dp |
| Hithpael | Hit̲pa$^{c}$ēl | Hith. | HtD |
| Hiphil | Hifil, Hip̄$^{c}$îl | Hiph.; Hif.; Hi. | H; C |
| Hophal | Hofal, Hop̄$^{c}$al | Hoph.; Hof.; Ho. | Hp; Cp |

Most grammars and dictionaries present the verbs in the above order. In this textbook, however, the active patterns (Qal, Pi., Hi.) will be studied first because they occur far more frequently than the passive and reflexive ones (Ni., Pu., Hith., Ho.).

The student should note, too, that the dictionaries ordinarily list each verb under its Qal Perfect 3 ms form (e.g., אָהַב). Roots that are II-Wāw/ Yōd̲, however, are listed under the Qal Infinitive Construct form (e.g., בּוֹא; קוּם, בִּין).

## 2. Root Types

We have already learned in IV.1.c that root types are classified according to the *I-II-III* system. However, traditional grammars and dictionaries, again, use פעל as the model root. According to this system, the letter פ refers to the first radical (i.e., *I*), ע refers to the second (i.e., *II*), and ל to the third (i.e, *III*). Thus, for instance, I-Nûn roots are called פ״ן (Pē-Nûn), II-Wāw types are ע״ו ($^{c}$Áyin-Wāw), III-$^{\supset}$Ā́lep̄ types are ל״א (Lā́med̲-$^{\supset}$Ā́lep̄), and so forth. In addition, roots that are II-Wāw/ Yōd̲ are called "Hollow" or "Middle Weak" (Mediae Infirmae) and those that are original III-Wāw-Yōd̲ (that is III-Hē) are called "Third Weak" (Tertiae Infirmae). Clearly, the I-II-III nomenclature is less confusing. Nevertheless, because the dictionaries and grammars do use these terms regularly, it is necessary to become familiar with them. The following are the names of the Hebrew root types.

| *Root types* | *Alternative names* |
|---|---|
| I-Guttural | פ-Guttural (Pē-Guttural); First Guttural |
| II-Guttural | ע-Guttural (ʿÁyin-Guttural); Second-Guttural |
| III-Guttural | ל-Guttural (Lā́med-Guttural); Third-Guttural |
| II = III | Geminate; Double ע; ע״ע; Middle-Geminate |
| I-Nûn | פ״ן (Pē-Nûn) |
| I-ʾA̅́lep̄ | פ״א (Pē-ʾA̅́lep̄) |
| I-Wāw | פ״ו (Pē-Wāw) |
| I-Yōḏ | פ״י (Pē-Yōḏ) |
| II-Wāw | ע״ו (ʿÁyin-Wāw); Hollow (-Wāw); Middle-Weak (-Wāw) |
| II-Yōḏ | ע״י (ʿÁyin-Yōḏ); Hollow(-Yōḏ); Middle-Weak (-Yōḏ) |
| III-ʾA̅́lep̄ | ל״א (Lā́meḏ-ʾA̅́lep̄) |
| III-Hē | ל״ה (Lā́meḏ-Hē); Third-Weak |

# Lesson IX

## 1. The Independent Personal Pronouns

**a.** Forms

Pronouns in Hebrew may occur as independent forms or as suffixes. The independent forms are as follows.

| | | | | | |
|---|---|---|---|---|---|
| *3 ms* | הוּא | he, it | *3 mp* | הֵם/הֵמָּה | they |
| *3 fs* | הִיא | she, it | *3 fp* | הֵנָּה | they |
| *2 ms* | אַתָּ/אַתָּה | you | *2 mp* | אַתֶּם | you |
| *2 fs* | אַתְּ | you | *2 fp* | אַתֵּן/אַתֵּנָה | you |
| *1 cs* | אֲנִי/אָנֹכִי | I | *1 cp* | אֲנַחְנוּ | we |

*Notes*:

i. The pronouns are characterized by distinct beginnings: **ʾan-* for the first person forms, **ʾan + t* for the second (thus *ʾatt-*; see IV.2.b), and *h-* for the third.

ii. In the Pentateuch (the first five books of the Bible), the 3 fs form is almost always written as הִוא (but pronounced as הִיא).

iii. In addition to the more common 2 fs form, אַתְּ, an archaic variant, אַתִּי, is attested.

iv. In addition to the more common 1 cp אֲנַחְנוּ, the variant forms נַחְנוּ and אֲנוּ are attested.

v. Forms in pause may be vocalized or stressed a little differently (see Excursus B). These are easily recognized: אָנִי, אָנֹכִי, אֲנָחְנוּ, אָתְּ, אָתָּה.

**b.** Uses

**i.** The independent personal pronoun is used most frequently as the subject of a verbless clause (see VI.8).

אֲנִי יְהוָה *I am* YHWH (Exod 6:2)

נָבִיא הוּא *He is* a prophet (Gen 20:7)

אַתָּה הָאִישׁ *You are* the man (2 Sam 12:7)

צַדִּיק אַתָּה *You* are righteous (Jer 12:1)

מֵחָרָן אֲנָחְנוּ *We are* from Haran (Gen 29:4)

It is clear that the independent personal pronoun may precede or follow the noun. Although it may not always be evident in translation, the Hebrew word order in each case may indicate some emphasis. Thus, the statement **מֵחָרָן אֲנַחְנוּ** "we are from Haran" (Gen 29:4) answers the question, "from where do you come?" On the other hand, had the question been "who is / are from Haran?" one might expect the answer, **אֲנַחְנוּ מֵחָרָן** ("we are from Haran").

**ii.** The independent pronoun is also used for emphasis.

יְהוָה הוּא הָאֱלֹהִים YHWH is God (Deut 4:35)

אַתָּה־הוּא הָאֱלֹהִים You are God (2 Sam 7:28)

In these examples, the pronoun **הוּא** appears in addition to the subject and has an emphatic function. Here the pronoun may signify something like "the one," "the very one," "that one." In the same way, the independent personal pronoun may be used to emphasize the direct or indirect object.

אִתָּנוּ אֲנַחְנוּ with us, *even us* (Deut 5:3)

לָכֶם אַתֶּם for you, *even you* (Hag 1:4)

**iii.** The third person pronoun is sometimes used to refer emphatically to someone just mentioned and means something like "the same," "the aforementioned," or "that."

הוּא עֶזְרָא that (the aforementioned) Ezra (Ezr 7:6)

**iv.** The 3 ms and 3 fs forms are sometimes used to introduce an explanation or clarification of what precedes.

עֵשָׂ֖ו ה֥וּא אֱדֽוֹם׃ Esau, that is, Edom (Gen 36:1)

**v.** As we will learn later, the independent personal pronoun may be used to indicate a change of the speaker or actor, particularly in parenthetical comments (see XIII.4.b.ii).

## 2. The Suffixed Pronouns

Whereas the independent personal pronoun is used for the subject, the suffixed pronouns (or "pronominal suffixes") may refer to the noun as the indirect or direct object. In terms of form, three sets of suffixed pronouns may be identified.

**a.** Type A

The prepositions בְּ (in) and לְ (to, for) take suffixes of this type.

| | | | | |
|---|---|---|---|---|
| *3 ms* | לוֹ | to him | בּוֹ | in him |
| *3 fs* | לָהּ | to her | בָּהּ | in her |
| *2 ms* | לְךָ | to you | בְּךָ | in you |
| *2 fs* | לָךְ | to you | בָּךְ | in you |
| *1 cs* | לִי | to me | בִּי | in me |
| *3 mp* | לָהֶם | to them | בָּהֶם | in them |
| *3 fp* | לָהֶן | to them | בָּהֶן | in them |
| *2 mp* | לָכֶם | to you | בָּכֶם | in them |
| *2 fp* | לָכֶן | to you | בָּכֶן | in you |
| *1 cp* | לָ֫נוּ | to us | בָּ֫נוּ | in us |

*Notes*:

i. For the 3 mp one finds the variant ָם– occurring along with ָהֶם–, e.g., בָּם (in them). By analogy, one expects the 3 fp to have ָן– suffix, in addition to ָהֶם–. Although unattested with prepositions, this suffix is in fact found in other contexts and should be learned as a possible form.

ii. When in pause, the 2 ms form is usually ָךְ– (-*āḵ*). One must take special note of this, since the form is identical to the 2 fs suffix.

iii. The accent on the 1 cp suffix is important; without the penultimate stress, the word may mean something else. Compare: בָּ֫נוּ (in us), בָּנוּ (they built).

The prepositions עִם (with), אֵת (with), and בֵּין (between) take suffixed pronouns of this type. Since עִם and אֵת are derived from geminate roots, however, the suffixes are added to the base forms *ᶜimm* and *ʾitt*-, respectively.

| | | |
|---|---|---|
| *3 ms* | אִתּוֹ with him | עִמּוֹ with him |
| *3 fs* | אִתָּהּ with her | עִמָּהּ with her |
| *2 ms* | אִתְּךָ with you | עִמְּךָ with you |
| *2 fs* | אִתָּךְ with you | עִמָּךְ with you |
| *1 cs* | אִתִּי with me | עִמִּי/עִמָּדִי with me |
| *3 mp* | אִתָּם with them | עִמָּם/עִמָּהֶם with them |
| *3 fp* | –not attested– | –not attested– |
| *2 mp* | אִתְּכֶם with you | עִמָּכֶם with you |
| *2 fp* | –not attested– | –not attested– |
| *1 cp* | אִתָּ֫נוּ with us | עִמָּ֫נוּ with us |

*Note*: The 1 cs form עִמָּדִי is peculiar, but well attested.

**b.** Type B

The prepositions כְּ (like) and מִן (from) take suffixed pronouns of this type.

| | | | | |
|---|---|---|---|---|
| *3 ms* | כָּמֹ֫והוּ | like him | מִמֶּ֫נּוּ | from him |
| *3 fs* | כָּמֹ֫והָ | like her | מִמֶּ֫נָּה | from her |
| *2 ms* | כָּמֹ֫וךָ | like you | מִמְּךָ | from you |
| *2 fs* | כָּמוֹךְ | like you | מִמֵּךְ | from you |
| *1 cs* | כָּמֹ֫ונִי | like me | מִמֶּ֫נִּי / מִנִּי | from me |
| *3 mp* | כָּהֶם | like them | מֵהֶם | from them |
| *3 fp* | כָּהֶן / כָּהֵ֫נָּה | like them | מֵהֶן / מֵהֵ֫נָּה | from them |
| *2 mp* | כָּכֶם | like you | מִכֶּם | from you |
| *2 fp* | כָּכֶן | like you | מִכֶּן | from you |
| *1 cp* | כָּמֹ֫ונוּ | like us | מִמֶּ֫נּוּ | from us |

*Note*: Whereas the 1 cp form *mimménnû* is simply **mimmén-nû*, the 3 ms **mimmén-hû* becomes *mimménnû*. By the same token, the form *mimménnā*(*h*) is derived from **mimmén-hā*. The preposition עוֹד (still, yet) takes suffixes of this type: thus, עוֹדְךָ (you are still); עוֹדֶ֫נִּי (I am still); עוֹדֶ֫נּוּ (we are / he is still).

**c.** Type C

The prepositions אֶל־ (to) and עַל־ (on) take suffixed pronouns of this type.

| | | |
|---|---|---|
| *3 ms* | אֵלָיו to him | עָלָיו upon him/it |
| *3 fs* | אֵלֶ֫יהָ to her | עָלֶ֫יהָ upon her/it |
| *2 ms* | אֵלֶ֫יךָ to you | עָלֶ֫יךָ upon you |
| *2 fs* | אֵלַ֫יִךְ to you | עָלַ֫יִךְ upon you |
| *1 cs* | אֵלַי to me | עָלַי upon me |
| *3 mp* | אֲלֵיהֶם to them | עֲלֵיהֶם upon them |
| *3 fp* | אֲלֵיהֶן to them | עֲלֵיהֶן upon them |
| *2 mp* | אֲלֵיכֶם to you | עֲלֵיכֶם upon you |
| *2 fp* | –not attested– | עֲלֵיכֶן upon you |
| *1 cp* | אֵלֵ֫ינוּ to us | עָלֵ֫ינוּ upon us |

The prepositions עַד־ (until), תַּ֫חַת (under), אַחֲרֵי (after), לִפְנֵי (before), and סָבִיב (around) all take suffixed pronouns like אֶל־ and עַל־. The preposition לִפְנֵי, however, appears as לְפָנ– in all the singular and the 1 cp forms (thus לְפָנָיו, לְפָנֶ֫יךָ, etc.; but לִפְנֵיהֶם, לִפְנֵיכֶם).

## Summary of Pronominal Suffixes

| | *Type A* | *Type B* | *Type C* |
|---|---|---|---|
| *3 ms* | ־וֹ | ־הוּ | ־ָיו |
| *3 fs* | ־ָהּ | ־הָ | ־ֶ֫יהָ |
| *2 ms* | ־ְךָ | ־ךָ | ־ֶ֫יךָ |
| *2 fs* | ־ָךְ | ־ךְ | ־ַ֫יִךְ |
| *1 cs* | ־ִי | ־נִי | ־ַי |

| | *Type A* | *Type B* | *Type C* |
|---|---|---|---|
| *3 mp* | –ָם/–הֶם | –הֶם | –ֵיהֶם |
| *3 fp* | –ָן/–הֶן | –הֶן | –ֵיהֶן |
| *2 mp* | –כֶם | –כֶם | –ֵיכֶם |
| *2 fp* | –כֶן | –כֶן | –ֵיכֶן |
| *1 cp* | –נוּ | –נוּ | –ֵ֫ינוּ |

## 3. The Marker of Definite Direct Object

**a.** Almost always in Hebrew prose, and less commonly in poetry, an untranslatable particle אֶת־/אֵת is used to mark the definite direct object of the verb. A noun is said to be definite when it is a proper name, a noun with a definite article, or a noun with a suffixed pronoun (see Lesson XII).

שֹׁלֵחַ אֶת־מֹשֶׁה sending Moses

שֹׁלֵחַ אֶת־הָעֶ֫בֶד sending the servant

שֹׁלֵחַ אֶת־עַבְדִּי sending my servant

The indefinite direct object, however, is not so marked.

שֹׁלֵחַ עֶ֫בֶד sending a servant

*Note*: The marker of the definite direct object looks just like the preposition אֶת־/אֵת (with). One must determine the usage from the context.

**b.** The marker of the definite direct object must immediately precede the object and ordinarily comes after the verb and the subject.

אֲנִי שֹׁלֵחַ אֶת־עַבְדִּי I am sending my servant

If an indirect object (marked by the preposition לְ) is involved, the indirect object ordinarily precedes the direct object.

אֲנִי שֹׁלֵחַ לָכֶם אֶת־עַבְדִּי I am sending you my servant

## 4. The Object Pronouns

When the direct object of a verb is a pronoun, it may be indicated by the marker of definite direct object with a pronominal suffix of Type A.

**a.** Forms

| | | | |
|---|---|---|---|
| *3 ms* | אֹתוֹ him, it | *3 mp* | אֶתְהֶם/אֹתָם them |
| *3 fs* | אֹתָהּ her, it | *3 fp* | אֶתְהֶן/אֹתָן them |
| *2 ms* | אֹתְךָ you | *2 mp* | אֶתְכֶם you |
| *2 fs* | אֹתָךְ you | *2 fp* | –not attested– |
| *1 cs* | אֹתִי me | *1 cp* | אֹתָ֫נוּ us |

*Note*: Unlike the preposition אֶת־ / אֵת (with), which has the base form ʾ*itt*- before the suffix, the marker of direct definite object has the base form ʾ*ōṯ*- or ʾ*eṯ*-.

**b.** Use

The independent object pronoun functions as the direct object of a clause.

אֲנִי שֹׁלֵחַ אֹתוֹ I am sending *him*

הוּא שֹׁלֵחַ אֹתִי he is sending *me*

## 5. הִנֵּה

**a.** Form

The particle הִנֵּה (also הֶן־ / הֵן) may appear independently or take suffixed pronouns of Type A, as follows.

| | | | |
|---|---|---|---|
| *3 ms* | הִנּוֹ | *3 mp* | הִנָּם |
| *3 fs* | –not attested– | *3 fp* | –not attested– |
| *2 ms* | הִנְּךָ | *2 mp* | הִנְּכֶם |
| *2 fs* | הִנָּךְ/הִנֵּךְ | *2 fp* | –not attested– |
| *1 cs* | הִנְנִי | *1 cp* | הִנְנוּ |

*Note*: The 1 cs form הִנְנִי and 1 cp הִנְנוּ are derived from הִנְּנִי and הִנְּנוּ respectively – with the loss of the strong *dāgēš* (VI.7).

**b.** Uses

There is no equivalent of הִנֵּה in English. It has traditionally been translated as "Lo!" or "Behold!" But הִנֵּה is not really a demonstrative particle. Rather, it indicates the presence of someone or something, or the immediacy of an event or situation. It is very often used to introduce the circumstances of something that is happening.

Study the following examples.

| | |
|---|---|
| הִנֵּנִי | *Here I am* (Gen 22:1) |
| הִנֵּה הָאֵשׁ וְהָעֵצִים | *Here are* the fire and the wood (Gen 22:7) |
| הִנֵּה בֵין־קָדֵשׁ וּבֵין בָּרֶד | *It is* between Kadesh and Bered (Gen 16:14) |
| וַיֹּאמֶר לָבָן הֵן לוּ יְהִי כִדְבָרֶךָ | And Laban said: "*Very well*, let it be according to your word" (Gen 30:34) |
| הִנְּךָ יָפֶה דוֹדִי | *You are* handsome, my love (Song 1:16) |
| הִנְנִי נֹתֵן לוֹ אֶת־בְּרִיתִי שָׁלוֹם | *I am* giving him my covenant of peace (Num 25:12) |

## Vocabulary

*Prepositions*:

אֵת / אֶת־ with, together with. Also the marker of definite direct object.

סָבִיב around. Also used as an adjective (round about, around)

עִם with

*Verbs*:

זָבַח to sacrifice. *Nouns*: מִזְבֵּחַ (mp. מִזְבְּחוֹת) altar; זֶ֫בַח sacrifice

כָּרַת to cut. Also used in the idiom כָּרַת בְּרִית "to make a covenant" (lit.: to cut a covenant)

שָׁלַח to send, stretch out, let go

*Nouns*:

אֵשׁ (fs) fire

גִּבּוֹר hero, warrior. גְּבוּרָה strength, might

דּוֹר (pl. usually דּוֹרוֹת) generation

זֶ֫רַע seed. *Verb*: זָרַע to sow

מִדְבָּר desert, wilderness, wasteland

נָהָר (pl. נְהָרוֹת or נְהָרִים) river

עֵץ (pl. עֵצִים) tree, wood

פַּרְעֹה pharaoh (the king of Egypt)

שָׂדֶה (pl. שָׂדוֹת) field, country

שֵׁם (pl. שֵׁמוֹת) name

שָׁנָה (fp. שָׁנִים) year

*Proper Names:*

אֵלִיָּה Elijah

רִבְקָה Rebecca

דָּנִאֵל Daniel

## Exercise 9

**a.** Translate into English:

1. לָהֶם
2. בָּהּ
3. מִמֶּנִּי
4. אִתְּכֶם
5. עִמִּי
6. כָּמוֹהוּ
7. עִמָּדִי
8. בָּם
9. מֵהֵנָּה
10. עִמָּהֶם
11. תַּחְתַּי
12. אֲלֵיכֶם
13. לְפָנֶיךָ
14. עָלַיִךְ
15. לְפָנַי

**b.** Translate into Hebrew:

1. in me
2. from him
3. from us
4. to(ward) me
5. upon you (fs)
6. from you (mp)
7. from you (fp)
8. like her
9. upon me
10. for you (ms)
11. for you (fs)
12. for her
13. like them (mp)
14. for us
15. like him

**c.** Write the following in Hebrew:

1. I am a prophet like you (ms)
2. I am doing a new thing
3. I am making a covenant
4. like a consuming fire
5. the matter is too heavy for you (ms)
6. an angel sent to (אֶל־) them
7. a hand that is stretched out against me
8. you (ms) are more righteous than I

9. you (ms) and they (mp) alike
10. lo, you are wiser than Daniel

**d.** Translate the following into English:

1. עִמָּנוּ אֵל (Isa 8:10)
2. הוּא אִתִּי (Gen 30:33)
3. הִנְּךָ יָפֶה (Song 1:16)
4. הִנָּךְ יָפָה (Song 1:15)
5. הָעֹלִים עִמִּי (Ezr 8:1)
6. הַשֹּׁמְרִים אֹתִי (Zech 11:11)
7. הָאֹכְלִים אִתּוֹ (Gen 43:32)
8. רוּחַ אַחֶרֶת עִמּוֹ (Num 14:24)
9. הֵם אִתָּנוּ (Gen 34:21)
10. וְאַבְרָהָם הֹלֵךְ עִמָּם (Gen 18:16)
11. הִנֵּה הָאֵשׁ וְהָעֵצִים (Gen 22:7)
12. הִנֵּה־רִבְקָה לְפָנֶיךָ (Gen 24:51)

**e.** Read Gen 41:17–20 out loud and translate the passage with the help of a dictionary and these notes.

*Notes*:

v 17: וַיְדַבֵּר (subject) spoke; בַּחֲלֹמִי in my dream; שְׂפַת הַיְאֹר the bank of the river (i.e., the Nile).

v 18: בְּרִיאוֹת בָּשָׂר lit.: sturdy of flesh; וִיפֹת תֹּאַר lit.: and beautiful of form; וַתִּרְעֶינָה and they were feeding.

v 19: וְרָעוֹת תֹּאַר מְאֹד lit.: and very ugly of form; וְרַקּוֹת בָּשָׂר lit.: and thin of flesh; בְּכָל־אֶרֶץ מִצְרָיִם in all the land of Egypt.

v 20: וַתֹּאכַלְנָה and (subject) ate.

# Lesson X

## 1. The Demonstratives

A demonstrative is a word that points to someone or something to make that referent more specific: *this*, *that*, *these*, *those*. It may be used as an adjective (e.g., *this woman*) or as a pronoun (e.g., *this is the woman*).

**a.** Forms

Whereas English distinguishes between near demonstratives (this, these) and far (that, those), Hebrew uses only one set. The demonstrative simply points to something or someone, whether near or far.

| | | | | | | | | |
|---|---|---|---|---|---|---|---|---|
| *ms* | זֶה | this | *fs* | **זֹאת** | this | *cp* | אֵ֫לֶּה | these |

*Notes*:

i. In addition to the normal fs form **זֹאת**, the variants **זֹה** and **זוֹ** are attested for the fs.

ii. The form אֵל is found as a variant of **אֵ֫לֶּה.**

iii. The ms forms הַלָּז and הַלָּ֫זֶה and the fs הַלֵּ֫זוּ are also used as demonstratives.

**b.** Uses

**i.** The demonstrative may be used as an adjective. Compare the following two sets.

| *With adjective* | | *With demonstrative* | |
|---|---|---|---|
| הָאִישׁ הַטּוֹב | the good man | הָאִישׁ הַזֶּה | this man |
| הָאִשָּׁה הַטּוֹבָה | the good woman | הָאִשָּׁה הַזֹּאת | this woman |
| הָאֲנָשִׁים הַטּוֹבִים | the good men | הָאֲנָשִׁים הָאֵ֫לֶּה | these men |
| הַנָּשִׁים הַטּוֹבוֹת | the good women | הַנָּשִׁים הָאֵ֫לֶּה | these women |

When the demonstrative is used with adjectives (and participles functioning as adjectives), it stands in the final position – after the adjective(s).

| | |
|---|---|
| הַגּוֹי הַגָּדוֹל הַזֶּה | *this* great nation (Deut 4:6) |
| לָעִיר הַגְּדוֹלָה הַזֹּאת | to *this* great city (Jer 22:8) |
| הַשָּׁנִים הַטֹּבֹת הַבָּאֹת הָאֵלֶּה | *these* coming good years (Gen 41:35) |

A third person independent pronoun may be used emphatically (see IX.1.b.ii) to take the place of a demonstrative adjective. When it does, an article may appear before the pronoun: הָאִישׁ הַהוּא the man, the very one = that man.

| | |
|---|---|
| בַּיָּמִים הָהֵם וּבָעֵת הַהִיא[1] | in *those* days and at *that* time (Jer 33:15) |

**ii.** The demonstrative may be used as a pronoun. Compare the following two sets:

| *With pronoun* | | *With demonstrative* | |
|---|---|---|---|
| הוּא הָאִישׁ | he is the man | זֶה הָאִישׁ | this is the man |
| הִיא הָאִשָּׁה | she is the woman | זֹאת הָאִשָּׁה | this is the woman |
| הֵם הָאֲנָשִׁים | they are the men | אֵלֶּה הָאֲנָשִׁים | these are the men |

**iii.** The repetition of the same demonstrative may indicate reciprocity or contrast.

| | |
|---|---|
| זֶה אֶל־זֶה | this one to that one = one to another (Isa 6:3) |
| זֹאת אֹמֶרֶת...וְזֹאת אֹמֶרֶת | this one was saying ... but that one was saying (1 Kgs 3:23) |

1. Contrary to the rule given in Lesson VI.1.b.ii, the definite article before הֵם and הֵנָּה shows compensatory lengthening; the singular forms הוּא and הִיא, however, show virtual doubling.

## 2. Relative Clauses

We have already seen in Lesson VIII that the participle used as an attributive adjective or substantive may be rendered in English by the relative pronouns "who ... " or "that ... " (e.g., **הָאִישׁ הָעֹמֵד** the man who is standing; **הַתּוֹרָה הַכְּתוּבָה** the instruction *that* is written). There are other ways of expressing the relative in Hebrew, however.

**a.** Relative clauses in Hebrew prose are commonly introduced by the particle **אֲשֶׁר** (that, who, which, when). The particle may refer to an antecedent of any gender, number, or case. Its precise translation, therefore, depends on the context. Study the following examples.

| | |
|---|---|
| אֶל־הָאָרֶץ אֲשֶׁר אָנֹכִי נֹתֵן לָהֶם | to the land *which* I am giving them (Josh 1:2) |
| וְהַיָּמִים אֲשֶׁר מָלַךְ דָּוִד | the days *when* David reigned (1 Kgs 2:11) |
| הָאִשָּׁה אֲשֶׁר נָתַתָּה עִמָּדִי | the woman *whom* you put beside me (Gen 3:12) |

There is often a resumptive element at the end of the relative clause which is redundant in English and best left untranslated.

| | |
|---|---|
| הַמָּקוֹם אֲשֶׁר אַתָּה עוֹמֵד עָלָיו | the place *where* you are standing *on it* = the place on *which* you stand (Exod 3:5) |
| עַל־הָאָרֶץ אֲשֶׁר אַתֶּם יֹשְׁבִים בָּהּ | upon the land *where* you are dwelling *in it* = upon the land in *which* you dwell (Num 33:55) |
| מִן־הַמָּקוֹם אֲשֶׁר־אַתָּה שָׁם | from the place *where* you are *there* = from the place *where* you are (Gen 13:14) |

**b.** Relative clauses may also be introduced by –שֶׁ / –שַׁ, with doubling of the following consonant (where permissible). There is no difference in meaning between -שֶׁ / -שַׁ and אֲשֶׁר; they appear to be dialectal variants.

שֶׁהַנְּחָלִים הֹלְכִים *where* the streams flow (Eccl 1:7)

**c.** In archaic poetry, זֶה and the related forms זוּ (ms) and זֹה / זוֹ (fs) may be found instead of אֲשֶׁר or -שֶׁ / -שַׁ.

הַר־צִיּוֹן זֶה ׀ שָׁכַנְתָּ בּוֹ Mount Zion *wherein* you dwell (Ps 74:2)

עַם־זוּ גָּאָלְתָּ a people *whom* you redeemed (Exod 15:13)

**d.** A relative clause is sometimes expressed without explicit markers. Such clauses are said to be *asyndetic* (without connector). Only the context will determine that the clause is relative.

בְּאֶרֶץ לֹא לָהֶם in a land *that* is not theirs (Gen 15:13)

## 3. The Particle of Existence יֵשׁ

**a.** To express the existence of something or someone, the particle יֵשׁ / יֶשׁ־ is used. This particle is simply translated as "is/are" or "there is / are."

יֵשׁ נָבִיא בְּיִשְׂרָאֵל *there is* a prophet in Israel (2 Kgs 5:8)

יֵשׁ יְהוָה בַּמָּקוֹם הַזֶּה YHWH *is* (present) in this place (Gen 28:16)

יֵשׁ צַדִּיקִים *there are* righteous ones (Eccl 8:14)

**b.** To express existence of a person or persons, Hebrew sometimes uses יֵשׁ with pronominal suffixes of Type A (IX.2.a), except that the 3 ms form is יֶשְׁנוֹ, instead of *יֵשׁוֹ, as one might expect.

אֶת־אֲשֶׁר יֶשְׁנוֹ פֹּה with the one who *is* here (Deut 29:14)

*Note*: To express continuing presence, one uses the adverb עוֹד (still) with pronominal suffixes of Type B (see IX.2.b).

וְהוּא עוֹדֶנּוּ שָׁם and he was still there (Gen 44:14)

**c.** To express possession, the idiom X יֶשׁ־לְ may be used.

יֵשׁ אֱלֹהִים לְיִשְׂרָאֵל Israel *has* a God (1 Sam 17:46)

יֶשׁ־לִי תִקְוָה I *have* hope (Ruth 1:12)

## 4. The Particle of Negation אֵין

**a.** To express non-existence or absence, the particle אֵין (אַ֫יִן when stressed) is used.

אֵין אִישׁ עִמָּנוּ *there is no* one with us (Gen 31:50)

אֵין כָּמֹנִי *there is none* like me (Exod 9:14)

**b.** To express absence of a person or persons, Hebrew sometimes uses אֵין with suffixes of Type B (IX.2.b) or Type A (IX.2.a).

יוֹסֵף אֵינֶנּוּ Joseph *is not here* (Gen 42:36)

אֵינֶנִּי בְּקִרְבְּכֶם *I will not be* in your midst (Deut 1:42)

**c.** To express non-possession, the idiom X אֵין לְ may be used.

אֵין לוֹ בֵּן he *has no* son (Num 27:4)

## 5. אֵין vs. לֹא

**a.** The negative particle אֵין typically negates verbless clauses. Participles, because they may function as substantives, are negated in this way.

אֵינֶנִּי נֹתֵן לָכֶם תֶּבֶן *I am not* giving you straw! (Exod. 5:10)

אֵינָם יֹדְעִים *they do not* know (2 Kgs. 17:26)

**b.** The negative particle לֹא is used for verbal clauses (about which we will learn later). This particle, however, also negates single words.

לֹא־אֵל *not* God (Deut 32:21)

וְלֹא חָכָם *not* wise (Deut 32:6)

## 6. Interrogative Clauses

**a.** Questions are sometimes not indicated as such in the text (that is, there are no special markers or punctuation). Presumably in speech such questions were originally indicated by intonation.

שָׁלוֹם לַנַּעַר Is the boy well? (2 Sam 18:29)

**b.** Most frequently, questions are introduced by a prefixed interrogative particle (ה) found in the following forms.

**i.** Before most consonants, including ר, it is הֲ.

הֲיֵשׁ לָכֶם אָח Do you have a brother? (Gen 43:7)

הֲזֶה אוֹ־זֶה whether this or that? (Eccl 11:6)

**ii.** Before a guttural it is ordinarily הַ.

הַאַתָּה יוֹאָב Are you Joab? (2 Sam 20:17)

**iii.** Before any consonant with a *šĕwāʾ* it is הַ.

הַמְעַט מִכֶּם Is it too little for you? (Isa 7:13)

**iv.** Before a guttural with ָ it is הֶ.

הֶאָמוּר Should it be said? (Mic 2:7)

*Note*: In contrast to the definite article, the interrogative ה does *not* call for the doubling of the following radical. Only in a few instances does a *dāgēš* appear anomalously.

**c.** The personal interrogative pronoun (who?) is מִי, which may refer to an animate noun of any gender, number, or case (i.e., who? whose? whom?).

מִי־הָאִישׁ הַלָּזֶה *Who* is that man? (Gen 24:65)

מִי־אֵלֶּה *Who* are these? (Gen 33:5)

לְמִי־אַתָּה *To whom* do you belong? (Gen 32:18)

Less frequently, מִי may be translated by the indefinite "whoever, whosoever."

מִי לַיהוָה *Whoever* is for YHWH (Exod 32:26)

**d.** The impersonal interrogative pronoun (what?) is מה, which may refer to an inanimate noun, whether singular or plural. It is vocalized in various ways, but is always easy to recognize.

**i.** The form is ordinarily מַה־ plus doubling of the following radical.

מַה־שְּׁמוֹ  *What* is his name? (Exod 3:13)

**ii.** Before א and ר it is מָה.

מָה אַתֶּם עֹשִׂים  *What* are you doing? (Judg 18:18)

**iii.** Before ח and ע it is usually מֶה.

מֶה־עֲוֹנִי  *What* is my guilt? (1 Sam 20:1)

**iv.** Before ה it is either מָה or מֶה.

מֶה הַחֲלוֹם הַזֶּה  *What* is this dream? (Gen 37:10)

מֶה־הֹוֶה לָאָדָם  *What* exists for the human? (Eccl 2:22)

Various prepositions may be combined with מה. The following should be committed to memory.

בַּמֶּה / בַּמָּה / בַּמַּה־  by what? = how?

כַּמֶּה / כַּמָּה  like what? = how many, how much?

לָמֶה / לָמָה / לָ֫מָּה  for what? = why?

עַד־מָה  until what? = how long?

עַל־מָה  upon what = why?

Less frequently, מה may be translated by the indefinite "whatever, whatsoever."

מַה־בַּבָּיִת  *whatever* (is) in the house (Gen 39:8)

**e.** The interrogative adverb of manner (how?) is אֵיכָה / אֵיךְ.

אֵיךְ נָשִׁיר  *how* shall we sing? (Ps 137:4)

**f.** The most common interrogative adverb of place (where?) is אַיֵּה / אֵי.

| | |
|---|---|
| אֵי הֶבֶל | *where* is Abel? (Gen. 4:9) |
| אַיֵּה שָׂרָה | *where* is Sarah? (Gen 18:9) |
| אַיֵּה הָאֲנָשִׁים | *where* are the men? (Gen 19:5) |

This adverb may take suffixes of Type A (IX.2.a): אַיֶּכָּה (where are you?), אַיּוֹ (where is he?), אַיָּם (where are they?). In addition to אַיֵּה / אֵי, the form מֵאַיִן (from where?) must be learned.

| | |
|---|---|
| מֵאַיִן אַתֶּם | Where are you from? (Gen 29:4) |

## 7. Exclamations and Emphatic Questions

**a.** As in English, certain interrogative words may become exclamatory.

i. אֵיכָה / אֵיךְ (how!)

| | |
|---|---|
| אֵיךְ נָפַלְתָּ מִשָּׁמַיִם | *How* you have fallen from heaven! (Isa 14:12) |

ii. מֶה / מָה / מַה־ (how!)

| | |
|---|---|
| מָה רַב־טוּבְךָ | *How* abundant is your goodness! (Ps 31:20) |

**b.** Often זֶה or זֹאת is added to make a question emphatic.

| | |
|---|---|
| מַה־זֹּאת עָשִׂינוּ | *Whatever* have we done? (Exod 14:5) |
| לָמָּה זֶּה אַתֶּם עֹבְרִים | *Why* (indeed) are you transgressing? (Num 14:41) |

## 8. אֲשֶׁר as a Conjunction

Sometimes אֲשֶׁר (also שֶׁ– / שַׁ–) may be used as a conjunction meaning "that, so that, since, because, for."

| | |
|---|---|
| אֲשֶׁר אָנֹכִי שֹׁמֵעַ | *for* I hear (1 Sam 2:23) |

| | |
|---|---|
| אֲשֶׁר הֵם חַיִּים | *so that* they are living (Deut 4:10) |
| טוֹב אֲשֶׁר לֹא־תִדֹּר | better *that* you do not vow (Eccl 5:4) |

The conjunctive use of אֲשֶׁר (also –שֶׁ/–שַׁ) is especially evident when it is used with certain prepositions. The following combinations of אֲשֶׁר with other prepositions should be committed to memory.

| | |
|---|---|
| בַּאֲשֶׁר | in that, inasmuch as |
| כַּאֲשֶׁר | as, even as, when |
| עֵקֶב אֲשֶׁר | because, because of |
| יַעַן אֲשֶׁר | because, because of |
| אַחֲרֵי אֲשֶׁר | after |

## Vocabulary

*Nouns*:

| | |
|---|---|
| אוֹת | (ms; but fp: אוֹתוֹת) sign, mark |
| בַּד | solitude. *Adverb*: [לְבַד] alone. Takes suffixes of Type A (IX.2.a): לְבַדּוֹ (by himself, he alone); לְבַדִּי (by myself, I alone). |
| כִּסֵּא | (pl. כִּסְאוֹת) throne, chair |
| נַעַר | lad |
| עֵת | (fs) time, season. *Adverb*: עַתָּה now |
| שָׁלוֹם | peace, well-being, wholeness. Note the idioms: שָׁאַל שָׁלוֹם to ask about (someone's) well being; הֲשָׁלוֹם is (subject) well? |
| שֶׁמֶשׁ | (usually regarded as fs) sun |
| תּוֹרָה | instruction, law. *Verb*: יָרָה to teach, instruct, cast |

*Verbs*:

| | |
|---|---|
| בָּכָה | to weep |
| בָּרָא | to create |
| יָצַר | to form |
| מָשַׁל | (takes object marked by בְּ) to govern, dominate |
| נָפַל | to fall |
| שָׁכַב | to lie down |

*Adverbs*:

| | |
|---|---|
| גַּם | also, even, morever, yea, although. גַּם ... גַּם both ... and |
| מַדּוּעַ | why? |
| עוֹד | still, yet, again, else |
| פֹּה | here |
| שָׁם | there |

*Conjunction*:

| | |
|---|---|
| כִּי | for, because, that, indeed, surely, when (sometimes כִּי simply introduces a quotation) |

## Exercise 10

**a.** Translate the following into Hebrew:

1. this great nation
2. who is wise?
3. is this the man?
4. who is the woman?
5. where are the men?
6. these cities
7. these great signs
8. these are the wicked
9. we have no food
10. where are you (ms)?
11. whoever is for YHWH
12. there is no king and no prince
13. who is like you (ms)?
14. a man lying with a woman
15. what are you (mp) doing?
16. the lad is not with (אֵת) us
17. is this the great city?
18. a man governing Israel
19. YHWH is in this place
20. do you (mp) have a brother?

**b.** Translate the following into English:

1. שָׁל֥וֹם ׀ שָׁל֖וֹם וְאֵ֥ין שָׁלֽוֹם (Jer 6:14)
2. אֵין־ט֤וֹב לָֽאָדָם֙ תַּ֣חַת הַשֶּׁ֔מֶשׁ (Eccl 8:15)
3. הָאָ֗רֶץ אֲשֶׁ֤ר אַתָּה֙ שֹׁכֵ֣ב עָלֶ֔יהָ (Gen 28:13)
4. יֵשׁ־אֱ֝לֹהִ֗ים שֹׁפְטִ֥ים בָּאָֽרֶץ (Ps 58:12)
5. כַּמָּ֣ה לִ֭י עֲוֺנ֣וֹת וְחַטָּא֑וֹת (Job 13:23)
6. מָ֛ה הָאֲבָנִ֥ים הָאֵ֖לֶּה לָכֶֽם (Josh 4:6)
7. מִֽי־יוֹדֵ֡עַ מַה־טּוֹב֩ לָֽאָדָ֨ם בַּֽחַיִּ֜ים (Eccl 6:12)
8. גַּם־אַתָּ֕ה גַּם־הָעָ֥ם הַזֶּ֖ה אֲשֶׁ֣ר עִמָּ֑ךְ (Exod 18:18)
9. כִּֽי־כָבֵ֤ד מִמְּךָ֙ הַדָּבָ֔ר (Exod 18:18)
10. הַֽאֵינְךָ֣ רֹאֶ֔ה מָ֛ה הֵ֥מָּה עֹשִׂ֖ים (Jer 7:17)
11. ה֛וּא וְהָאֲנָשִׁ֥ים אֲשֶׁר־עִמּ֖וֹ (Gen 24:54)
12. מָֽה־הַדָּבָ֤ר הָרָע֙ הַזֶּ֨ה אֲשֶׁ֤ר אַתֶּם֙ עֹשִׂ֔ים (Neh 13:17)

13. מָֽה־הַדָּבָ֤ר הַזֶּה֙ אֲשֶׁ֤ר אַתָּה֙ עֹשֶׂ֣ה לָעָ֔ם (Exod 18:14)
14. מַדּ֗וּעַ אַתָּ֤ה יוֹשֵׁב֙ לְבַדֶּ֔ךָ (Exod 18:14)
15. לֹ֣א זֶ֣ה הַדֶּ֗רֶךְ וְלֹ֣א זֹ֣ה הָעִיר֒ (2 Kgs 6:19)
16. אֵינֶ֨נּוּ גָד֜וֹל בַּבַּ֣יִת הַזֶּה֮ מִמֶּנִּי֒ (Gen 39:9)
17. מִ֣י זֹ֗את עֹלָה֙ מִן־הַמִּדְבָּ֔ר (Song 8:5)
18. הִנֵּ֨ה אָנֹכִ֜י שֹׁלֵ֤חַ מַלְאָךְ֙ לְפָנֶ֔יךָ (Exod 23:20)
19. וְאַ֨בְרָהָ֔ם עוֹדֶ֥נּוּ עֹמֵ֖ד לִפְנֵ֥י יְהוָֽה (Gen 18:22)
20. אֲנִ֥י יְהוָ֖ה וְאֵ֥ין עֽוֹד׃
    יוֹצֵ֥ר אוֹר֙ וּבוֹרֵ֣א חֹ֔שֶׁךְ
    עֹשֶׂ֥ה שָׁל֖וֹם וּב֣וֹרֵא רָ֑ע (Isa 45:6–7)

**c.** Read Deut 29:12–14 out loud and translate the passage with the help of a dictionary and these notes.

*Notes*:

v 12: לְמַ֣עַן הָקִֽים so that he (i.e., YHWH) may establish; יִֽהְיֶה will be; דִּבֶּר he spoke; נִשְׁבַּע֙ he swore; לַאֲבֹתֶ֔יךָ to your forebears.

v 14: אֱלֹהֵ֑ינוּ our God.

# Lesson XI

## 1. The Construct Chain

There is no word in Biblical Hebrew that corresponds in every way to the English preposition "of." To say "a son of a man" in Hebrew, then, one would ordinarily juxtapose the nouns, and sometimes link them with the *maqqēp̄*, e.g., בֶּן־אִישׁ "a son of a man." In this construction, the noun בֶּן־ is said to be in the *construct state*, whereas the noun אִישׁ is said to be in the *absolute state*. The words in such a construct chain are thought to be so closely related that they are read as if they constituted one long word.

There may be three or even four nouns in a construct chain, e.g., בֶּן־אִישׁ־חָ֫יִל "a son *of* a man *of* valor." In any case, only the last noun in the chain is in the absolute state; all the others are construct nouns.

Nouns in the construct state cannot, as a rule, take the definite article. Nouns in the absolute state, on the other hand, may be indefinite or definite. The definiteness of the noun in the absolute state determines the definiteness of the entire chain. Thus,

**a.** the construct chain is indefinite if the absolute noun is indefinite.

אִישׁ מִלְחָמָה *a* man of war (Exod 15:3)

**b.** the construct chain is definite if the absolute noun is definite

אֲרוֹן הַבְּרִית *the* ark of the covenant (Josh 4:9)

עֶ֫בֶד אַבְרָהָם *the* servant of Abraham (Gen 24:34)

בֵּית אָבִי *the* house of my father (1 Kgs 2:31)

Since construct nouns as a rule do not take the definite article, a construct noun with a prefixed preposition (בְּ, כְּ, לְ) will also not have the definite article: בְּבֵית אָבִי in *the* house of my father (Judg 6:15).

Adjectives and demonstratives do not normally interrupt the

construct chain; even if they qualify the construct noun, they will stand after the absolute. The adjective and/or demonstrative will, of course, agree in gender and number with the noun it qualifies. Compare the following.

בֶּן־הָאִשָּׁה הַטּוֹבָה הַזֹּאת the son of this good woman

בֶּן־הָאִשָּׁה הַטּוֹב הַזֶּה this good son of the woman

It is clear, then, that the absolute noun determines the definiteness of the entire construct chain. The construct chain is not, therefore, employed to express a relationship of possession between an indefinite noun and a definite noun. Instead, the preposition לְ (to, for, belonging to) is used.

בֵּן לְיִשַׁי son of Jesse (1 Sam 16:18)

Since proper names are considered definite, the simple juxtaposition of the nouns without the intervening לְ would make the phrase definite. Thus, whereas בֶּן־יִשַׁי (1 Sam 20:27) means "*the* son of Jesse," בֵּן לְיִשַׁי means "*a* son of Jesse" (1 Sam 16:18). By the same token, עֶבֶד אֲדֹנִי (Dan 10:17) means "*the* servant of my lord," but עֶבֶד לַאדֹנִי (Gen 44:33) means "*a* servant of my lord." In short, the addition of לְ breaks the construct chain.

## 2. Construct Noun Forms

Many nouns manifest no difference in form between the construct and the absolute. But since nouns in construct (except for singular segolates) tend to lose their primary stress, certain changes may be expected. The following rules account for most of the changes.

**a.** The vowel ֵ (*ē*) in a monosyllabic noun frequently becomes ֶ (*e*) when that noun is joined to the following word(s) by means of the *maqqēp̄*.

| *Absolute* | *Construct* |
|---|---|
| בֵּן son | בֶּן־ son of |
| לֵב heart | לֶב־ / לֵב־ heart of |

**b.** The vowel ָ (*ā*) in a final closed syllable becomes ַ (*a*).

| *Absolute* | *Construct* |
|---|---|
| יָד hand | יַד hand of |
| מַלְאָךְ angel | מַלְאַךְ angel of |

**c.** The masculine plural (ִים–) or dual ending (ַיִם–) changes to ֵי (*ê*)

| *Absolute* | *Construct* |
|---|---|
| אֲדֹנִים lords | אֲדֹנֵי lords of |
| מַיִם waters | מֵי waters of |

**d.** In an open syllable ָ (*ā*) or ֵ (*ē*) reduces to *šĕwāʾ*.

| *Absolute* | *Construct* |
|---|---|
| שָׁלוֹם peace | שְׁלוֹם peace of |
| שֵׁמוֹת names | שְׁמוֹת names of |

*Notes:*

i. In some nouns, long *ā* or *ē* is not reduced. This is so because the long vowel is the result of compensatory lengthening (IV.2.a.i.α) or the root is II-Wāw/Yōḏ (IV.2.c.vi).

| *Absolute* | *Construct* |
|---|---|
| שָׂרִים (שׂרר) princes | שָׂרֵי (not *שְׂרֵי) rulers of |
| עָבִים (עוב) clouds | עָבֵי (not *עֲבֵי) clouds of |
| עֵדִים (עוד) witnesses | עֵדֵי (not *עֲדֵי) witnesses of |

ii. If the reduction of a vowel results in two vocal *šĕwāʾ*'s in immediate succession, the *Rule of Šĕwāʾ* applies (see VI.3).

| *Absolute* | *Construct* |
|---|---|
| דְּבָרִים words | דִּבְרֵי < *דְּבְרֵי < *דְּבָרֵי words of |
| אֲנָשִׁים men | אַנְשֵׁי < *אֲנְשֵׁי < *אֲנָשֵׁי men of |
| אֲרָצוֹת lands | אַרְצוֹת < *אֲרְצוֹת lands of |

**e.** The feminine ending ָה– changes to ַת–.

| *Absolute* | *Construct* |
|---|---|
| תּוֹרָה instruction | תּוֹרַת instruction of |

**f.** Final ֶה– becomes ֵה–.

| *Absolute* | *Construct* |
|---|---|
| מַעֲשֶׂה deed | מַעֲשֵׂה deed of |

**g.** Original **aw* contracts to *ô*, since the stress is lost (see IV.2.c.iii.β).

| *Absolute* | *Construct* |
|---|---|
| מָוֶת death | מוֹת death of |

**h.** Original **ay* contracts to *ê*, since the stress is lost (see IV.2.c.iv.β).

| *Absolute* | *Construct* |
|---|---|
| בַּ֫יִת house | בֵּית house of |

**j.** Segolate plurals retain their **qaṭl*, **qiṭl*, or **qoṭl* (**quṭl*) bases (see V.2). Thus, the three different types are discernible in the plural construct.

i. **qaṭl*

| *Absolute* | *Construct* |
|---|---|
| מְלָכִים kings | מַלְכֵי kings of |
| נְפָשׁוֹת lives | נַפְשׁוֹת lives of |

ii. **qiṭl*

| *Absolute* | *Construct* |
|---|---|
| סְפָרִים books | סִפְרֵי books of |

iii. **qoṭl* (**quṭl*)

| *Absolute* | *Construct* |
|---|---|
| חֳדָשִׁים new moons | חָדְשֵׁי new moons of |
| גֳּרָנוֹת threshing floors | גָּרְנוֹת threshing floors of |

**k.** Nouns of the *qāṭēl* pattern become *qĕṭal*.

| *Absolute* | *Construct* |
|---|---|
| זָקֵן elder | זְקַן elder of |

A few nouns have construct forms that are unpredictable. The following should be committed to memory.

| *Absolute* | *Construct* |
|---|---|
| אִשָּׁה wife | אֵשֶׁת wife of |
| אָב father | אֲבִי father of |
| אָח brother | אֲחִי brother of |
| אַחִים brothers | אֲחֵי brothers of |
| יָרֵךְ thigh | יֶרֶךְ thigh of |
| כָּתֵף shoulder | כֶּתֶף shoulder of |
| מִלְחָמָה battle | מִלְחֶמֶת battle of |
| בְּהֵמָה beast | בֶּהֱמַת beast of |
| מִשְׁפָּחָה family | מִשְׁפַּחַת family of |
| עָרִים cities | עָרֵי cities of |
| פֶּה mouth | פִּי mouth of |
| רָאשִׁים heads | רָאשֵׁי heads of |

## 3. Participles and Adjectives in Construct Chains

Participles and adjectives also appear in construct chains, since they may be used as substantives.

**a.** Participles

| | |
|---|---|
| חֹלֵם חֲלוֹם | a *dreamer* of a dream (Deut 13:2) |
| חוֹלֵם הַחֲלוֹם | the *dreamer* of the dream (Deut 13:4) |
| בֹּנֵי שְׁלֹמֹה | Solomon's *builders* (I Kgs 5:32) |

**b.** Adjectives

| | |
|---|---|
| יְפֵה־תֹאַר וִיפֵה מַרְאֶה | *handsome* in form and *handsome* in appearance (Gen 39:6) |
| כְבַד־פֶּה וּכְבַד לָשׁוֹן | *heavy* of mouth and *heavy* of tongue (Exod 4:10) |

## 4. Translation of the Construct Chain

Although genitive relation is expressed by the construct chain, it does not mean that the construct chain must always be translated by the English preposition *of*. One must determine from the context the proper function of the absolute. Consider the following examples.

| | |
|---|---|
| זָבַת חָלָב וּדְבָשׁ | *flowing with* milk and honey (Exod 3:8) |
| חוֹלַת אַהֲבָה | *sick with* love (Song 2:5) |
| יוֹרְדֵי־בוֹר | *those who go down to* the pit (Isa 38:18) |

Very frequently, the construct chain takes the place of an adjectival construction:

| | |
|---|---|
| זֶרַע קֹדֶשׁ | seed of holiness = a holy seed (Isa 6:13) |
| בְּרִית עוֹלָם | covenant of eternity = eternal covenant (Gen 9:16) |

## 5. The Forms and Uses of כֹּל

**a.** The word כֹּל (any, all, each, every) may appear in three forms.

**i.** Independent form: כֹּל.

כֹּל יְמֵי חַיֶּיךָ all the days of your life (Gen 3:17)

**ii.** With the *maqqēp̄*: ־כָּל (*kol-*).

כָּל־עֵץ every tree (Gen 2:9)

**iii.** With pronominal suffix of Type A (IX.2.a): –כֻּל.

כֻּלָּנוּ all of us (Deut 5:3)

כֻּלָּם all of them (Gen 43:34)

**b.** The translation of כֹּל depends on the definiteness of the noun it qualifies.

**i.** It may be a substantive, used independently with the meaning "everyone, everything, all." The word may appear with or without the definite article.

כֹּל אֲשֶׁר־בָּאָרֶץ *everything* that is on earth (Gen 6:17)

יָדוֹ בַכֹּל וְיַד כֹּל בּוֹ his hand is against *everyone*, and *every one*'s hand is against him (Gen 16:12)

**ii.** It may appear in the construct state with a definite noun, in which case it means "all of" or "the whole of."

כָּל־הָעֵדָה *the whole* congregation (Num 16:3)

כֹּל גּוֹיֵי הָאָרֶץ *all* (of) the nations of the earth (Gen 18:18)

**iii.** It may appear in the construct state with an indefinite noun, in which case it may be translated as "every," or "each."

כֹּל צִפּוֹר כָּל־כָּנָף *every* bird, *every* winged thing (Gen 7:14)

בְּכָל־יוֹם on *each* day (Ps 7:12)

## 6. The Superlative

Hebrew has no special form or ending for the superlative (e.g., tallest, greatest). Rather, the superlative may be expressed in a variety of ways.

**a.** By an adjective that is definite in form or in sense.

הַקָּטֹן the *youngest* (Gen 42:13)

קְטַן בָּנָיו the *youngest* of his sons (2 Chron 21:17)

*Note*: In the first example, of course, one must determine from context if the word means "the youngest" or simply "the young one."

**b.** By the adjective + the preposition בְּ with a plural noun.

הַיָּפָה בַּנָּשִׁים the *most beautiful* among women (Song 1:8)

**c.** By means of a construct chain.

קֹדֶשׁ הַקֳּדָשִׁים the *holiest* place (Exod 26:33)

עֶבֶד עֲבָדִים *lowliest* slave (Gen 9:25)

The superlative may be intended even if the construct and absolute are not semantically related.

חַכְמֵי יֹעֲצֵי פַרְעֹה *the wisest* of Pharaoh's advisors (Isa 19:11)

וְאֶבְיוֹנֵי אָדָם *the neediest* of humanity (Isa 29:19)

**d.** By means of the מִן (used as a comparative) with כֹּל.

עָרוּם מִכֹּל חַיַּת הַשָּׂדֶה the *most cunning* of all the wild animals of the field (Gen 3:1)

## Vocabulary

*Nouns*:

בֶּ֫גֶד (mp cs: בִּגְדֵי) garment

בָּקָר large cattle

בֹּ֫קֶר (pl.: בְּקָרִים) morning

חוֹמָה wall

חוּץ (pl. חוּצוֹת) street, outside. מִחוּץ outside (often in contrast with מִבַּ֫יִת *inside*)

יַ֫יִן wine

כָּנָף (fs) wing, skirt

כְּרוּב cherub (a winged sphinx)

מָ֫וֶת death

מָטָר rain

מְלָאכָה (cs: מְלֶ֫אכֶת) mission, work

נְאֻם oracle. Occurs almost exclusively in the construct state: "oracle of."

סֵ֫פֶר book, scroll, letter

עֵדָה congregation

עָפָר dust

צֹאן flock, sheep and goats, small cattle

צָבָא (pl. צְבָאוֹת) host, army

תָּ֫וֶךְ midst

*Verb*:

שׁוּב to turn, to return

*Adverb*:

אָז then, at that time; מֵאָז since (that time)

## Exercise 11

**a.** Give the construct forms of the following:

1. מָקוֹם
2. יָם
3. שָׂדֶה
4. בָּֽתִּים
5. אֲנָשִׁים
6. אֲרָצוֹת
7. עַמִּים
8. עֲבָדִים
9. אָב
10. אַחִים
11. תָּ֫וֶךְ
12. שֵׁמוֹת
13. נְפָשׁוֹת
14. פָּנִים
15. רָאשִׁים
16. כֵּלִים
17. שָׂרִים
18. עֵדָה
19. יַ֫יִן
20. מַעֲשֶׂה
21. עָפָר
22. סְפָרִים
23. רַגְלַ֫יִם
24. בָּנוֹת

**b.** Give the absolute forms of the following:

1. אֲחֵי
2. דִּבְרֵי
3. אָהֳלֵי
4. דַּרְכֵי
5. כַּנְפֵי
6. דְּמֵי
7. מְלֶ֫אכֶת
8. אֵ֫שֶׁת
9. נְשֵׁי
10. מִלְחֶ֫מֶת
11. יְמֵי
12. יַמֵּי
13. מֵי
14. עֵינֵי
15. כְּלֵי
16. אֵיל
17. עָרֵי
18. אֲחִי
19. חוֹמַת
20. שְׁנֵי
21. שְׁמֵי
22. פִּי
23. זְקַן
24. מוֹת

**c.** Translate the following into English:

1. וְאֵ֨לֶּה שְׁמוֹת֙ בְּנֵ֣י יִשְׂרָאֵ֔ל (Exod 1:1)
2. אָנֹכִ֕י אֱלֹהֵ֖י אַבְרָהָ֣ם (Gen 26:24)
3. אַחֲרֵ֖י מ֣וֹת מֹשֶׁ֣ה עֶ֣בֶד יְהוָ֑ה (Josh 1:1)
4. מַעֲשֵׂ֖ה יְדֵ֣י אָדָ֑ם (Deut 4:28)
5. כְּמַרְאֵ֛ה מַלְאַ֥ךְ הָאֱלֹהִ֖ים (Judg 13:6)
6. וְלֶ֤חֶם אֵין֙ בְּכָל־הָאָ֔רֶץ כִּֽי־כָבֵ֥ד הָרָעָ֖ב מְאֹ֑ד (Gen 47:13)
7. וְהִנֵּה֙ מַלְאֲכֵ֣י אֱלֹהִ֔ים עֹלִ֥ים וְיֹרְדִ֖ים בּֽוֹ (Gen 28:12)
8. וּמַרְאֵה֙ כְּב֣וֹד יְהוָ֔ה כְּאֵ֥שׁ אֹכֶ֖לֶת בְּרֹ֣אשׁ הָהָ֑ר (Exod 24:17)
9. לָ֥מָּה זֶּ֛ה אַתֶּ֥ם עֹבְרִ֖ים אֶת־פִּ֣י יְהוָ֑ה (Num 14:41)
10. הַנֹּתֵ֣ן מָ֭טָר עַל־פְּנֵי־אָ֑רֶץ וְשֹׁ֥לֵֽחַ מַ֝֗יִם עַל־פְּנֵ֥י חוּצֽוֹת (Job 5:10)
11. הַֽאֵינְךָ֣ רֹאֶ֔ה מָ֛ה הֵ֥מָּה עֹשִׂ֖ים בְּעָרֵ֣י יְהוּדָ֑ה וּבְחֻצ֖וֹת יְרוּשָׁלִָֽם (Jer 7:17)
12. וְכָל־אִ֣ישׁ יְהוּדָ֡ה וְכָל־יֹשְׁבֵ֨י יְרוּשָׁלִַ֜ם אִתּ֗וֹ וְהַכֹּֽהֲנִים֙ וְהַנְּבִיאִ֔ים וְכָל־
הָעָ֖ם לְמִקָּטֹ֣ן וְעַד־גָּד֑וֹל (2 Kgs 23:2)

**d.** Read 2 Chron 5:1–10 out loud and translate the passage with the help of a dictionary and the following notes.

*Notes*:

v 1: וַתִּשְׁלַם֙ when (subject) was completed; עָשָׂ֥ה (subject) accomplished; וַיָּבֵ֨א (subject) brought; אָבִ֗יו his father; נָתַ֕ן he put.

v 2: יַקְהֵ֨יל (subject) assembled; לְהַעֲל֞וֹת to bring up.

v 3: וַיִּקָּהֲל֣וּ (subject) assembled themselves.

v 4: וַיָּבֹ֕אוּ (subject) came; וַיִּשְׂא֥וּ and (subject) carried.

v 5: וַיַּעֲלוּ and (subject) brought (object) up; הֶעֱלוּ they brought (object) up.

v 6: הַנּוֹעָדִים who had gathered themselves; מְזַבְּחִים were sacrificing; לֹא־יִסָּפְרוּ could not be counted; וְלֹא יִמָּנוּ and could not be numbered; מֵרֹב (= רֹב + מִן) because of (their) abundance.

v 7: וַיָּבִאוּ and (subject) brought (object) in; מְקוֹמוֹ its place.

v 8: וַיִּהְיוּ and (subject) were; וַיְכַסּוּ and (subject) covered; מִלְמָעְלָה from above.

v 9: וַיַּאֲרִכוּ and (subject) extended out; וַיֵּרָאוּ and (subject) were visible; וְלֹא יֵרָאוּ but they were not visible; וַיְהִי and it has been.

v 10: רַק only; שְׁנֵי the two; נָתַן (subject) gave; כָּרַת (subject) had made (i.e., the covenant); בְּצֵאתָם when they went out.

# Excursus D
# Reference Grammars

The student will no doubt notice that the rules given in this book are often qualified by words like "probably," "ordinarily," and the like. This is so because there are, more often than not, exceptions to the rules. There are anomalous forms and constructions which, for pedagogical and practical reasons, cannot be treated in an elementary grammar. Moreover, there are nuances of certain constructions which are not mentioned in the simplified explanations of an introductory textbook. These are the sort of fine points that may be discussed in reference grammars.

## 1. Reference Grammars in English

For most of this century, the standard work in the English-speaking world has been *Gesenius' Hebrew Grammar*, which, as the title suggests, was based on a work by the great German scholar Wilhelm Gesenius. This eighteenth-century grammar was edited and expanded by E. Kautzsch and, subsequently, by A. E. Cowley. Hence, it is known as Gesenius-Kautzsch-Cowley, or abbreviated as GKC (2nd English Edition; Oxford: Clarendon, 1910). The volume includes paradigms, subject index, and scripture index. Although outdated, it is still a useful work that is widely used.

Along with GKC, scholars this century often cite a grammar published by the French scholar Paul Joüon in 1922. Now, thanks to the efforts of T. Muraoka, we have an English translation of that grammar, revised and enlarged as *A Grammar of Biblical Hebrew* (2 Volumes; Subsidia Biblica 14 / 1–2; Rome: Editrice Pontificio Istituto Biblico, 1993). Also with full paradigms, subject index, and scripture index, this grammar may become a standard work for years to come.

Another important grammar is B. K. Waltke and M. O'Connor's *An Introduction to Biblical Hebrew Syntax* (Winona Lake, Indiana: Eisenbrauns, 1990). As the title suggests, it is not a full reference grammar but a volume dedicated to issues of Hebrew syntax, something which other grammars do not present as fully or as lucidly. Beginners will find this book quite accessible. The explanations are easy to follow and there are plenty of examples of the various constructions, each duly translated. Copious notes and an extensive bibliography point to further studies. Besides the usual indexes that characterize reference grammars, there is also a helpful glossary of technical terms.

R. J. Williams' *Hebrew Syntax*: *An Outline* (Second Edition; Toronto: University of Toronto, 1976) is not a reference grammar in the sense that the other books mentioned here are; it is much abbreviated. Rather, it falls in the category of what one may call a "Quick Reference" on Hebrew syntax. Published in paperback, it is an inexpensive and perhaps indispensable handbook.

## 2. Using the Grammars

Only specialists and the most advanced students will attempt to study the reference grammars systematically. Most people will turn to these books for information on some aspect of Hebrew grammar, as the need arises. In that case, it may suffice to look for the pertinent section or sections in the grammar in the table of contents, various indexes, or the paradigms.

On occasion one may want to know more about a certain topic. For instance, it is possible to learn a lot more about the construct nouns than we have been able to cover in this book: the possible origin of the construction, more rules on morphology, the nuances, exceptions, and so forth. GKC and Joüon-Muraoka discuss this topic in various places, sometimes focussing on the forms, and other times on syntax. Waltke-O'Connor has an extensive discussion in the chapter on "Genitive Function," where the authors attempt to discern the various nuances of the construct noun. Williams treats the topic under "Bound Structure," where he notes, among other things, that a construct chain may be interrupted under certain conditions. To find the appropriate sections where a topic is discussed, one needs only to look at the table of contents and the subject index.

Most often, however, one begins not with questions about a specific topic, but with problems in translation. For instance, someone reading Jer 25:26 may be troubled by the construction כָּל־הַמַּמְלְכוֹת הָאָרֶץ, apparently meaning "all *the* kingdoms *of* the earth." This is a violation of the rules (see XI.1), if they are strictly applied. One may want to know if the rules are ever broken and, if so, under what circumstances. The Scripture Index in GKC directs one to §127.g, where the phrase is explained as a conflation of two readings, הַמַּמְלָכוֹת and מַמְלְכוֹת הָאָרֶץ. But, then, one notes that there are other examples, which GKC also tries to explain, although not always convincingly. Joüon-Muraoka and Waltke-O'Connor do not have our passage in the scripture index. Williams says simply that the construct form "should be anarthrous" (i.e., without the article), but cites a Phoenician text and gives eight examples, including Jer 25:26, where a definite article apparently appears with a construct noun.

As another example, in 1 Kgs 7:14, one finds אֶת־הַחָכְמָה as the apparent object of the passive verb "he was filled." The question there is whether אֶת־, which is supposed to mark the definite direct object, can be used with a passive verb. Checking the scripture index in Joüon-Muraoka, one is referred to a section in the grammar that explains that verbs of abundance (to be full, be sated) and scarcity (to be lacking, be deprived) regularly take the direct object. The scripture index in Waltke-O'Connor also leads one to a discussion of the various uses of אֶת־.

Sometimes the problem is with a particular Hebrew form, in which case one looks under the index of Hebrew words in either GKC or Joüon-Muraoka. The irregular plural בָּתִּים (pl. of בַּיִת), for example, is listed here.

*A Suggestion*: Prepositions in Hebrew are often problematic for the beginner because they tend to have a much wider range of meaning than their English counterparts. It will prove immensely helpful, therefore, if one takes some time to read the discussions on prepositions in the grammars.

# Lesson XII

## 1. Nouns with Pronominal Suffixes

Personal possession in Hebrew (e.g., my horse) is usually indicated by a suffixed pronoun. For singular nouns, suffixes of Type A (IX.2.a) are used, with only minor changes in the 2 fs and 1 cp forms. For plural and dual nouns, suffixes of Type C (IX.2.c) are used. In general the suffixes are attached to the construct nouns, for סוּסִי "*my* horse" means the same thing as "*the* horse *of mine*."

**a.** Masculine nouns with suffixes

| | *Singular noun* | | *Plural noun* | |
|---|---|---|---|---|
| *abs.* | סוּס | horse | סוּסִים | horses |
| *cs.* | סוּס | horse of | סוּסֵי | horses of |
| *3 ms* | סוּסוֹ | his horse | סוּסָיו | his horses |
| *3 fs* | סוּסָהּ | her horse | סוּסֶ֫יהָ | her horses |
| *2 ms* | סוּסְךָ | your horse | סוּסֶ֫יךָ | your horses |
| *2 fs* | סוּסֵךְ | your horse | סוּסַ֫יִךְ | your horses |
| *1 cs* | סוּסִי | my horse | סוּסַי | my horses |
| *3 mp* | סוּסָם | their horse | סוּסֵיהֶם | their horses |
| *3 fp* | סוּסָן | their horse | סוּסֵיהֶן | their horses |
| *2 mp* | סוּסְכֶם | your horse | סוּסֵיכֶם | your horses |
| *2 fp* | סוּסְכֶן | your horse | סוּסֵיכֶן | your horses |
| *1 cp* | סוּסֵ֫נוּ | our horse | סוּסֵ֫ינוּ | our horses |

**b.** Feminine nouns with suffixes

| | *Singular noun* | | *Plural noun* | |
|---|---|---|---|---|
| *abs.* | סוּסָה | mare | סוּסוֹת | mares |
| *cs.* | סוּסַת | mare of | סוּסוֹת | mares of |
| *3 ms* | סוּסָתוֹ | his mare | סוּסוֹתָיו | his mares |
| *3 fs* | סוּסָתָהּ | her mare | סוּסוֹתֶיהָ | her mares |
| *2 ms* | סוּסָתְךָ | your mare | סוּסוֹתֶיךָ | your mares |
| *2 fs* | סוּסָתֵךְ | your mare | סוּסוֹתַיִךְ | your mares |
| *1 cs* | סוּסָתִי | my mare | סוּסוֹתַי | my mares |
| *3 mp* | סוּסָתָם | their mare | סוּסוֹתֵיהֶם | their mares |
| *3 fp* | סוּסָתָן | their mare | סוּסוֹתֵיהֶן | their mares |
| *2 mp* | סוּסַתְכֶם | your mare | סוּסוֹתֵיכֶם | your mares |
| *2 fp* | סוּסַתְכֶן | your mare | סוּסוֹתֵיכֶן | your mares |
| *1 cp* | סוּסָתֵנוּ | our mare | סוּסוֹתֵינוּ | our mares |

## 2. Forms of the Noun before Suffixes

### a. Polysyllabic Nouns

The addition of the suffix causes the noun to shift its accent forward, and vowel reduction takes place according to the rules set forth in III.2.a.

| *Independent noun* | | *Noun with pronominal suffix* | |
|---|---|---|---|
| דָּבָר | word | דְּבָרוֹ | his word |
| אָדוֹן | lord | אֲדוֹנוֹ | his lord |
| שָׁנָה | year | שְׁנָתוֹ | his year |
| לֵבָב | heart | לְבָבוֹ | his heart |
| חֵמָה | anger | חֲמָתוֹ | his anger |
| גֹּאֵל | redeemer | גֹּאֲלוֹ | his redeemer |
| מִשְׁפָּט | judgment | מִשְׁפָּטוֹ | his judgment |

If, as a result of such a reduction, two vocal *šēwāʾ*'s should stand in immediate succession, the *Rule of Šēwāʾ* (VI.3) applies (compare XI.2.d.ii).

| | |
|---|---|
| דִּבְרֵיהֶם < דְּבְרֵיהֶם* < דְּבָרֵיהֶם* | their words |
| צִדְקָתוֹ < צְדְקָתוֹ* < צְדָקָתוֹ* | his righteousness |
| אַדְמָתוֹ < אֲדְמָתוֹ* < אֲדָמָתוֹ* | his ground |
| אַנְשֵׁיהֶם < אֲנְשֵׁיהֶם* < אֲנָשֵׁיהֶם* | their men |

Study the following examples of the polysyllabic nouns דָּבָר (word), חָצֵר (court), and צְדָקָה (righteousness).

*Singular noun*

| | | | |
|---|---|---|---|
| *cs.* | דְּבַר | חֲצַר | צִדְקַת |
| *3 ms* | דְּבָרוֹ | חֲצֵרוֹ | צִדְקָתוֹ |
| *3 fs* | דְּבָרָהּ | חֲצֵרָהּ | צִדְקָתָהּ |
| *2 ms* | דְּבָרְךָ | חֲצֵרְךָ | צִדְקָתְךָ |
| *2 fs* | דְּבָרֵךְ | חֲצֵרֵךְ | צִדְקָתֵךְ |
| *1 cs* | דְּבָרִי | חֲצֵרִי | צִדְקָתִי |
| *3 mp* | דְּבָרָם | חֲצֵרָם | צִדְקָתָם |
| *3 fp* | דְּבָרָן | חֲצֵרָן | צִדְקָתָן |
| *2 mp* | דְּבַרְכֶם | חֲצַרְכֶם | צִדְקָתְכֶם |
| *2 fp* | דְּבַרְכֶן | חֲצַרְכֶן | צִדְקָתְכֶן |
| *1 cp* | דְּבָרֵ֫נוּ | חֲצֵרֵ֫נוּ | צִדְקָתֵ֫נוּ |

*Plural noun*

| | | | |
|---|---|---|---|
| *cs.* | דִּבְרֵי | חַצְרֵי | צִדְקוֹת |
| *3 ms* | דְּבָרָיו | חֲצֵרָיו | צִדְקוֹתָיו |
| *3 fs* | דְּבָרֶ֫יהָ | חֲצֵרֶ֫יהָ | צִדְקוֹתֶ֫יהָ |
| *2 ms* | דְּבָרֶ֫יךָ | חֲצֵרֶ֫יךָ | צִדְקוֹתֶ֫יךָ |
| *2 fs* | דְּבָרַ֫יִךְ | חֲצֵרַ֫יִךְ | צִדְקוֹתַ֫יִךְ |
| *1 cs* | דְּבָרַי | חֲצֵרַי | צִדְקוֹתַי |
| *3 mp* | דִּבְרֵיהֶם | חַצְרֵיהֶם | צִדְקוֹתֵיהֶם |
| *3 fp* | דִּבְרֵיהֶן | חַצְרֵיהֶן | צִדְקוֹתֵיהֶן |
| *2 mp* | דִּבְרֵיכֶם | חַצְרֵיכֶם | צִדְקוֹתֵיכֶם |
| *2 fp* | דִּבְרֵיכֶן | חַצְרֵיכֶן | צִדְקוֹתֵיכֶן |
| *1 cp* | דְּבָרֵ֫ינוּ | חַצְרֵ֫ינוּ | צִדְקוֹתֵ֫ינוּ |

**b.** Geminate Nouns

Nouns that were originally **qall*, **qill*, or **qull* and those that have become associated with nouns of this group by virtue of the assimilation of a Nûn, behave according to rules (see V.1). Study the following examples of geminate nouns עַם (people), חֵץ (arrow), and חֹק (statute).

**Singular Noun**

| | **Qall* | **Qill* | **Qull* |
|---|---|---|---|
| *cs.* | עַם | חֵץ | חֹק |
| *3 ms* | עַמּוֹ | חִצּוֹ | חֻקּוֹ |
| *3 fs* | עַמָּהּ | חִצָּהּ | חֻקָּהּ |
| *2 ms* | עַמְּךָ | חִצְּךָ | חֻקְּךָ |
| *2 fs* | עַמֵּךְ | חִצֵּךְ | חֻקֵּךְ |
| *1 cs* | עַמִּי | חִצִּי | חֻקִּי |
| *3 mp* | עַמָּם | חִצָּם | חֻקָּם |
| *3 fp* | עַמָּן | חִצָּן | חֻקָּן |
| *2 mp* | עַמְּכֶם | חִצְּכֶם | חֻקְּכֶם |
| *2 fp* | עַמְּכֶן | חִצְּכֶן | חֻקְּכֶן |
| *1 cp* | עַמֵּ֫נוּ | חִצֵּ֫נוּ | חֻקֵּ֫נוּ |

## Plural Noun

| | **Qall* | **Qill* | **Qull* |
|---|---|---|---|
| *cs.* | עַמֵּי | חִצֵּי | חֻקֵּי |
| *3 ms* | עַמָּיו | חִצָּיו | חֻקָּיו |
| *3 fs* | עַמֶּיהָ | חִצֶּיהָ | חֻקֶּיהָ |
| *2 ms* | עַמֶּיךָ | חִצֶּיךָ | חֻקֶּיךָ |
| *2 fs* | עַמַּיִךְ | חִצַּיִךְ | חֻקַּיִךְ |
| *1 cs* | עַמַּי | חִצַּי | חֻקַּי |
| *3 mp* | עַמֵּיהֶם | חִצֵּיהֶם | חֻקֵּיהֶם |
| *3 fp* | עַמֵּיהֶן | חִצֵּיהֶן | חֻקֵּיהֶן |
| *2 mp* | עַמֵּיכֶם | חִצֵּיכֶם | חֻקֵּיכֶם |
| *2 fp* | עַמֵּיכֶן | חִצֵּיכֶן | חֻקֵּיכֶן |
| *1 cp* | עַמֵּינוּ | חִצֵּינוּ | חֻקֵּינוּ |

**c.** Segolate Nouns

Nouns that were originally **qaṭl*, **qiṭl*, or **quṭl* (V.2) retain their original bases in the singular forms with suffixes. Plural nouns, however, retain their bases only when they take plural suffixes. Study the following examples of the segolate nouns מֶלֶךְ (king), נֶדֶר (vow), and חֹדֶשׁ (month).

## Singular Noun

| | *Qaṭl | *Qiṭl | *Quṭl |
|---|---|---|---|
| *cs.* | מֶ֫לֶךְ | נֵ֫דֶר | חֹ֫דֶשׁ |
| *3 ms* | מַלְכּוֹ | נִדְרוֹ | חָדְשׁוֹ |
| *3 fs* | מַלְכָּהּ | נִדְרָהּ | חָדְשָׁהּ |
| *2 ms* | מַלְכְּךָ | נִדְרְךָ | חָדְשְׁךָ |
| *2 fs* | מַלְכֵּךְ | נִדְרֵךְ | חָדְשֵׁךְ |
| *1 cs* | מַלְכִּי | נִדְרִי | חָדְשִׁי |
| *3 mp* | מַלְכָּם | נִדְרָם | חָדְשָׁם |
| *3 fp* | מַלְכָּן | נִדְרָן | חָדְשָׁן |
| *2 mp* | מַלְכְּכֶם | נִדְרְכֶם | חָדְשְׁכֶם |
| *2 fp* | מַלְכְּכֶן | נִדְרְכֶן | חָדְשְׁכֶן |
| *1 cp* | מַלְכֵּ֫נוּ | נִדְרֵ֫נוּ | חָדְשֵׁ֫נוּ |

## Plural Noun

| | *Qaṭl | *Qiṭl | *Quṭl |
|---|---|---|---|
| *cs.* | מַלְכֵי | נִדְרֵי | חָדְשֵׁי |
| *3 ms* | מְלָכָיו | נְדָרָיו | חֳדָשָׁיו |
| *3 fs* | מְלָכֶ֫יהָ | נְדָרֶ֫יהָ | חֳדָשֶׁ֫יהָ |
| *2 ms* | מְלָכֶ֫יךָ | נְדָרֶ֫יךָ | חֳדָשֶׁ֫יךָ |
| *2 fs* | מְלָכַ֫יִךְ | נְדָרַ֫יִךְ | חֳדָשַׁ֫יִךְ |
| *1 cs* | מְלָכַי | נְדָרַי | חֳדָשַׁי |
| *3 mp* | מַלְכֵיהֶם | נִדְרֵיהֶם | חָדְשֵׁיהֶם |
| *3 fp* | מַלְכֵיהֶן | נִדְרֵיהֶן | חָדְשֵׁיהֶן |
| *2 mp* | מַלְכֵיכֶם | נִדְרֵיכֶם | חָדְשֵׁיכֶם |
| *2 fp* | מַלְכֵיכֶן | נִדְרֵיכֶן | חָדְשֵׁיכֶן |
| *1 cp* | מַלְכֵ֫ינוּ | נִדְרֵ֫ינוּ | חָדְשֵׁ֫ינוּ |

Related to these three types are a few penultimately stressed feminine nouns that end in ֶת– or ַת– (III.1.b.iii,iv).

i. *a*-class

| | | | |
|---|---|---|---|
| מִשְׁמֶ֫רֶת | obligation | מִשְׁמַרְתּוֹ | his obligation |

ii. *i*-class

| | | | |
|---|---|---|---|
| גְּבֶ֫רֶת | mistress | גְּבִרְתִּי | my mistress |

iii. *u*-class

| | | | |
|---|---|---|---|
| נְחֹ֫שֶׁת | bronze | נְחָשְׁתִּי | my bronze |
| | | נְחֻשְׁתָּם | their bronze |

**d.** Nouns with diphthongs

Diphthongs in nouns contract according to the principles given in IV.2.c.iii.β, iv.β:

| | | | |
|---|---|---|---|
| מָ֫וֶת | death | מוֹתוֹ | his death |
| בַּ֫יִת | house | בֵּיתוֹ | his house |

**e.** Nouns with III-Wāw/Yōḏ Roots

**i.** Monosyllabic nouns with III-Wāw/Yōḏ Roots (IV.2.c.vii.γ) have construct forms with final *-î* (ִי–).

| | *Singular noun* | | |
|---|---|---|---|
| *cs.* | אֲבִי | אֲחִי | פִּי |
| *3 ms* | אָבִיו | אָחִיו | פִּיו |
| | אָבִיהוּ | אָחִיהוּ | פִּיהוּ |
| *3 fs* | אָבִיהָ | אָחִיהָ | פִּיהָ |
| *2 ms* | אָבִיךָ | אָחִיךָ | פִּיךָ |
| *2 fs* | אָבִיךְ | אָחִיךְ | פִּיךְ |
| *1 cs* | אָבִי | אָחִי | פִּי |
| *3 mp* | אֲבִיהֶם | אֲחִיהֶם | פִּיהֶם |
| *3 fp* | אֲבִיהֶן | אֲחִיהֶן | פִּיהֶן |
| *2 mp* | אֲבִיכֶם | אֲחִיכֶם | פִּיכֶם |
| *2 fp* | אֲבִיכֶן | אֲחִיכֶן | פִּיכֶן |
| *1 cp* | אָבִינוּ | אָחִינוּ | פִּינוּ |

*Notes*:

i. With the exception of the alternative 3 ms ending (ו–) and the 1 cs (ִי–), the suffixes are those of Type B (IX.2.b).

ii. Singular nouns that end in ֶה– (IV.2.c.vii.α), except for פֶּה (mouth), lose the ֶה– ending and take the suffixes of Type A (IX.2.a), except that the 3 ms suffix for the singular noun is ֵהוּ– instead of ֹו–. Plural forms are regular.

| | | | |
|---|---|---|---|
| מַעֲשֶׂה | deed | מַעֲשֵׂהוּ | his deed |
| | | מַעֲשֵׂינוּ | our deeds |
| שָׂדֶה | field | שָׂדֵהוּ | his field |
| | | שָׂדִי | my field |
| | | שָׂדֵינוּ | our fields |

iii. Nouns like חֲצִי (half), פְּרִי (fruit), and עֳנִי (affliction) treat the final י as a consonant whenever the suffix is added (IV.2.c.vii.β). They take suffixes of Type A (IX.2.a). When the suffix is added, the vowel in the first syllable is difficult to predict. Study the following attested suffixal forms of the nouns חֲצִי (half), פְּרִי (fruit), and עֳנִי (affliction).

*Singular noun*

| | | | |
|---|---|---|---|
| *3 ms* | חֶצְיוֹ | פִּרְיוֹ | עָנְיוֹ |
| *3 fs* | חֶצְיָהּ | פִּרְיָהּ | עָנְיָהּ |
| *2 ms* | | פֶּרְיְךָ | |
| *2 fs* | | פִּרְיֵךְ | עָנְיֵךְ |
| *1 cs* | | פִּרְיִי | עָנְיִי |
| *3 mp* | חֶצְיָם | פִּרְיָם | עָנְיָם |
| *3 fp* | | פִּרְיָן | |
| *2 mp* | | פֶּרְיְכֶם | |
| *1 cp* | חֶצְיֵנוּ | | |

*Note*: The alternate forms פְּרִיהֶם (their fruit) and פְּרִיהֶן (with 3 fp suffix) are attested, as is the 2 mp suffixal form for שְׁבִיכֶם (your captive).

**f.** The nouns בֵּן (son) and שֵׁם (name)

These nouns reduce the stem vowel ( ֵ ) before the suffix. If, as a result of this reduction, two vocal *šĕwā*ʾ's stand in immediate succession, the *Rule of Šĕwā*ʾ applies.

| | | | |
|---|---|---|---|
| בֵּן | son | בְּנוֹ | his son |
| | | בִּנְךָ < בְּנְךָ* | your son |
| שֵׁם | name | שְׁמוֹ | his name |
| | | שִׁמְךָ < שְׁמְךָ* | your name |

**g.** The nouns אִשָּׁה (woman, wife) and בַּת (daughter)

The pre-suffix forms of אִשָּׁה and בַּת are –אִשְׁתּ (*ʾišt-*) and –בִּתּ (*bitt-*) respectively.

| | |
|---|---|
| אִשָּׁה wife | אִשְׁתּוֹ his wife |
| בַּת daughter | בִּתּוֹ his daughter |

## Vocabulary

*Nouns*:

אַף (ms; md: אַפַּ֫יִם) nose, face, anger

חֵמָה heat, rage

חֲצִי half, middle. *Verb*: חָצָה to divide

חָצֵר (pl. חֲצֵרִים or חֲצֵרוֹת) court

חֹק (also חֻקָּה) statute

כֹּחַ strength, power

מִגְדָּל (pl. מִגְדָּלִים or מִגְדָּלוֹת) tower

מִנְחָה gift, offering

מִצְוָה (fp מִצְוֹת *miṣwōṯ*) commandment

מִשְׁפָּחָה (cs. מִשְׁפַּ֫חַת) family, clan

נֵ֫דֶר (also נֶ֫דֶר) vow. *Verb*: נָדַר to vow

נַחֲלָה inheritance

עֹז strength. *Adjective*: עַז strong

עָנָן cloud

רֵעַ friend

רֵעֶה friend, companion

שֵׁן (fs; du. שִׁנַּ֫יִם) tooth, ivory

תִּפְאֶ֫רֶת glory, beauty, splendor

*Verbs*:

חָנָה  to camp. *Noun*: מַחֲנֶה (pl. מַחֲנִים, מַחֲנוֹת) camp, army

*Other*:

לֵאמֹר  saying (introduces a quotation)

## Exercise 12

**a.** Write the following in Hebrew:

1. her nose
2. his men
3. his field
4. their fruit
5. my fruit
6. our king
7. his wife
8. my name
9. her strength
10. his wives
11. your cities
12. my people
13. our father
14. his hands
15. his mouth
16. our deeds
17. your (mp) spirit
18. a heavy cloud
19. my daughter
20. your (ms) staff
21. your (ms) brother
22. your (ms) brothers
23. your (ms) seed
24. her garments

**b.** Translate the following into English:

1. רוּחַ אַפֵּינוּ
2. אֲרוֹן עֻזֶּךָ
3. מִגְדַּל־עֹז
4. בָּתֵּי הַשֵּׁן
5. אָבִינוּ זָקֵן
6. בִּגְדֵי תִפְאַרְתֵּךְ
7. בִּגְדֵי הַקֹּדֶשׁ
8. כָּל־יְמֵי חַיַּי
9. כְּמִגְדַּל הַשֵּׁן
10. כִּסֵּא־שֵׁן גָּדוֹל
11. כָּל־אַנְשֵׁי בֵיתוֹ
12. עֲנָנְךָ עֹמֵד עֲלֵיהֶם
13. אֱלֹהִים אֲבוֹתֵינוּ
14. רוּחַ חַיִּים בְּאַפָּיו
15. אִמֹּתָם הַיֹּלְדוֹת אֹתָם

**c.** Translate the following into English:

1. מִי־יוֹדֵעַ עֹז אַפֶּךָ (Ps 90:11)
2. כִּי־טוֹב חַסְדְּךָ מֵחַיִּים (Ps 63:4)
3. מַחֲנֵה אֱלֹהִים זֶה (Gen 32:3)

4. וְחַסְדְּכֶם֙ כַּעֲנַן־בֹּ֔קֶר (Hos 6:4)
5. אֵין־כָּמ֖וֹךָ בָאֱלֹהִ֥ים ׀ אֲדֹנָ֗י וְאֵ֣ין כְּֽמַעֲשֶֽׂיךָ (Ps 86:8)
6. בֵּ֧ית קָדְשֵׁ֣נוּ וְתִפְאַרְתֵּ֗נוּ (Isa 64:10)
7. אֵין־נֹטֶ֥ה ע֙וֹד֙ אָהֳלִ֔י (Jer 10:20)
8. מִגְדַּל־עֹ֭ז שֵׁ֣ם יְהוָ֑ה (Prov 18:10)
9. חֻקַּ֥ת עוֹלָ֛ם ל֖וֹ וּלְזַרְע֥וֹ אַחֲרָֽיו (Exod 28:43)
10. וְרוּחִ֖י עֹמֶ֣דֶת בְּתוֹכְכֶ֑ם (Hag 2:5)
11. אָנֹכִ֤י יְהוָה֙ עֹ֣שֶׂה כֹּ֔ל נֹטֶ֤ה שָׁמַ֙יִם֙ לְבַדִּ֔י (Isa 44:24)
12. הִנְנִ֨י נֹתֵ֧ן דְּבָרַ֛י בְּפִ֖יךָ לְאֵ֑שׁ (Jer 5:14)
13. וְאֵינָ֣ם עֹשִׂ֗ים כְּחֻקֹּתָם֙ וּכְמִשְׁפָּטָ֔ם וְכַתּוֹרָ֣ה וְכַמִּצְוָ֔ה (2 Kgs 17:34)
14. הִנֵּה֙ אֲר֣וֹן הַבְּרִ֔ית אֲד֖וֹן כָּל־הָאָ֑רֶץ עֹבֵ֥ר לִפְנֵיכֶ֖ם (Josh 3:11)
15. כָּל־עַבְדֵ֤י פַרְעֹה֙ זִקְנֵ֣י בֵית֔וֹ וְכֹ֖ל זִקְנֵ֥י אֶֽרֶץ־מִצְרָֽיִם (Gen 50:7)

**d.** Read out loud Psalm 121 and translate the passage with the help of a dictionary and these notes.

*Notes*:

v 1: אֶשָּׂ֣א I will lift up; יָבֹ֣א will come.

v 3: אַל־יִתֵּ֣ן לַמּ֣וֹט may he not permit (object) to stumble.

v 3: אַל־יָ֝נ֗וּם may (subject) not slumber.

v 4: לֹ֣א יָ֭נוּם וְלֹ֣א יִישָׁ֑ן he will not slumber and he will not sleep.

v 6: לֹֽא־יַכֶּ֗כָּה will not smite you.

v 7: יִשְׁמָרְךָ֥ will keep you; יִ֝שְׁמֹ֗ר he will keep.

v 8: יִשְׁמָר־צֵאתְךָ֥ וּבוֹאֶ֑ךָ will guard your going and coming.

# Lesson XIII

## 1. The Afformatives of the Perfect

The first full inflection of the finite verb in Hebrew is called the *perfect*. The third person masculine singular (3 ms) form in this inflection has no special markers. Otherwise, endings called *afformatives* are appended to the base form to indicate gender, person, and number. The same set of afformatives is used for all verbs in the perfect, regardless of their verbal patterns ("conjugations").

| | | | |
|---|---|---|---|
| *3 ms* | – | *3 cp* | וּ– |
| *3 fs* | ָה– | | |
| *2 ms* | תָּ– | *2 mp* | תֶּם– |
| *2 fs* | תְּ– | *2 fp* | תֶּן– |
| *1 cs* | תִּי– | *1 cp* | נוּ– |

*Notes*:

i. An archaic afformative תִּי– is attested for the 2 fs (compare the variant 2 fs independent pronoun אַתִּי in IX.1.a.iii).

ii. There is no distinction between the masculine and the feminine genders in the third person plural and all first person forms.

## 2. The Qal Perfect

The 3 ms of the perfect of strong roots may have one of three variations: *qāṭal*, *qāṭēl*, *qāṭōl*. The *qāṭal* type is by far the most common of the three. Verbs belonging to this group are typically *dynamic*; they involve some sort of action, whether transitive (taking a direct object) or intransitive (not taking a direct object), e.g., כָּתַב (to write), שָׁמַר (to keep), נָפַל (to fall), יָרַד (to descend). The *qāṭēl* and *qāṭōl* types are much smaller groups of verbs that are typically *stative*. In contrast to verbs of action, stative verbs describe a state or condition, e.g., כָּבֵד (to be heavy, important), זָקֵן (to be old), יָרֵא (to be afraid, fearful), קָטֹן (to be small), יָכֹל (to be able). Some verbs appear in Qal in both *qāṭal* and *qāṭēl* forms, e.g. לָבַשׁ (to clothe) and לָבֵשׁ (to be clothed). A rigid semantic categorization of the types must be avoided, however. A few verbs of the *qāṭal* pattern are stative (e.g., חָכַם to be wise). Moreover, some verbs of the *qāṭēl* pattern may exhibit qualities of a dynamic verb (e.g., שָׂנֵא to hate), or the original distinction between the dynamic and stative forms may have been lost (e.g., קָרַב and קָרֵב both meaning "to draw near").

The forms of the Qal perfect of שָׁמַר (to keep), כָּבֵד (to be heavy), and קָטֹן (to be small) are as follows.

| | *qāṭal* | *qāṭēl* | *qāṭōl* |
|---|---|---|---|
| *3 ms* | שָׁמַר | כָּבֵד | קָטֹן |
| *3 fs* | שָֽׁמְרָה | כָּֽבְדָה | קָֽטְנָה |
| *2 ms* | שָׁמַ֫רְתָּ | כָּבַ֫דְתָּ | קָטֹ֫נְתָּ |
| *2 fs* | שָׁמַרְתְּ | כָּבַדְתְּ | קָטֹנְתְּ |
| *1 cs* | שָׁמַ֫רְתִּי | כָּבַ֫דְתִּי | קָטֹ֫נְתִּי |
| *3 cp* | שָֽׁמְרוּ | כָּֽבְדוּ | קָֽטְנוּ |
| *2 mp* | שְׁמַרְתֶּם | כְּבַדְתֶּם | קְטָנְתֶּם |
| *2 fp* | שְׁמַרְתֶּן | כְּבַדְתֶּן | קְטָנְתֶּן |
| *1 cp* | שָׁמַ֫רְנוּ | כָּבַ֫דְנוּ | קָטֹ֫נּוּ |

*Notes*:

i. The original characteristic *ē* vowel in the *qāṭēl* perfect is preserved only in the 3 ms; elsewhere the forms cannot be distinguished from the qal perfect, except when the verb is in pause (e.g., כָּבֵ֫דָה).

ii. The *qāṭōl* type preserves the characteristic *ō* vowel in the second syllable whenever that syllable is stressed. In the 2 mp and 2 fp forms, the vowel is shortened: thus *qĕṭontem* and *qĕṭonten*.

iii. If the final radical of the stem is the same as the consonant of the afformative, the consonant is written only once, but doubling is indicated by a strong *dāgēš*.

| | | | |
|---|---|---|---|
| קָטְנוּ | they were small | קָטֹנּוּ | we were small |
| נָתְנוּ | they gave | נָתַנּוּ | we gave |
| כָּרְתָה | she cut | כָּרַתָּ | you cut |

The important verb נָתַן not only shows doubling in the 1 cp form, but the final Nûn also assimilates whenever it precedes the consonant ת of the suffix.

| | | | |
|---|---|---|---|
| *נָתַנְתָּ > נָתַתָּ | you gave | *נָתַנְתִּי > נָתַתִּי | I gave |

The final Nûn radical of other III-Nûn verbs, however, does not assimilate: זָקַנְתִּי; קָטֹנְתִּי.

## 3. Uses of the Perfect

Biblical Hebrew does not have tenses in the strict sense of the word. Time of occurrence is indicated in context by certain adverbs (time words) and, as we shall see in later lessons, by the way the sentence is constructed. The finite verbs themselves do not indicate tense, but *aspect* – that is, whether the situation is viewed by the speaker/writer as an outsider looking at a situation as a complete whole ("perfect"), or as an insider looking at a situation as it develops ("imperfect"). For example, a narrator recounting a battle may depict the event from the perspective of an outsider who knows the entire situation from beginning to end. If so, the narrator would ideally use verbs in the perfect. A participant in the battle, on the other hand, would probably use verbs in the imperfect, as would a narrator, if that narrator attempts to describe the events as if he or she were personally present when the events unfolded.

**a.** Since the perfect is most commonly used to express a situation that is viewed as *complete whole*, with the beginning and the end of the situation in view, one usually renders the perfect with the English simple past or present perfect.

עָמַדְתָּ לִפְנֵי יְהוָה *you stood* before YHWH (Deut 4:10)

שָׁכַח אֵל God *has forgotten* (Ps 10:11)

In reference to an event prior to a narrative situation, one may render the Hebrew perfect with the English past perfect.

וַיהוָה פָּקַד אֶת־שָׂרָה כַּאֲשֶׁר אָמָר Now YHWH visited Sarah, even as *he had said* (Gen 21:1)

**b.** The perfect of stative verbs may indicate the *condition* of the subject. In such instances one may translate the perfect by the English present of the verb *to be*.

אֲנִי זָקַנְתִּי *I am old* (Josh 23:2)

**c.** The perfect of verbs of attitude, perception, or experience may also be rendered by the English present.

אָהַבְתִּי אֶת־אֲדֹנִי *I love* my master (Exod 21:5)

עַתָּה יָדַעְתִּי now *I know* (Gen 22:12)

**d.** In statements of general truths, the perfect may be rendered by the English present. This is called the *proverbial perfect*.

יָבֵשׁ חָצִיר נָבֵל צִיץ grass *withers*, flowers *fade* (Isa 40:7)

**e.** Some verbs suggesting *instantaneous occurrence* are regularly rendered by the English present.

כִּי יָעַצְתִּי so *I advise* ... (2 Sam 17:11)

**f.** In the language of communication, a writer sometimes assumes the perspective of the recipient. Thus, the perfect is used, but the verb should be translated by the English present continuous. This usage has been called the *epistolary perfect*.

שָׁלַחְתִּי לְךָ שֹׁחַד *I am sending* you a gift (1 Kgs 15:19)

**g.** In some instances, the *certainty* of occurrence in the mind of the speaker is enough to justify the use of the perfect. This usage of the perfect is especially common in prophecies, promises, and threats. In such cases, one should render the Hebrew perfect by the English present, or even future.

גָּוַעְנוּ אָבַדְנוּ *We are finished! We are lost!* (Num 17:27)

עָזַבְתִּי אֶתְכֶם *I shall abandon* you (2 Chron 12:5)

It is important to remember that tense is not conveyed by the verb itself; one must consider other elements in the sentence and know something of the context to translate accurately. The perfect simply indicates the assumed or real perspective of the speaker/writer as an outsider who views the situation as a complete whole.

## 4. Syntax of the Verbal Clause

**a.** Normal Word Order

In Hebrew prose, the normal word order in a verbal clause is as follows.

**i.** *Circumstance.* Any adverb or adverbial phrase that places a narrative in context (then, now, at that time, after these events, moreover, etc.) takes the first position. The particle הִנֵּה (see IX.5), frequently used to indicate background circumstances, also comes first.

**ii.** *Verb.* The verb stands before the nominal subject, if any.

**iii.** *Subject.* Since the subject of a verb is often indicated in the verb itself, it is possible that neither a noun nor independent pronoun may be stated. When a noun is explicitly named as subject, however, it ordinarily comes after the verb.

**iv.** *Indirect Object.* When the indirect object (usually indicated by the prepositions לְ or אֶל־) is involved, it usually comes after the subject, but before the direct object.

**v.** *Direct Object.* When there is a direct object, it comes after the verb and indirect object, if any.

Study the following examples carefully,

| | |
|---|---|
| *iv iii ii i*<br>אָז שָׁמַע הַמֶּלֶךְ אֲלֵיהֶם | then the king listened to them (2 Chron 24:17) |
| *v iv iii ii*<br>נָתַן יְהוָה לָכֶם אֶת־הָאָרֶץ | YHWH has given you the land (Josh 2:9) |

**b.** Disrupted Word Order

Although the rules for proper word order are not strictly adhered to in every instance, they do provide a norm for good Hebrew prose. The normal word order in Hebrew prose may be disrupted for various reasons. If a connecting ו is present before a non-verb in a disrupted sequence, that ו is likely to be *disjunctive*, and may be translated as "but," "now," or the like.

**i.** When a *new subject* is introduced, the normal order of verb-subject may be reversed.

| | |
|---|---|
| וְהָאָדָם יָדַע אֶת־חַוָּה אִשְׁתּוֹ | *Now* Adam knew Eve, his wife (Gen 4:1) |

**ii.** A redundant independent personal pronoun is frequently put before a verb, particularly in *parenthetical comments*.

| | |
|---|---|
| וְהֵם לֹא יָדְעוּ כִּי שֹׁמֵעַ יוֹסֵף | *Now* they did not know that Joseph was listening (Gen 42:23) |
| וְהַמְּדָנִים מָכְרוּ אֹתוֹ אֶל־מִצְרָיִם | *Meanwhile*, the Midianites sold him in Egypt (Gen 37:36) |

**iii.** Sometimes the normal word order is disrupted for *emphasis*.

אֹתוֹ אָהַב אֲבִיהֶם מִכָּל־אֶחָיו their father loved *him* above all his brothers (Gen 37:4)

**iv.** Sometimes the word order is disrupted to sharpen *contrast*.

וְלוֹט יָשַׁב בְּעָרֵי הַכִּכָּר *but* Lot dwelled in the cities of the plain (Gen 13:12)

*Note*: The rules above apply only to Hebrew prose. In poetic texts, word order may vary for purely stylistic reasons (see Excursus E).

**c.** Agreement of Subject

The verb normally agrees with the subject in gender, number, and person.

יָשַׁב שְׁלֹמֹה Solomon sat (1 Kgs 1:46)

יָרְדָה אֵשׁ מִן־הַשָּׁמַיִם a fire descended from heaven (2 Kgs 1:14)

אַתָּה יָדַעְתָּ you know (Ps 69:6)

הָאֲנָשִׁים אֲשֶׁר הָלְכוּ the men who went (Gen 14:24)

*Notes*:

i. Collective nouns may take the singular or plural verb.

הָלְכוּ הָעָם or הָלַךְ הָעָם the people went

ii. Nouns that are plural in form but singular in meaning usually take the singular verb.

הָלַךְ הָאֱלֹהִים God went

iii. When more than one noun is named as subject, the verb may be plural or singular (agreeing with the first noun).

הָלְכוּ מֹשֶׁה וְאַהֲרֹן or הָלַךְ מֹשֶׁה וְאַהֲרֹן

Moses and Aaron went

## 5. Negation of the Perfect

The perfect is negated by the particle לֹא placed immediately before the verb.

לֹ֣א שָׁמַ֔עְתָּ בְּקוֹל֙ יְהוָ֣ה you did *not* obey the voice of YHWH (Deut 28:45)

## 6. The Directive ָה–

An unaccented final ָה– is frequently appended to a noun to indicate direction of motion, ordinarily, motion *toward*. It may be found with common nouns, even those with the definite article, or with proper nouns. When the noun receives the directive ָה– it may be vocalized slightly differently. Nouns with the feminine ending ָה– change their ending to ָת–, as in the fs noun with pronominal suffix (XII.1.b).

| | | | |
|---|---|---|---|
| בַּ֫יִת | house | הַבַּ֫יְתָה | toward the house |
| הַר | mountain | הָ֫רָה | toward the mountain |
| תִּרְצָה | Tirzah | תִּרְצָ֫תָה | toward Tirzah |
| קֶ֫דֶם | front, east | קֵ֫דְמָה | toward the east |
| אָן | where? | אָ֫נָה | toward where? |
| הֵן | here | הֵ֫נָּה | toward here |
| שָׁם | there | שָׁ֫מָּה | toward there |

*Note*: In a few instances, the directive element is ֶה–, instead of ָה–: e.g., נֹ֫בֶה toward Nob.

Less frequently, the directive ָה– may occur after a prepositional phrase: אֶל־הַצָּפוֹנָה (toward the north). Indeed, the directive element may be used with a variety of prepositions to indicate motion in any direction.

| | | | |
|---|---|---|---|
| מִצָּפ֫וֹנָה | from the north | לְמַ֫עְלָה | upward |

Direction of movement is sometimes expressed without a preposition or the directive הָ–. In this case, the noun of place has an adverbial function.

| | |
|---|---|
| מִן־הָאָ֥רֶץ הַהִ֖וא יָצָ֣א אַשּׁ֑וּר | from that land he went *to* Assyria (Gen 10:11) |
| עָל֖וּ רֹ֥אשׁ הַגִּבְעָֽה | they went up *to* the top of the mountain (Exod 17:10) |

## 7. Construct Chains (*continued*)

**a.** The link between a construct and an absolute may be broken in a few instances.

**i.** by the directive הָ–

| | |
|---|---|
| אַ֫רְצָה מִצְרָ֑יִם | to the land of Egypt (Exod 4:20) |
| בֵּ֫יתָה יוֹסֵ֔ף | into the house of Joseph (Gen 44:14) |

**ii.** by a preposition

| | |
|---|---|
| הָרֵ֣י בַגִּלְבֹּ֗עַ | the mountains of Gilboa (2 Sam 1:21) |
| אֱלֹהֵ֖י מֵרָחֹֽק | a god from afar off (Jer 23:23) |
| כְּשִׂמְחַ֣ת בַּקָּצִ֔יר | joy at the harvest (Isa 9:2) |

**iii.** by a suffixed pronoun

| | |
|---|---|
| בְּרִיתִ֣י הַיּ֔וֹם | my covenant with the day (Jer 33:20) |

**b.** A construct noun is sometimes bound not to a noun but to an entire relative clause.

| | |
|---|---|
| מְק֕וֹם אֲשֶׁ֥ר יוֹסֵ֖ף אָס֥וּר שָֽׁם | the place where Joseph was imprisoned (Gen 40:3) |
| אֶל־מְק֗וֹם שֶׁ֤הַנְּחָלִים֙ הֹֽלְכִ֔ים | to the place where the streams flow (Eccl 1:7) |

## Vocabulary

*Nouns*:

אֶבְיוֹן poor, needy. *Verb*: אָבָה to be willing, want, consent

אֹיֵב enemy

מִשְׁכָּן tabernacle; שָׁכֵן neighbor. *Verb*: שָׁכַן to dwell

עֳנִי affliction. *Adjective*: עָנִי afflicted, humble

פַּר bull

צָפוֹן north, Zaphon

קֶ֫דֶם east, antiquity, front

רֹעֶה shepherd. *Verb*: רָעָה to tend, feed

תֵּימָן south, Teman

*Verbs*:

זָכַר to remember

יָרֵא to fear, be afraid. *Noun*: יִרְאָה fear

כָּבֵד to be(come) weighty, important, rich

לָקַח to receive, take

מָשַׁח to anoint. *Noun*: מָשִׁיחַ anointed

עָזַב to abandon, leave, forsake

*Adverbs*:

אָן where?

כֹּה thus, here

## Exercise 13

**a.** Write the following in Hebrew:

1. I ate
2. we wrote
3. I gave
4. we cut
5. I took
6. we gave
7. I went
8. they gave
9. he anointed
10. he prevailed
11. they took
12. I am old
13. they took
14. they forsook
15. she prevailed
16. she feared
17. we remember
18. you (fs) kept
19. you (ms) cut
20. you (mp) remember
21. she remembers
22. you (ms) went
23. she is important
24. you (mp) took

**b.** Translate the following into English:

1. הִנֵּה֙ יָ֣רְדָה אֵ֔שׁ מִן־הַשָּׁמַ֔יִם (2 Kgs 1:14)
2. כִּ֣י אֲמַרְתֶּ֗ם כָּרַ֤תְנוּ בְרִית֙ אֶת־מָ֔וֶת (Isa 28:15)
3. אָהַ֣בְתָּ רָּ֣ע מִטּ֑וֹב (Ps 52:5)
4. ה֣וּא הַלֶּ֔חֶם אֲשֶׁ֨ר נָתַ֧ן יְהוָ֛ה לָכֶ֖ם (Exod 16:15)
5. הֲזֶה֙ אֲחִיכֶ֣ם הַקָּטֹ֔ן אֲשֶׁ֥ר אֲמַרְתֶּ֖ם אֵלָ֑י (Gen 43:29)
6. הִנֵּ֣ה ׀ נָתַ֣תִּי לְךָ֗ לֵ֚ב חָכָ֣ם (1 Kgs 3:12)
7. לֹ֤א אָֽכַל֙ לֶ֔חֶם כָּל־הַיּ֖וֹם וְכָל־הַלָּֽיְלָה (1 Sam 28:20)
8. שָׁמַ֗ע כִּ֥י אֹת֛וֹ מָשְׁח֥וּ לְמֶ֖לֶךְ תַּ֣חַת אָבִ֑יהוּ (1 Kgs 5:15)
9. מָלַ֣ךְ אֱ֭לֹהִים עַל־גּוֹיִ֑ם אֱלֹהִ֗ים יָשַׁ֤ב ׀ עַל־כִּסֵּ֬א קָדְשֽׁוֹ (Ps 47:9)
10. זָקַ֔נְתִּי לֹ֥א יָדַ֖עְתִּי י֥וֹם מוֹתִֽי (Gen 27:2)

**c.** Read Ps 136 out loud and translate it with the help of a dictionary and these notes.

*Notes*:

v 1: הוֹדוּ give thanks!; טֹוב is good (here טוב is the Qal Perf. 3 ms of טוב to be good, pleasing).

v 4: נִפְלָאוֹת wonders.

v 10: לְמַכֵּה to the one who smites.

v 11: וַיּוֹצֵא and lead.

v 14: וְהֶעֱבִיר and he caused (object) to pass through.

v 15: וְנִעֵר and he threw off.

v 16: לְמוֹלִיךְ to the one who leads.

v 17: לְמַכֵּה to the one who smites.

v 18: וַיַּהֲרֹג and he killed.

v 19: לְסִיחוֹן the preposition לְ here and in v 20 marks the person against whom an action is directed. See BDB, pp. 511–12 (3.b)

v 23: שֶׁבְּשִׁפְלֵנוּ = שֶׁ + בְּ + שֵׁפֶל + 1 cp suffix

v 24: וַיִּפְרְקֵנוּ and he tore us away.

# Excursus E
# Poetic Hebrew

As one might expect, poetic Hebrew differs noticeably from standard Hebrew prose, and archaic poetry differs from later poetic styles. For our purposes, it is necessary to note only the most prominent features of poetic Hebrew.

## 1. Infrequency of Prose Particles

There are certain particles that occur regularly in prose but are absent or rare in the oldest poetic texts and are only infrequently attested in later poetry.

**a.** The definite article is frequently absent; in the oldest texts it is present only as a result of tendencies to make the Hebrew more prosaic.

| | |
|---|---|
| אֶרֶץ רָעָשָׁה גַּם־שָׁמַיִם נָטָפוּ | the earth quaked, also the heavens dripped (Judg 5:4) |
| מַלְכֵי־אֶרֶץ | the kings of the earth (Ps 2:2) |

**b.** The relative particle **אֲשֶׁר** is absent from the oldest poetic texts and is uncommon in standard poetry. Instead, one finds asyndetic (unmarked) relative clauses, and **זוּ**, **זוֹ**, **זֶה** used in its place (see X.2.c, d).

| | |
|---|---|
| בְּשַׁחַת עָשׂוּ ... בְּרֶשֶׁת־זוּ טָמָנוּ | in the pit *which* they made ... in the net *where* they hid (Ps 9:16) |

**c.** The marker of definite direct object is frequently absent, especially in the oldest poetic texts.

| | |
|---|---|
| שָׁמַרְתִּי דַּרְכֵי יְהוָה וְלֹא־רָשַׁעְתִּי מֵאֱלֹהָי | For I have kept the ways of YHWH, I have not acted wickedly, away from my God (Ps 18:22) |

## 2. Longer Forms of Prepositions

Perhaps for metrical reasons, longer forms of several prepositions are found in some poetic texts: בְּמוֹ = בְּ; כְּמוֹ = כְּ; לְמוֹ = לְ; אֱלֵי = אֶל־; עֲדֵי = עַד; עֲלֵי = עַל.

| | |
|---|---|
| יָרְדוּ בִמְצוֹלֹת כְּמוֹ־אָבֶן | they sank into (the) deep like stone (Exod 15:5) |
| כַּאֲרָזִים עֲלֵי־מָיִם | like cedars by (the) waters (Num 24:6) |

## 3. Longer forms of the 3 mp Pronominal Suffix

Again, perhaps for aesthetic reasons, the 3 mp suffixes מוֹ– / ָמוֹ– / ֵמוֹ– are found in poetic texts, instead of the regular 3 mp suffixes.

| | |
|---|---|
| חֶלְבָּמוֹ ... פִּימוֹ | *their* fat (heart) ... *their* mouth (Ps 17:10) |

## 4. Anomalous Final ִי– and וֹ– After Construct Nouns

An additional ִי– known as *ḥîreq compaginis* or "linking *ḥîreq*" is frequently attached to the construct noun.

| | |
|---|---|
| עֹזְבִי הַצֹּאן | the deserter of the flock (Zech 11:17) |

*Notes*:

i. The *–î* at the end must not be confused with the 1 cs suffix.
ii. There is vowel reduction in the form before the suffix (compare XII.2.a). Thus, עֹזֵב (one who deserts / abandons), but עֹזְבִי.

The *wāw compaginis* (וֹ–) is less certainly attested.

## 5. Variable Word Order

Whereas the rules for word order in XIII.4 apply to Hebrew prose, poetic texts may take license for stylistic reasons. The following is a good example of variations in word order in Hebrew poetry.

| | |
|---|---|
| יְהוָה֙ מִצִּיּ֣וֹן יִשְׁאָ֔ג | YHWH roars from Zion; |
| וּמִירוּשָׁלִַ֖ם יִתֵּ֣ן קוֹל֑וֹ | He gives forth his voice from Jerusalem. |
| וְאָֽבְלוּ֙ נְא֣וֹת הָרֹעִ֔ים | The pastures of the shepherds languish; |
| וְיָבֵ֖שׁ רֹ֥אשׁ הַכַּרְמֶֽל | Yea, the top of Carmel dries up. (Amos 1:2) |

This example also illustrates the most important rhetorical feature in Hebrew poetry: parallelism. In the first pair, Zion and Jerusalem are, of course, not two different places; they are parallel terms. Moreover one can see here that in Hebrew poetry, ו is not necessarily a conjunction and should not, therefore, be translated as "and" in this case. Here ו merely serves to introduce, or even to emphasize, the parallel line (see also XXV.6.c, d). A well known example both of parallelism and of the non-conjunctive use of ו is in Zech 9:9, regarding the triumphal entry of a king.

| | |
|---|---|
| עָנִי֙ וְרֹכֵ֣ב עַל־חֲמ֔וֹר | humble and riding on a he-ass, |
| וְעַל־עַ֖יִר בֶּן־אֲתֹנֽוֹת | on the foal of she-asses. |

A later tradition (Matt 21:5), missing the significance of the parallelism and the function of ו in Hebrew poetry, took the Hebrew to mean that the king would come riding on two animals!

## 6. Double-Duty Preposition

In Hebrew poetry, a single preposition in one line may also govern a noun in the parallel line. Thus the preposition is said to do "double-duty."

| | |
|---|---|
| יַעֲשֶׂה֙ חֶפְצוֹ֙ בְּבָבֶ֔ל | he will do his will *against* Babylon, |
| וּזְרֹע֖וֹ כַּשְׂדִּֽים | and his arm shall be (*against*) the Chaldeans (Isa 48:14) |

# Lesson XIV

## 1. The Qal Perfect of Guttural Verbs

**a.** I-Guttural Verbs

These are regular, except that the *šĕwāʾ* under the guttural is ֲ (see IV.2.a.ii).

| | *Strong verb* | *I-Guttural verb* |
|---|---|---|
| 2 *mp* | קְטַלְתֶּם | עֲמַדְתֶּם |
| 2 *fp* | קְטַלְתֶּן | עֲמַדְתֶּן |

*Note*: The verbs הָיָה (to be, become) and חָיָה (to live) have ֱ instead of ֲ in the 2 mp and 2 fp forms.

**b.** II-Guttural Verbs

These are regular, except that the *šĕwāʾ* under the guttural is ֲ (see IV.2.a.ii).

| | *Strong verb* | *II-Guttural verb* |
|---|---|---|
| 3 *fs* | קָֽטְלָה | בָּֽחֲרָה |
| 3 *cp* | קָֽטְלוּ | בָּֽחֲרוּ |

**c.** III-Guttural Verbs

These are regular, except that the 2 fs is שָׁמַ֫עַתְּ instead of *שָׁמַעְתְּ.

## 2. The Qal Perfect of III-ʾÁlep̄ Verbs

Since א normally quiesces when it closes a syllable (II.11), any short vowel preceding it is lengthened, and the afformative ת is spirantized. The forms of the Qal perfect of מָצָא (to find), then, are as follows.

| | | | |
|---|---|---|---|
| *3 ms* | מָצָא | *3 cp* | מָצְאוּ |
| *3 fs* | מָצְאָה | | |
| *2 ms* | מָצָ֫אתָ | *2 mp* | מְצָאתֶם |
| *2 fs* | מָצָאת | *2 fp* | מְצָאתֶן |
| *1 cs* | מָצָ֫אתִי | *1 cp* | מָצָ֫אנוּ |

*Note*: Occasionally, the **א** is omitted in spelling, e.g., מָצָ֫תִי for מָצָ֫אתִי, מָלֵ֫תִי for מָלֵ֫אתִי. This phenomenon is observable not only in the Qal perfect, but also in other inflections and other verbal patterns.

## 3. The Qal Perfect of III-Hē Verbs

**a.** The forms of the Qal perfect of גָּלָה (to uncover) are as follows.

| | | | |
|---|---|---|---|
| *3 ms* | גָּלָה | *3 cp* | גָּלוּ |
| *3 fs* | גָּלְתָה | | |
| *2 ms* | גָּלִ֫יתָ | *2 mp* | גְּלִיתֶם |
| *2 fs* | גָּלִית | *2 fp* | גְּלִיתֶן |
| *1 cs* | גָּלִ֫יתִי | *1 cp* | גָּלִ֫ינוּ |

*Notes*:

i. The final ָה– of the 3 ms must not be confused with the fs ending.

ii. The 3 fs has an additional marker of the feminine, ת–.

iii. The first and second person forms have a י after the second radical.

iv. The afformative תּ is spirantized (> ת).

**b.** The verbs הָיָה (to be) and חָיָה (to live) are at once I-Guttural and III-Hē. The forms of the Qal perfect of הָיָה (to be), then, are as follows.

| | | | |
|---|---|---|---|
| *3 ms* | הָיָה | *3 cp* | הָיוּ |
| *3 fs* | הָיְתָה | | |
| *2 ms* | הָיִיתָ | *2 mp* | הֱיִיתֶם |
| *2 fs* | הָיִית | *2 fp* | הֱיִיתֶן |
| *1 cs* | הָיִיתִי | *1 cp* | הָיִינוּ |

*Notes*: The composite *šĕwāʾ* under the first radical is ֱ rather than ֲ. After the conjunction ו, however, it is silent: וִהְיִיתֶם; וִחְיִיתֶם.

## 4. The Qal Perfect of II-Wāw/Yōd Verbs

**a.** Verbs with II-Wāw/Yōḏ usually show only two radicals in the Qal perfect. The weak middle radical disappears, so that there is no distinction between II-Wāw and II-Yōḏ forms. The forms of the Qal perfect of קוּם (to arise), שִׂים (to set), and בּוֹא (to come), then, are as follows.

| | | | |
|---|---|---|---|
| *3 ms* | קָם | שָׂם | בָּא |
| *3 fs* | קָ֫מָה | שָׂ֫מָה | בָּ֫אָה |
| *2 ms* | קַ֫מְתָּ | שַׂ֫מְתָּ | בָּ֫אתָ |
| *2 fs* | קַמְתְּ | שַׂמְתְּ | בָּאת |
| *1 cs* | קַ֫מְתִּי | שַׂ֫מְתִּי | בָּ֫אתִי |
| *3 cp* | קָ֫מוּ | שָׂ֫מוּ | בָּ֫אוּ |
| *2 mp* | קַמְתֶּם | שַׂמְתֶּם | בָּאתֶם |
| *2 fp* | קַמְתֶּן | שַׂמְתֶּן | בָּאתֶן |
| *1 cp* | קַ֫מְנוּ | שַׂ֫מְנוּ | בָּ֫אנוּ |

*Notes*:

i. The verb בּוֹא also shows the characteristics of a III-ʾĀ́lep̄ verb.

ii. There is no difference in form between the 3 ms Qal perfect and the ms Qal active participle. Proper understanding of the form depends on the context. Word order may be instructive, however. If the form stands before a nominal subject, it is more likely to be the perfect 3 ms (see XIII.4.a.ii); if it stands after a named subject, it is likely the participle.

iii. The only formal difference between the 3 fs perfect (קָ֫מָה) and the Qal act. ptc. fs. (קָמָה) is in the accentuation.

iv. The accent in the 3 cp is on the first syllable. This distinguishes it from the 3 cp of a III-Hē verb (see 3.a). Thus, for example, שָׁ֫בוּ (3 cp of שׁוּב) means "they returned," but שָׁבוּ (3 cp of שָׁבָה) means "they captured."

**b.** The forms of the Qal perfect of the stative verbs מוּת (to die) and בּוֹשׁ (to be ashamed) are as follows.

| *3 ms* | מֵת | בֹּשׁ |
|---|---|---|
| *3 fs* | מֵ֫תָה | בֹּ֫ושָׁה |
| *2 ms* | מַ֫תָּה | בֹּ֫שְׁתָּ |
| *2 fs* | מַתְּ | בֹּשְׁתְּ |
| *1 cs* | מַ֫תִּי | בֹּ֫שְׁתִּי |
| *3 cp* | מֵ֫תוּ | בֹּ֫שׁוּ |
| *2 mp* | מַתֶּם | בָּשְׁתֶּם |
| *2 fp* | מַתֶּן | בָּשְׁתֶּן |
| *1 cp* | מַ֫תְנוּ | בֹּ֫שְׁנוּ |

*Notes*:

i. The third radical (ת) of the root מות assimilates into the afformative תּ, e.g., 1 cs מַ֫תִּי (*máttî*).

ii. The stative verb טוֹב (be good) belongs with this group: thus, טוֹב (he is good), טֹ֫בוּ (they are good).

## 5. Stative Verbs

As we have learned in XIII.2, stative verbs are those that describe a state or condition, rather than an action. In general they tend to be of *qāṭēl* and *qāṭōl* patterns, rather than *qāṭal*. The 3 ms forms, therefore, are identical to the adjectives of the same root. Thus, כָּבֵד can mean "he is heavy, important" (Qal Perf. 3 ms) or "heavy, important" (adjective) and קָטֹן can mean "he is small" (Qal Perf. 3 ms) or "small" (adjective). One cannot, however, rely on the form of a verb to tell if it is stative or not. In the course of history the distinction between stative and non-stative meanings often became blurred. Thus, the root שׁכן has the Qal perfect forms שָׁכֵן and שָׁכַן. Originally the former may have meant "he is situated" (stative), whereas the latter meant "he dwelled" (active). But no distinction is made now between the patterns; both words simply mean "he dwelled." Since stative verbs describe state rather than action, one should not expect them to have participles. Yet, there are forms that cannot be distinguished from adjectives but that clearly function as participles. Some of these even take the direct object.

| | |
|---|---|
| מִפְּנֵי מֶלֶךְ בָּבֶל אֲשֶׁר־אַתֶּם יְרֵאִים | the king of Babylon whose presence you *fear* (Jer 42:11) |
| וְשׁוּלָיו מְלֵאִים אֶת־הַהֵיכָל | and his flowing hem *was filling* the temple (Isa 6:1) |

Moreover, like the participle, these words may also be used as substantives. Thus, **יָרֵא** means "one who is afraid" and, hence, "a fearer."

| | |
|---|---|
| יְרֵא אֱלֹהִים | a God-fearer (Gen 22:12) |

## 6. Uses of הָיָה

There is no present tense verb "to be" in Hebrew. Simple predication (e.g., "the man is king") is accomplished by a juxtaposition of words (VI.8). Existence of someone or something in the present time is expressed by the particle **יֵשׁ** (X.3) or **הִנֵּה** (IX.5.b); absence is expressed by the particle **אֵין / אַיִן** (X.4).

**a.** Although a simple juxtaposition of words may also be adequate to state a past fact, Hebrew commonly uses the perfect of the verb **הָיָה** (to be, become) for it.

| | |
|---|---|
| עֲבָדִים הָיִינוּ | we *were* slaves (Deut 6:21) |

**b.** To indicate the existence of someone or something in the past, the verb **הָיָה** is used.

| | |
|---|---|
| אִישׁ הָיָה בְאֶרֶץ־עוּץ | *there was* a man in the land of Uz (Job 1:1) |

Conversely, to indicate the absence of something or someone in the past, the verb **הָיָה** is simply negated by the particle **לֹא**.

לֹא־הָיָה מֶלֶךְ כָּמֹהוּ *there was no* king like him (Neh 13:26)

**c.** To indicate possession in a past time, the idiom **הָיָה לְ**– is used.

וְלוֹ־הָיָה בֵן and he *had* a son (1 Sam 9:2)

**d.** **הָיָה** may also be translated as "to come," "to come to pass," "to become," "to happen," or the like.

הָיָה דְבַר־יְהוָה אֶל־אַבְרָם the word of YHWH *came* to Abram (Gen 15:1)

מֶה־הָיָה הַדָּבָר בְּנִי How *did* the matter *go*, my son? (1 Sam 4:16)

וְהוּא הָיָה לְאָבֶן and he *became* as a stone (1 Sam 25:37)

## 7. Impersonal Constructions

**a.** The 3 ms verb is sometimes used impersonally. In such cases, it is often best to translate the Hebrew with a passive phrase in English.

עַל־כֵּן קָרָא שְׁמָהּ בָּבֶל therefore *one called* its name Babel = therefore its name *is called* Babel (Gen 11:9)

**b.** The 3 cp verb may also refer to an indefinite subject.

שָׁמָּה קָבְרוּ אֶת־אַבְרָהָם וְאֵת שָׂרָה אִשְׁתּוֹ there *they buried* Abraham and Sarah, his wife = there Abraham and Sarah, his wife, *were buried* (Gen 49:31)

**c.** With certain verbs of emotion, an impersonal construction with the 3 ms may be used, and the one who experiences the emotion is indicated by the preposition לְ.

וְרָוַח לְשָׁאוּל וְטוֹב לוֹ *it was spacious* for Saul and *it was good* for him
= Saul *was relieved* and *he felt good* (1 Sam 16:23)

**d.** In expressions of natural phenomena, the third person singular may also be used impersonally (as in English "it is raining").

וְאוֹר לָכֶם when *it is light* (enough) for you (1 Sam 29:10)

**e.** As we have learned in VIII.4.d, participles may also be used to refer to an impersonal subject.

קֹרֵא מִשֵּׂעִיר someone *calls* from Seir (Isa 21:11)

בָּאִים לְהָרְגֶךָ some (people) *are coming* to kill you (Neh 6:10)

## Vocabulary

*Nouns*:

אֹרֶךְ length. *Verb*: אָרֵךְ to be long.

רֹחַב width, breadth. *Verb*: רָחַב to be wide, broad

*Verbs*:

בּוֹשׁ to be ashamed. *Noun*: בֹּשֶׁת shame

בָּחַר to choose (object usually indicated by marker or בְּ)

גּוּר to sojourn (i.e., live as a resident alien). *Nouns*: מָגוֹר (mp: מְגוּרִים) sojourning place, sojourning; גֵּר sojourner

הָיָה to be, come to pass, come about, happen

חָיָה to live

מוּת to die

מָלֵא to be full

נָשָׂא to lift up, raise, bear, forgive

סוּר to turn aside

קוּם to arise

שִׂים to place, put, set

שָׁבַר to break

*Conjunctions*:

אוֹ or

אִם if, or, either. כִּי אִם rather, except, yet

*Adverbs*:

אַךְ however, surely, indeed

אַף also, even, indeed

רַק only

## Exercise 14

**a.** Parse the following forms:

| | | |
|---|---|---|
| 1. מָלֵ֫אתִי | 6. בָּאָה | 11. הָיוּ |
| 2. עָשִׂ֫יתָ | 7. בָּ֫אָה | 12. חֹטֵאת |
| 3. בֹּ֫שְׁתִּי | 8. גָּ֫רוּ | 13. מַ֫תִּי |
| 4. הָיִ֫יתִי | 9. הָֽיְתָה | 14. סַ֫רְתִּי |
| 5. מֵ֫תָה | 10. חָטָאת | 15. מַ֫תְנוּ |

**b.** Write the following in Hebrew:

| | | |
|---|---|---|
| 1. they chose | 6. you (mp) were | 11. you (ms) entered |
| 2. she set | 7. you (ms) died | 12. he sojourned |
| 3. I made | 8. she went up | 13. you (ms) lifted |
| 4. they set | 9. you (mp) did | 14. we are ashamed |
| 5. he died | 10. you (ms) lived | 15. you (mp) left |

**c.** Translate the following into English:

1. אַיֵּה הָאֲנָשִׁים אֲשֶׁר־בָּאוּ אֵלֶיךָ הַלָּיְלָה (Gen 19:5)
2. בֹּשְׁנוּ מְאֹד כִּי־עָזַבְנוּ אָרֶץ (Jer 9:18)
3. לֹא יָדַעְנוּ מֶה־הָיָה לוֹ (Exod 32:1)
4. הֶן־כֹּל רָאֲתָה עֵינִי שָׁמְעָה אָזְנִי (Job 13:1)
5. וְזֹאת הַתּוֹרָה אֲשֶׁר־שָׂם מֹשֶׁה לִפְנֵי בְּנֵי יִשְׂרָאֵל (Deut 4:44)
6. אֲדֹנִי שָׁאַל אֶת־עֲבָדָיו לֵאמֹר הֲיֵשׁ־לָכֶם אָב אוֹ־אָח (Gen 44:19)
7. וְאַתֶּם יְדַעְתֶּם אֶת־נֶפֶשׁ הַגֵּר כִּי־גֵרִים הֱיִיתֶם בְּאֶרֶץ מִצְרָיִם (Exod 23:9)
8. הֶהָיְתָה זֹּאת בִּימֵיכֶם וְאִם בִּימֵי אֲבֹתֵיכֶם (Joel 1:2)
9. וְכָמֹהוּ לֹא־הָיָה לְפָנָיו מֶלֶךְ אֲשֶׁר־שָׁב אֶל־יְהוָה בְּכָל־לְבָבוֹ (2 Kgs 23:25)
10. אַךְ בַּת־פַּרְעֹה עָלְתָה מֵעִיר דָּוִד אֶל־בֵּיתָהּ אֲשֶׁר בָּנָה־לָהּ (1 Kgs 9:24)

**d.** Translate Eccl 2:4–10 with the help of a dictionary and these notes.

*Notes*:

v 4: הִגְדַּלְתִּי I accomplished (greatly).

v 6: לְהַשְׁקוֹת to irrigate.

v 7: הָיָה לִי / הָיָה לִי there was to me (impersonal use);
הַרְבֵּה abundantly.

v 9: וְהוֹסַפְתִּי and I increased.

# Excursus F
# Orientation to the Hebrew Bible

## 1. The Massoretic Text

The Hebrew text in most editions of the Bible is known as the *Massoretic Text*, abbreviated as MT. The name comes from the Hebrew word *massōrā(h)* "tradition." Hence, the Jewish traditionalists who helped preserve the text (between 600–1000 CE) are called "Massoretes."

The original Hebrew texts had no verse or chapter numberings; Christian scholars introduced them from the thirteenth century onwards. Moreover, the Pentateuch (the five books, Genesis-Deuteronomy) is divided into sections, marked by the signs פ (for פְּתוּחָה *opened*) and ס (for סְתוּמָה *closed*) at the end of each to indicate the relationship of the section to the next. In addition, the Massoretes wrote their observations in the margins of every page (called "marginal Massorah") and at the end of books (called "final Massorah"). A small circle above the line usually calls attention to a certain form or construction, which is then commented on in the margin. Since these comments are in Post-biblical Hebrew and Aramaic, and often in abbreviations, these notes are not accessible to beginning students.

## 2. *Kĕṯîḇ-Qĕrê*

A phenomenon that we have already encountered in our readings so far is the occasional discrepancy between the consonantal text and the vocalization. This peculiarity of the Hebrew Bible stems from the great reverance of the consonantal text on the part of the Massoretes. Only in the most extreme situations (and usually for serious theological reasons) was the consonantal texts deliberately altered. In most cases, the Massoretes simply superimposed on the consonantal text what ought to be read. In so doing, they were recommending what should be read and ignoring the consonants. The resulting combination of consonants and the vowel points is known as *Kĕṯîḇ-Qĕrê* (Aramaic for "what is written" and "to be read," respectively). That is, the text is written one way, but it is to be read another.

Some words *always* appear as *Kĕṯîḇ-Qĕrê*. For instance, the name of Israel's God is always spelled as יהוה, but the vowels tell the reader to pronounce the name as *ʾăḏōnāy*, or, in some cases, as *ʾĕlōhîm* (see p. 61 above).

We have learned, too, that the 3 fs in the Pentateuch is usually written as הוא but vocalized as הִיא (hence הִוא), and the name Jerusalem is usually written as ירושלם (assuming the pronunciation *yĕrûšālēm*) but vocalized as *yĕrûšāláyim* (hence יְרֻשָׁלַ͏ִם). These are examples of the so-called "perpetual *Kĕṯîḇ-Qĕrê*'s." In these and many other instances, the variants make no difference in our understanding of the texts. Often the *Qĕrê* makes a correction, according to what was understood to be the proper form or pronunciation, or the *Qĕrê* may simply offer a variant without attempting to replace the *Kĕṯîḇ*. There are some cases, however, where the variance is more substantive, and one is forced to choose one interpretation over another. Occasionally, too, the *Qĕrê* ignores a word by not vocalizing it (see ידרך in Jer 51:3), or it inserts a word by supplying the vowels (see ָ ִֽ for בָּאִים in Jer 31:38). The former is an example of dittography, where something is inadvertantly written twice. The latter is an instance where a word has accidentally dropped out. In each case, a small circle above the form in question points one to the marginal notes which elaborate on the problem.

## 3. The Critical Apparatus in *BHS*

There are several editions of the Hebrew Bible. The critical edition that is most commonly used by students and scholars today is *Biblia Hebraica Stuttgartensia* edited by K. Elliger and W. Rudolph (Stuttgart: Deutsche Bibelgesellschaft, 1967–77), popularly abbreviated to *BHS*. It is the third edition of *Biblica Hebraica*, first edited by Rudolph Kittel (*BHK*), and is based on the Leningrad Codex known as B19[A]. Since *BHS* is a *critical* edition, it comes with a critical apparatus at the bottom of each page with the editors' notes on variant readings and various proposals. For the beginner, the morass of details, presented in abbreviations of Latin and through symbols, can be quite intimidating. It is necessary, therefore, to have a brief orientation to the critical apparatus, not so that one might instantly know how to do textual criticism, but so that one might know what the critical apparatus is for and, perhaps, turn to it from time to time. Fortunately, *BHS* now comes with an English key to the symbols and abbreviations.

To illustrate very briefly how the critical apparatus works, we may turn to Eccl 2:7, which we have just translated in Exercise 15. The superscript "a" after קָנִ֫יתִי points us to the first note at the bottom of the page, which says "mlt Mss S + לִי." This means that many manuscripts and the Syriac version add לִי after קָנִ֫יתִי. One may have to decide, then, whether the לִי is authentic and has accidentally dropped out of the text in the process of transmission, or whether the variant cited by BHS is in fact a secondary addition. One of the rules of thumb in Hebrew textual criticism is that the shorter text is to be preferred, since there was a tendency for scribes to add and harmonize. Apparently some scribe added לִי in an attempt to harmonize this sentence with the rest of the passage, for elsewhere in this passage we have the perfect 1 cs form + לִי.

The superscript "b" after הָיָה points us to the note that tells us that a few (abbreviation pc for *pauci*) manuscripts, and the Greek (𝔊) and Syriac (S) versions read הָיוּ. One may have to choose between the reading הָיָה and הָיוּ. The latter is the easier reading, since the subject seems to be וּבְנֵי־בַיִת; the text flows better with הָיוּ as the verb. But that is precisely why one must be careful, since people tend to "correct" the text – that is, make it easier. The reading הָיָה can, in fact, be explained in some other way (see GKC 145.u). Indeed, the more awkward reading is probably the more original! In textual criticism this is called the principle *lectio difficilior* – that is, the more difficult reading is to be preferred.

# Lesson XV

## 1. The Piel Perfect

The Piel verbal pattern is characterized by the *doubling* of the second radical in all its inflections. The forms of the Piel perfect are as follows.

| | | | |
|---|---|---|---|
| *3 ms* | קִטֵּל | *3 cp* | קִטְּלוּ |
| *3 fs* | קִטְּלָה | | |
| *2 ms* | קִטַּ֫לְתָּ | *2 mp* | קִטַּלְתֶּם |
| *2 fs* | קִטַּלְתְּ | *2 fp* | קִטַּלְתֶּן |
| *1 cs* | קִטַּ֫לְתִּי | *1 cp* | קִטַּ֫לְנוּ |

*Notes*:

i. The *ē*-vowel in *qiṭṭēl* is typical of all inflections of the Piel verbal pattern, but in the perfect it is preserved only in the 3 ms. Moreover, for some verbs the 3 ms form is *qiṭṭal*, instead of *qiṭṭēl* (e.g., לִמַּד he taught), while others (mostly with final ר) have *e* instead of *ē* (e.g., דִּבֶּר he spoke).

ii. In a few instances, the *dāgēš* in the middle radical is lost when a *šĕwāʾ* stands under it (VI.7): thus, *בִּקְּשָׁה > בִּקְשָׁה (she sought).

## 2. The Meaning of Verbs in Piel

**a.** *Factitive*. Roots that are stative or intransitive in Qal may become transitive in Piel. One may compare the ending *-ize* in English (e.g., be normal :: normal*ize*).

| *Root* | *Qal* | *Piel* |
|---|---|---|
| טהר | to be clean | to cleanse |
| קדשׁ | to be holy | to consecrate |
| אבד | to perish | to destroy |

**b.** *Intensive.* Many verbs in Piel suggest multiple, repeated, or busy action.

| *Root* | *Qal* | *Piel* |
|---|---|---|
| הלך | to walk | to walk around |
| קבר | to bury | to bury many |
| שׁאל | to ask | to beg |
| שׁבר | to break | to shatter |

**c.** *Denominative.* Some verbs are derived from nouns and adjectives. One may compare the English prefix *en-* (danger :: to *en*danger).

| *Root* | *Noun* | *Piel verb* |
|---|---|---|
| כהן | priest | to act as priest |
| שׁרשׁ | root | to uproot |

**d.** *Declarative.* Some verbs declare a state of being.

| *Root* | *Adjective* | *Piel verb* |
|---|---|---|
| נקה | innocent | to declare innocent |
| צדק | righteous | to declare righteous |

It is not always possible to fit a Piel verb into one of these categories. Sometimes there is no obvious reason why a certain verb occurs in Piel. Often, too, a verb may occur in both Qal and Piel, with no discernible difference in meaning. Sometimes a verb may be both transitive and intransitive in Qal, but in Piel it is always transitive.

## 3. The Piel Perfect of II-Guttural and II-Rêš Verbs

**a.** Since gutturals and Rêš cannot be doubled by a *dāgēš* (IV.2.a), we get the following.

**i.** Compensatory lengthening before א and ר.

**ii.** Virtual doubling of ה, ח, and ע.

**b.** When a vocal *šĕwāʾ* is expected under a guttural, one finds ◌ֲ instead of ◌ְ (II.7). Even ר sometimes takes ◌ֲ (e.g., בֵּרֲכוּ "they blessed").

**c.** The inflections of the Piel perfect of מֵאֵן (to refuse) and מִהַר (to hasten), representing the type with compensatory lengthening and the type with virtual doubling, respectively, are as follows.

| | | |
|---|---|---|
| *3 ms* | מֵאֵן | מִהַר |
| *3 fs* | מֵאֲנָה | מִהֲרָה |
| *2 ms* | מֵאַנְתָּ | מִהַרְתָּ |
| *2 fs* | מֵאַנְתְּ | מִהַרְתְּ |
| *1 cs* | מֵאַנְתִּי | מִהַרְתִּי |
| *3 cp* | מֵאֲנוּ | מִהֲרוּ |
| *2 mp* | מֵאַנְתֶּם | מִהַרְתֶּם |
| *2 fp* | מֵאַנְתֶּן | מִהַרְתֶּן |
| *1 cp* | מֵאַנּוּ | מִהַרְנוּ |

## 4. The Piel Perfect of III-ʾÁlep̄ Verbs

Verbs of this type show the expected quiescence of א, the lengthening of the preceding vowel, and the spirantization of the afformative ת (XIV.2). The characteristic *ē*-vowel in the second syllable, however, is preserved beyond the 3 ms form (contrast 1.note i): מִלֵּ֫אתָ (you filled), מִלֵּ֫אתִי (I filled), and so forth.

## 5. The Piel Perfect of III-Hē Verbs

Apart from the characteristic doubling of the second radical and the *i* vowel in the first syllable, the Piel perfect of III-Hē verbs is inflected like its Qal counterpart (XIV.3): גִּלָּה (he uncovered), גִּלְּתָה (she uncovered), and so forth.

## 6. The Piel Perfect of II Wāw/ Yōḏ Verbs

Such verbs are rare in Piel; for these verbs, the functions of the Piel are assumed by other verbal patterns (see Lesson XXX). A few forms are attested, however (e. g., עִוֵּר he blinded).

## 7. The Piel Participle

The Piel participle is marked by a prefix –מְ, a *páṯaḥ* under the first radical, and the characteristic doubling of the second radical: מְקַטֵּל.

## Synopsis of Forms of the Piel Participle

| *Root* | *ms* | *mp* | *fs* | *fp* |
|---|---|---|---|---|
| קטל | מְקַטֵּל | מְקַטְּלִים | מְקַטֶּ֫לֶת | מְקַטְּלוֹת |
| מאן | מְמָאֵן | מְמָאֲנִים | מְמָאֶ֫נֶת | מְמָאֲנוֹת |
| מהר | מְמַהֵר | מְמַהֲרִים | מְמַהֶ֫רֶת | מְמַהֲרוֹת |
| שׁלח | מְשַׁלֵּחַ | מְשַׁלְּחִים | מְשַׁלַּ֫חַת | מְשַׁלְּחוֹת |
| מלא | מְמַלֵּא | מְמַלְּאִים | מְמַלֵּאת | מְמַלְּאוֹת |
| גלה | מְגַלֶּה | מְגַלִּים | מְגַלָּה | מְגַלּוֹת |
| ילד | מְיַלֵּד | מְיַלְּדִים | מְיַלֶּ֫דֶת | מְיַלְּדוֹת |

*Note*: The *dāḡēš* in the second radical may be lost when it is followed by ְ (see VI.7 and 1. Note ii above). Thus, *מְבַקְּשִׁים > מְבַקְשִׁים (*mĕḇaqšîm*).

## Vocabulary

*Verbs*:[1]

בָּקַשׁ Pi.: to seek

בָּרַךְ Pi.: to bless; Qal only in the pass. ptc. forms. *Noun*: בְּרָכָה blessing; בֶּ֫רֶךְ (fs; fd: בִּרְכַּ֫יִם) knee

גָּדַל to grow up, become great; Pi.: to bring up, raise, make great

דָּבַר to speak

הָלַל Pi.: to praise, boast. *Noun*: תְּהִלָּה praise, song of praise

כָּלָה to be complete, be finished; Pi.: to complete, finish

כָּסָה to cover, conceal

1. We follow the convention in BDB of giving the lexical form of the verb as the Qal Perf. 3 ms, even if the form is unattested in that verbal pattern.

מָאֵן Pi.: to refuse, reject

מָהַר Pi.: to hurry, hasten

סָפַר to count, write; Pi.: to recount, relate, tell. *Noun*: מִסְפָּר number. *Idioms*: אֵין מִסְפָּר innumerable, infinite; יֵשׁ מִסְפָּר numerable

פָּעַל to work, perform, accomplish. *Noun*: פֹּ֫עַל deed

צָוָה Pi.: to command, charge, appoint. *Noun*: מִצְוָה commandment

קָדַשׁ to be holy, consecrated; Pi.: to sanctify, consecrate. *Noun*: מִקְדָּשׁ sanctuary

שָׁרַת Pi.: to serve, minister

*Nouns*:

בָּשָׂר flesh

נַ֫חַל wadi, stream

נְחֹ֫שֶׁת bronze, copper

*Adverb*:

כֵּן so, thus, therefore, accordingly; עַל־כֵּן for this reason, therefore

## Exercise 15

**a.** Parse the following forms:

| | | |
|---|---|---|
| 1. בִּקַּשְׁתֶּם | 6. מְדַבֶּ֫רֶת | 11. הִלַּלְתֶּם |
| 2. דִּבַּ֫רְתָּ | 7. בֵּרֲכוּ | 12. מְכַלֶּה |
| 3. כִּלּוּ | 8. בִּקְשָׁה | 13. מְבַקְשִׁים |
| 4. כִּלְּתָה | 9. כִּלִּ֫ינוּ | 14. כִּסִּ֫יתִי |
| 5. כִּסִּ֫יתָ | 10. דִּבַּרְתְּ | 15. מְבָרֵךְ |

**b.** Write the following in Hebrew:

1. I blessed
2. he sought
3. they hurried
4. I filled
5. she hurried
6. they ministered
7. they recounted
8. he completed
9. I commanded
10. they performed
11. you (mp) completed
12. you (mp) counted
13. you (ms) hastened
14. you (mp) consecrated
15. he commanded

**c.** Translate the following into English:

1. חָטָאנוּ כִּי־דִבַּרְנוּ בַיהוָה וָבָךְ (Num 21:7)
2. כִּי־מֵתוּ כָּל־הָאֲנָשִׁים הַמְבַקְשִׁים אֶת־נַפְשֶׁךָ (Exod 4:19)
3. אַתֶּם רְאִיתֶם כִּי מִן־הַשָּׁמַיִם דִּבַּרְתִּי עִמָּכֶם (Exod 20:22)
4. הַשָּׁמַיִם מְסַפְּרִים כְּבוֹד־אֵל (Ps 19:2)
5. כַּאֲשֶׁר צִוָּה יְהוָה אֹתָם כֵּן עָשׂוּ (Exod 7:6)
6. הַאַתָּה הָאִישׁ אֲשֶׁר־דִּבַּרְתָּ אֶל־הָאִשָּׁה (Judg 13:11)
7. בֵּאלֹהִים הִלַּלְנוּ כָל־הַיּוֹם (Ps 44:9)
8. נָשָׂאתָ עֲוֹן עַמֶּךָ כִּסִּיתָ כָל־חַטָּאתָם (Ps 85:3)
9. רַבִּים מְבַקְשִׁים פְּנֵי־מוֹשֵׁל וּמֵיְהוָה מִשְׁפַּט־אִישׁ (Prov 29:26)
10. וְזֹאת הַבְּרָכָה אֲשֶׁר בֵּרַךְ מֹשֶׁה אִישׁ הָאֱלֹהִים אֶת־בְּנֵי יִשְׂרָאֵל
    לִפְנֵי מוֹתוֹ (Deut 33:1)

**d.** Read Jer 45:1–5 out loud and translate the passage with the help of a dictionary and these notes.

*Notes*:

v 1: בְּכָתְבוֹ when he wrote

v 3: אוֹי־נָא woe.

v 4: תֹּאמַר you shall say.

v 5: תְּבַקֶּשׁ־לְךָ will you seek (object) for yourself?; אַל־תְּבַקֵּשׁ do not seek; מֵבִיא am bringing; וְנָתַתִּי and I will give; תֵּלֵךְ־שָׁם lit.: you shall go there.

# Lesson XVI

## 1. The Hiphil Perfect

The Hiphil verbal pattern is characterized by a prefixed *h* in the perfect. An *î*-vowel appears in the second syllable of all the third person forms, but elsewhere it is replaced by an *a*-vowel (i.e., *páṯaḥ*).

The forms of the Hiphil perfect, then, are as follows.

| | | | |
|---|---|---|---|
| *3 ms* | הִקְטִיל | *3 cp* | הִקְטִ֫ילוּ |
| *3 fs* | הִקְטִ֫ילָה | | |
| *2 ms* | הִקְטַ֫לְתָּ | *2 mp* | הִקְטַלְתֶּם |
| *2 fs* | הִקְטַלְתְּ | *2 fp* | הִקְטַלְתֶּן |
| *1 cs* | הִקְטַ֫לְתִּי | *1 cp* | הִקְטַ֫לְנוּ |

## 2. The Meaning of Verbs in Hiphil

**a.** *Causative.* Most frequently the Hiphil verb is used as a causative; the verb in Hiphil causes something to happen or to be.

| *Root* | *Qal* | *Hiphil* |
|---|---|---|
| מלך | to reign | to cause to reign |
| בטח | to trust | to cause to trust |

Sometimes it is possible to translate the Hebrew causative with a single English word. Thus, הֶאֱכִיל he caused to eat = he fed.

| *Root* | *Qal* | *Hiphil* |
|---|---|---|
| אכל | to eat | to feed (cause to eat) |
| מות | to die | to kill (cause to die) |
| ראה | to see | to show (cause to see) |

**b.** *Factitive.* Roots that are stative or intransitive in Qal may become transitive in Hiphil.

| *Root* | *Qal* | *Hiphil* |
|---|---|---|
| גדל | to be great | to exalt (make great) |
| רחב | to be wide | to widen (make wide) |
| חיה | to live | to preserve (make live) |

**c.** *Denominative.* Some verbs are derived from nouns and adjectives.

| *Root* | *Noun* | *Hiphil verb* |
|---|---|---|
| אזן | ear | to pay attention |
| שׁרשׁ | root | to grow root |

**d.** *Declarative.* Some verbs declare a state of being.

| *Root* | *Adjective* | *Hiphil verb* |
|---|---|---|
| צדק | righteous | to declare righteous |
| רשׁע | wicked | to declare wrong |

There is obviously some semantic overlap between the Hiphil and Piel verbal patterns. Hence, some verbs are found in both verbal patterns with no discernible difference in meaning. Other verbs cannot be classified under one of the above categories. Some verbs are related to adjectives but are, even in Hiphil, still stative or intransitive.

| *Root* | *Adjective* | *Hiphil verb* |
|---|---|---|
| זקן | old | to become old |
| טוב | good | to do well |

Some verbs in this group are, curiously, both transitive and intransitive. For instance, the Hiphil of יטב may mean either "to do well" (intransitive) or "to make (something) good" (transitive).

## 3. The Hiphil Perfect of I-Guttural Verbs

When the first radical is a guttural, a composite *šĕwāʾ* ( ֱ ) takes the place of the simple silent *šĕwāʾ* ( ְ ) under the first radical. Moreover, the vowel with the prefixed ה is influenced by the composite *šĕwāʾ* ( ֱ ), so that it is changed from ִ to ֶ (thus, הֶעֱמִיד). The forms are otherwise regular.

## 4. The Hiphil Perfect of III-Guttural Verbs

In verbs of this type, the *furtive páṯaḥ* appears as expected, whenever הּ, ח, or ע stands at the end of the form (II.10). In the perfect, this situation occurs only in the 3 ms form (thus, הִשְׁלִיחַ). The other forms are all regular.

## 5. The Hiphil Perfect of III-ʾÁlep̄ Verbs

Verbs of this type show the expected quiescence of א, the lengthening of the preceding vowel, and the spirantization of the ת of the afformative (see XIV.2). It should be noted, however, that the characteristic vowel in the second syllable is *ē* in all first and second person forms: thus, הִמְצִיא, הִמְצִ֫יאָה *but* הִמְצֵ֫אתָ, הִמְצֵ֫אתִי.

## 6. The Hiphil Perfect of III-Hē Verbs

The forms of the Hiphil perfect of גָּלָה (to uncover) are as follows.

| | | | |
|---|---|---|---|
| *3 ms* | הִגְלָה / הֶגְלָה | *3 cp* | הִגְלוּ |
| *3 fs* | הִגְלְתָה | | |
| *2 ms* | הִגְלִ֫יתָ / הִגְלֵ֫יתָ | *2 mp* | הִגְלִיתֶם / הִגְלֵיתֶם |
| *2 fs* | הִגְלִית / הִגְלֵית | *2 fp* | הִגְלִיתֶן / הִגְלֵיתֶן |
| *1 cs* | הִגְלִ֫יתִי / הִגְלֵ֫יתִי | *1 cp* | הִגְלִ֫ינוּ |

## 7. The Hiphil Perfect of I-Nûn Verbs

The Nûn is assimilated into the following consonant, as expected when there is no intervening vowel (IV.2.b). The forms of the Hiphil perfect of נָגַד (to tell) are as follows.

| | | | |
|---|---|---|---|
| *3 ms* | הִגִּיד | *3 cp* | הִגִּ֫ידוּ |
| *3 fs* | הִגִּ֫ידָה | | |
| *2 ms* | הִגַּ֫דְתָּ | *2 mp* | הִגַּדְתֶּם |
| *2 fs* | הִגַּדְתְּ | *2 fp* | הִגַּדְתֶּן |
| *1 cs* | הִגַּ֫דְתִּי | *1 cp* | הִגַּ֫דְנוּ |

I-Nûn verbs that are also II-Guttural are uncommon. The attested roots do not show the assimilation of Nûn, e.g., הִנְחַ֫לְתִּי (I bequeathed). The combination of I-Nûn with other weak radicals occasions no surprise; they are according to the rules for both weak radicals, e.g., *הִנְכָה > הִכָּה (he struck).

## 8. The Hiphil Perfect of I-Wāw Verbs

**a.** The forms of the Hiphil perfect יָשַׁב (original *ושב dwell) are as follows.

| | | | |
|---|---|---|---|
| *3 ms* | הוֹשִׁיב | *3 cp* | הוֹשִׁ֫יבוּ |
| *3 fs* | הוֹשִׁ֫יבָה | | |
| *2 ms* | הוֹשַׁ֫בְתָּ | *2 mp* | הוֹשַׁבְתֶּם |
| *2 fs* | הוֹשַׁבְתְּ | *2 fp* | הוֹשַׁבְתֶּן |
| *1 cs* | הוֹשַׁ֫בְתִּי | *1 cp* | הוֹשַׁ֫בְנוּ |

*Note*: The Hiphil prefix (*hô*- instead of *hi*-) here may seem surprising, but it can be explained. The original Hiphil prefix was actually **ha*-, but it has generally become *hi*- (through a complicated process). In the Hiphil of I-Wāw verbs, however, the old **ha*- prefix, in combination with the initial *w*, yields the contracted diphthong *ô*, in accordance with IV.2.c.iii.β: thus, **hawšīb* > *hôšîḇ*.

**b.** The verb הָלַךְ (walk) behaves as if it were *ולך in all inflections of the Hiphil (thus, הוֹלִיךְ, הוֹלִ֫יכָה, etc.).

**c.** A few verbs (almost always with צ as the second radical) regularly behave like I-*Nûn* verbs – that is, the initial radical is assimilated. The following verbs are the most important.

יצג to set down הִצִּיג, הִצִּיגָה, הִצַּגְתָּ, etc.

יצק to pour out הִצִּיק, הִצִּיקָה, הִצַּקְתָּ, etc.

יצת to kindle הִצִּית, הִצִּיתָה, הִצַּתָּ, etc.

## 9. The Hiphil Perfect of I-Yōḏ Verbs

The forms of the Hiphil perfect of יָטַב (be good) are as follows.

| | | | |
|---|---|---|---|
| *3 ms* | הֵיטִיב | *3 cp* | הֵיטִיבוּ |
| *3 fs* | הֵיטִיבָה | | |
| *2 ms* | הֵיטַבְתָּ | *2 mp* | הֵיטַבְתֶּם |
| *2 fs* | הֵיטַבְתְּ | *2 fp* | הֵיטַבְתֶּן |
| *1 cs* | הֵיטַבְתִּי | *1 cp* | הֵיטַבְנוּ |

*Note*: As in original I-Wāw verbs, traces of the old **ha-* prefix are evident. Here **ha-* has combined with the initial radical (*y*) and the contraction of **hay-* > *hê-* is in accordance with IV.2.c.iv.β (thus, **hayṭīb* > *hêṭîḇ*, etc.). Verbs of this type are actually quite rare. Most verbs listed as I-Yōḏ in the dictionaries are original I-Wāw. The following, however, are genuine I-Yōḏ verbs occurring in Hiphil.

| *Root* | *Qal* | *Hiphil* |
|---|---|---|
| יטב | to please, do well | to treat well, make good |
| ינק | to suck | to suckle, nurse |
| ילל | –not attested– | to wail, howl |
| ימן | –not attested– | to go to the right |
| ישר | to be level | to level |

The verb יָבֵשׁ (to be dry) behaves like a I-Yōḏ verb in Qal, but it is like original I-Wāw in Hiphil (thus, הוֹבִישׁ he caused to dry up).

## 10. The Hiphil Perfect of II-Wāw/ Yōḏ Verbs

There is no distinction between II-Wāw and II-Yōḏ verbs in the Hiphil perfect. The forms of the Hiphil perfect of קוּם (to arise) are as follows.

| | | | |
|---|---|---|---|
| *3 ms* | הֵקִים | *3 cp* | הֵקִ֫ימוּ |
| *3 fs* | הֵקִ֫ימָה | | |
| *2 ms* | הֲקִימ֫וֹתָ | *2 mp* | הֲקִימוֹתֶם |
| *2 fs* | הֲקִימוֹת | *2 fp* | הֲקִימוֹתֶן |
| *1 cs* | הֲקִימ֫וֹתִי | *1 cp* | הֲקִימ֫וֹנוּ |

*Notes*:

i. The characteristic –הִ prefix becomes –הֵ, which, in the second and first person forms reduces to –הֲ (see III.2.a.i). In some instances, however, one finds ֱ instead of ֲ (e.g., הֱשִׁיב֫וֹתָ you restored).

ii. An additional *ô* (וֹ) precedes every consonantal afformative, thus opening the syllable and causing the spirantization of afformative ת. Not infrequently, however, the וֹ is omitted.

הֵבֵ֫אתָ instead of הֲבִיא֫וֹתָ

הֵבֵ֫אתִי instead of הֲבִיא֫וֹתִי

הֲמִתֶּם instead of הֲמִיתוֹתֶם*

## 11. Hiphil Verbs as Causatives

As we have seen in 1.a above, the Hiphil is used most commonly as a causative. If the basic verbal idea expressed by the root is already transitive (taking an object), the Hiphil verb may be doubly transitive – that is, it takes two objects.

| | |
|---|---|
| הֶרְאָה אֹתִי אֱלֹהִים גַּם אֶת־זַרְעֶךָ | God has shown *me* even *your seed* (Gen 48:11) |
| וַאדֹנָי הִשְׁמִיעַ ׀ אֶת־מַחֲנֵה אֲרָם קוֹל רֶכֶב קוֹל סוּס קוֹל חַיִל גָּדוֹל | The Lord caused the *Aramean camp* to hear *the sound* of chariotry, *the sound* of horses, and *the sound* of a great army (2 Kgs 7:6) |

It is common, however, to have only a single object.

| | |
|---|---|
| כַּאֲשֶׁר הֶרְאָה אֹתְךָ בָּהָר | just as he showed *you* on the mountain (Exod 27:8) |
| אַתָּה הִמְלַכְתָּ אֶת־עַבְדְּךָ | you caused *your servant* to reign (1 Kgs 3:7) |

If there is no personal object mentioned, a literal translation may be a passive construction in English (e.g., "cause to *be known*"), but it is better to render the phrase in more idiomatic style.

| | |
|---|---|
| הוֹדִיעַ יְהוָה יְשׁוּעָתוֹ | YHWH has caused his salvation to be known = YHWH has proclaimed his salvation (Ps 98:2) |

## 12. The Hiphil Participle

Hiphil participles are typically marked by a prefixed –מַ (*ma*-). The characteristic *h* of this verbal pattern is no longer evident in the participle because it has been lost, probably in a manner not unlike the loss of the definite article after a prefixed preposition (VI.2.b).

## Synopsis of Forms of the Hiphil Participle

| *Root* | *ms* | *mp* | *fs* | *fp* |
|---|---|---|---|---|
| קטל | מַקְטִיל | מַקְטִילִים | מַקְטֶלֶת | מַקְטִילוֹת |
| עמד | מַעֲמִיד | מַעֲמִידִים | מַעֲמֶדֶת | מַעֲמִידוֹת |
| שׁלח | מַשְׁלִיחַ | מַשְׁלִיחִים | מַשְׁלַחַת | מַשְׁלִיחוֹת |
| גלה | מַגְלֶה | מַגְלִים | מַגְלָה | מַגְלוֹת |
| נגד | מַגִּיד | מַגִּידִים | מַגֶּדֶת | מַגִּידוֹת |
| ישׁב | מוֹשִׁיב | מוֹשִׁיבִים | מוֹשֶׁבֶת | מוֹשִׁיבוֹת |
| יטב | מֵיטִיב | מֵיטִיבִים | מֵיטֶבֶת | מֵיטִיבוֹת |
| קום | מֵקִים | מְקִימִים | מְקִימָה | מְקִימוֹת |

*Notes*:

i. The fs participle is of the מַקְטֶלֶת pattern, except for III-Hē verbs (מַגְלָה) and II-Wāw/Yōḏ verbs (מְקִימָה).

ii. The prefix for I-Wāw verbs is מוֹ– (see 8.Note) and for I-Yōḏ it is מֵי– (see 9. Note).

iii. II-Wāw/Yōḏ has מֵי– as the prefix, but in the forms with endings, the *ē* vowel is reduced (see III.2.a.i).

## Vocabulary

*Nouns*:

בְּכֹר first-born

כַּף (fs) palm, sole

פֶּתַח opening, entrance. *Verb*: פָּתַח to open

רֶכֶב chariotry; מֶרְכָּבָה chariot. *Verb*: רָכַב to ride, mount

שֶׁקֶר deception, falsehood

*Verbs*:

דָּרַשׁ to inquire, demand

הָרַג to kill

יָטַב to do well; please; suit; Hi.: to make good, treat well

יָשַׁע Hi.: to save, help. *Nouns*: יְשׁוּעָה, יֵ֫שַׁע, תְּשׁוּעָה deliverance, salvation

נָגַד Hi.: to tell, announce, report

נָחַל to inherit, possess; Hi.: to bequeath, assign inheritance

נָטַע to plant

נָכָה Hi.: to strike, smite, defeat. *Noun*: מַכָּה blow, strike

נָצַל Hi.: to rescue, snatch, deliver

צָעַק to cry out. *Noun*: צְעָקָה cry

רָבָה to become great, numerous; Pi.: increase, bring up; Hi.: to multiply, increase. *Adverb*: הַרְבֵּה abundantly

שָׁחַת Pi.: to ruin, destroy; Hi.: to ruin, destroy

שָׁלַךְ Hi.: to throw, cast

שָׁתָה to drink. *Noun*: מִשְׁתֶּה banquet

## Exercise 16

**a.** Parse the following forms:

1. הֵיטִיב
2. הִגַּ֫דְתִּי
3. הוֹצֵ֫אתָ
4. נְטַעְתֶּם
5. הִכֵּ֫יתִי
6. הִנְחַ֫לְתִּי
7. הֵיטַ֫בְנוּ
8. הִגִּ֫ידוּ
9. רָֽבְתָה
10. רָבוּ
11. הִרְבֵּ֫יתִי
12. שִׁחֲתוּ
13. רִבִּ֫יתָ
14. הִשְׁחִ֫יתוּ
15. צֹעֲקִים

**b.** Write the following in Hebrew:

1. I planted
2. he snatched
3. he struck
4. they struck
5. she cast out
6. she inquired
7. they cast out
8. they cried out
9. you (ms) saved
10. she announced
11. you (ms) killed
12. you (fs) drank

**c.** Translate the following into English:

1. אָנֹכִי הִגַּדְתִּי וְהוֹשַׁעְתִּי וְהִשְׁמַעְתִּי (Isa 43:12)
2. וְאֵלֶּה ׀ מַלְכֵי הָאָרֶץ אֲשֶׁר הִכּוּ בְנֵי־יִשְׂרָאֵל (Josh 12:1)
3. וְלֹא הִגִּיד לְאָבִיו וּלְאִמּוֹ אֵת אֲשֶׁר עָשָׂה (Judg 14:6)
4. הִגִּיד לְךָ אָדָם מַה־טּוֹב וּמָה־יְהוָה דּוֹרֵשׁ מִמְּךָ (Mic 6:8)
5. וַיהוָה הִשְׁלִיךְ עֲלֵיהֶם אֲבָנִים גְּדֹלוֹת מִן־הַשָּׁמַיִם (Josh 10:11)
6. מַה־זֹּאת עָשִׂיתָ לִּי לָמָּה לֹא־הִגַּדְתָּ לִּי כִּי אִשְׁתְּךָ הִוא
(Gen 12:18)
7. אַתֶּם הֲמִתֶּם אֶת־עַם יְהוָה (Num 17:6)
8. וְלָמָה יְהוָה מֵבִיא אֹתָנוּ אֶל־הָאָרֶץ הַזֹּאת (Num 14:3)
9. כִּי אֲנִי יְהוָה אֱלֹהֶיךָ קְדוֹשׁ יִשְׂרָאֵל מוֹשִׁיעֶךָ (Isa 43:3)
10. הוֹצִיא יְהוָה אֶתְכֶם בְּיָד חֲזָקָה (Deut 7:8)
11. וַיהוָה הִכָּה כָל־בְּכוֹר בְּאֶרֶץ מִצְרַיִם (Exod 12:29)
12. וַאֲנִי הִנְנִי מֵקִים אֶת־בְּרִיתִי אִתְּכֶם וְאֶת־זַרְעֲכֶם אַחֲרֵיכֶם
(Gen 9:9)
13. הוּא הַדָּבָר אֲשֶׁר דִּבַּרְתִּי אֶל־פַּרְעֹה אֲשֶׁר הָאֱלֹהִים עֹשֶׂה
הֶרְאָה אֶת־פַּרְעֹה (Gen 41:28)
14. זֹאת אוֹת־הַבְּרִית אֲשֶׁר הֲקִמֹתִי בֵּינִי וּבֵין כָּל־בָּשָׂר אֲשֶׁר עַל־
הָאָרֶץ (Gen 9:17)
15. וְלֹא אָמְרוּ אַיֵּה יְהוָה הַמַּעֲלֶה אֹתָנוּ מֵאֶרֶץ מִצְרָיִם הַמּוֹלִיךְ
אֹתָנוּ בַּמִּדְבָּר (Jer 2:6)

**d.** Read 1 Kgs 8:12–21 out loud and translate the passage with the help of a dictionary and these notes.

*Notes*:

v 12: לִשְׁכֹּן to dwell

v 13: בָּנֹה בָנִיתִי I have indeed built; לְשִׁבְתְּךָ for you to dwell

v 14: וַיַּסֵּב then (subject) turned around; וַיְבָרֶךְ and blessed; וְכָל־קְהַל while all the assembly of (the וְ here introduces a circumstantial clause; thus it should not be translate simply as "and")

v 15: וַיֹּאמֶר and he said

v 16: לִבְנוֹת to build; לִהְיוֹת for (subject) to be; וָאֶבְחַר and I chose; לִהְיוֹת to be

v 17: וַיְהִי now it was; לִבְנוֹת to build

v 18: וַיֹּאמֶר and (subject) said

v 19: לֹא תִבְנֶה you will not build; כִּי אִם־ but rather; יִבְנֶה will build

v 20: וַיָּקֶם and (subject) established; וָאָקֻם I have risen; וָאֵשֵׁב and I have sat; וָאֶבְנֶה and I have built

v 21: וָאָשִׂם and I have set; בְּהוֹצִיאוֹ when he brought out.

# Lesson XVII

## 1. The Perfect with Object Suffixes

In addition to the marker of the definite direct object with the pronominal suffix (IX.4), an object pronoun may be indicated by an object suffix appended directly to the verb. These are merely alternate ways of indicating an object; no difference in meaning may be discerned between the two. Thus הוֹצֵאתִי אֹתְךָ and הוֹצֵאתִיךָ both mean "I brought you out"; the 2 ms suffix ךָ– simply takes the place of אֹתְךָ.

As with the addition of the possessive suffix to a noun (XII.2), certain changes are to be expected in the verb forms with object suffixes.

**a.** Afformatives

**i.** The 3 fs ending is תַ– / תָ– instead of הָ–.

| *Without object suffix* | | *With object suffix* | |
|---|---|---|---|
| יָלְדָה | she bore | יְלָדַתְךָ | she bore you |
| בִּקְשָׁה | she sought | בִּקְשָׁתַם | she sought them |

**ii.** The 2 ms ending is simply תּ–.

| *Without object suffix* | | *With object suffix* | |
|---|---|---|---|
| כִּבַּדְתָּ | you honored | כִּבַּדְתַּנִי | you honored me |
| כִּבַּדְתָּ | you honored | כִּבַּדְתּוֹ | you honored him |
| כִּבַּדְתָּ | you honored | כִּבַּדְתָּם | you honored them |

**iii.** The 2 fs ending תִּי–

| *Without object suffix* | *With object suffix* |
|---|---|
| נָתַתְּ you gave | נְתַתִּ֫יהוּ you gave him |

*Notes*:

α. The תִּי– afformative is similar to the less common variant of the 2 fs independent pronoun (IX.1.a.iii) and the 2 fs perfect without object suffix (XIII.1.Note i). In the form before the object suffix, however, the תִּי– form is normative.

β. The afformative is frequently spelled defectively, e.g., רִמִּיתִ֫נִי (you deceived me).

γ. Obviously, the afformative is easily confused with the 1 cs. One can tell only from context which is intended.

**iv.** The 2 mp afformative is תוּ–, which is usually spelled defectively as תֻּ–.

| *Without object suffix* | *With object suffix* |
|---|---|
| הַעֲלִיתֶם you brought up | הֶעֱלִיתֻ֫נוּ you brought us up |

**b.** Before the afformatives

Since the addition of a suffix often causes the accent to advance, the verb forms may be different from those without object suffixes. The following rules account for most forms.

**i.** There is no change in a syllable if it is unchangeably long (i.e., has a *mater*), is closed, or has compensatory lengthening.

| *Without object suffix* | *With object suffix* |
|---|---|
| הוֹשַׁ֫עְתִּי I saved | הוֹשַׁעְתִּ֫יךָ I saved you |
| בֵּרַ֫כְתִּי I blessed | בֵּרַכְתִּ֫יךָ I blessed you |

**ii.** Apart from rule i, a long vowel in an open syllable is reduced to *šĕwāʾ*.

| *Without object suffix* | *With object suffix* |
|---|---|
| יָדַ֫עְתִּי I knew | יְדַעְתִּ֫יךָ I knew you |
| בֵּרֵךְ he blessed | בֵּרְכוֹ he blessed him |

**iii.** A long vowel becomes a short vowel if the syllable is closed and unstressed.

| *Without object suffix* | *With object suffix* |
|---|---|
| שִׁחֵת he destroyed | שִׁחֶתְךָ he destroyed you |
| בֵּרֵךְ he blessed | בֵּרַכְךָ he blessed you |

**iv.** The vocal *šĕwāʾ* in the Qal perfect 3 fs and 3 cp is restored to a full vowel.

| *Without object suffix* | *With object suffix* |
|---|---|
| אָֽכְלָה she devoured | אֲכָלַ֫תְהוּ she devoured him |
| יָֽדְעוּ they knew | יְדָעוּם they knew them |

**v.** A short vowel is lengthened, if the syllable becomes open.

| *Without object suffix* | *With object suffix* |
|---|---|
| יָדַע he knew | יְדָעוֹ he knew him |

*Note*: In the Piel, however, a short *a*-vowel in forms like לִמַּד is reduced: לִמְּדוֹ (he taught him).

**c.** The forms of the perfect before the addition of the object suffixes, then, are as follows:

| | *Qal* | *Piel* | *Hiphil* |
|---|---|---|---|
| *3 ms* | קְטָל־ | קִטְּל־ | הִקְטִיל־ |
| *3 fs* | קְטָלַת־ | קִטְּלַת־ | הִקְטִילַת־ |
| *2 ms* | קְטַלְתּ־ | קִטַּלְתּ־ | הִקְטַלְתּ־ |
| *2 fs* | קְטַלְתִּי־ | קִטַּלְתִּי־ | הִקְטַלְתִּי־ |
| *1 cs* | קְטַלְתִּי־ | קִטַּלְתִּי־ | הִקְטַלְתִּי־ |
| *3 cp* | קְטָלוּ־ | קִטְּלוּ־ | הִקְטִילוּ־ |
| *2 mp* | קְטַלְתּוּ־ | קִטַּלְתּוּ־ | הִקְטַלְתּוּ־ |
| *2 fp* | קְטַלְתּוּ־ | קִטַּלְתּוּ־ | הִקְטַלְתּוּ־ |
| *1 cp* | קְטַלְנוּ־ | קִטַּלְנוּ־ | הִקְטַלְנוּ־ |

*Notes*:

i. Apart from the afformatives, the Hiphil forms of the strong verb are unchanged (according to b.i). On the other hand, forms like הֵבֵאתִי will show reduction of the first vowel, according to b.ii: thus, הֵבֵאתִי (I brought in) *but* הֲבֵאתִיהָ (I brought her in). In these cases, the reduced vowel may be either ◌ֲ or ◌ֱ (e.g, הֱשִׁיבְךָ / הֲשִׁיבְךָ he restored you).

ii. Apart from the afformatives, most forms of the Piel are unchanged (according to b.i), but the 3 ms the *ē*-vowel reduces to *ĕ* (b.ii) or shortens to *e* (b.iii).

iii. Apart from the afformatives, the following changes are evident in the Qal forms.

  α. The first vowel is reduced (b.ii).

  β. The second vowel in the 3 ms is lengthened (b.v).

  γ. The second vowel in 3 fs and cp is restored and lengthened (b.iv, v).

**d.** The object suffixes used with the perfects come in various forms, depending on what immediately precedes them (whether a consonant or a vowel). The attested forms are provided below for reference, with the upper case letters indicating the subject and the lower case letters the object. The student should not try to memorize the entire chart.

| | | a<br>*3ms* | b<br>*3fs* | c<br>*2ms* | d<br>*2fs* | e<br>*1cs* | f<br>*3cp* | g<br>*3fp* | h<br>*2mp* | i<br>*1cp* |
|---|---|---|---|---|---|---|---|---|---|---|
| A | *3 ms* | ◌ָ֫הוּ/וֹ | ◌ָהּ | ◌ְךָ | ◌ֵךְ | ◌ַ֫נִי | ◌ָם | ◌ָן | | ◌ָ֫נוּ |
| B | *3 fs* | הוּ/תּוּ | תָּה | ךָ | ◌ֶךְ | נִי | ◌ַם | | | נוּ |
| C | *2 ms* | ◌ָ֫הוּ/וֹ | ◌ָהּ | | | ◌ַ֫נִי | ◌ָם | | | ◌ָנוּ |
| D | *2 fs* | הוּ | הָ | | | ◌ַ֫נִי | ם | | | נוּ |
| E | *1 cs* | הוּ/ו | הָ | ךָ | ךְ | | ם | ן | כֶם | |
| F | *3 cp* | הוּ | הָ | ךָ | ךְ | נִי | ם | ן | | נוּ |
| G | *2 mp* | הוּ | | | | נִי | | | | נוּ |
| H | *2 fp* | הוּ | | | | נִי | | | | נוּ |
| I | *1 cp* | הוּ | הָ | ךָ | ךְ | | ם | | כֶם | |

*Notes*:

i. The 3 ms object suffix used with the 3 fs perfect (a-B on the grid) is הוּ–, as expected, but also תּוּ. The latter is apparently developed from *-áthû*, i.e., *-áthû* > *-áttû*. The 3 fs object suffix used with the 3 fs perfect (b-B on the grid) is **-áthā(h)* > *-áttā(h)*.

ii. Forms in pause may vary slightly in vocalization (e.g., 1 cs ◌ָ֫נִי instead of ◌ַ֫נִי; 2 ms ◌ֶ֫ךָ– instead of ◌ְךָ–).

Study the following examples carefully, referring to the grid above (e.g., 1 cs subject + 3 ms object = E-a in the grid).

| *Form* | *Subject* | *Object* | *Translation* |
|---|---|---|---|
| הוֹצִיאַ֫נִי | 3 ms | 1 cs | he brought me out |
| הוֹצִיאֲךָ | 3 ms | 2 ms | he brought you out |
| הוֹצִיאָ֫נוּ | 3 ms | 1 cp | he brought us out |
| הוֹצִיאָם | 3 ms | 3 mp | he brought them out |
| הוֹצֵאתַ֫נִי | 2 ms | 1 cs | you brought me out |
| הוֹצֵאתָ֫נוּ | 2 ms | 1 cp | you brought us out |
| הוֹצֵאתוֹ | 2 ms | 3 ms | you brought him out |
| הוֹצֵאתִ֫יךָ | 1 cs | 2 ms | I brought you out |
| הוֹצֵאתִ֫יהָ | 1 cs | 3 fs | I brought her out |
| הוֹצֵאתִים | 1 cs | 3 mp | I brought them out |

| *Form* | *Subject* | *Object* | *Translation* |
|---|---|---|---|
| יְדָעוֹ | 3 ms | 3 ms | he knew him |
| יְדָעָהּ | 3 ms | 3 fs | he knew her |
| יְדָעוּם | 3 mp | 3 mp | they knew them |
| יְדַעְתּוֹ | 2 ms | 3 ms | you knew him |
| יְדַעְתָּם | 2 ms | 3 mp | you knew them |
| יְדַעְתִּ֫יךָ | 1 cs | 2 ms | I knew you |
| יְדַעְתִּיו | 1 cs | 3 ms | I knew him |
| יְדַעְתִּ֫יהָ | 1 cs | 3 fs | I knew her |
| יְדַעְתִּים | 1 cs | 3 mp | I knew them |
| יְדַעְתִּין | 1 cs | 3 fp | I knew them |

| *Form* | *Subject* | *Object* | *Translation* |
|---|---|---|---|
| נְתָנַ֫נִי | 3 ms | 1 cs | he gave me |
| נְתָנָ֫נוּ | 3 ms | 1 cp | he gave us |
| נְתַתִּ֫יהוּ | 2 fs | 3 ms | you gave him |
| נְתַתִּים | 1 cs | 3 mp | I gave them |
| נְתַתִּיךְ | 1 cs | 2 fs | I gave you |
| נְתַתִּיו | 1 cs | 3 ms | I gave him |
| נְתַתִּ֫יהוּ | 1 cs | 3 ms | I gave him |

| *Form* | *Subject* | *Object* | *Translation* |
|---|---|---|---|
| אֲכָלַ֫תְהוּ | 3 fs | 3 ms | she devoured him |
| אֲכָלָ֫תַם | 3 fs | 3 mp | she devoured them |
| הֶעֱלָ֫תַם | 3 fs | 3 mp | she brought them up |
| יְלָדַ֫תּוּ | 3 fs | 3 ms | she bore him |
| אֲחָזָ֫תָּה | 3 fs | 3 fs | she seized her |
| הֶעֱלִיתָ֫נוּ | 2 ms | 1 cp | you brought us up |
| הֶעֱלִיתֻ֫נוּ | 2 mp | 1 cp | you brought us up |

## 2. The Perfect of III-Hē Verbs with Suffixes

**a.** Apart from the 3 ms and 3 fs, the perfect of III-Hē verbs are regular for their type.

| | |
|---|---|
| רָאִ֫יתִי I saw | רָאִיתִ֫יךָ I saw you |
| רָאוּ they saw | רָא֫וּךָ they saw you |

**b.** In the 3 ms perfect of all verbal patterns, the final weak radical is lost before the object suffix.

| | | | |
|---|---|---|---|
| רָאָה | he saw | רָאָהוּ | he saw him/it |
| צִוָּה | he commanded | צִוָּהוּ | he commanded him |
| הֶרְאָה | he showed | הֶרְאֲךָ | he showed you |

**c.** The 3 fs perfect is doubly marked for gender in the form of the verb without object suffix (XIV.3.a.ii). When the verb takes an object suffix, however, the 3 fs perfect is marked as feminine only by ת.

| | | | |
|---|---|---|---|
| רָאֲתָה | she saw | רָאָתְךָ | she saw you |
| צִוְּתָה | she commanded | צִוַּתָּה | she commanded her |

*Note*: The form צִוַּתָּה is derived from צִוַּתְהָ (see 1.d.Note i).

## 3. Irregular Vocalization

In a few instances, the Qal perfect of the *qāṭal* type has an *i* ( ִ ), *ē* ( ֵ ), or *e* ( ֶ ) vowel in the second syllable, instead of *a* ( ַ ).

| | | |
|---|---|---|
| ילד | יְלִדְתִּנִי | you have begotten me |
| | יְלִדְתִּיךָ | I have begotten you |
| | יְלִדְתִּיהוּ | I have begotten him |
| ירשׁ | יְרִשְׁתֶּם | you possessed them |
| | יְרִשְׁתָּהּ | you possessed it |
| | יְרֵשׁוּךָ | they possessed you |
| שׁאל | שְׁאֶלְתֶּם | you asked |
| | שְׁאִלְתִּיו | I asked him |
| | שְׁאֵלוּנוּ | they asked us |

## 4. Redundant Object Suffix

Sometimes an object suffix may be resumptive and need not be translated in English.

אֱלֹהִים אֲחֵרִים אֲשֶׁר לֹא־יְדַעְתָּם other gods whom you have not known (lit. "not known *them*") (Deut 13:3)

## Vocabulary

*Nouns*:

יָמִין right side, right hand

לָשׁוֹן tongue

שָׂפָה lip, edge, language

שִׁפְחָה female servant

תּוֹעֵבָה abomination

*Verbs*:

בָּטַח to trust; Hi.: to make secure

בָּרַח to flee

לָבַשׁ to clothe; also לָבֵשׁ to be clothed

לָמַד to learn; Pi.: to teach

מָלַט Pi.: to save, let (someone) escape

עָנָה to answer, reply

שָׂנֵא to hate. *Noun*: שִׂנְאָה hatred

שָׁבַר to break

שָׁכַח (also שָׁכֵחַ) to forget

*Adjectives*:

רָחוֹק far. *Verb*: רָחַק to be far

רַק thin

*Adverb*:

יַחְדָּו together

לָכֵן therefore

מְעַט little, few (also as adjective and substantive); עוֹד מְעַט soon; כִּמְעַט almost

תָּמִיד always, constantly

## Exercise 17

**a.** Parse the following forms; e.g., יְדַעְתִּ֫יךָ Qal perf. 1 cs of יָדַע + obj. sfx. 2 ms.

| | | |
|---|---|---|
| 1. צִוִּיתִיו | 6. סְפָרָם | 11. קִדַּשְׁתּוֹ |
| 2. שְׁלָחוֹ | 7. הֲרַגְתֶּ֫ם | 12. כִּלַּ֫תּוּ |
| 3. כִּלֵּיתִים | 8. צִוַּתָּה | 13. אֲהֵבַ֫תְהוּ |
| 4. אֲהֵבוֹ | 9. כִּלִּיתָם | 14. הִקְדַּשְׁתִּ֫יךָ |
| 5. כִּלָּם | 10. צִוָּם | 15. אֲהֵבוּם |

**b.** Write the following in Hebrew, using only the perfect + object suffix.

1. I hate him
2. he killed me
3. I love you (fs)
4. he answered them (mp)
5. I charged you (ms)
6. I hated them (mp)
7. you (ms) have forgotten me
8. they praised you (ms)
9. I killed you (fs)
10. you (ms) commanded us

**c.** Translate the following into English:

1. שְׁכֵחֻנִי עַמִּי (Jer 18:15)
2. לִמְּדוּם אֲבוֹתָם (Jer 9:13)
3. אֲנִי הַיּוֹם יְלִדְתִּיךָ (Ps 2:7)
4. הִלְבִּישַׁנִי בִּגְדֵי־יֶשַׁע (Isa 61:10)
5. וְלֹא־לָמַדְתִּי חָכְמָה (Prov 30:3)
6. כָּל־מוֹצְאֵיהֶם אֲכָלוּם (Jer 50:7)
7. הֱבִיאַנִי אֶל־בֵּית הַיָּיִן (Song 2:4)
8. חַיָּה רָעָה אֲכָלָתְהוּ (Gen 37:20)
9. אֵלִי אֵלִי לָמָה עֲזַבְתָּנִי (Ps 22:2)
10. אֲנִי יְדַעְתִּיךָ בַּמִּדְבָּר (Hos 13:5)

**d.** Translate the following into English:

1. שְׂנֵאתַנִי וְלֹא אֲהַבְתָּנִי (Judg 14:16)
2. וְלָמָה הֶעֱלִיתֻנוּ מִמִּצְרַיִם (Num 20:5)
3. כִּי יְהוָה אֱלֹהֶיךָ בֵּרַכְךָ בְּכֹל מַעֲשֵׂה יָדֶךָ (Deut 2:7)
4. לִמַּדְתִּי אֶתְכֶם חֻקִּים וּמִשְׁפָּטִים כַּאֲשֶׁר צִוַּנִי יְהוָה אֱלֹהָי (Deut 4:5)
5. יוֹם אֲשֶׁר־יְלָדַתְנִי אִמִּי (Jer 20:14)
6. לֹא־דִבַּרְתִּי אֶת־אֲבוֹתֵיכֶם וְלֹא צִוִּיתִים (Jer 7:22)
7. שָׂמַנִי אֱלֹהִים לְאָדוֹן לְכָל־מִצְרָיִם (Gen 45:9)
8. הַמֶּלֶךְ הִצִּילָנוּ ׀ מִכַּף אֹיְבֵינוּ (2 Sam 19:10)
9. כִּי גְדוֹלָה הַשִּׂנְאָה אֲשֶׁר שְׂנֵאָהּ מֵאַהֲבָה אֲשֶׁר אֲהֵבָהּ (2 Sam 13:15)

10. אָנֹכִי מְשַׁחְתִּיךָ לְמֶלֶךְ עַל־יִשְׂרָאֵל וְאָנֹכִי הִצַּלְתִּיךָ מִיַּד שָׁאוּל
(2 Sam 12:7)

11. וְלֹא הִטִּיתֶם אֶת־אָזְנְכֶם וְלֹא שְׁמַעְתֶּם אֵלָי (Jer 35:15)

12. הוּא צִוָּנִי וְהוּא שָׂם בְּפִי שִׁפְחָתְךָ אֵת כָּל־הַדְּבָרִים הָאֵלֶּה
(2 Sam 14:19)

13. מֹשֶׁה הָאִישׁ אֲשֶׁר הֶעֱלָנוּ מֵאֶרֶץ מִצְרַיִם לֹא יָדַעְנוּ מֶה־הָיָה לוֹ
(Exod 32:1)

14. אָנֹכִי יְהוָה אֱלֹהֶיךָ אֲשֶׁר הוֹצֵאתִיךָ מֵאֶרֶץ מִצְרַיִם מִבֵּית
עֲבָדִים (Exod 20:1)

15. עָשָׂה דָוִד אֶת־הַיָּשָׁר בְּעֵינֵי יְהוָה וְלֹא־סָר מִכֹּל אֲשֶׁר־צִוָּהוּ כֹּל
יְמֵי חַיָּיו (1 Kgs 15:5)

**e.** Translate Song 3:1–5 with the help of a dictionary and these notes.

*Notes*:

v 2: אָקוּמָה נָּא וַאֲסוֹבְבָה I will arise and roam about;
אֲבַקְשָׁה I will seek.

v 4: אֲרַפֶּנּוּ I will not let him go; הוֹרָתִי Qal perf. fs ptc. of הָרָה (to conceive) + 1 cs possessive sfx.

v 5: אִם־תָּעִירוּ do no not stir; וְאִם־תְּעוֹרְרוּ and do not rouse;
עַד שֶׁתֶּחְפָּץ until it please.

# Lesson XVIII

## 1. The Imperfect Inflection

The second full inflection of the finite verb in Hebrew is called the *imperfect*. Whereas the gender, number, and person of a verb in the perfect are indicated by afformatives, in the imperfect they are indicated by preformatives (elements *before* the stem), sometimes in combination with afformatives, as follows.

| | | | |
|---|---|---|---|
| *3 ms* | י--- | *3 mp* | י---וּ |
| *3 fs* | תּ--- | *3 fp* | תּ---נָה |
| *2 ms* | תּ--- | *2 mp* | תּ---וּ |
| *2 fs* | תּ---י | *2 fp* | תּ---נָה |
| *1 cs* | א--- | *1 cp* | נ--- |

*Notes*:

i. Whereas no distinction is made in the perfect between masculine and feminine of the third person plural (XIII.1.ii), gender is clearly distinguished in the imperfect: יִקְטְלוּ (3 mp) versus תִּקְטֹלְנָה (3 fp).

ii. The 3 mp and 2 mp forms frequently have an additional Nûn at the end, i.e., וּן– instead of וּ–.

## 2. The Qal Imperfect

In the Qal perfect we recognized three types: *qāṭal*, *qāṭēl*, *qāṭōl*. In the Qal imperfect, only two types are discernible: *yiqṭōl* and *yiqṭal*. Verbs that are *dynamic* (e.g., שָׁמַר to keep; נָפַל to fall) generally belong to the first type, whereas verbs that are *stative* (e.g., כָּבֵד to be heavy; קָטֹן to be small) belong to the second type. Thus, we have the following situation.

| *Perfect* | *Imperfect* |
|---|---|
| *qāṭal* | *yiqṭōl* |
| *qāṭēl* | *yiqṭal* |
| *qāṭōl* | *yiqṭal* |

A rigid classification of the verb types must be avoided, however. It is true that verbs that have *yiqṭōl* imperfects are almost always dynamic, but verbs with *yiqṭal* imperfects are not limited to statives. Many dynamic verbs with II- or III-Guttural have imperfect of the *yiqṭal* type. A few others with strong radicals also have the *yiqṭal* pattern.

The inflections of the Qal Imperfect of שָׁמַר (to keep) and כָּבֵד (to be heavy) are as follows.

| | | |
|---|---|---|
| *3 ms* | יִשְׁמֹר | יִכְבַּד |
| *3 fs* | תִּשְׁמֹר | תִּכְבַּד |
| *2 ms* | תִּשְׁמֹר | תִּכְבַּד |
| *2 fs* | תִּשְׁמְרִי | תִּכְבְּדִי |
| *1 cs* | אֶשְׁמֹר | אֶכְבַּד |
| | | |
| *3 mp* | יִשְׁמְרוּ | יִכְבְּדוּ |
| *3 fp* | תִּשְׁמֹרְנָה | תִּכְבַּדְנָה |
| *2 mp* | תִּשְׁמְרוּ | תִּכְבְּדוּ |
| *2 fp* | תִּשְׁמֹרְנָה | תִּכְבַּדְנָה |
| *1 cp* | נִשְׁמֹר | נִכְבַּד |

*Notes*:

i. The second vowel is said to be *thematic*. This vowel is retained when the syllable is stressed; otherwise, it is reduced. 3 mp and 2 mp forms with the additional Nûn (see 1. Note ii above) sometimes retain the thematic vowels as *ō* or *ā*, e.g., יִשְׁמָעוּן; יִלְקֹטוּן.

ii. When the imperfect of the *yiqṭōl* type is linked to the following word by the *maqqēp̄*, the *ō* thematic vowel is shortened to *o* (see Excursus B.4).

יִשְׁפֹּט *but* יִשְׁפָּט־שָׁם (*yišpoṭ-šām*)

iii. Occasionally the forms with final נָה– (i.e., 2 fs or 3 fp) may be spelled without the final ה–.

תִּלְבַּשְׁןְ for regular תִּלְבַּשְׁנָה

## 3. The Uses of the Imperfect

As we have learned in Lesson XIII, Hebrew verbs by themselves do not indicate *tense*. Rather, they indicate how a situation is viewed by the speaker/writer. In the perfect, the speaker/writer is an outsider considering the situation as a whole, with the beginning and the end both in view. In the imperfect, the speaker/writer views a situation from the inside, making explicit reference to the internal temporal structure of the situation, without explicit reference to the beginning or the end.

**a.** In most instances, the imperfect in isolation may simply be rendered by the English *future*.

| | |
|---|---|
| אֲדֹנִיָּהוּ יִמְלֹךְ אַחֲרָי | Adonijah *will be king* after me (1 Kgs 1:24) |

**b.** The imperfect may have reference to a *habit* or *custom*. If the context suggests a custom or habit in the past, one translates with English "used to ... " or "would."

| | |
|---|---|
| וּבְחֵיקוֹ תִשְׁכָּב | and it (the ewe) *used to lie* in his bosom (2 Sam 12:3) |

עַל־כֵּן יֹאמְרוּ הַמֹּשְׁלִים — therefore, the bards *used to say* (Num 21:27)

חֲכָמִים יִצְפְּנוּ־דָעַת — wise men *store up* knowledge (Prov 10:14)

**c.** The imperfect is frequently rendered by the English *modal* (may, should, could, would, etc.).

מִי יְהוָה אֲשֶׁר אֶשְׁמַע בְּקֹלוֹ — Who is YHWH that *I should heed* his voice? (Exod 5:2)

פֶּן־יִשְׁלַח יָדוֹ — lest *he should stretch forth* his hand (Gen 3:22)

*Note*: After the particle **טֶרֶם** (not yet, before), or the preposition **עַד** (until), the imperfect is usually rendered by the English past or present perfect.

טֶרֶם יִשְׁכָּבוּן — before *they lay down* (Josh 2:8)

עַד־יִגְדַּל שֵׁלָה בְנִי — until Shelah my son *has grown up* (Gen 38:11)

## 4. Expressions of Will

Corresponding in some ways to the modal use, the imperfect may also be used to express the speaker's will to have a situation occur.

**a.** The first person forms used in this way are called *cohortatives*. The cohortative is usually marked by a final ָה–. The addition of this final element to an imperfect base form ordinarily causes the accent to advance and the thematic vowel to reduce.

אֶעְבְּרָה בְאַרְצֶךָ — *let me pass* through your land (Num 21:22)

נִכְרְתָה בְרִית — *let us make* a covenant (Gen 31:44)

*Note*: This final ָה– sometimes appears with various forms of the imperfect, without any particular significance.

**b.** The third person forms used in this way are called *jussives*. For most roots there is no distinction between the jussives and the corresponding imperfect forms.

יִשְׁפֹּט יְהוָה בֵּינִי וּבֵינֶיךָ — *May* YHWH *judge* between you and me! (Gen 16:5)

מִי־חָכָם וְיִשְׁמָר־אֵלֶּה — whoever is wise, *let him observe* these things (Ps 107:43)

**c.** Since the second person verb is addressed directly to the subject of the verb, it may function as a command: thus, "may you hear" = "you shall hear!"

תִּשְׁמָעוּ — you shall hear! (Isa 18:3)

וְאַתָּה אֶת־בְּרִיתִי תִשְׁמֹר — As for you, you shall keep my covenant! (Gen 17:9)

## 5. Negation of Imperfects, Jussives, and Cohortatives

**a.** Like the perfect, the imperfect is negated by **לֹא**.

וְלֹא־יִשְׁמַע אֲלֵכֶם פַּרְעֹה — But Pharaoh *will not listen* to you (Exod 7:4)

**b.** The negative particle **לֹא** may be used with the second person imperfect for *general prohibition*. This construction should be translated in English as "you shall not...."

לֹא תִּרְצָח — *You shall not murder!* (Exod 20:13)

**c.** The negative particle **אַל** is used with the second person imperfect in negative commands. This construction is used to forbid or prevent a *specific action*. It should be translated in English as "Do not...."

אַל־תִּשְׂמַח יִשְׂרָאֵל — *Do not rejoice*, O Israel! (Hos 9:1)

The cohortatives and jussives are also negated by the negative particle אַל.

אַל־יִמְשְׁלוּ־בִי Do not let them dominate me! (Ps 19:14)

## 6. The נָא Particle

With commands and various expressions of will, a נָא particle is frequently found. It is common to take this as a particle of entreaty or exhortation, which is interpreted to have the force of "I (we) pray" or "please!" In many instances, however, the particle clearly has nothing to do with entreaties or exhortation. The significance of the נָא particle is, in fact, not entirely clear and it is best to leave it untranslated.

*Note*: With negative commands, the נָא particle usually comes immediately after the negative particle אַל.

אַל־נָא נֹאבְדָה Do not let us perish! (Jonah 1:14)

## Vocabulary

*Nouns*:

מָחֳרָת the morrow; the next day; time to come. מָחָר the morrow; time to come (also as an *adverb*: tomorrow)

עֶ֫צֶם (fs.) bone, substance, self. *Adjective*: עָצוּם mighty, numerous

עֶ֫רֶב evening

*Verbs*:

בָּלַע to swallow

בָּעַר to burn, consume

גָּאַל to redeem

זָעַק to cry out

| | |
|---|---|
| יָדָה | to throw; Hi.: to confess, give thanks. *Noun*: תּוֹדָה thanksgiving |
| כָּפַר | to cover; Pi.: to cover, atone. *Nouns*: כֹּפֶר atonement |
| פָּקַד | to visit, appoint, inspect |
| קָבַץ | to gather |
| קָבַר | to bury. *Noun*: קֶ֫בֶר grave |
| קָטַר | Pi.; Hi.: to burn incense. *Noun*: קְטֹ֫רֶת incense |
| רָדַף | to pursue, follow |
| שָׂמַח | (also שָׂמֵחַ) to rejoice, be happy. *Noun*: שִׂמְחָה joy |
| שָׂרַף | to burn. *Noun*: שָׂרָף Saraph (a winged-cobra) |
| שָׁפַךְ | to pour out |

*Conjunctions*:

| | |
|---|---|
| לְמַ֫עַן | in order that, so that |
| פֶּן־ | lest |

*Adverb*:

| | |
|---|---|
| טֶ֫רֶם | not yet, before (also בְּטֶ֫רֶם) |

## Exercise 18

**a.** Parse the following forms:

| | | |
|---|---|---|
| 1. אֶכְתֹּב | 6. תִּכְתְּבוּ | 11. יִמְשְׁחוּ |
| 2. יִשְׁאַל | 7. יִשְׁכְּבוּ | 12. תִּשְׁמַ֫עְנָה |
| 3. יִבְחַר | 8. תִּזְכְּרִי | 13. תִּבְטְחִי |
| 4. נִכְרֹת | 9. תִּכְרְתוּ | 14. אֶזְבְּחָה |
| 5. יִמְשַׁח | 10. נִדְרֹשׁ | 15. תִּשְׁלַ֫חְנָה |

**b.** Write the following in Hebrew:

1. you (fs) will keep
2. you (ms) ask
3. let him govern
4. I will lie down
5. let us sacrifice
6. let me send
7. let him remember
8. I will not listen to them (mp)
9. Do not stretch out your (ms) hand
10. you (ms) shall not sacrifice

**c.** Translate the following into English:

1. מִי־יִשְׁכֹּן בְּהַר קָדְשֶׁךָ (Ps 15:1)
2. יִזְכֹּר לְעוֹלָם בְּרִיתוֹ (Ps 111:5)
3. אָנֹכִי אֶשְׂמַח בַּיהוָה (Ps 104:34)
4. יִשְׁכַּב עִמָּךְ הַלַּיְלָה (Gen 30:15)
5. הַאִישׁ כָּמוֹנִי יִבְרָח (Neh 6:11)
6. בִּי מְלָכִים יִמְלֹכוּ (Prov 8:15)
7. יִשְׁלַח מַלְאָכוֹ (Gen 24:7)
8. נִשְׁלְחָה אֲנָשִׁים (Deut 1:22)
9. אֶת־מִי אֶשְׁלַח (Isa 6:8)
10. וְאַל־תִּשְׁלַחְנָה (Obad 13)
11. אֶרְדּוֹף אוֹיְבַי (Ps 18:38)
12. נִכְרֹת עֵצִים (2 Chron 2:15)

**d.** Translate the following into English:

1. וְאַתָּה תִּמְלֹךְ עַל־יִשְׂרָאֵל (1 Sam 23:17)
2. לְךָ־אֶזְבַּח זֶבַח תּוֹדָה (Ps 116:17)
3. וְאֶכְרְתָה לָכֶם בְּרִית עוֹלָם (Isa 55:3)

4. שָׁ֣ם יִזְבְּח֣וּ זִבְחֵי־צֶ֑דֶק (Deut 33:19)

5. אֱלֹהֵ֙ינוּ֙ הֲלֹ֣א תִשְׁפָּט־בָּ֔ם (2 Chron 20:12)

6. וְאָזְנֶ֙יךָ֙ תִּשְׁמַ֣עְנָה דָבָ֔ר מֵאַחֲרֶ֖יךָ לֵאמֹ֑ר זֶ֤ה הַדֶּ֙רֶךְ֙ (Isa 30:21)

7. פֶּן־נִשְׂרֹ֥ף אוֹתָ֛ךְ וְאֶת־בֵּ֥ית אָבִ֖יךְ בָּאֵ֑שׁ (Judg 14:15)

8. מִ֤י יְהוָה֙ אֲשֶׁ֣ר אֶשְׁמַ֣ע בְּקֹל֔וֹ (Exod 5:2)

9. לֹֽא־אֶמְשֹׁ֤ל אֲנִי֙ בָּכֶ֔ם וְלֹֽא־יִמְשֹׁ֥ל בְּנִ֖י בָּכֶ֑ם יְהוָ֖ה יִמְשֹׁ֥ל בָּכֶֽם (Judg 8:23)

10. כִּ֣י זֹ֣את הַבְּרִ֡ית אֲשֶׁ֣ר אֶכְרֹת֩ אֶת־בֵּ֨ית יִשְׂרָאֵ֜ל (Jer 31:33)

**e.** Translate Deut 13:1-6 with the help of a dictionary and these notes.

*Notes*:

v 1: לַעֲשׂ֑וֹת to do; לֹֽא־תֹסֵ֣ף you shall not add.

v 2: יָק֣וּם Qal impf. 3 ms of **קוּם**; וְנָתַ֥ן and he gives.

v 3: וּבָ֥א and (subject) comes (i.e., comes to pass); נֵלְכָ֞ה Qal coh. 1 cp of **הָלַךְ**; וְנָעָבְדֵֽם and let us serve them.

v 4: לָדַ֗עַת to know; הֲיִשְׁכֶ֣ם = הֲ + **יֶשְׁכֶם**.

v 5: תֵּלֵ֖כוּ Qal impf. 2 mp of **הָלַךְ**; תִירָ֑אוּ Qal impf. 2 mp of **יָרֵא**; תַעֲבֹ֖דוּ Qal impf. 2 mp of **עָבַד**.

v 6: יוּמָ֗ת shall be put to death; לְהַדִּֽיחֲךָ֙ to divert you; לָלֶ֣כֶת to walk; וּבִעַרְתָּ֥ so you shall purge.

# Lesson XIX

## 1. The Qal Imperfect of I-Guttural Verbs

**a.** As in the strong verb, there are verbs with the ō thematic vowel (i.e., *yiqṭōl* type) and those with *a* (i.e., *yiqṭal* type): יַעֲמֹד (he will stand); יֶחֱזַק (he will be strong).

**b.** Since gutturals generally prefer the composite *šĕwāʾ* (IV.2.a.ii) instead of the simple silent ְ under the first radical, one finds ֲ for verbs with the thematic vowel ō and ֱ for verbs with the thematic vowel *a*: יַעֲמֹד (he will stand); יֶחֱזַק (he will be strong). Not infrequently, however, the simple silent ְ may be retained; e.g., יַחְשֹׂךְ (he will refrain); יֶחְכַּם (he will be wise).

**c.** I-ʾÁlep̄ verbs behave normally, except for the following: אָמַר (to say), אָכַל (to eat), אָבַד (to perish), אָפָה (to bake), אָבָה (to be willing). For these verbs, the vowel in the preformative is always ō, and the א quiesces.

**d.** The inflections of the Qal imperfect of עָמַד (to stand), חָזַק (to be strong), and אָכַל (to eat) are as follows.

| | | | |
|---|---|---|---|
| *3 ms* | יַעֲמֹד | יֶחֱזַק | יֹאכַל |
| *3 fs* | תַּעֲמֹד | תֶּחֱזַק | תֹּאכַל |
| *2 ms* | תַּעֲמֹד | תֶּחֱזַק | תֹּאכַל |
| *2 fs* | תַּעַמְדִי | תֶּחֶזְקִי | תֹּאכְלִי |
| *1 cs* | אֶעֱמֹד | אֶחֱזַק | אֹכַל |
| *3 mp* | יַעַמְדוּ | יֶחֶזְקוּ | יֹאכְלוּ |
| *3 fp* | תַּעֲמֹ֫דְנָה | תֶּחֱזַ֫קְנָה | תֹּאכַ֫לְנָה |
| *2 mp* | תַּעַמְדוּ | תֶּחֶזְקוּ | תֹּאכְלוּ |
| *2 fp* | תַּעֲמֹ֫דְנָה | תֶּחֱזַ֫קְנָה | תֹּאכַ֫לְנָה |
| *1 cp* | נַעֲמֹד | נֶחֱזַק | נֹאכַל |

*Notes*:

i. When a composite *šĕwā*ʾ precedes a simple vocal *šĕwā*ʾ, the former becomes a full short vowel and the latter becomes silent.

| | |
|---|---|
| *תַּעֲמְדִי < תַּעַמְדִי | *תֶּחֱזְקִי < תֶּחֶזְקִי |
| *יַעֲמְדוּ < יַעַמְדוּ | *יֶחֱזְקוּ < יֶחֶזְקוּ |
| *תַּעֲמְדוּ < תַּעַמְדוּ | *תֶּחֱזְקוּ < תֶּחֶזְקוּ |

ii. I-ʾĀlep̄ verbs of the אָכַל type frequently have *ē* instead of *a* as the thematic vowel: יֹאכֵל, תֹּאכֵל, etc.

iii. The 1 cs of I-ʾĀlep̄ verbs of the אָכַל type show the development *אאכַל > אֹכַל – that is, the א of the preformative and the first radical have merged. The 1 cs imperfect should not be confused with the Qal active participle (ms).

אֹכַל I will eat אֹכֵל (one) eating

## 2. The Qal Imperfect of III-ʾĀlep̄ Verbs

The inflection of the Qal imperfect of מָצָא (to find) is as follows.

| | | | |
|---|---|---|---|
| *3 ms* | יִמְצָא | *3 mp* | יִמְצְאוּ |
| *3 fs* | תִּמְצָא | *3 fp* | תִּמְצֶאנָה |
| *2 ms* | תִּמְצָא | *2 mp* | תִּמְצְאוּ |
| *2 fs* | תִּמְצְאִי | *2 fp* | תִּמְצֶאנָה |
| *1 cs* | אֶמְצָא | *1 cp* | נִמְצָא |

*Notes*:

i. Since the א quiesces when it closes a syllable, the preceding vowel is lengthened: *יִמְצַא > יִמְצָא.

ii. The 3 fp/2 fp form is תִּמְצֶאנָה not *תִּמְצָאנָה, as one might expect.

## 3. The Qal Imperfect of III-Hē Verbs

The inflections of גָּלָה (to uncover) and הָיָה (to be) are as follows.

| | | |
|---|---|---|
| *3 ms* | יִגְלֶה | יִהְיֶה |
| *3 fs* | תִּגְלֶה | תִּהְיֶה |
| *2 ms* | תִּגְלֶה | תִּהְיֶה |
| *2 fs* | תִּגְלִי | תִּהְיִי |
| *1 cs* | אֶגְלֶה | אֶהְיֶה |
| *3 mp* | יִגְלוּ | יִהְיוּ |
| *3 fp* | תִּגְלֶ֫ינָה | תִּהְיֶ֫ינָה |
| *2 mp* | תִּגְלוּ | תִּהְיוּ |
| *2 fp* | תִּגְלֶ֫ינָה | תִּהְיֶ֫ינָה |
| *1 cp* | נִגְלֶה | נִהְיֶה |

## 4. The Qal Imperfect of I-Nûn Verbs

**a.** The Nûn is typically assimilated into the following radical (IV.2.b): יִפֹּל (*yinpōl > yippōl) he will fall; יִסַּע (*yinsaᶜ > yissaᶜ) he will set out. With roots that are both I-Nûn and II-Guttural, however, the Nûn radical is retained, e.g., יִנְחַל (he will inherit).

**b.** The verb נָתַן (to give) has *ē* as the thematic vowel, instead of *ō* or *a*, e.g., יִתֵּן (he will give).

**c.** The inflections of the Qal imperfect of נָפַל (to fall), נָחַל (to inherit), נָסַע (to set out), and נָתַן (to give) are as follows.

| | | | | |
|---|---|---|---|---|
| *3 ms* | יִפֹּל | יִנְחַל | יִסַּע | יִתֵּן |
| *3 fs* | תִּפֹּל | תִּנְחַל | תִּסַּע | תִּתֵּן |
| *2 ms* | תִּפֹּל | תִּנְחַל | תִּסַּע | תִּתֵּן |
| *2 fs* | תִּפְּלִי | תִּנְחֲלִי | תִּסְּעִי | תִּתְּנִי |
| *1 cs* | אֶפֹּל | אֶנְחַל | אֶסַּע | אֶתֵּן |
| *3 mp* | יִפְּלוּ | יִנְחֲלוּ | יִסְּעוּ | יִתְּנוּ |
| *3 fp* | תִּפֹּ֫לְנָה | תִּנְחַ֫לְנָה | תִּסַּ֫עְנָה | תִּתֵּ֫נָּה |
| *2 mp* | תִּפְּלוּ | תִּנְחֲלוּ | תִּסְּעוּ | תִּתְּנוּ |
| *2 fp* | תִּפֹּ֫לְנָה | תִּנְחַ֫לְנָה | תִּסַּ֫עְנָה | תִּתֵּ֫נָּה |
| *1 cp* | נִפֹּל | נִנְחַל | נִסַּע | נִתֵּן |

**d.** The verb לָקַח (to take) behaves like a I-Nûn verb in the Qal imperfect. Thus, it is inflected like נָסַע, with the assimilation of ל (as if it were Nûn): יִקַּח, תִּקַּח, etc.

*Note*: The strong *dāḡēš* representing the assimilated Nûn often disappears when a *šĕwāʾ* stands under the consonant (VI.7): thus, יִסְּעוּ > יִסְעוּ; יִקְּחוּ > יִקְחוּ, and so forth.

## 5. The Qal Imperfect of I-Wāw Verbs

**a.** Three important features characterize the Qal imperfect of most I-Wāw verbs.

**i.** The absence of the first radical.

**ii.** The vowel of the preformative is *ē*.

**iii.** The thematic vowel is ordinarily *ē*, except in the 3 fp/2 fp form, which has *a*. III-Guttural verbs also have *a* as the thematic vowel.

**b.** The imperfect forms of יָשַׁב (to sit, dwell) and יָדַע (to know) are as follows.

| | | |
|---|---|---|
| *3 ms* | יֵשֵׁב | יֵדַע |
| *3 fs* | תֵּשֵׁב | תֵּדַע |
| *2 ms* | תֵּשֵׁב | תֵּדַע |
| *2 fs* | תֵּשְׁבִי | תֵּדְעִי |
| *1 cs* | אֵשֵׁב | אֵדַע |
| *3 mp* | יֵשְׁבוּ | יֵדְעוּ |
| *3 fp* | תֵּשַׁ֫בְנָה | תֵּדַ֫עְנָה |
| *2 mp* | תֵּשְׁבוּ | תֵּדְעוּ |
| *2 fp* | תֵּשַׁ֫בְנָה | תֵּדַ֫עְנָה |
| *1 cp* | נֵשֵׁב | נֵדַע |

**c.** The verb הָלַךְ (to walk, go) behaves like an original I-Wāw verb in the Qal and Hiphil (see also XVI.8.b). The Qal imperfect of הָלַךְ, therefore, is inflected like יָשַׁב (thus, יֵלֵךְ, תֵּלֵךְ, etc.). Imperfect forms of הָלַךְ that do not behave like I-Wāw verbs are also attested (e.g., יַהֲלֹךְ, אֶהֱלֹךְ), but they are relatively uncommon.

**d.** A small group of original I-Wāw verbs may retain the first radical, but as י, not ו – that is, they behave like I-Yōḏ verbs (see section 6 below). The most important examples of these are the verbs יָרַשׁ (to possess) and יָרֵא (to fear, be afraid).

**e.** I-Wāw verbs that behave like I-Nûn (see XVI.8.c) are sporadically attested, e.g., יָצַת (perfect), but יִצַּת (imperfect).

## 6. The Qal Imperfect of I-Yōḏ Verbs

**a.** Original I-Yōḏ verbs are treated like any strong verb with the *yiqṭal* imperfect, except that the silent *šĕwāʾ* under the first radical is lost: thus, *יְיְטַב > יִיטַב (see VI.3.a).

**b.** The inflection of the Qal imperfect of יָטַב (to go well) is as follows.

| | | | |
|---|---|---|---|
| *3 ms* | יִיטַב | *3 mp* | יִיטְבוּ |
| *3 fs* | תִּיטַב | *3 fp* | תִּיטַבְנָה |
| *2 ms* | תִּיטַב | *2 mp* | תִּיטְבוּ |
| *2 fs* | תִּיטְבִי | *2 fp* | תִּיטַבְנָה |
| *1 cs* | אִיטַב | *1 cp* | נִיטַב |

*Note*: Occasionally the imperfects of this type (including the few I-Wāw verbs that behave like I-Yōḏ) are spelled defectively. When they are so written, the *méṯeḡ* is usually added to the vowel of the preformative to indicate that it is long, e.g., יִֽרַשׁ (for יִירַשׁ). The defective form יִֽרְאוּ (Qal impf. 3 mp of יָרֵא) may be confused with יָרְאוּ (Qal perf. 3 cp of רָאָה), except that the *méṯeḡ* in the former indicates that it is defective for יִירְאוּ.

## 7. The Qal Imperfect of II-Wāw/ Yōḏ Verbs

**a.** The vowel of the preformative in the Qal imperfect of II-Wāw/ Yōḏ verbs is normally *ā*, which is reduced when it is propretonic. Less commonly it is *ē* instead of *ā* (e.g., יֵבוֹשׁ he will be ashamed).

**b.** The inflections of the Qal imperfect of קוּם (to arise), שִׂים (to place), and בּוֹא (to come) are as follows.

| | | | |
|---|---|---|---|
| *3 ms* | יָקוּם | יָשִׂים | יָבוֹא |
| *3 fs* | תָּקוּם | תָּשִׂים | תָּבוֹא |
| *2 ms* | תָּקוּם | תָּשִׂים | תָּבוֹא |
| *2 fs* | תָּקוּמִי | תָּשִׂימִי | תָּבוֹאִי |
| *1 cs* | אָקוּם | אָשִׂים | אָבוֹא |
| *3 mp* | יָקוּמוּ | יָשִׂימוּ | יָבוֹאוּ |
| *3 fp* | תְּקוּמֶינָה | תְּשִׂימֶינָה | תְּבֹאֶינָה |
| *2 mp* | תָּקוּמוּ | תָּשִׂימוּ | תָּבוֹאוּ |
| *2 fp* | תְּקוּמֶינָה | תְּשִׂימֶינָה | תְּבֹאֶינָה |
| *1 cp* | נָקוּם | נָשִׂים | נָבוֹא |

*Notes*:

i. The variant forms תָּקֹמְנָה (instead of תְּקוּמֶינָה) and תָּבֹאנָה (instead of תְּבֹאֶינָה) are attested.

ii. Although the distinction between II-Wāw and II-Yōḏ is usually clear, there is considerable mixing of the two types. For instance, one finds the imperfect יָשׂוּם, along with יָשִׂים.

## 8. The Verb יָכֹל

The Qal perfect of the verb יָכֹל (be able) behaves regularly as a *qāṭōl* type (XIII.2). The Qal imperfect of יָכֹל, however, is unique.

| | | | |
|---|---|---|---|
| *3 ms* | יוּכַל | *3 mp* | יוּכְלוּ |
| *3 fs* | תּוּכַל | *3 fp* | –not attested– |
| *2 ms* | תּוּכַל | *2 mp* | תּוּכְלוּ |
| *2 fs* | תּוּכְלִי | *2 fp* | –not attested– |
| *1 cs* | אוּכַל | *1 cp* | נוּכַל |

## Vocabulary

*Nouns*:

חֵן grace, favor. *Verb*: חָנַן to be gracious, favor

עֵצָה counsel, plan, advice. *Verb*: יָעַץ to advise

שֵׁ֫בֶט rod, tribe

שַׁ֫עַר gate

*Verbs*:

אָבַד to perish

אָחַז to seize

אָמַן to confirm, support; Hi.: to believe, trust. *Noun*: אֱמוּנָה truth

אָסַר to bind. *Noun*: אָסִיר prisoner

חָדַל to cease, stop (doing something)

חָלַק to divide, apportion. *Noun*: חֵ֫לֶק portion, lot

חָפֵץ to delight, desire. *Noun*: חֵ֫פֶץ desire, pleasure

חָשַׁב to think, reckon. *Noun*: מַחֲשָׁבָה (cs. מַחֲשֶׁ֫בֶת) thought

יָכֹל to be able (to do something), prevail

יָרַשׁ to possess, dispossess

נוּס to flee

נָסַע to set out, travel, depart

קָרַב to approach, draw near. *Adjective*: קָרוֹב near

רוּץ to run

שָׁאַר to remain, be left over

שָׁלֵם to be whole, healthy, complete, at peace; Pi.: to make whole, make amends, recompense

## Exercise 19

**a.** Parse the following forms:

| | | | | | |
|---|---|---|---|---|---|
| 1. | יֹאחֵז | 9. | יַחֲלֹק | 17. | נֶחְדַּל |
| 2. | נִקַּח | 10. | יַחְפְּצוּ | 18. | יַחֲשֹׁבוּן |
| 3. | תֹּאבֶה | 11. | יִירְשׁוּ | 19. | תִּתְּנִי |
| 4. | אֶחְדַּל | 12. | תַּחְלְקוּ | 20. | אָסוּרָה |
| 5. | יֶאְסֹר | 13. | יִסְעוּ | 21. | יִפְּלוּ |
| 6. | אוּכַל | 14. | נָבוֹא | 22. | אָנוּסָה |
| 7. | תֵּשְׁבִי | 15. | תִּירְאִי | 23. | תְּבוֹאֶינָה |
| 8. | אֵדַע | 16. | נֵלְכָה | 24. | יִקְחוּ |

**b.** Write the following in Hebrew:

1. we will build
2. let us run
3. we will be able
4. we will possess
5. I will say
6. I will give
7. I will go
8. I will take
9. you (mp) will possess
10. they (mp) will be
11. they (mp) will flee
12. they (fp) will say
13. you (fs) will be able
14. they (mp) will stand
15. they (fp) will stand
16. he will be willing

**c.** Translate the following into English:

1. לֹא־תֹאבַד תּוֹרָה מִכֹּהֵן וְעֵצָה מֵחָכָם וְדָבָר מִנָּבִיא (Jer 18:18)
2. אֶת־בְּנֹתָם נִקַּח־לָנוּ לְנָשִׁים וְאֶת־בְּנֹתֵינוּ נִתֵּן לָהֶם (Gen 34:21)
3. בֵּאלֹהִים בָּטַחְתִּי לֹא אִירָא מַה־יַּעֲשֶׂה אָדָם לִי (Ps 56:12)
4. הֲיִפְּלוּ וְלֹא יָקוּמוּ אִם־יָשׁוּב וְלֹא יָשׁוּב (Jer 8:4)

5. וְנָק֥וּמָה וְנֵלֵ֖כָה וְנִחְיֶה֙ וְלֹ֣א נָמ֔וּת (Gen 43:8)

6. בַּבַּ֣יִת הַזֶּ֗ה וּבִירוּשָׁלַ֙͏ִם֙ אֲשֶׁ֤ר בָּחַ֙רְתִּי֙ מִכֹּל֙ שִׁבְטֵ֣י יִשְׂרָאֵ֔ל אָשִׂ֥ים
אֶת־שְׁמִ֖י לְעוֹלָֽם (2 Kgs 21:7)

7. וְאַֽחֲרֵי־כֵ֗ן יִסְע֖וּ בְּנֵ֣י יִשְׂרָאֵ֑ל וּבִמְק֗וֹם אֲשֶׁ֤ר יִשְׁכָּן־שָׁם֙ הֶֽעָנָ֔ן שָׁ֥ם יַחֲנ֖וּ
בְּנֵ֥י יִשְׂרָאֵֽל (Num 9:17)

8. וְעַתָּ֗ה בִּתִּי֙ אַל־תִּ֣ירְאִ֔י כֹּ֥ל אֲשֶׁר־תֹּאמְרִ֖י אֶֽעֱשֶׂה־לָּ֑ךְ כִּ֤י יוֹדֵ֙עַ֙
כָּל־שַׁ֣עַר עַמִּ֔י כִּ֛י אֵ֥שֶׁת חַ֖יִל אָֽתְּ (Ruth 3:11)

9. הוּא֙ יִהְיֶה־לְּךָ֣ לְפֶ֔ה וְאַתָּ֖ה תִּֽהְיֶה־לּ֥וֹ לֵאלֹהִֽים׃
וְאֶת־הַמַּטֶּ֥ה הַזֶּ֖ה תִּקַּ֣ח בְּיָדֶ֑ךָ אֲשֶׁ֥ר תַּעֲשֶׂה־בּ֖וֹ אֶת־הָאֹתֹֽת׃
(Exod 4:16–17)

10. אִם־תִּתֶּן־לִי֙ אֶת־חֲצִ֣י בֵיתֶ֔ךָ לֹ֥א אָבֹ֖א עִמָּ֑ךְ וְלֹֽא־אֹ֤כַל לֶ֙חֶם֙ וְלֹ֣א
אֶשְׁתֶּה־מַּ֔יִם בַּמָּק֖וֹם הַזֶּֽה׃ כִּֽי־כֵ֣ן ׀ צִוָּ֣ה אֹתִ֗י בִּדְבַ֤ר יְהוָה֙ לֵאמֹ֔ר
לֹא־תֹ֥אכַל לֶ֖חֶם וְלֹ֣א תִשְׁתֶּה־מָּ֑יִם וְלֹ֣א תָשׁ֔וּב בַּדֶּ֖רֶךְ אֲשֶׁ֥ר הָלָֽכְתָּ׃
(1 Kgs 13:8–9)

**d.** Translate Exod 3:1–14 with the help of a dictionary and these notes.

*Notes*:

v 1: וַיִּנְהַג and he drove; וַיָּבֹא and he came.

v 2: וַיֵּרָא (subject) appeared; וַיַּרְא and he saw; אֻכָּל consumed.

v 3: וַיֹּאמֶר (subject) said.

v 4: וַיַּרְא (subject) saw; לִרְאוֹת to see; וַיִּקְרָא and (subject) called; וַיֹּאמֶר and he said.

v 5: שַׁל remove.

v 6: וַיַּסְתֵּר (subject) hid; מֵהַבִּיט to look (lit. of looking).

v 7: רָאֹה רָאִיתִי I have indeed seen.

v 8: וָאֵרֵד I have descended; לְהַצִּילוֹ to rescue them; וּלְהַעֲלֹתוֹ
and to bring them up.

v 10: לְכָה וְאֶשְׁלָחֲךָ come, let me send you; וְהוֹצֵא bring out.

v 11: אוֹצִיא I should bring out.

v 12: בְּהוֹצִיאֲךָ when you bring out.

v 13: וְאָמַרְתִּי and I will say; וְאָמְרוּ and they will say.

# Lesson XX

## 1. The Preterite

We have learned so far (XIII.3) that a situation viewed by an outsider as a complete whole is generally expressed by verbs in the afformative inflection (*qāṭal*). On the other hand, a situation that is viewed as if "from the inside" (XVIII.3) is expressed by the preformative inflection (*yiqṭōl*).[1] We have seen, therefore, that situations that are perceived to be complete tend to be described by verbs in the perfect. This is only partially correct, however. In fact, the *yiqṭōl* form has two different origins: **yaqṭulu* for the imperfect and **yaqṭul* for the preterite (referring to past situations). But early in the evolution of the Hebrew language, final short vowels disappeared and so the imperfect form (**yaqṭulu* > **yaqṭul*) became identical to the preterite (**yaqṭul*). In time, **yaqṭul* (i.e., either imperfect or preterite) developed to *yiqṭōl*. Thus, the *yiqṭōl* form may be imperfect or preterite. In its latter function, of course, there is some overlap with the perfect.

The preterite use of the *yiqṭōl* form is clearly evident in the following situations.

**a.** In poetic, and especially archaic, texts.

שָׁמְעוּ עַמִּים יִרְגָּזוּן the peoples heard, *they trembled* (Exod 15:14)

*Note*: Here the preterite meaning of the *yiqṭōl* form (יִרְגָּזוּן) is evident in its close association with a *qāṭal* form.

**b.** After the adverb אָז (then, at that time).

אָז תִּפְשַׁע לִבְנָה at that time, Libnah *revolted* (2 Kgs 8:22)

**c.** In the *wayyiqṭōl* form (see below).

וַיִּנְהַג אֶת־הַצֹּאן and *he drove* the flock (Exod 3:1)

1. For simplicity's sake, we refer to the afformative inflections in general as *qāṭal* and the preformative inflections as *yiqṭōl*, but one must remember that there are variations for different verbs types and verbal patterns.

## 2. Discourse on Past Situations

Even though Hebrew verbs do not by themselves indicate tense, they may be found in certain constructions to refer to specific situations in the past or the future.

**a.** In the narration of past situations, the sequence *qāṭal* + *wayyiqṭōl* is used. Since the *wayyiqṭōl* form follows the perfect in this sequence and refers to a past situation, it is sometimes said to be "converted" (i.e., by the perfect). Hence, the *wayyiqṭōl* form is called the *wāw-conversive* or *wāw-consecutive*, although the form is really from an original **yaqṭul* (i.e., the preterite) and has not been "converted."

וְנֹבַח הָלַךְ וַיִּלְכֹּד אֶת־קְנָת   Nobah went *and captured* Kenath (Num 32:42)

The meaning of the *wayyiqṭōl* verb is not necessarily tied to such a sequence, however. Even when it does not follow a *qāṭal* form, the *wayyiqṭōl* must be interpreted as referring to a past situation.

וַיִּקְרָא אֶל־מֹשֶׁה   (YHWH) *called* to Moses (Lev 1:1)

**b.** The ו used with the consecutive form appears as follows.

**i.** It is normally וַ (*wa–*) + doubling of the next radical: וַיִּקְרָא and he called.

**ii.** If the next radical has a *šĕwāʾ*, it is וַ without doubling (see VI.7): וַיְדַבֵּר and he spoke.

**iii.** If the preformative of the verb is א, it is וָ without doubling: וָאֹכֵל and I ate.

The *wayyiqṭōl* form should not be confused with the simple conjunction + imperfect (i.e., *wĕyiqṭōl*). Compare the following.

| | | |
|---|---|---|
| *wāw-consecutive*: | וַיִּשְׁמַע | and he heard |
| *simple wāw*: | וְיִשְׁמַע | and he will hear |

*Note*: The וַ– became a convenient way to distinguish the preterite from the imperfect. It should not, therefore, be translated slavishly as "and"; sometimes it is best to leave it untranslated.

## 3. Discourse on Future Situations

**a.** Since the *qāṭal* + *wayyiqṭōl* sequence is used in the narration of past situations, the *yiqṭōl* + *wĕqāṭal* sequence may be perceived to be its logical opposite. Thus, in contrast to the *wayyiqṭōl* form (which overlaps in function with the perfect), the *wĕqāṭal* form in a *yiqṭōl* + *wĕqāṭal* sequence is understood to refer to an imperfective situation.

| | |
|---|---|
| **אֵצֵא** וְהָיִיתִי רוּחַ שֶׁקֶר | I will go forth, and *I will be* a lying spirit (1 Kgs 22:22) |

*Note*: In the 2 ms and 1 cs of the *wĕqāṭal* form, the accent is usually on the ultima, rather than the preceding syllable. Compare:

| *Simple perfect* | | *Consecutive perfect* | |
|---|---|---|---|
| וְהָלַכְתִּי | and I went | וְהָלַכְתִּי | and I will go |
| וְהָלַכְתָּ | and you went | וְהָלַכְתָּ | and you will go |

**b.** A *wĕqāṭal* form following a participle may refer to something that is not yet complete.

| | |
|---|---|
| הִנְנִי עֹמֵד לְפָנֶיךָ שָּׁם ׀ עַל־הַצּוּר בְּחֹרֵב וְהִכִּיתָ בַצּוּר וְיָצְאוּ מִמֶּנּוּ מַיִם | I will stand before you on the rock at Horeb and *you shall strike* the rock, and water *shall flow* from it (Exod 17:6) |

## 4. The Wāw-Consecutive Forms

The Wāw-consecutive forms of the prefixed verbal forms are easy to recognize because they are always preceded by *wa*– (plus *dāgēš*) or *wā*– (see 2.b above), as opposed to *wĕ*–. For most verbs, there is no distinction in form between the imperfect and the Wāw-consecutive forms.

| *Imperfect* | *Wāw-consecutive* | |
|---|---|---|
| יִמְצָא | וַיִּמְצָא | (and) he found |
| יִפֹּל | וַיִּפֹּל | (and) he fell |

The following peculiarities should be noted, however.

**a.** The I-ʾÁlep̄ verbs אָכַל (to eat) and אָמַר (to say) show a retraction of the accent from the ultima to the penultima in the forms without endings. This retraction results in a slight change in vocalization for the verb אָמַר, but not אָכַל.

| *Imperfect* | *Wāw-consecutive* | |
|---|---|---|
| יֹאמַר | וַיֹּ֫אמֶר | (and) he said |
| יֹאכַל | וַיֹּ֫אכַל | (and) he ate |

**b.** I-Wāw verbs usually show a retraction of the accent in the forms without endings. This retraction typically results in the shortening of the final vowel from ◌ֵ to ◌ֶ.

| *Imperfect* | *Wāw-consecutive* | |
|---|---|---|
| יֵשֵׁב | וַיֵּ֫שֶׁב | (and) he dwelled/sat |
| תֵּלֵד | וַתֵּ֫לֶד | (and) she bore |

*Note*: The verb הָלַךְ (to go) behaves like a I-Wāw verb (thus, וַיֵּ֫לֶךְ he went).

**c.** II-Wāw/Yōd̲ verbs without endings generally show a retraction of the accent and the consequent shortening of *û* to *o* and *î* to *e*.

| *Imperfect* | *Wāw-consecutive* | |
|---|---|---|
| יָקוּם | וַיָּקָם | (and) he arose |
| יָשִׂים | וַיָּשֶׂם | (and) he placed |

There is no retraction of accent, however, in the Wāw-consecutive form of בּוֹא (thus, וַיָּבֹא). A few verbs with III-Guttural show a retraction of accent, but the final vowel is shortened to *a*, not to *o* or *e*.

| *Imperfect* | *Wāw-consecutive* | |
|---|---|---|
| יָנוּחַ | וַיָּנַח | (and) he rested |
| יָנוּעַ | וַיָּנַע | (and) he wandered |
| יָסוּר | וַיָּסַר | (and) he turned aside |

**d.** The III-Hē forms are characterized by three things.

**i.** Apocope (cutting off) of the final ה.

**ii.** After the apocope of ה, a *sĕgôl* is usually inserted to prevent a consonant cluster at the end of the new form.

**iii.** The retraction of the accent.

| *Imperfect* | *Wāw-consecutive* | |
|---|---|---|
| יִגְלֶה | וַיִּגֶל < יִגְל* | (and) he uncovered |
| יִבְנֶה | וַיִּבֶן < יִבְן* | (and) he built |

Beyond these basic characteristics, however, the forms of III-Hē verbs are quite unpredictable. Even within the same root there may be differences in vocalization. Some III-Hē verbs have *ē* (..) in the preformative (instead of *i*) and no *sĕgôl* inserted.

| *Imperfect* | *Wāw-consecutive* | |
|---|---|---|
| יִבְכֶּה | *יִבְךְּ > וַיֵּבְךְּ (not *וַיִּבֶךְ) | he wept |
| יִשְׁתֶּה | *יִשְׁתְּ > וַיֵּשְׁתְּ (not *וַתִּשֶׁת) | he drank |

III-Hē verbs that are also I-Guttural generally have *páṯaḥ* instead of *sĕḡôl* inserted, although there is some variation in the vocalization of the preformative (sometimes an *i*-vowel appears instead of the expected *a*-vowel).

| *Imperfect* | *Wāw-consecutive* | |
|---|---|---|
| יַעֲנֶה | *יַעֲן > וַיַּעַן | (and) he answered |
| יַעֲשֶׂה | *יַעֲשׂ > וַיַּעַשׂ | (and) he made/did |
| יַחֲנֶה | *יַחֲן > וַיִּחַן | (and) he camped |

The verbs הָיָה (to be) and חָיָה (to live) are peculiar in their Wāw-consecutive forms. Because they occur frequently, they should be memorized.

| *Imperfect* | *Wāw-consecutive* | |
|---|---|---|
| יִחְיֶה | וַיְחִי | (and) he lived |
| אֶהְיֶה | וָאֱהִי | (and) I was |

III-Hē verbs that are also I-Nûn may pose a problem to the beginning student: in addition to the apocope of Hē, the form may also lose the *dāḡēš* in the second radical which normally indicates the assimilated Nûn (compare V.1).

| *Imperfect* | *Wāw-consecutive* | |
|---|---|---|
| *יְנְטֶה < יֵטֶּה | וַיֵּט | (and) he stretched out |
| *יְנְזֶה < יִזֶּה | וַיִּז | (and) he sprinkled |

Finally, it should be noted that the Wāw-consecutive form of רָאָה (to see) is וַיַּרְא. Since this form occurs very frequently, it should be committed to memory. The 3 fs/2 ms form, however, is וַתֵּרֶא.

## 5. Narrative Contexts

In a discourse, context may be provided in a number of ways. A past event is typically introduced by וַיְהִי, literally, "and it was/came to pass." Future events are introduced by וְהָיָה, literally, "and it shall be." Further indication of the context usually follows: a prepositional or adverbial expression giving a specific time (e.g., after these things), a reference to some event introduced by כַּאֲשֶׁר (even as) or כִּי (when), or the like. The event that happened or will happen is then introduced by the conjunction –ו. Literally, the sequence –ו ... וַיְהִי means "(and) it came to pass ... that," and the sequence –ו ... וְהָיָה means "(and) it shall be ... that." It is often best, however, to avoid a literal translation. Study the following examples.

**a.** Past Events

| | |
|---|---|
| וַיְהִי בָעֶרֶב וַיִּקַּח אֶת־לֵאָה בִתּוֹ | In the evening, he took Leah his daughter (Gen 29:23) |
| וַיְהִי ׀ בַּיּוֹם הַהוּא וַיָּבֹאוּ עַבְדֵי יִצְחָק | On that day, the servants of Isaac came (Gen 26:32) |
| וַיְהִי בָּעֵת הַהִוא וַיֵּרֶד יְהוּדָה | At that time, Judah went down (Gen 38:1) |
| וַיְהִי כַּאֲשֶׁר יָלְדָה רָחֵל אֶת־יוֹסֵף וַיֹּאמֶר יַעֲקֹב | When Rachel bore Joseph, Jacob said (Gen 30:25) |

| | |
|---|---|
| וַיְהִ֗י כִּי־בָ֙אנוּ֙ אֶל־הַמָּל֔וֹן וַנִּפְתְּחָה֙ אֶת־אַמְתְּחֹתֵ֔ינוּ | When we came to the lodge, we opened our saddle bags (Gen 43:21) |

**b.** Future Events

| | |
|---|---|
| וְהָיָ֖ה בַּיּ֣וֹם הַה֑וּא וְקָרָ֣אתִי לְעַבְדִּ֔י | On that day, I will summon my servant (Isa 22:20) |
| וְהָיָ֞ה כִּֽי־תָבֹ֣אוּ אֶל־הָאָ֗רֶץ אֲשֶׁ֨ר יִתֵּ֧ן יְהוָ֛ה לָכֶ֖ם כַּאֲשֶׁ֣ר דִּבֵּ֑ר וּשְׁמַרְתֶּ֖ם אֶת־הָעֲבֹדָ֥ה הַזֹּֽאת | When you enter the land which YHWH will give to you, even as he has spoken, you shall keep this service (Exod 12:25) |

## 6. Concomitant Circumstances

Clauses describing circumstances concomitant with the main event may be introduced by the conjunction ־ו, in which case the conjunction may be translated as "while," "when," or "as."

| | |
|---|---|
| וַיִּפֹּ֛ל עַל־צַוְּארֵ֥י בִנְיָמִֽן־אָחִ֖יו וַיֵּ֑בְךְּ וּבִנְיָמִ֕ן בָּכָ֖ה עַל־צַוָּארָֽיו | He fell on the neck of Benjamin his brother and wept, *as* Benjamin wept on his neck (Gen 45:14) |
| וַ֠יָּבֹאוּ שְׁנֵ֨י הַמַּלְאָכִ֤ים סְדֹ֙מָה֙ בָּעֶ֔רֶב וְל֖וֹט יֹשֵׁ֣ב בְּשַֽׁעַר־סְדֹ֑ם | The two angels came to Sodom in the evening, *while* Lot was sitting by the gate of Sodom (Gen 19:1) |
| וַיָּבֹ֤א אֱלִישָׁע֙ דַּמֶּ֔שֶׂק וּבֶן־הֲדַ֥ד מֶֽלֶךְ־אֲרָ֖ם חֹלֶ֑ה | Elisha came to Damascus *when* Ben-Hadad the king of Aram was sick (2 Kgs 8:7) |

As noted in IX.5.b, הִנֵּה very often introduces the circumstances of something that is happening.

| | |
|---|---|
| וַיָּבֹא֙ אֶל־הָאִ֔ישׁ וְהִנֵּ֛ה עֹמֵ֥ד עַל־הַגְּמַלִּ֖ים | He came to the man *while* (he was) standing by the camels (Gen 24:30) |

## Vocabulary

*Nouns*:

בְּהֵמָה (cs: בֶּהֱמַת; with sfx. בְּהֶמְתּוֹ) wild animal, beast, cattle

חֲמוֹר (he-)ass

מִגְרָשׁ pasture land

קָצֶה (also קָצָה) extremity, end

שֶׂה lamb, kid

שַׂק sack

שֶׁ֫מֶן oil, fat

*Verbs*:

אָבַד to perish

בָּקַע to split

זָנָה to act like a prostitute, be promiscuous. *Noun*: זוֹנָה prostitute, promiscuous woman

חָזָה to see (a vision). *Noun*: חָזוֹן vision

חָשַׂךְ to restrain, withhold

מָאַס to reject

נָגַע to touch, strike (object of the verb usually indicated by בְּ). *Idiom*: נָגַע אֶל־ reach. *Noun*: נֶ֫גַע plague, stroke

צוּם to fast. *Noun*: צוֹם fast, fasting

*Prepositions*:

בַּעֲבוּר for the sake of, on account of

לִקְרַאת toward, against

מַ֫עַל above

## Exercise 20

**a.** Parse the following forms.

| | | | | | | | |
|---|---|---|---|---|---|---|---|
| 1. | וַתִּזְנִ֫י | 6. | וַתֵּ֫לֶךְ | 11. | וַיַּ֫עַן | 16. | וַנָּ֫שָׁב |
| 2. | וַיֵּ֫שֶׁב | 7. | וַיֵּ֫דַע | 12. | וַיָּ֫שָׁב | 17. | וָאֹכֵל |
| 3. | וַיֵּ֫לֶךְ | 8. | וַיֵּ֫בְךְּ | 13. | וַיָּ֫סַר | 18. | וַתֹּאבַ֫דְנָה |
| 4. | וַיִּקַּח | 9. | וַתַּ֫חַז | 14. | וַיַּ֫רְא | 19. | וַתִּזְנֶ֫ינָה |
| 5. | וַיְהִי | 10. | וַיִּ֫בֶן | 15. | וַיַּ֫עַשׂ | 20. | וָאִירָא |

**b.** Write the following in Hebrew, using only consecutive forms.

1. (and) he rejected
2. (and) she touched
3. (and) he fasted
4. (and) she went
5. (and) we came
6. (and) she saw
7. (and) she sat
8. (and) he was afraid
9. (and) he saw
10. (and) I took
11. (and) he died
12. (and) she came
13. (and) you (ms) said
14. (and) he gave
15. (and) he went up
16. (and) he camped

**c.** Translate Gen 22:1–15 with the help of a dictionary and these notes.

*Notes*:

v 2: קַח־נָא take!; וְלֶךְ־לְךָ go! וְהַעֲלֵהוּ and offer him up!

v 3: וַיַּשְׁכֵּם (subject) got up early; אֶת־שְׁנֵי two of; וַיְבַקַּע he split.

v 5: שְׁבוּ־לָכֶם you stay!; וְנִשְׁתַּחֲוֶה and we will worship.

v 8: שְׁנֵיהֶם the two of them.

v 10: לִשְׁחֹט to slay.

v 13: נֶאֱחַז caught; וַיַּעֲלֵהוּ and offered it up.

v 14: יֵאָמֵר it is said; יֵרָאֶה it will be seen.

# Lesson XXI

## 1. Distinctive Qal Jussive Forms

We have already learned in XVIII.4.b that there is no difference between the jussives and the corresponding imperfect forms of most verbs. For two root types, however, the jussives are clearly distinguished: III-Hē and II-Wāw/Yōḏ.

**a.** The jussives of III-Hē verbs are usually identical to the corresponding Wāw-consecutive forms without the conjunction (see XX.4.d).

| *Root* | *Imperfect* | *Wāw-consec.* | *Jussive* | |
|---|---|---|---|---|
| בנה | יִבְנֶה | וַיִּ֫בֶן | יִ֫בֶן | let him build |
| גלה | יִגְלֶה | וַיִּ֫גֶל | יִ֫גֶל | let him uncover |
| היה | יִהְיֶה | וַיְהִי | יְהִי | let him be, become |
| חיה | יִחְיֶה | וַיְחִי | יְחִי | let him live |
| חרה | יֶחֱרֶה | וַיִּ֫חַר | יִ֫חַר | let him him be angry |
| נטה | יִטֶּה | וַיֵּט | יֵט | let him stretch |
| עלה | יַעֲלֶה | וַיַּ֫עַל | יַ֫עַל | let him go up |
| עשׂה | יַעֲשֶׂה | וַיַּ֫עַשׂ | יַ֫עַשׂ | let him do, make |
| שׁתה | יִשְׁתֶּה | וַיֵּשְׁתְּ | יֵשְׁתְּ | let him drink |

For the verb רָאָה (to see), however, there is a slight difference in vocalization between Wāw-consecutive and 3 ms jussive forms.

וַיַּרְא (and) he saw          יֵ֫רֶא let him see

**b.** The jussives of II-Wāw/Yōḏ verbs are normally distinguished from the Wāw-consecutive forms.

| *Root* | *Imperfect* | *Wāw-consec.* | *Jussive* | |
|---|---|---|---|---|
| מות | יָמוּת | וַיָּ֫מָת | יָמֹת | let him die |
| רום | יָרוּם | וַיָּ֫רָם | יָרֹם | let him be exalted |
| שׁוב | יָשׁוּב | וַיָּ֫שָׁב | יָשֹׁב | let him return |
| גיל | יָגִיל | וַיָּ֫גֶל | יָגֵל | let him rejoice |
| ריב | יָרִיב | וַיָּ֫רֶב | יָרֵב | let him quarrel |
| שׂים | יָשִׂים | וַיָּ֫שֶׂם | יָשֵׂם | let him set |

## 2. The Qal Cohortative of Weak Verbs

The Qal cohortative forms of weak verbs occasion no surprises, but a few forms are noteworthy.

| | | | |
|---|---|---|---|
| אֶעֶמְדָה | let me stand | נַעַמְדָה | let us stand |
| אֹכְלָה | let me eat | נֹאכְלָה | let us eat |
| אֶרְאֶה | let me see | נִרְאֶה | let us see |

*Notes*:

i. The cohortatives of I-Guttural verbs like עָמַד are formed according to rules (see XIX.1.d.i).

*אֶעֱמְדָה > אֶעֶמְדָה let me stand

*נַעֲמְדָה > נַעַמְדָה let us stand

ii. The 1 cs cohortatives of I-ʾÁlep̄ verbs like אָכַל are formed according to rules (see XIX.1.d.iii).

*אאכְלָה > אֹכְלָה let me eat

iii. Instead of special cohortative forms, III-Hē verbs use the appropriate imperfect forms; they are without the final ָה– that marks most cohortatives.

נִרְאֶה we will see (imperfect) or let us see (cohortative)

## 3. The Qal Imperative

It is easiest at this stage to think of the imperative forms as related to the corresponding imperfect forms, inasmuch as the preformative is lacking in the imperative.

| | *Imperfect* | *Imperative* | |
|---|---|---|---|
| 2 *ms* | תִּקְטֹל | קְטֹל | (see II.6.a.i) |
| 2 *fs* | תִּקְטְלִי | קִטְלִי < קְטְלִי* | (see II.6.a.i; VI.3.a) |
| 2 *mp* | תִּקְטְלוּ | קִטְלוּ < קְטְלוּ* | (see II.6.a.i; VI.3.a) |
| 2 *fp* | תִּקְטֹלְנָה | קְטֹלְנָה | (see II.6.a.i) |

**a.** The Qal imperatives of the strong verbs שָׁמַר (to keep) and שָׁכַב (to lie down) are inflected as follows.

| | | |
|---|---|---|
| *ms* | שְׁמֹר | שְׁכַב |
| *fs* | שִׁמְרִי | שִׁכְבִי |
| *mp* | שִׁמְרוּ | שִׁכְבוּ |
| *fp* | שְׁמֹרְנָה | שְׁכַבְנָה |

**b.** The Qal imperatives of the I-Guttural verbs עָמַד (to stand), חָזַק (to be strong), and אָכַל (to eat) are inflected as follows.

| | | | |
|---|---|---|---|
| *ms* | עֲמֹד | חֲזַק | אֱכֹל |
| *fs* | עִמְדִי | חִזְקִי | אִכְלִי |
| *mp* | עִמְדוּ | חִזְקוּ | אִכְלוּ |
| *fp* | עֲמֹדְנָה | חֲזַקְנָה | אֱכֹלְנָה |

*Notes*:

i. Although the 2 ms imperfect of חָזַק is תֶּחֱזַק, the imperative is חֲזַק, not *חֱזַק.

ii. In I-ʾĀlep̄ verbs, the vowel in the first syllable is ֱ .

iii. Regardless of the guttural, the fs and mp forms have the *i*-vowel in the first syllable.

עִמְדִי not *עֲמְדִי > *עַמְדִי (see XIX.1.d.i)

חִזְקִי not *חֱזְקִי or *חֲזְקִי

**c.** The Qal imperative of the II-Guttural verb בָּחַר (choose) is inflected as follows.

| | |
|---|---|
| *ms* | בְּחַר |
| *fs* | בַּחֲרִי |
| *mp* | בַּחֲרוּ |
| *fp* | בְּחַ֫רְנָה |

*Note*: The fs and mp are formed according to rules (see VI.3.b): thus, *בְּחֲרִי > בַּחֲרִי; *בְּחֲרוּ > בַּחֲרוּ.

**d.** The Qal imperatives of the III-Hē verbs בָּנָה (to build), עָשָׂה (to do), and הָיָה (to be) are inflected as follows.

| | | | |
|---|---|---|---|
| *ms* | בְּנֵה | עֲשֵׂה | הֱיֵה |
| *fs* | בְּנִי | עֲשִׂי | הֱיִי |
| *mp* | בְּנוּ | עֲשׂוּ | הֱיוּ |
| *fp* | בְּנֶ֫ינָה | עֲשֶׂ֫ינָה | הֱיֶ֫ינָה |

*Notes*:

i. The ending in the ms is always ֵה–, not ֶה–, as in the imperfect 2 ms.

ii. For the verbs הָיָה (to be) and חָיָה (to live), the first syllable is ֱ, not ֲ. After the conjunction ו, however, it is silent: וֶחְיֵה *weḥyē(h)*; וִחְיוּ *wiḥyû*.

**e.** The Qal imperative of the I-Wāw verbs יָשַׁב (to dwell) and יָדַע (to know), and the verb הָלַךְ are inflected as follows.

| | | | |
|---|---|---|---|
| *ms* | שֵׁב | דַּע | לֵךְ |
| *fs* | שְׁבִי | דְּעִי | לְכִי |
| *mp* | שְׁבוּ | דְּעוּ | לְכוּ |
| *fp* | שֵׁ֫בְנָה | דַּ֫עְנָה | לֵ֫כְנָה |

*Notes*:

i. As in the imperfect (XIX.5.a.i), the first radical does not appear in the imperative.

ii. As previously noted (XIX.5.c), the verb הָלַךְ behaves like an original I-Wāw verb in the Qal imperfect. So, too, it is treated like a I-Wāw verb in the imperative.

iii. The 3 fp/2 fp imperfect of יָשַׁב is תֵּשַׁ֫בְנָה, but the imperative is שֵׁ֫בְנָה, not *שַׁ֫בְנָה (also תֵּלַ֫כְנָה but לֵ֫כְנָה). The imperfect 3 fp/2 fp of יָצָא is תֵּצֶ֫אנָה, but the corresponding imperative is irregular, צְאֶ֫ינָה.

iv. Although יָרַשׁ (to possess) behaves like an original I-Yōḏ verb in the imperfect (see XIX.5.d), the imperatives are, with only one exception, typical of I-Wāw verbs (i.e., רֵשׁ, רְשׁוּ). The verb יָרֵא (to be afraid), on the other hand, does not lose the first radical in the imperative (יְרָא; יִרְאוּ).

**f.** The Qal imperatives of the I-Nûn verbs נָפַל (to fall), נָסַע (to set out), and נָתַן (to give) are inflected as follows.

| | | | |
|---|---|---|---|
| *ms* | נְפֹל | סַע | תֵּן |
| *fs* | נִפְלִי | סְעִי | תְּנִי |
| *mp* | נִפְלוּ | סְעוּ | תְּנוּ |
| *fp* | נְפֹ֫לְנָה | סַ֫עְנָה | תֵּ֫נָּה |

*Notes*:

i. There are two basic types of I-Nûn verbs evident in the Qal imperative forms: those with the first radical (like נְפֹל), and those that lose the first radical (like סַע and תֵּן).
ii. The verb לָקַח (to take) behaves like a I-Nûn verb: thus, קַח (ms), קְחִי (fs), קְחוּ (mp). The fp form is unattested.

**g.** The Qal imperatives of the II-Wāw verbs קוּם (to arise) and בּוֹא (to come), and the II-Yōḏ verb שִׂים (to put) are inflected as follows.

| | | | |
|---|---|---|---|
| *ms* | קוּם | בּוֹא | שִׂים |
| *fs* | ק֫וּמִי | בּ֫וֹאִי | שׂ֫ימִי |
| *mp* | ק֫וּמוּ | בּ֫וֹאוּ | שׂ֫ימוּ |
| *fp* | ק֫מְנָה | – | – |

*Notes*:

i. II-Wāw verbs are clearly distinguished from II-Yōḏ verbs.
ii. The fp form of קוּם is ק֫מְנָה, even though the 2 fp imperfect is usually תְּקוּמ֫ינָה.

An imperative form may be vocalized slightly differently in certain situations. When linked to a following word or particle by means of the *maqqēp̄*, it loses its stress and the last syllable may be shortened from *ō* to *o* or from *ē* to *e*.

שְׁמֹר but שְׁמָר־לְךָ Keep!

שֵׁב but שֶׁב־שָׁם Stay there!

When the imperative is in pause, the thematic vowel may not be reduced; it may, in fact, be lengthened.

שְׁבוּ but שֵׁ֫בוּ Stay!

שְׁמַע but שְׁמָ֫ע Hear!

אִכְלוּ but אֱכֹ֫לוּ Eat!

## 4. Imperative Forms with Final הָ –

**a.** The ms of the imperative may take the final הָ–, like the cohortative. When it does, the base form is shortened, contracted, or reduced before the final הָ–, unless it is a II-Wāw/Yōḏ verb, in which case it remains unchanged. There is no difference in meaning between an imperative with the final הָ– and one without.

**b.** The following are the forms of the Qal imperative with the final הָ–.

| *Root* | *Without* הָ– | *With* הָ– | |
|---|---|---|---|
| שמר | שְׁמֹר | שָׁמְרָה | Keep! |
| עמד | עֲמֹד | עָמְדָה | Stand! |
| אכל | אֱכֹל | אָכְלָה | Eat! |
| שלח | שְׁלַח | שִׁלְחָה | Send! |
| ישב | שֵׁב | שְׁבָה | Sit! |
| ידע | דַּע | דְּעָה | Know! |
| נפל | נְפֹל | נָפְלָה | Fall! |
| נסע | סַע | סְעָה | Set out! |
| נתן | תֵּן | תְּנָה | Give! |
| קום | קוּם | קוּמָה | Arise! |
| בוא | בּוֹא | בֹּאָה | Come! |
| שׂים | שִׂים | שִׂימָה | Place! |

*Note*: The III-Hē imperative never takes the final הָ– (compare 2. Note iii above).

## 5. Negative Commands

The imperative forms are *not* negated in Hebrew. For negative commands, the negative particles לֹא and אַל are used with the second person imperfect (see XVIII.5.b-c).

| | |
|---|---|
| לֹא תִּרְצָח | You shall not murder! (not *לֹא רְצַח) |
| אַל־תִּשְׂמַח | Do not rejoice! (not *לֹא שְׂמַח) |

## 6. Imperatives as Interjections

A few imperative forms are used as interjections and, therefore, should not be taken literally. When so used, the imperative form may be masculine singular even though the subject may be feminine or plural.

**a.** רָאָה (see)

| | |
|---|---|
| רְאֵה רֵיחַ בְּנִי כְּרֵיחַ שָׂדֶה אֲשֶׁר בֵּרֲכוֹ יְהוָה | *Ah!* The smell of my son is like the smell of a field which YHWH has blessed! (Gen 27:27) |

**b.** קוּם (arise)

| | |
|---|---|
| קוּם־נָא שְׁבָה וְאָכְלָה | *Come on!* Sit up and eat! (Gen 27:19) |

**c.** יָהַב (give)

| | |
|---|---|
| הָבָה־נָּא אָבוֹא אֵלַיִךְ | *Come!* Let me come into you! (Gen 38:16) |

**d.** הָלַךְ (go)

| | |
|---|---|
| לְכָה נִכְרְתָה בְרִית | *Come on!* Let us make a covenant! (Gen 31:44) |

## 7. The Imperative with a Redundant ל

After the imperative, the preposition ל with the second person pronominal suffix may occur redundantly to indicate the subject of the action commanded. In any case, this redundant ל is normally not translated into English.

לֶךְ־לְךָ מֵאַרְצְךָ — Go from your country (Gen 12:1)

וְקוּם בְּרַח־לְךָ אֶל־לָבָן אָחִי — Now go on! *Flee* to Laban my brother (Gen 27:43)

## 8. Commands in Narrative Sequence

**a.** A series of imperatives or imperatival phrases may occur, with or without the conjunction ו– linking them.

לְכוּ שִׁבְרוּ וֶאֱכֹלוּ וּלְכוּ שִׁבְרוּ בְּלוֹא־כֶסֶף — Come, buy food and eat! Come buy food without money! (Isa 55:1)

In such a sequence, the imperatives joined by ו– may or may not be consequent to one another.

**b.** By analogy with other narrative sequences (XX.2–3), an imperative form preceding a perfect, causes the perfect to have an imperative force.

לֵךְ וּבָאתָ־לְּךָ אֶרֶץ יְהוּדָה — Go on and *enter* the land of Judah (1 Sam 22:5)

שְׁמַע בְּקוֹלָם וְהִמְלַכְתָּ לָהֶם מֶלֶךְ — Heed their voice and *cause* a king *to reign* for them (1 Sam 8:22)

In this sequence, the *wĕqāṭal* form is consequent to the imperative form: Go (and then) enter! Heed (and then) cause a king to reign!

**c.** If the imperative is followed by an imperfect or cohortative, the latter begins a purpose or result clause and should, therefore, be translated by "that ..." or "so that ..."

וְתֶן־זֶרַע וְנִחְיֶה וְלֹא נָמוּת — Provide the seed *so that* we may live and not die! (Gen 47:19)

Like the imperative, the jussive may be followed by an imperfect or cohortative. In this case, the imperfect or cohortative also introduces a purpose or result clause.

| | |
|---|---|
| יָבֹא־נָא אֵלַי וְיֵדַע כִּי יֵשׁ נָבִיא בְּיִשְׂרָאֵל | Let him come to me *that* he may know there is a prophet in Israel (2 Kgs 5:8) |

**d.** The jussive may also be followed by an imperative. In this sequence, the imperative introduces a result or purpose clause and should not, therefore, be translated as a command.

| | |
|---|---|
| יִתֵּן יְהוָה לָכֶם וּמְצֶאןָ מְנוּחָה | May YHWH grant *that you may find* a resting place (Ruth 1:9) |

## Vocabulary

*Nouns*:

אַמָּה cubit

אֱמֶת (with sfx.: אֲמִתּוֹ) truth, reliability, firmness

בָּמָה high place (a sanctuary)

חֲלוֹם (pl. חֲלוֹמוֹת) dream. *Verb*: חָלַם to dream

יֶתֶר remainder, excess

כֶּבֶשׂ lamb

לוּחַ (pl. לוּחוֹת) tablet

עֹשֶׁר wealth. *Adjective*: עָשִׁיר rich

*Verbs*:

אָסַף to gather, remove

טָהֵר to be clean. *Adjective*: טָהוֹר clean, pure

יָהַב to give, ascribe (occurs only in the imperative forms)

יָצַק to pour out (see XVI.8.c)

כָּבַס to wash, clean

כָּשַׁל to stumble

נוּחַ to rest. *Noun*: מְנוּחָה rest

נָצַר to watch

שִׁיר to sing. *Noun*: שִׁיר song

שִׁית to put, set

## Exercise 21

**a.** Parse the following forms:

1. וַיִּצֹק
2. הָ֫בָה
3. עֲלִי
4. יָשֵׂם
5. יַ֫עַל
6. תְּנָה
7. נְצֹר
8. הָ֫בוּ
9. יַ֫עַשׂ
10. עֲלֵה
11. וַתָּ֫נַח
12. יָשֵׁת
13. תֵּט
14. שִׁיתָה
15. וַיָּ֫שֶׁת
16. שִׁ֫ירוּ
17. זָכְרָה
18. יָקֹם
19. שׁוּבָה
20. וַיִּצְקוּ
21. וָאֶטְהַר

**b.** Write the following forms:

1. Qal impv. ms of שִׁיר
2. Qal impv. ms of בָּנָה
3. Qal juss. 3 ms of מוּת
4. Qal impv. ms of מוּת
5. Qal impv. ms of שָׁתָה
6. Qal impv. mp of עָשָׂה
7. Qal juss. 3 fs of שׁוּב
8. Qal impv. mp of רָאָה
9. Qal impv. ms of חָיָה
10. Qal impv. mp of הָיָה
11. Qal impv. ms of נָטָה
12. Qal juss. 3 ms of יָשַׁב
13. Qal impv. mp of יָשַׁב
14. Qal impv. mp of שׁוּב
15. Qal impv. fs of יָשַׁב
16. Qal impv. fp of שׁוּב
17. Qal impv. fs of הָלַךְ
18. Qal impv. ms of לָקַח
19. Qal impv. mp of נָסַע
20. Qal impv. mp of נָתַן

**c.** Translate 1 Kgs 3:4–15 with the help of a dictionary and these notes.

*Notes*:

v 4: לִזְבֹּחַ to sacrifice; יַעֲלֶה (subject) offered.

v 5: נִרְאָה (subject) appeared.

v 7: צֵאת וָבֹא to go out and to come in.

v 8: לֹא־יִמָּנֶה וְלֹא יִסָּפֵר cannot be numbered and cannot be counted.

v 9: לִשְׁפֹּט to judge; לְהָבִין to discern.

v 11: הָבִין לִשְׁמֹעַ discernment (lit. discerning) to hear.

v 12: וְנָבוֹן and intelligent.

v 14: לִשְׁמֹר to keep.

v 15: וַיִּקַץ = וַיִּיקַץ; וַיַּעַל and he offered up.

# Lesson XXII

## 1. The Imperfect and Imperative with Object Suffixes

As with the perfect (XVII), imperfect and imperative forms may indicate direct objects by means of suffixed pronouns.

אֶשְׁלַח אֹתְךָ = אֶשְׁלָחֲךָ I will send you

שְׁלַח אֹתִי = שְׁלָחֵנִי Send me!

**a.** The imperfect form may undergo certain vowel changes before the object suffix.

**i.** The *ō* thematic vowel is reduced to *šĕwāʾ* before the object suffix, if it is not already reduced.

יִשְׁמֹר he will keep *but* יִשְׁמְרֵנִי he will keep me

Before the 2 ms and 2 mp suffixes, however, *ō* is usually not reduced. Instead, *ō* is shortened to *o*: thus, יִשְׁמָרְךָ (he will keep you); יִשְׁמָרְכֶם (he will keep you).

**ii.** The thematic *ē* vowel is reduced to *šĕwāʾ* before the object suffix, if it is not already reduced.

יִתֵּן he will give *but* יִתְּנֵנִי he will give me

Before the 2 ms and 2 mp suffixes, however, *ē* is usually not reduced. Instead, *ē* is shortened to *e*. Thus, יִתֶּנְךָ (he will give you); יִתֶּנְכֶם (he will give you).

**iii.** The *a* thematic vowel is not reduced. It is lengthened to *ā* before the object suffix.

יִשְׁמַע he will hear *but* יִשְׁמָעֵנִי he will hear me

**b.** The imperative form may undergo certain changes before the object suffix.

**i.** The Qal ms imperative of the *qĕṭōl* type becomes *qoṭl-* before the object suffix.

שְׁמֹר Keep! *but* שָׁמְרֵנִי Keep me!

The mp (*qiṭlû*) and fs (*qiṭlî*), however, remain unchanged: thus, דִּרְשׁ֫וּנִי (Seek me!).

**ii.** All Qal imperative forms of the *qĕṭal* type lengthen the *a* vowel to *ā* before the object suffix.

שְׁמַע Hear! *but* שְׁמָעֵ֫נִי Hear me! שְׁמָע֫וּנִי Hear me!

So, too, all imperatives with the *a*-vowel will lengthen that vowel to *ā* before the object suffix.

דַּע Know! *but* דָּעֵ֫הוּ Know him!

קַח Take! *but* קָחֵ֫הוּ Take him!

**iii.** The *ē*-vowel is normally reduced to *šĕwāʾ*.

תֵּן Give! *but* תְּנֵ֫הוּ Give it!

**c.** The same set of object suffixes is used with the imperfect and imperative. The suffixes are essentially those of Type B in IX.2.b, except for the 3 mp and 3 fp forms. If a "connecting vowel" appears before the object suffix, it will be either ֵ or ֶ (as opposed to the *a*-vowel used to connect object suffixes to verbs in the perfect). The object suffixes are as follows.

| | | | |
|---|---|---|---|
| *3 ms* | –ֵ֫הוּ | *3 mp* | –ֵם |
| *3 fs* | –ֶ֫הָ | *3 fp* | –ֵן |
| *2 ms* | –ךָ | *2 mp* | –כֶם |
| *2 fs* | –ֵךְ | *2 fp* | –not attested– |
| *1 cs* | –ֵ֫נִי | *1 cp* | –ֵ֫נוּ |

*Notes:*

i. If the imperfect or imperative form ends in a vowel (i.e., in the 2 fs, 2 mp, 3 mp), the "connecting vowel" is omitted.

ii. The 3 fp/2 fp imperfect and imperative forms (i.e., תִּקְטֹ֫לְנָה, קְטֹ֫לְנָה) are not attested with object suffixes; they are replaced by their mp counterparts (i.e., יִקְטְלוּ; קִטְלוּ).

Like the preposition מִן, which also take suffixes of Type B in IX.2.b, the object suffixes used with imperfects and imperatives may have an additional *-en-* element before the suffix. The following forms of the object suffixes (with *-en-*) are attested.

| | | |
|---|---|---|
| *3 ms* | ֶ֫נּוּ– | (*-*énhû* > -*énnû*) |
| *3 fs* | ֶ֫נָּה– | (*-*énhā*[*h*] > -*énnā*[*h*]) |
| *2 ms* | ֶ֫ךָּ– | (*-*énkā* > -*ékkā*) |
| *1 cs* | ֶ֫נִּי– | (-*énnî*) |
| *1 cp* | ֶ֫נּוּ– | (-*énnû*) |

There is no difference in meaning between the suffixes with the additional *-en-* element and those without.

יִשְׁלָחֶ֫נּוּ = יִשְׁלָחֵ֫הוּ he will send him

**d.** III-Hē verbs drop the Hē before the object suffix.

| | |
|---|---|
| אֶבְנֶה I will build | אֶבְנֵךְ I will build you |
| יִרְאֶה he will see | יִרְאֵ֫נִי He will see me |
| עֲנֵה answer! | עֲנֵ֫נִי Answer me! |

## 2. The Qal Infinitive Absolute

There are two forms in Hebrew that are called infinitives: the infinitive absolute and the infinitive construct. The infinitive construct will be treated in the Lesson XXIII.

The infinitive absolute is not inflected for gender, number, or person.

**a.** The proper form of the Qal infinitive absolute is קָטֹל, but it is most often written as קָטוֹל.

**b.** The weak roots occasion no surprises, but note the following.

**i.** In III-Guttural roots, the Qal infinitive absolute has the *furtive pátaḥ*, as one would expect, e.g, שָׁמוֹעַ.

**ii.** In III-Hē roots, the Qal infinitive absolute is either like גָּלוֹ or גָּלֹה.

**iii.** There is no distinction in the Qal infinitive absolute between II-Wāw and II-Yōḏ verbs, e.g., קוֹם, שׂוֹם.

## 3. Uses of the Infinitive Absolute

The infinitive absolute is used in the following ways.

**a.** It may simply be a *verbal noun*.

| | |
|---|---|
| הָרֹ֣ג ׀ בָּקָ֗ר וְשָׁחֹ֣ט צֹ֔אן | *slaying* cattle and *slaughtering* sheep (Isa 22:13) |
| אָכֹ֣ל דְּבַ֣שׁ הַרְבּ֣וֹת לֹא־ט֑וֹב | *eating* honey abundantly is not good = It is not good *to eat* much honey (Prov 25:27) |

**b.** Most commonly the infinitive absolute stands before a finite verb of the same root to emphasize the *certainty* or *decisiveness* of the verbal idea of the root.

| | |
|---|---|
| מ֥וֹת תָּמֽוּת | You shall *certainly* die (Gen 2:17) |
| שׁ֨וֹב אָשׁ֤וּב | I will *certainly* return (Gen 18:10) |

Occasionally, however, the infinitive absolute may also come after the finite verb.

| | |
|---|---|
| יֵצֵ֣א יָצ֔וֹא | he would *surely* come out (2 Kgs 5:11) |

**c.** The infinitive absolute may come after an imperative to *intensify* it.

| | |
|---|---|
| הָרְגֵ֤נִי נָא֙ הָרֹ֔ג | Kill me *right away!* (Num 11:15) |
| שִׁמְע֨וּ שָׁמ֤וֹעַ אֵלַי֙ | *Really* listen to me! (Isa 55:2) |

**d.** Frequently two different infinitive absolute forms are used, with the second one indicating an action occurring *simultaneously* with the first.

| | |
|---|---|
| וַיֵּלֶךְ הָלוֹךְ וְאָכֹל | And he went along eating (Judg 14:9) |
| הָלְכוּ הָלֹךְ וְגָעוֹ | they went along lowing (1 Sam 6:12) |

Probably because of the frequent use of הָלוֹךְ in such constructions, this particular form functions as an adverb indicating *continuance*.

| | |
|---|---|
| וְהַמַּיִם הָיוּ הָלוֹךְ וְחָסוֹר | Now, the water was continually abating (Gen 8:5) |

*Note*: In some instances, the participle form הֹלֵךְ is used in place of the infinitive absolute form הָלוֹךְ, with no discernible difference in meaning. Compare the following examples.

| | |
|---|---|
| וַיֵּלֶךְ הָלוֹךְ וְקָרֵב | he kept approaching (2 Sam 18:25) |
| וַיֵּלֶךְ הַפְּלִשְׁתִּי הֹלֵךְ וְקָרֵב | the Philistine kept approaching (1 Sam 17:41) |

**e.** The infinitive absolute is frequently used as a substitute for an *imperative*.

| | |
|---|---|
| זָכוֹר אֶת־יוֹם הַשַּׁבָּת | *Remember* the sabbath day! (Exod 20:8) |
| שָׁמוֹר אֶת־יוֹם הַשַּׁבָּת | *Observe* the sabbath day! (Deut 5:12) |

In a narrative sequence, an infinitive absolute used as a substitute for an imperative form will also cause a *wĕqāṭal* form following it to have an imperative force (see XXI.8.b).

| | |
|---|---|
| הָלוֹךְ וְדִבַּרְתָּ אֶל־דָּוִד | Go and speak to David (2 Sam 24:12) |

**f.** An infinitive absolute may describe an action occurring concurrently with the main verb and, thus, may take the place of a finite verb, whether perfect or imperfect.

| | |
|---|---|
| וַיַּרְכֵּב אֹתוֹ בְּמִרְכֶּבֶת הַמִּשְׁנֶה... וְנָתוֹן אֹתוֹ עַל כָּל־אֶרֶץ מִצְרָיִם | He made him ride in the chariot of (his) second-in-command ... and *set* him over all the land of Egypt (Gen 41:43) |

## Vocabulary

*Nouns*:

| | |
|---|---|
| אָוֶן | wickedness, trouble, sorrow |
| אֹמֶר | (also אִמְרָה) word, saying |
| בִּינָה | understanding, perception. *Verb*: בִּין to understand, perceive |
| בַּעַל | lord, master, husband, owner; frequently used as proper name of a god, Baal. *Verb*: בָּעַל to rule, lord, marry |
| גְּבוּל | territory, boundary |
| חֵיק | bosom |
| צָרָה | distress. *Verb*: צָרַר to be hard pressed, be in distress |
| קֶרֶב | inward part, inner parts, middle, midst |
| רֵאשִׁית | first |
| רַחַם/רֶחֶם | (fs; fd: רַחְמָתַיִם)/womb, mercy. רַחֲמִים compassion. *Verb*: רָחַם Pi.: to have compassion |
| רִיב | controversy, dispute. *Verb*: רִיב to dispute, be in law-suit |

*Verbs*:

| | |
|---|---|
| זוּר | to be a stranger (ptc. זָר, זָרָה, etc.: stranger, foreigner; also ptc. as adjective "strange, foreign") |
| חָגַר | to gird |
| טָמֵא | to be unclean |

יָסַף to add; Hi.: to continue, increase

יָסַר to discipline, chasten. *Noun*: מוּסָר discipline; chastening

יָרָה to throw, cast; Hi.: to throw, teach, point

קָנָה to acquire, buy, create. *Nouns*: מִקְנֶה possession, property; קִנְיָן property.

*Preposition*:

אֵ֫צֶל near, beside. Also with suffixes: אֶצְלִי near me, etc.

## Exercise 22

**a.** Parse the following forms:

| | | |
|---|---|---|
| 1. נָתוֹן | 6. שְׁמָרֵךְ | 11. אֶבְנֶ֫נָּה |
| 2. קָנוֹ | 7. שָׁמְרֵ֫נִי | 12. יְשִׂימֵ֫נִי |
| 3. יִתֶּנְךָ | 8. שָׁמְרוֹ | 13. תִּשְׁמְרֵם |
| 4. תִּנֵ֫הוּ | 9. יִבְנֵ֫הוּ | 14. שְׁמָעֵ֫נִי |
| 5. תְּנֵם | 10. יִקְנֵ֫הוּ | 15. יַחְגְּרֶ֫הָ |

**b.** Translate the following with the help of a dictionary.

1. Prov 4:1–6

*Notes*:

v 1: וְהַקְשִׁיבוּ and pay attention.

v 4: וַיֹּ֫רֵנִי he instructed me.

2. Amos 7:10–17

*Notes*:

v 10: לְהָכִיל to endure.

v 12: תִּנָּבֵא you may prophesy.

v 13: לֹא־תוֹסִיף you shall not continue; לְהִנָּבֵא to prophesy.

v 15: הִנָּבֵא Prophesy!

v 16: לֹא תִנָּבֵא you shall not prophesy; וְלֹא תַטִּיף you shall not preach.

v 17: תְּחֻלָּק shall be divided up.

c. Translate 1 Kgs 3:16–28 with the help of a dictionary.

*Notes*:

v 16: שְׁתַּיִם two.

v 17: בִּי אֲדֹנִי Please, my lord! (an introductory formula used to begin conversation with a male superior).

v 18: לְלִדְתִּי of my child-bearing; זוּלָתִי except; שְׁתַּיִם two.

v 20: וַתַּשְׁכִּיבֵהוּ and she laid him.

v 21: לְהֵינִיק to nurse; וָאֶתְבּוֹנֵן I looked closely.

v 22: וַתְּדַבֵּרְנָה and they spoke.

v 24: וַיָּבִאוּ and they brought.

v 25: לִשְׁנָיִם into two.

v 26: נִכְמְרוּ (subject) were moved; אַל־תְּמִיתֻהוּ do not kill him.

v 27: לֹא תְמִיתֻהוּ you shall not kill him.

v 28: לַעֲשׂוֹת to do.

# Lesson XXIII

## 1. The Qal Infinitive Construct

**a.** The regular form of the Qal infinitive construct is קְטֹל.

| | | | |
|---|---|---|---|
| שְׁמֹר | to keep, keeping | בְּחֹר | to choose, choosing |

*Note*: A *qĕṭal* type infinitive construct is attested very rarely (e.g., שְׁכַב to lie down, lying down).

**b.** In contrast to the infinitive absolute, the infinitive construct may take a suffixed pronoun. Since the infinitive is a verbal noun, the suffixes used are normally those attached to nouns (XII.1). Certain changes to the base form may take place in the *presuffix* form.

**i.** The infinitive construct usually becomes קָטְל– (*qoṭl-*), but before the 2 ms and 2 mp suffixes it is קְטָל– (*qĕṭol-*).

| | | | |
|---|---|---|---|
| שָׁמְרִי | my keeping | שְׁמָרְךָ | your keeping |
| עָמְדִי | my standing | עֲמָדְךָ | your standing |
| אָכְלִי | my eating | אֲכָלְךָ | your eating |

**ii.** The infinitive construct of III-Guttural roots remains as *qoṭl-* throughout; it does not change to (*qĕṭol-*) before the 2 ms and 2 mp suffix.

| | | | |
|---|---|---|---|
| שָׁמְעִי | my hearing | שָׁמְעֲךָ | your hearing |
| שָׁלְחִי | my sending | שָׁלְחֲךָ | your sending |

**iii.** Infrequently, the infinitive construct form before the suffix is *qiṭl-* or *qaṭl-* instead of *qoṭl-*.

| | | | |
|---|---|---|---|
| בִּטְחֲךָ | your trusting | זַעֲקֵךְ | your crying |

**c.** The suffix appended to the infinitive construct may be subjective or objective. One must rely on context to determine which is the case. Thus, the 2 fs suffix in the first example below indicates the subject (the one who abandons), but in the second example the 2 fs suffix indicates the object (the one abandoned).

| | |
|---|---|
| עָזְבֵךְ֙ אֶת־יְהוָ֣ה | your abandoning YHWH (Jer 2:17) |
| לְעָזְבֵ֖ךְ לָשׁ֣וּב מֵאַחֲרָ֑יִךְ | to abandon you, to turn from following you (Ruth 1:16) |

Occasionally, clarity is achieved when a verbal object suffix (XXII.1.c) is used instead of a suffix used with nouns (XII.1).

| | | | |
|---|---|---|---|
| לְהָרְגֵ֫נִי | to kill me | לְדָרְשֵׁ֫נִי | to seek me |

## 2. The Qal Infinitive Construct of Weak Verbs

**a.** The Qal infinitive construct forms of verbs with gutturals are predictable, except that I-ʾÁlep̄ roots have ֱ instead of ֲ in the first syllable.

| | | | |
|---|---|---|---|
| עֲמֹד | to stand, standing | בְּחֹר | to choose, choosing |
| אֱכֹל | to eat, eating | שְׁלֹחַ | to send, sending |

**b.** The infinitive construct of III-Hē verbs always ends with וֹת–.

| | | | |
|---|---|---|---|
| גְּלוֹת | to uncover, uncovering | עֲשׂוֹת | to make, making |
| בְּנוֹת | to build, building | הֱיוֹת | to be, being |

**c.** The infinitive construct of I-Wāw verbs generally does not show the initial radical (see XIX.5.a.i). It also takes an anomalous ת– ending. The resulting forms (with ת at the end acting like the third radical) behave like *qiṭl*-segolates (see V.2.b; XII.2.c). Verbs that are the III-Guttural, however, are like *qaṭl*-segolates.

| | | | |
|---|---|---|---|
| שֶׁ֫בֶת | to dwell, dwelling | שִׁבְתִּי | my dwelling |
| לֶ֫דֶת | to bear, bearing | לִדְתִּי | my bearing |
| צֵאת | to go out, going out | צֵאתִי | my going out |
| רֶ֫שֶׁת | to possess, possessing | רִשְׁתִּי | my possessing |
| דַּ֫עַת | to know, knowing | דַּעְתִּי | my knowing |

*Notes*:

i. The verb הָלַךְ (to go, walk) behaves like a I-Wāw verb. Hence, the Qal infinitive construct is usually לֶ֫כֶת (the infinitive construct form הֲלֹךְ is attested rarely). With a suffix it is always לֶכְתּ–, not *לְכֶת–, as one might expect: thus, לֶכְתִּי, לֶכְתְּךָ, etc.

ii. The Qal infinitive construct of יָצָא (to go forth) shows the quiescence of א: thus, *צְאת > צֵאת.

iii. The Qal infinitive construct of יָרַשׁ (to possess) is regular: רֶ֫שֶׁת.

iv. The verb יָרֵא (to be afraid, fear), which behaves like a I-Yōḏ verb in the imperfect and imperative (XIX.5.d; XXI.3.e.iv), has יְרֹא twice as the infinitive construct. More commonly the function of the infinitive is taken over by the noun יִרְאָה (fearing).

v. The Qal infinitive construct of יָכֹל (to be able) is irregular: יְכֹ֫לֶת.

**d.** There are two types of Qal infinitive construct for I-Nûn verbs.

**i.** Most I-Nûn verbs retain the first radical.

| | | | |
|---|---|---|---|
| נְפֹל | to fall, falling | נָפְלוֹ | his falling |
| נְגֹף | to strike, striking | נָגְפוֹ | his striking, striking him |
| נְסֹעַ | to set out, setting out | נָסְעָם | their setting out |

**ii.** Some I-Nûn verbs lose the initial נ. These behave like I-Wāw verbs. The verb לָקַח (to take), which behaves like a I-Nûn verb in the Qal imperfect and imperatives (XIX.4.d; XXI.3.f.ii), also loses the initial radical.

| | | | |
|---|---|---|---|
| גַּ֫עַת/נְגֹעַ | to touch, touching | נָגְעוֹ | his touching, touching him |
| נְשֹׂא/שְׂאֵת/שֵׂאת | to lift, lifting | שְׂאֵתוֹ | his lifting, lifting him |
| נְתֹן/תֵּת | to give, giving | תִּתִּי | my giving, giving me |
| גֶּ֫שֶׁת | to draw near, drawing near | גִּשְׁתָּם | their drawing near, drawing near them |
| קַ֫חַת | to take, taking | קַחְתִּי | my taking, taking me |

*Notes*:

i. שֵׂאת is derived from original *שְׂאֵת (see 2.c.ii, above); שְׂאֵת is a variant of שֵׂאת.

ii. תֵּת is derived from original **tint* (i.e., **tint* > **titt* > *tēṯ*).

**e.** Whereas no distinction is made between II-Wāw and II-Yōḏ verbs in the Qal infinitive absolute, the infinitive construct forms of these two types are clearly distinguished.

| | |
|---|---|
| קוּם to arise, arising | קוּמִי my arising |
| בּוֹא to come, coming | בּוֹאִי my coming |
| שִׂית to put, putting | שִׂיתִי my putting |

## 3. Uses of the Infinitive Construct

The infinitive construct may be used in the following ways.

**a.** It may simply be a verbal noun.

| | |
|---|---|
| שְׁמֹעַ מִזֶּבַח טוֹב | *obeying* is better than sacrifice (1 Sam 15:22) |
| לֹא אֵדַע צֵאת וָבֹא | I do not know *going out* or *coming in* = I do not know (how) *to go out* or *come in* (1 Kgs 3:7) |

**b.** Most commonly it stands after לְ to express intention.

| | |
|---|---|
| סָר לִרְאוֹת | he had turned aside *to see* (Exod 3:4) |
| לָלֶכֶת אַרְצָה כְּנַעַן | *to go* to the land of Canaan (Gen 12:5) |

**c.** Sometimes the infinitive construct after לְ elaborates on a preceding statement and clarifies it.

| | |
|---|---|
| הִנֵּה הָעָם חֹטְאִים לַיהוָה לֶאֱכֹל עַל־הַדָּם | the people are sinning against YHWH *by eating* (meat) with blood (1 Sam 14:33) |
| צִוִּיתִיךָ לֵאמֹר לֹא תֹאכַל מִמֶּנּוּ | I commanded you, (by) *saying*, "You shall not eat from it!" (Gen 3:17) |

**d.** Sometimes the infinitive construct after ל indicates an event that is about to happen.

גַּם־בָּבֶל לִנְפֹּל Babylon is about to fall (Jer 51:49)

וַיְהִי הַשֶּׁמֶשׁ לָבוֹא the sun was about to set (Gen 15:12)

**e.** The infinitive construct is used very frequently in temporal clauses. The clause may be introduced by בּ or כּ together with an adverbial expression followed by an infinitive construct, or simply by בּ or כּ with the infinitive construct. In such cases, the temporal clause should be introduced in translation by "when …" or "as…."

בְּיוֹם אֲכָלְךָ מִמֶּנּוּ *when you eat* from it … (Gen 2:17)

וַיְהִי בִּשְׁכֹּן יִשְׂרָאֵל בָּאָרֶץ הַהִוא *when* Israel *dwelled* in that land … (Gen 35:22)

וַיְהִי כְּבוֹא אַבְרָם מִצְרָיְמָה *as* Abram *was entering* Egypt … (Gen 12:14)

## 4. The Negation of Infinitives

**a.** The infinitive construct is usually negated by לְבִלְתִּי (not).

צִוִּיתִיךָ לְבִלְתִּי אֲכָל־מִמֶּנּוּ I commanded you *not to eat* from it (Gen 3:11)

**b.** Much less frequently, the infinitive construct may be negated by בְּלֹא (without), or מִבְּלִי/בְּלִי (without).

בְּלֹא רְאוֹת *without seeing* (Num 35:23)

מִבְּלִי יְכֹלֶת יְהוָה *without* YHWH *being able* … (Deut 9:28)

## 5. Synopsis of Verbs in Qal

We have now learned all the "principle parts" of the verb. The following synopsis is provided to aid the student in learning the various forms. Some forms below are not attested and have been reconstructed by analogy from extant verbs of the same class.

| *Root* | *Perf.* | *Impf.* | *Juss.* | *Impv.* | *Inf. Abs.* | *Inf. Cs.* | *Ptc.* |
|---|---|---|---|---|---|---|---|
| שׁמר | שָׁמַר | יִשְׁמֹר | יִשְׁמֹר | שְׁמֹר | שָׁמוֹר | שְׁמֹר | שֹׁמֵר |
| כבד | כָּבֵד | יִכְבַּד | יִכְבַּד | כְּבַד | כָּבוֹד | כְּבֹד | כָּבֵד |
| קטן | קָטֹן | יִקְטַן | יִקְטַן | קְטַן | קָטוֹן | קְטֹן | קָטֹן |
| עמד | עָמַד | יַעֲמֹד | יַעֲמֹד | עֲמֹד | עָמוֹד | עֲמֹד | עֹמֵד |
| חזק | חָזַק | יֶחֱזַק | יֶחֱזַק | חֲזַק | חָזוֹק | חֲזֹק | חָזֵק |
| אכל | אָכַל | יֹאכַל | יֹאכַל | אֱכֹל | אָכוֹל | אֱכֹל | אֹכֵל |
| בחר | בָּחַר | יִבְחַר | יִבְחַר | בְּחַר | בָּחוֹר | בְּחֹר | בֹּחֵר |
| שׁלח | שָׁלַח | יִשְׁלַח | יִשְׁלַח | שְׁלַח | שָׁלוֹחַ | שְׁלֹחַ | שֹׁלֵחַ |
| מצא | מָצָא | יִמְצָא | יִמְצָא | מְצָא | מָצוֹא | מְצֹא | מֹצֵא |
| גלה | גָּלָה | יִגְלֶה | יִ֫גֶל | גְּלֵה | גָּלֹה/גָּלוֹ | גְּלוֹת | גֹּלֶה |
| נפל | נָפַל | יִפֹּל | יִפֹּל | נְפֹל | נָפוֹל | נְפֹל | נֹפֵל |
| נסע | נָסַע | יִסַּע | יִסַּע | סַע | נָסוֹעַ | סַ֫עַת/נְסֹעַ | נֹסֵעַ |
| נתן | נָתַן | יִתֵּן | יִתֵּן | תֵּן | נָתוֹן | תֵּת | נֹתֵן |
| ישׁב | יָשַׁב | יֵשֵׁב | יֵ֫שֶׁב | שֵׁב | יָשׁוֹב | שֶׁ֫בֶת | יֹשֵׁב |
| יטב | יָטַב | יִיטַב | יִיטַב | יְטַב | יָטוֹב | יְטֹב | יֹטֵב |
| קום | קָם | יָקוּם | יָקֹם | קוּם | קוֹם | קוּם | קָם |
| בוא | בָּא | יָבוֹא | יָבֹא | בּוֹא | בּוֹא | בּוֹא | בָּא |
| שׁית | שָׁת | יָשִׁית | יָשֵׁת | שִׁית | שׁוֹת | שִׁית | שָׁת |
| מות | מֵת | יָמוּת | יָמֹת | מוּת | מוֹת | מוּת | מֵת |

## Vocabulary

*Verbs*:

| | |
|---|---|
| הָפַךְ | to turn, overturn |
| יָבֵשׁ | to be dry. *Noun*: יַבָּשָׁה dry ground |
| יָכַח | Hi.: to reprove |
| כָּעַס | to be irritated, angry |
| לִין/לוּן | to lodge. *Noun*: מָלוֹן lodging place |
| לָכַד | to capture |
| פָּגַע | to meet, befall, encounter. *Noun*: פֶּ֫גַע happening |
| פָּדָה | to ransom |
| פָּרַץ | to break, breach, increase |
| פָּרַשׂ | to spread out |
| צָלַח | to succeed, prosper; Hi.: to make prosperous |
| קָרַע | to rend, tear |
| רָפָא | to heal |
| רָצָה | to be pleased |
| רָצַח | to murder, slay |
| צָחַק/שָׂחַק | to laugh; Pi.: to play, make fun of |
| שָׁכַם | Hi.: to do something early, arise early |
| תָּפַשׂ | to catch, seize |

## Exercise 23

**a.** Give the Qal infinitive construct form of the following:

1. שָׁמַר
2. שָׁמַע
3. זָכַר
4. לָקַח
5. יָצָא
6. יָלַד
7. יָרַשׁ
8. נָתַן
9. יָדַע
10 בָּחַר

11. עָמַד
12. נָפַל
13. בָּנָה
14. גָּלָה
15. עָשָׂה
16. הָלַךְ
17. יָשַׁב
18. חָזַק
19. יָרַד
20. אָכַל

21. שָׁמַר + 3 ms sfx.
22. נָתַן + 1 cs sfx.
23. נָתַן + 3 ms sfx.
24. הָלַךְ + 3 ms sfx.
25. יָשַׁב + 1 cs sfx.
26. יָרַשׁ + 3 ms sfx.
27. בּוֹא + 2 ms sfx.
28. מָצָא + 2 ms sfx.
29. אָכַל + 2 ms sfx.
30. לָקַח + 1 cs sfx.

**b.** Translate Eccl 3:1–9 with the help of a dictionary.

*Notes*:

v 5: לְהַשְׁלִיךְ for casting (also in v 6); מֵחַבֵּק from embracing.

v 6: לְבַקֵּשׁ for seeking; לְאַבֵּד for destroying.

v 7: לְדַבֵּר for speaking.

**c.** Translate Josh 1:1–9 with the help of a dictionary.

*Notes*:

v 5: לֹא־יִתְיַצֵּב אִישׁ no one shall stand (lit.: a man shall not stand); לֹא אַרְפְּךָ I will not fail you.

v 6: תַּנְחִיל you will cause (object) to inherit; נִשְׁבַּעְתִּי I swore.

v 7: תַּשְׂכִּיל you will have success (also in v 8).

v 8: תַּצְלִיחַ you will make (object) prosper.

v 9: וְאַל־תֵּחָת do not be dismayed.

**d.** Translate Gen 3:1–14 with the help of a dictionary.

*Notes*:

v 5: וְנִפְקְחוּ and (subject) will open.

v 6: וְנֶחְמָד and desirable; לְהַשְׂכִּיל to make wise/successful.

v 7: וַתִּפָּקַחְנָה and (subject) opened; שְׁנֵיהֶם two of them.

v 8: מִתְהַלֵּךְ walking about; וַיִּתְחַבֵּא (subject) hid himself.

v 10: וָאֵחָבֵא and I hid myself.

# Lesson XXIV

## 1. The Piel Imperfect

As in the Piel perfect and participle, the Piel imperfect is characterized by the doubling of the second radical (XV).

**a.** Strong Verbs

The Piel imperfect of the strong verb is inflected as follows.

| | | | |
|---|---|---|---|
| *3 ms* | יְקַטֵּל | *3 mp* | יְקַטְּלוּ |
| *3 fs* | תְּקַטֵּל | *3 fp* | תְּקַטֵּ֫לְנָה |
| *2 ms* | תְּקַטֵּל | *2 mp* | תְּקַטְּלוּ |
| *2 fs* | תְּקַטְּלִי | *2 fp* | תְּקַטֵּ֫לְנָה |
| *1 cs* | אֲקַטֵּל | *1 cp* | נְקַטֵּל |

*Notes*:

i. In addition to the characteristic doubling of the second radical, the Piel imperfect is marked by the *šĕwāʾ* in the preformative and the *a*-vowel under the first radical.

ii. In a few verbs, the *dāḡēš* may be lost if the second radical takes a *šĕwāʾ* (VI.7).

**b.** II-Guttural and II-Rêš Verbs

Since gutturals and Rêš do not take the *dāḡēš*, the Piel imperfect forms of such verbs will have either compensatory lengthening or virtual doubling (see XV.3.a), e.g., יְמָאֵן (he will refuse); יְמַהֵר (he will hurry).

**c.** III-ʾĀlep̄ Verbs

The Piel imperfect forms of these verbs are regular, except that the 3 fp/2 fp form is תְּמַלֶּ֫אנָה, not *תְּמַלֵּ֫אנָה, as one might expect.

**d.** III-Guttural Verbs

Since gutturals prefer *a*-class vowels, the Piel imperfect forms of these verbs tend to have the *yĕqaṭṭal* pattern, instead of *yĕqaṭṭēl* (e.g., יְשַׁלַּח; יְבַקַּע). In pause, however, the *yĕqaṭṭēl* pattern is found, but, of course, with the *furtive páṭaḥ* (e.g., יְשַׁלֵּחַ; יְבַקֵּעַ).

**e.** III-Hē Verbs

The imperfect forms of these verbs are regular for their type (see XIX.3). The Piel imperfect of גָּלָה (to uncover) is inflected as follows.

| | | | |
|---|---|---|---|
| *3 ms* | יְגַלֶּה | *3 mp* | יְגַלּוּ |
| *3 fs* | תְּגַלֶּה | *3 fp* | תְּגַלֶּ֫ינָה |
| *2 ms* | תְּגַלֶּה | *2 mp* | תְּגַלּוּ |
| *2 fs* | תְּגַלִּי | *2 fp* | תְּגַלֶּ֫ינָה |
| *1 cs* | אֲגַלֶּה | *1 cp* | נְגַלֶּה |

**f.** I-Wāw Verbs

Original I-Wāw verbs merge with those of I-Yōḏ in the imperfect, even though the first radical (original **w*) is no longer in the initial position (IV.2.c.ii). Thus, we get forms like יְיַסֵּר (he will discipline), instead of *יְוַסֵּר, as one might expect. Otherwise, the Piel imperfect of I-Wāw verbs is inflected regularly.

## 2. The Piel Jussive, Wāw-Consecutive, and Cohortative

**a.** The Piel jussive and Wāw-consecutive forms are predictable. In general they are similar to their corresponding imperfect forms (XVIII.4.b). The forms of III-Hē verbs, however, are without the final Hē (XX.4.d.i). As a result of this loss of Hē, the *dāgēš* is also lost because Hebrew does not tolerate a word ending in a doubled consonant (II.6.b.i. Note), e.g., *יְגַלּ > יְגַל. The resulting forms, thus, are without the expected doubling, the most conspicuous marker of the Piel verbal pattern. The *šĕwāʾ* under the preformative and the *a*-vowel, however, remain as valuable indicators.

**b.** The Piel cohortative is regular: אֲקַטְּלָה.

## 3. The Piel Imperative

We learned in XXI.3 that the Qal imperative forms are like their corresponding forms in the imperfect, except that the preformative is lacking in the imperative. The Piel imperative forms, likewise, correspond to the forms of the imperfect – minus the preformative.

The following is a synopsis of the Piel imperative forms.

| *Root* | בקשׁ | מאן | מהר | שׁלח | מלא | גלה | יסר |
|---|---|---|---|---|---|---|---|
| *ms* | בַּקֵּשׁ | מָאֵן | מַהֵר | שַׁלַּח | מַלֵּא | גַּלֵּה | יַסֵּר |
| *fs* | בַּקְּשִׁי | מָאֲנִי | מַהֲרִי | שַׁלְּחִי | מַלְּאִי | גַּלִּי | יַסְּרִי |
| *mp* | בַּקְּשׁוּ | מָאֲנוּ | מַהֲרוּ | שַׁלְּחוּ | מַלְּאוּ | גַּלּוּ | יַסְּרוּ |
| *fp* | בַּקֵּשְׁנָה | מָאֵנָּה | מַהֵרְנָה | שַׁלַּחְנָה | מַלֶּאנָה | גַּלֶּינָה | יַסֵּרְנָה |

*Note*: In some verbs, the *dāgēš* may be lost (VI.7), e.g., *מַלְּאוּ > מַלְאוּ (fill!). On the other hand, we have forms like שַׁלְּחוּ (send!), where the *dāgēš* is retained. Moreover, we get the form בַּקְּשׁוּ (seek!), even though the 2 mp imperfect is תְּבַקְשׁוּ (with loss of the *dāgēš*). The ms Piel imperative may also take the final ָה– (XXI.4). In that case, the *ē*-vowel under the second radical reduces to *šĕwāʾ*: thus, סַפֵּר but סַפְּרָה (tell!); מַהֵר but מַהֲרָה (hurry!).

## 4. The Piel Infinitives

There is normally no distinction in form between the Piel infinitive absolute and the infinitive construct; the form *qaṭṭēl* may be either absolute or construct.

| *Abs.* | *Cs.* | *Cs. with Suffixes* |
|---|---|---|
| גַּדֵּל | גַּדֵּל | גַּדֶּלְךָ, גַּדְּלוֹ |
| בָּרֵךְ | בָּרֵךְ | בָּרֶכְךָ, בָּרֲכוֹ |
| בַּעֵר | בַּעֵר | בַּעֶרְךָ, בַּעֲרוֹ |
| שַׁלֵּחַ | שַׁלַּח | שַׁלַּחֲךָ, שַׁלְּחוֹ |
| קַנֹּא | קַנֵּא | קַנַּאֲךָ, קַנְּאוֹ |
| צַוֵּה | צַוּוֹת | צַוּוֹתְךָ, צַוּוֹתוֹ |
| יַסֹּר | יַסֵּר | יַסֶּרְךָ, יַסֵּרוֹ |

*Notes*:

i. Besides the regular *qaṭṭēl* infinitive absolute, a *qaṭṭōl* type is attested for a few verbs (e.g., קַנֹּא; יַסֹּר).

ii. The infinitive construct of III-Guttural verbs is usually like שַׁלַּח, but the form for זָבַח (to sacrifice) is זַבֵּחַ.

iii. For III-Hē verbs, in addition to the infinitive absolute of the צַוֵּה type, there is also קַוֹּה.

iv. The infinitive absolute form מַהֵר is used as an adverb meaning "quickly."

## 5. Synopsis of Verbs in Piel

The following is a synopsis of the forms of the verbs in Piel.

| *Root* | *Perf.* | *Impf.* | *Juss.* | *Impv.* | *Inf. Abs.* | *Inf. Cs.* | *Ptc.* |
|---|---|---|---|---|---|---|---|
| בקשׁ | בִּקֵּשׁ | יְבַקֵּשׁ | יְבַקֵּשׁ | בַּקֵּשׁ | בַּקֵּשׁ | בַּקֵּשׁ | מְבַקֵּשׁ |
| מאן | מֵאֵן | יְמָאֵן | יְמָאֵן | מָאֵן | מָאֵן | מָאֵן | מְמָאֵן |
| מהר | מִהַר | יְמַהֵר | יְמַהֵר | מַהֵר | מַהֵר | מַהֵר | מְמַהֵר |
| שׁלח | שִׁלַּח | יְשַׁלַּח | יְשַׁלַּח | שַׁלַּח | שַׁלֵּחַ | שַׁלַּח | מְשַׁלֵּחַ |
| מלא | מִלֵּא | יְמַלֵּא | יְמַלֵּא | מַלֵּא | מַלֹּא | מַלֵּא | מְמַלֵּא |
| גלה | גִּלָּה | יְגַלֶּה | יְגַל | גַּלֵּה/גַּל | גַּלֵּה/גָּלוֹ | גַּלּוֹת | מְגַלֶּה |
| יסר | יִסַּר | יְיַסֵּר | יְיַסֵּר | יַסֵּר | יַסֹּר | יַסֵּר | מְיַסֵּר |

## 6. The Numerals

There are two sets of numerals in Hebrew: the cardinals (one, two, three, etc.) and the ordinals (first, second, third, etc.). In each set there are masculine and feminine forms. The cardinals also have absolute and construct forms.

**a.** The Cardinal Numbers

**i.** one to ten

| | *Masculine* | | *Feminine* | |
|---|---|---|---|---|
| | *Abs.* | *Cs.* | *Abs.* | *Cs.* |
| *one* | אֶחָד | אַחַד | אַחַת | אַחַת |
| *two* | שְׁנַ֫יִם | שְׁנֵי | שְׁתַּ֫יִם | שְׁתֵּי |
| *three* | שָׁלֹשׁ | שְׁלֹשׁ | שְׁלֹשָׁה | שְׁלֹ֫שֶׁת |
| *four* | אַרְבַּע | אַרְבַּע | אַרְבָּעָה | אַרְבַּ֫עַת |
| *five* | חָמֵשׁ | חֲמֵשׁ | חֲמִשָּׁה | חֲמֵ֫שֶׁת |
| *six* | שֵׁשׁ | שֵׁשׁ | שִׁשָּׁה | שֵׁ֫שֶׁת |
| *seven* | שֶׁ֫בַע | שְׁבַע | שִׁבְעָה | שִׁבְעַת |
| *eight* | שְׁמֹנֶה | שְׁמֹנֵה | שְׁמֹנָה | שְׁמֹנַת |
| *nine* | תֵּ֫שַׁע | תְּשַׁע | תִּשְׁעָה | תִּשְׁעַת |
| *ten* | עֶ֫שֶׂר | עֶ֫שֶׂר | עֲשָׂרָה | עֲשֶׂ֫רֶת |

*Notes:*

α. The Hebrew words for the number "one" are most frequently used as attributive adjectives. They normally follow the nouns they modify and agree with them in gender and definiteness.

אִישׁ אֶחָד one man — הָאִשָּׁה הָאַחַת one woman

הָאִישׁ הָאֶחָד the one man — הָאִשָּׁה הָאַחַת the one woman

These words may also be used as substantives in the construct state. In such cases, the absolute noun will typically be plural.

| | | | |
|---|---|---|---|
| אַחַד הָאֲנָשִׁים | one of the men | אַחַת הַנָּשִׁים | one of the women |

β. The Hebrew words for the number "two" are substantives. They may be in construct or in apposition with other nouns. In either case, there is agreement of gender.

| | | | |
|---|---|---|---|
| שְׁנֵי אֲנָשִׁים | two men | שְׁתֵּי נָשִׁים | two women |
| שְׁנֵי הָאֲנָשִׁים | the two men | שְׁתֵּי הַנָּשִׁים | the two women |
| שְׁנֵי אֲנָשָׁיו | his two men | שְׁתֵּי נָשָׁיו | his two women |
| שְׁנַ֫יִם אֲנָשִׁים | two men | שְׁתַּ֫יִם נָשִׁים | two women |
| אֲנָשִׁים שְׁנַ֫יִם | two men | נָשִׁים שְׁתַּ֫יִם | two women |

Note that שְׁנֵי and שְׁתֵּי may take the suffixed pronoun, e.g., שְׁנֵיהֶם two of them; שְׁתֵּיהֶם two of them

γ. The Hebrew words for "three" through "ten" are also treated as substantives, but there is no agreement in gender. The forms are singular but the nouns (except for collectives) are plural. Moreover, the feminine form of the number is always used with the masculine noun, and the masculine form is always used with the feminine noun. The construct form always precedes the noun it modifies. The absolute, which is in apposition, usually also precedes the noun.

| | | | |
|---|---|---|---|
| שְׁלֹ֫שֶׁת אֲנָשִׁים | three men | שְׁלֹשׁ נָשִׁים | three women |
| שְׁלֹשָׁה אֲנָשִׁים | three men | שָׁלֹשׁ נָשִׁים | three women |

**ii.** eleven through nineteen

| *With mp nouns* | *With fp nouns* | |
|---|---|---|
| אַחַד עָשָׂר | אַחַת עֶשְׂרֵה | eleven |
| עַשְׁתֵּי עָשָׂר | עַשְׁתֵּי עֶשְׂרֵה | |
| שְׁנֵים עָשָׂר | שְׁתֵּים עֶשְׂרֵה | twelve |
| שְׁנֵי עָשָׂר | שְׁתֵּי עֶשְׂרֵה | |
| שְׁלֹשָׁה עָשָׂר | שְׁלֹשׁ עֶשְׂרֵה | thirteen |
| אַרְבָּעָה עָשָׂר | אַרְבַּע עֶשְׂרֵה | fourteen |
| … etc. | | |

**iii.** tens

עֶשְׂרִים twenty

שְׁלֹשִׁים thirty

אַרְבָּעִים forty

… etc.

**iv.** hundreds

מֵאָה (cs. מְאַת) one hundred

מָאתַיִם two hundred

שְׁלֹשׁ מֵאוֹת three hundred

אַרְבַּע מֵאוֹת four hundred

… etc.

**v.** thousands

אֶלֶף one thousand

אַלְפַּיִם two thousand

שְׁלֹשֶׁת אֲלָפִים three thousand

אַרְבַּעַת אֲלָפִים four thousand

… etc.

**vi.** tens of thousands, myriads

רִבּוֹת/רְבָבָה ten thousand

רִבּוֹתַ֫יִם twenty thousand

שְׁלֹשׁ רִבּוֹת thirty thousand

אַרְבַּע רִבּוֹת forty thousand

... etc.

**b.** The Ordinal Numbers

i. first to tenth

| *Masc.* | *Fem.* | |
|---|---|---|
| רִאשׁוֹן | רִאשׁוֹנָה | first |
| שֵׁנִי | שֵׁנִית | second |
| שְׁלִישִׁי | שְׁלִישִׁיָּה/שְׁלִישִׁית | third |
| רְבִיעִי | רְבִיעִית | fourth |
| חֲמִישִׁי | חֲמִישִׁית | fifth |
| שִׁשִּׁי | שִׁשִּׁית | sixth |
| שְׁבִיעִי | שְׁבִיעִית | seventh |
| שְׁמִינִי | שְׁמִינִית | eighth |
| תְּשִׁיעִי | תְּשִׁיעִית | ninth |
| עֲשִׂירִי | עֲשִׂירִיָּה/עֲשִׂירִית | tenth |

*Notes*:

α. The ordinal numbers are treated as attributive adjectives. They stand after the noun and agree with the noun in gender and, usually, in definiteness.

בֵּן שֵׁנִי a second son — בַּת שֵׁנִית a second daughter

β. The cardinal number אֶחָד (one) may occasionally be used instead of רִאשׁוֹן.

**ii.** eleventh and beyond

Beyond the first ten numbers, Hebrew uses the cardinals to serve the function of ordinals.

## 7. The Distributive

**a.** The distributive is expressed by the repetition of substantives.

| | |
|---|---|
| שְׁנַיִם שְׁנַיִם | two by two (Gen 7:9) |
| שָׁנָה שָׁנָה | year by year/each year (Deut 14:22) |
| יוֹם ׀ יוֹם | day after day/each day (Gen 39:10) |
| שֵׁשׁ כְּנָפַיִם שֵׁשׁ כְּנָפַיִם | six wings each (Isa 6:2) |

**b.** The preposition לְ may also be used to indicate the distributive.

| | |
|---|---|
| לִשְׁלֹשֶׁת יָמִים | every three days (Amos 4:4) |
| לְשָׁלֹשׁ שָׁנִים | every three years (1 Kgs 10:22) |

**c.** The noun **אִישׁ** may be used idiomatically for *each* one.

| | |
|---|---|
| אִישׁ־אִישׁ מִמְּלַאכְתּוֹ | each one from his task (Exod 36:4) |
| אִישׁ לִלְשֹׁנוֹ | each one by his own language (Gen 10:5) |
| אִישׁ חֲלֹמוֹ | each his own dream (Gen 40:5) |

When **אִישׁ** is used in this way, it may refer not only to men, but also to women and inanimate objects. Only infrequently is **אִשָּׁה** used in this manner.

Related to this use of **אִישׁ** are the expressions of reciprocity **אִישׁ ... אָחִיו** (lit.: each ... his brother) and **אִישׁ ... רֵעֵהוּ** (lit.: each ... his friend).

| | |
|---|---|
| וַיֹּאמְרוּ אִישׁ אֶל־אָחִיו | they said one to another ... (Exod 16:15) |
| וְכָשְׁלוּ אִישׁ־בְּאָחִיו | and they shall stumble over one another (Lev 26:37) |
| וַיִּשְׁאֲלוּ אִישׁ־לְרֵעֵהוּ | they asked each other (Exod 18:7) |

## Vocabulary

*Nouns*:

אָמָה (irreg. pl. אֲמָהוֹת) female slave

אֹרַח (pl. אֳרָחוֹת) path

גָּאוֹן pride. *Verb*: גָּאָה to be proud, arrogant

גִּבְעָה (pl. גְּבָעוֹת) hill

זְרוֹעַ (fs; pl. usually זְרוֹעוֹת) arm

מוֹפֵת (ms) sign, omen

פֶּסֶל idol

קָהָל assembly. *Verb*: קָהַל to assemble

שָׁוְא emptiness, vanity. *Idiom*: לַשָּׁוְא in vain

שׁוֹר (irreg. pl. שְׁוָרִים) bull

שְׂמֹאל left, left hand, left side

שַׁבָּת (ms or fs; pl. שַׁבָּתוֹת) Sabbath, rest

*Verbs*:

חָרָה to be(come) angry. *Idioms*: חָרָה אַף לX, X became angry (lit.: the nose of X became hot); hence, also חָרָה לX, X became angry; but חָרָה בּX, be/become angry with X

נָגַשׁ to draw near, approach

נָשַׁק to kiss (object marked by ל)

עוּד Hi.: to bear witness, testify. *Nouns*: עֵד witness; עֵדוֹת testimonies.

*Adjective*:

קַנָּא jealous. *Verb*: קָנָא Pi.: to be jealous, be zealous. *Noun*: קִנְאָה jealousy.

## Exercise 24

**a.** Write the following forms in Hebrew:

1. Pi. impf. 3 ms of בָּקַע
2. Pi. impf. 2 fs of בָּקַשׁ
3. Pi. inf. cs. of בָּקַשׁ
4. Pi. impv. ms of בָּקַשׁ
5. Pi. coh. 1 cs of בָּקַשׁ
6. Pi. inf. cs. of מָאַן
7. Pi. impf. 3 cp of מָאַן
8. Pi. impf. 3 mp of מָהַר
9. Pi. impv. ms of מָהַר
10. Pi. impv. 2 fs of מָהַר
11. Pi. inf. cs. of מָהַר
12. Pi. impf. 3 fp of מָהַר
13. Pi. impf. 3 ms of בָּרַךְ
14. Pi. impf. 1 cs of בָּרַךְ
15. Pi. inf. cs. of בָּרַךְ
16. Pi. impv. fs of בָּרַךְ
17. Pi. impv. mp of בָּרַךְ
18. Pi. impf. 3 ms of כָּסָה
19. Pi. impf. 1 cs of כָּסָה
20. Pi. inf. cs. of כָּסָה
21. Pi. impv. mp of כָּלָה
22. Pi. impv. ms of צָוָה
23. Pi. inf. cs. of צָוָה
24. Pi. juss. 3 ms of צָוָה
25. Pi. impv. ms of יָסַר
26. Pi. impf. 3 ms of נָשַׁק
27. Pi. impv. mp of נָשַׁק
28. Pi. act. ptc. fs of יָלַד
29. Pi. impf. 3 ms of גָּלָה
30. Pi. impv. fs of גָּלָה

**b.** Translate Deut 5:1–33 with the help of a dictionary.

*Notes*:

v 5: לְהַגִּיד to tell.

v 9: לֹא־תִשְׁתַּחֲוֶה you shall not bow down; וְלֹא תָעָבְדֵם and you shall not be made to serve them.

v 15: וַיֹּצִאֲךָ but (subject) brought you out.

v 16: יַאֲרִיכֻן (subject) may be prolonged.

v 21: וְלֹא תִתְאַוֶּה you shall not covet.

v 27: וְאַתְּ (read וְאַתָּ).

v 29: מִי־יִתֵּן would that (or “if only...”; a common idiom).

# Lesson XXV

## 1. The Hiphil Imperfect

As in the Hiphil participle (XVI.12), the characteristic *h* is no longer apparent in the Hiphil imperfect; it has dropped out probably in a manner similar to the disappearance of the *h* of the definite article after a prefixed preposition (VI.2.b): thus, *יְהַקְטִיל > יַקְטִיל.

**a.** Strong Verbs

Unlike the Qal imperfect (XVIII.2), there is no distinction between the imperfect of dynamic and stative verbs. The Hiphil imperfect of all strong verbs is inflected the same way.

| | | | |
|---|---|---|---|
| *3 ms* | יַקְטִיל | *3 mp* | יַקְטִ֫ילוּ |
| *3 fs* | תַּקְטִיל | *3 fp* | תַּקְטֵ֫לְנָה |
| *2 ms* | תַּקְטִיל | *2 mp* | תַּקְטִ֫ילוּ |
| *2 fs* | תַּקְטִ֫ילִי | *2 fp* | תַּקְטֵ֫לְנָה |
| *1 cs* | אַקְטִיל | *1 cp* | נַקְטִיל |

*Note*: Whereas the long *î* in the perfect appears only in the third person forms (XVI.1), it appears in all forms of the imperfect, except the 3 fp/2 fp.

**b.** I-Guttural Verbs

Unlike the Qal imperfect (XIX.1), there is no distinction in the Hiphil imperfect between verbs of the עָמַד type and those of the חָזַק and אָכַל types. The Hiphil imperfect of the I-Guttural verb עָמַד (to stand) is inflected as follows.

| | | | |
|---|---|---|---|
| *3 ms* | יַעֲמִיד | *3 mp* | יַעֲמִ֫ידוּ |
| *3 fs* | תַּעֲמִיד | *3 fp* | תַּעֲמֵ֫דְנָה |
| *2 ms* | תַּעֲמִיד | *2 mp* | תַּעֲמִ֫ידוּ |
| *2 fs* | תַּעֲמִ֫ידִי | *2 fp* | תַּעֲמֵ֫דְנָה |
| *1 cs* | אַעֲמִיד | *1 cp* | נַעֲמִיד |

*Note*: Even though the Qal imperfect of עָמַד also has the *a*-vowel in the preformative, there should be no confusion between the imperfect forms of Qal and Hiphil. The thematic vowel in the Hiphil imperfect is always *î* or *ē*, whereas in Qal it is always *ō* or *a*.

| *Qal* | | *Hiphil* | |
|---|---|---|---|
| יַעֲמֹד | he will stand | יַעֲמִיד | he will cause to stand |
| תַּעֲמֹ֫דְנָה | they/you will stand | תַּעֲמֵ֫דְנָה | they/you will cause to stand |

In the 1 cs forms, the distinction between the Qal and Hiphil is clear in the preformative, as well.

| *Qal* | | *Hiphil* | |
|---|---|---|---|
| אֶעֱמֹד | I will stand | אַעֲמִיד | I will cause to stand |

c. III-Guttural Verbs

The Hiphil imperfect forms of such verbs are predictable: the *furtive pátaḥ* appears, as expected, e.g., יַשְׁלִיחַ.

**d.** III-ʾÁlep̄ Verbs

The Hiphil imperfect forms of such verbs are regular, except that the 3 fp/2 fp form is תַּמְצֶ֫אנָה, not *תַּמְצֵ֫אנָה, as one might expect.

**e.** III-Hē Verbs

The Hiphil imperfect forms of such verbs are regular for their type (XIX.3). The Hiphil imperfect of III-Hē verbs רָבָה (to be many) and עָלָה (to go up) are inflected as follows.

| | | |
|---|---|---|
| *3 ms* | יַרְבֶּה | יַעֲלֶה |
| *3 fs* | תַּרְבֶּה | תַּעֲלֶה |
| *2 ms* | תַּרְבֶּה | תַּעֲלֶה |
| *2 fs* | תַּרְבִּי | תַּעֲלִי |
| *1 cs* | אַרְבֶּה | אַעֲלֶה |
| *3 mp* | יַרְבּוּ | יַעֲלוּ |
| *3 fp* | תַּרְבֶּ֫ינָה | תַּעֲלֶ֫ינָה |
| *2 mp* | תַּרְבּוּ | תַּעֲלוּ |
| *2 fp* | תַּרְבֶּ֫ינָה | תַּעֲלֶ֫ינָה |
| *1 cp* | נַרְבֶּה | נַעֲלֶה |

*Note*: Whereas the Hiphil imperfect of רָבָה (i.e., יַרְבֶּה) is easily distinguished from the Qal (i.e., יִרְבֶּה), the same is not true for doubly weak verbs that are both I-Guttural and III-Hē (like עָלָה). In the case of such doubly weak verbs, the Hiphil imperfect forms (e.g., יַעֲלֶה) are generally identical to their Qal counterparts; only in the 1 cs forms are they distinguished from one another, since the vowel in the preformative of the Hiphil is *a*, whereas it is *e* in Qal.

| *Qal* | | *Hiphil* | |
|---|---|---|---|
| אֶעֱלֶה | I will go up | אַעֲלֶה | I will cause to go up |

**f.** I-Wāw Verbs

Given what we have learned so far of the Hiphil of I-Wāw verbs (see XVI.8), the imperfect forms are predictable. The first radical (*w*) contracts with the *a*-vowel of the preformative to form the diphthong *ô*, in accordance with IV.2.c.iii.β. For the root ישׁב (original **wšb*, dwell, sit), therefore, we get **yawšīb* > *yôšîḇ*. Thus, the Hiphil imperfect forms are יוֹשִׁיב, תּוֹשִׁיב, and so forth.

*Note*: The verb הָלַךְ behaves like a I-Wāw verb (XIX.5.c); the imperfect forms are יוֹלִיךְ, תּוֹלִיךְ, and so forth.

**g.** I-Yōḏ Verbs

Given what we have learned so far of the Hiphil of I-Yōḏ verbs (XVI.9), the imperfect forms are predictable. The first radical (*y*) contracts with the *a*-vowel of the preformative to form the diphthong *ê*, in accordance with IV.2.c.iv.β. For the root יטב (to do well), therefore, we get **yayṭīb* > *yêṭîḇ*. Thus, the Hiphil imperfect forms are יֵיטִיב, תֵּיטִיב, and so forth.

**h.** I-Nûn Verbs

Given what we have learned so far of the Hiphil of I-Nûn verbs (XVI.7), the imperfect forms are predictable: the first radical *n* is assimilated into the next radical. For the root נָגַד (to tell), we get **yangīd* > *yaggîḏ*. Hence, we have the forms יַגִּיד, תַּגִּיד, and so forth. Doubly weak verbs that are both I-Nûn and III-Hē will, of course, show characteristics of both root types. Thus, for the root נָכָה (smite), the imperfect forms are יַכֶּה, תַּכֶּה, and so forth.

**j.** II-Wāw/Yōḏ Verbs

Whereas the II-Wāw and II-Yōḏ verbs are distinguished in the Qal imperfect (XIX.7.b), they are not distinguished in the Hiphil imperfect. The forms of the Hiphil imperfect of קוּם (to arise) and שִׂים (to place) are as follows.

| | | |
|---|---|---|
| *3 ms* | יָקִים | יָשִׂים |
| *3 fs* | תָּקִים | תָּשִׂים |
| *2 ms* | תָּקִים | תָּשִׂים |
| *2 fs* | תָּקִ֫ימִי | תָּשִׂ֫ימִי |
| *1 cs* | אָקִים | אָשִׂים |
| *3 mp* | יָקִ֫ימוּ | יָשִׂ֫ימוּ |
| *3 fp* | תְּקִימֶ֫ינָה | תְּשִׂימֶ֫ינָה |
| *2 mp* | תָּקִ֫ימוּ | תָּשִׂ֫ימוּ |
| *2 fp* | תְּקִימֶ֫ינָה | תְּשִׂימֶ֫ינָה |
| *1 cp* | נָקִים | נָשִׂים |

*Notes*:

i. Occasionally, a shorter form of the 3 fp/2 fp form is found, e.g., תָּקֵ֫מְנָה instead of תְּקִימֶ֫ינָה.

ii. The vowel of the preformative is normally ָ, but when it is propretonic (as when a suffix is added), it is reduced to ְ.

יָקִים but תְּקִימֶ֫ינָה (Hi. impf. 3 fp/2 fp)

יָקִים but יְקִימֶ֫נּוּ (Hi. impf. 3 ms + obj. sfx. 3 ms/1 cp)

אָבִיא but אֲבִיאֶ֫נּוּ (Hi. impf. 1 cs + obj. sfx. 3 ms)

## 2. The Hiphil Jussive, Wāw-Consecutive, and Cohortative

**a.** Unlike the Qal and Piel, the Hiphil jussive and Wāw-consecutive forms are clearly distinguished from their counterparts in the imperfect inflection.

**i.** In most cases, the difference is merely a shift from *yaqṭîl* to *yaqṭēl*.

| *Root* | *Impf.* | *Juss.* | *Wāw consec.* | *Meaning of root* |
|---|---|---|---|---|
| שׁמד | יַשְׁמִיד | יַשְׁמֵד | וַיַּשְׁמֵד | to destroy |
| נגד | יַגִּיד | יַגֵּד | וַיַּגֵּד | to tell |

**ii.** Verbs that are III-Gutturals prefer the *a*-vowel instead of *ē*.

| *Root* | *Impf.* | *Juss.* | *Wāw consec.* | *Meaning of root* |
|---|---|---|---|---|
| שׁלח | יַשְׁלִיחַ | יַשְׁלַח | וַיַּשְׁלַח | to send |
| נגע | יַגִּיעַ | יַגַּע | וַיַּגַּע | to touch |
| נוח | יָנִיחַ | יָנַח | וַיָּנַח | to rest |

**iii.** III-Hē verbs lose the final ה, and the accent is retracted.

| *Root* | *Impf.* | *Juss.* | *Wāw consec.* | *Meaning of root* |
|---|---|---|---|---|
| רבה | יַרְבֶּה | יֶרֶב | וַיֶּרֶב | to be many |
| עלה | יַעֲלֶה | יַעַל | וַיַּעַל | to go up |
| נכה | יַכֶּה | יַךְ | וַיַּךְ | to strike |

*Notes*:

α. The form יֶרֶב developed as follows: *yarbe(h)* > **yarb* (XX.4.d.i; XXI.1.a) > *yéreḇ*. We may note that the development of **yarb* > *yéreḇ* is analogous to the development of **malk* > *méleḵ* (see V.2.a). By the same token, the form יַעַל, because of the presence of the guttural, developed like **na*$^c$*r* > *ná*$^c$*ar* (V.2.a.Note): **ya*$^c$*l* > *yá*$^c$*al*.

β. The Hiphil forms can often be distinguished from the Qal (see XX.4.d).

| *Qal* | | *Hiphil* | |
|---|---|---|---|
| וַיִּ֫רֶב | and he became many | וַיֶּ֫רֶב | and he multiplied |

However, many forms cannot be distinguished.

| *Qal* | | *Hiphil* | |
|---|---|---|---|
| וַיַּ֫עַל | and he went up | וַיַּ֫עַל | and he caused to go up |
| וַיַּ֫רְא | and he saw | וַיַּ֫רְא | and he showed |

γ. The form יַךְ (let him strike) developed as follows: **yanke(h)* > *yakke(h)* (IV.2.b) > **yakk* > *yak̠* (V.1.a).

**iv.** I-Wāw verbs generally show retraction of the accent in the Wāw-consecutive forms, but not in the jussive.

| *Root* | *Impf.* | *Juss.* | *Wāw consec.* | *Meaning of root* |
|---|---|---|---|---|
| ישב | יוֹשִׁיב | יוֹשֵׁב | וַיּ֫וֹשֶׁב | to dwell |
| ידע | יוֹדִיעַ | יוֹדַע | וַיּ֫וֹדַע | to know |
| ירה | יוֹרֶה | יוֹר | וַיּוֹר | to throw |

**b.** The Hiphil cohortative is predictable: אַקְטִ֫ילָה.

## 3. The Hiphil Imperative

**a.** As we have already learned, the Qal and Piel imperatives are closely related to their corresponding imperfect forms. In fact, it looks as if the imperative form is the imperfect without the preformative.

| | *Impf.* | *Impv.* |
|---|---|---|
| *Qal* | תִּקְטֹל | קְטֹל |
| *Piel* | תְּקַטֵּל | קַטֵּל |

The Hiphil imperative may be thought of in the same way, but one should also remember that the characteristic *h* of the Hiphil has disappeared in the imperfect. For instance, the 2 fp imperfect תַּקְטֵ֫לְנָה is derived from an earlier form, *תְּהַקְטֵ֫לְנָה. Thus, the fp imperative is הַקְטֵ֫לְנָה. In other words, the imperative is still marked by the characteristic *h*, even though the imperfect is not. The Hiphil imperative of strong verbs, therefore, is inflected as follows.

| | | | |
|---|---|---|---|
| *ms* | הַקְטֵל | *mp* | הַקְטִ֫ילוּ |
| *fs* | הַקְטִ֫ילִי | *fp* | הַקְטֵ֫לְנָה |

*Note*: The ms imperative is הַקְטֵל, even though the 2 ms imperfect is תַּקְטִיל.

**b.** The forms of the Hiphil imperative are as follows.

| *Root* | *ms* | *fs* | *mp* | *fp* |
|---|---|---|---|---|
| שׁמד | הַשְׁמֵד | הַשְׁמִ֫ידִי | הַשְׁמִ֫ידוּ | הַשְׁמֵ֫דְנָה |
| עמד | הַעֲמֵד | הַעֲמִ֫ידִי | הַעֲמִ֫ידוּ | הַעֲמֵ֫דְנָה |
| שׁלח | הַשְׁלַח | הַשְׁלִ֫יחִי | הַשְׁלִ֫יחוּ | הַשְׁלַ֫חְנָה |
| מצא | הַמְצֵא | הַמְצִ֫יאִי | הַמְצִ֫יאוּ | הַמְצֶ֫אנָה |
| רבה | הַרְבֵּה | הַרְבִּי | הַרְבּוּ | הַרְבֶּ֫ינָה |
| נגד | הַגֵּד | הַגִּ֫ידִי | הַגִּ֫ידוּ | הַגֵּ֫דְנָה |
| ישׁב | הוֹשֵׁב | הוֹשִׁ֫יבִי | הוֹשִׁ֫יבוּ | הוֹשֵׁ֫בְנָה |
| יטב | הֵיטֵב | הֵיטִ֫יבִי | הֵיטִ֫יבוּ | הֵיטֵ֫בְנָה |
| קום | הָקֵם | הָקִ֫ימִי | הָקִ֫ימוּ | הָקֵ֫מְנָה |

## 4. The Hiphil Infinitives

Whereas in other verbal patterns, the infinitive construct form tends to coincide with the ms imperative, in the Hiphil it is the infinitive absolute that coincides with the ms imperative.

| *Root* | *Impv.* | *Inf. abs.* | *Inf. cs.* |
|---|---|---|---|
| שׁמד | הַשְׁמֵד | הַשְׁמֵד | הַשְׁמִיד |
| גלה | הַגְלֵה | הַגְלֵה | הַגְלוֹת |
| נגד | הַגֵּד | הַגֵּד | הַגִּיד |
| ישׁב | הוֹשֵׁב | הוֹשֵׁב | הוֹשִׁיב |
| קום | הָקֵם | הָקֵם | הָקִים |

*Note*: The infinitive absolute form הַרְבֵּה (from רָבָה *be numerous*) is often used adverbially, meaning "abundantly" or "frequently."

## 5. Synopsis of Verbs in Hiphil

The following is a synopsis of the principle forms of verbs in the Hiphil verbal pattern.

| *Root* | *Perf.* | *Impf.* | *Juss.* | *Impv.* | *Inf. abs.* | *Inf. cs.* | *Ptc.* |
|---|---|---|---|---|---|---|---|
| שׁמד | הִשְׁמִיד | יַשְׁמִיד | יַשְׁמֵד | הַשְׁמֵד | הַשְׁמֵד | הַשְׁמִיד | מַשְׁמִיד |
| עמד | הֶעֱמִיד | יַעֲמִיד | יַעֲמֵד | הַעֲמֵד | הַעֲמֵד | הַעֲמִיד | מַעֲמִיד |
| שׁלח | הִשְׁלִיחַ | יַשְׁלִיחַ | יַשְׁלַח | הַשְׁלַח | הַשְׁלֵחַ | הַשְׁלִיחַ | מַשְׁלִיחַ |
| מצא | הִמְצִיא | יַמְצִיא | יַמְצֵא | הַמְצֵא | הַמְצֵא | הַמְצִיא | מַמְצִיא |
| רבה | הִרְבָּה | יַרְבֶּה | יֶ֫רֶב | הַרְבֵּה | הַרְבֵּה | הַרְבּוֹת | מַרְבֶּה |
| נגד | הִגִּיד | יַגִּיד | יַגֵּד | הַגֵּד | הַגֵּד | הַגִּיד | מַגִּיד |
| ישׁב | הוֹשִׁיב | יוֹשִׁיב | יוֹשֵׁב | הוֹשֵׁב | הוֹשֵׁב | הוֹשִׁיב | מוֹשִׁיב |
| יטב | הֵיטִיב | יֵיטִיב | יֵיטֵב | הֵיטֵב | הֵיטֵב | הֵיטִיב | מֵיטִיב |
| קום | הֵקִים | יָקִים | יָקֵם | הָקֵם | הָקֵם | הָקִים | מֵקִים |

## 6. Translation of ו

We have learned so far that the conjunction ו (in its various forms) means "and" or "but." However, it must also be apparent that ו cannot always be translated just so.

**a.** Often one must rely on the context to tell what the function of the ו is. It is, in fact, used in a variety of ways.

**i.** *copulative*, meaning "and"

מֹשֶׁה וְאַהֲרֹן  Moses *and* Aaron (Exod 4:29)

*Note*: In a series of nouns, the copulative ו is usually repeated before each noun. Occasionally, however, it may appear only with the last noun.

**ii.** *alternative*, meaning "or"

עַבְדְּךָ וַאֲמָתְךָ  your male servant *or* female servant (Exod 20:10)

**iii.** *adversative*, meaning "but"

יֶלֶד מִסְכֵּן וְחָכָם  a poor *but* wise youth (Eccl 4:13)

**iv.** *explicative*, meaning "that is"

בִּכְלִי הָרֹעִים אֲשֶׁר־לוֹ וּבַיַּלְקוּט  in the shepherds' vessel which he had, *that is*, in his pouch (1 Sam 17:40)

**v.** *circumstantial*, meaning "while," "when," or "with"

וַיֵּלֶךְ וְכָל־טוּב אֲדֹנָיו בְּיָדוֹ  and he went *with* all the wealth of his master in his charge (Gen 24:10)

וַיְהִי כְּשָׁמְעֲכֶם אֶת־הַקּוֹל מִתּוֹךְ הַחֹשֶׁךְ וְהָהָר בֹּעֵר בָּאֵשׁ  and when you heard the voice from the midst of the darkness, *while* the mountain was burning with fire (Deut 5:23)

דֹּבְרֵי שָׁלוֹם עִם־רֵעֵיהֶם
וְרָעָה בִּלְבָבָם

those who speak peace with their friends, *while* evil is in their heart (Ps 28:3)

In some instances, it is appropriate to translate the ו as if it were a relative particle.

וּלְרִבְקָה אָח וּשְׁמוֹ לָבָן

Now Rebecca had a brother *whose* name was Laban (Gen 24:29)

**b.** When ו links verbal clauses in a narrative sequence, there are often more clues as to their function.

**i.** ו + verb that is inflected for number and gender (including the Wāw-consecutive) indicates a *conjunctive* sequence. In this case, the conjunction may be translated as "and," "then," "that," or "so that" – according to the rules given in XX.2–3, 5; XXI.8; XXIII.3.e.

**ii.** ו + any other form – including participles, infinitives, the negative particle לֹא, and so forth – indicates a *disjunctive*. In that case, the ו may serve several functions (see XIII.4.b; XX.6).

**α.** to highlight contrast
**β.** to introduce a new scene
**γ.** to introduce a parenthetical comment

*Note*: Occasionally the disjunctive ו may clarify its preceding clause by giving a reason.

אַל־תְּאַחֲרוּ אֹתִי וַיהוָה
הִצְלִיחַ דַּרְכִּי

Do not detain me *since* YHWH has prospered my way (Gen 24:56)

**c.** In poetic texts, ו sometimes introduces a comparison.

שָׁמַיִם לָרוּם וָאָרֶץ לָעֹמֶק
וְלֵב מְלָכִים אֵין חֵקֶר

(As) the heaven for height and the earth for depth, *so* is the mind of kings unsearchable (Prov 25:3)

**d.** Sometimes ו is purely stylistic and should not be translated.

| | |
|---|---|
| וְעַתָּה שְׁמַע יַעֲקֹב עַבְדִּי וְיִשְׂרָאֵל בָּחַרְתִּי בוֹ | But now hear, O Jacob, my servant, Israel whom I have chosen (Isa 44:1) |

## Vocabulary

*Nouns*:

אֶרֶז cedar

בָּחוּר young man

בְּתוּלָה young woman

גַּיְא (pl. גֵּאָיוֹת) valley

חַג festival

יָרֵחַ moon

כּוֹכָב star

לְאֹם (pl.: לְאֻמִּים) people

מִזְרָח sunrise, east

מָרוֹם height, high place. *Verb*: רוּם to be high

נָשִׂיא prince

פַּעַם step, occurrence

שֻׁלְחָן table

*Verbs*:

הָגָה to mumble, meditate

נָחַם Pi.: to comfort

סָלַח to forgive

עָרַךְ to arrange, lay out

# Exercise 25

**a.** Write the following forms in Hebrew:

1. Hi. impf. 3 mp of שָׁמַע
2. Hi. impv. mp of שָׁמַע
3. Hi. impf. 3 fp of עָמַד
4. Qal impf. 3 fp of עָמַד
5. Hi. impf. 3 ms of עָלָה
6. Qal impf. 3 ms of עָלָה
7. Hi. impv. fs of עָלָה
8. Hi. impf. 1 cs of עָלָה
9. Qal impf. 1 cs of עָלָה
10. Hi. impf. 1 cs of יָשַׁב
11. Hi. impf. 1 cs of שׁוּב
12. Qal impf. 1 cs of שׁוּב
13. Hi. impv. ms of שׁוּב
14. Hi. inf. cs. of עָלָה
15. Hi. inf. abs. of עָלָה
16. Hi. impf. 3 ms of נָכָה
17. Hi. impf. 1 cs of נָכָה
18. Hi. juss. 3 ms of נָכָה
19. Hi. impf. 1 cp of נָגַד
20. Hi. impv. ms of נָגַד
21. Hi. inf. abs. of נָגַד
22. Hi. impf. 3 fp of בּוֹא
23. Qal impf. 3 fp of בּוֹא
24. Hi. juss. 3 ms of גָּלָה
25. Hi. juss. 3 ms of עָלָה
26. Qal juss. 3 ms of עָלָה
27. Hi. inf. cs. of יָטַב
28. Hi. impv. fs of יָטַב
29. Hi. impv. ms of רָבָה
30. Hi. inf. cs. of רָבָה

**b.** Translate Psalm 1 with the help of a dictionary.

**c.** Translate Psalm 23 with the help of a dictionary.

*Note*:

v 3: יְשׁוֹבֵב he restores.

**d.** Translate Psalm 148 with the help of a dictionary.

*Notes*:

v 5: וְנִבְרָאוּ and they were created.

v 13: נִשְׂגָּב exalted.

# Lesson XXVI

## 1. The Niphal Pattern

The Niphal verbal pattern is characterized by the presence of a Nûn that is either prefixed or infixed and assimilated.

**a.** The Nûn is prefixed in the perfect, participle, and one form of the infinitive absolute: נִקְטַל, נִקְטָל, נִקְטֹל.

**b.** The Nûn is infixed and assimilated in the imperfect, imperative, the infinitive construct, and one form of the infinitive absolute: יִקָּטֵל (< *יִנְקָטֵל), הִקָּטֵל (< *הִנְקָטֵל), etc.

## 2. The Meaning of Verbs in Niphal

**a.** *Reflexive.* The Niphal verb frequently indicates action for or concerning oneself. Thus, the subject is also the object of the verb.

נִמְכַּר he sold himself

נִסְגַּר he shut himself in

Also subsumed under this category are a few verbs that may be regarded as *tolerative*, where the subject allows an action to affect himself or herself.

נִזְהַר he let himself be warned

נִדְרַשׁ he let himself be sought

**b.** *Reciprocal.* In some instances, the Niphal verb suggests reciprocity.

נִדְבְּרוּ they spoke with one another

נִלְחֲמוּ they fought with one another

**c.** *Passive.* The Niphal is frequently used as the passive of a verb that is active in Qal.

נִקְבַּר he was buried　　נֶאֱכַל he was devoured

In many instances, the Niphal passive is impersonal – no subject is explicitly stated.

נֶאֱמַר it was said　　　　נֶאֱכַל it was eaten

**d.** *Resultative.* In some instances, the Niphal indicates a state resulting from the action produced by the verb. In this usage, the Niphal sometimes indicates potential.

נֶאֱכַל is eaten > is edible

נִרְאָה is seen > is visible

Since the Niphal may indicate resulting state, it is not surprising that many Niphal participles function as adjectives.

| *Root* | *Niphal Participle* |
|---|---|
| ירא to fear, be afraid | נוֹרָא feared, terrible |
| בין to perceive | נָבוֹן perceptive |
| אמן to be firm | נֶאֱמָן firm |

**e.** *Middle.* Some verbs are used in such a way that the object appears to be the active subject.

וְנִפְקְחוּ עֵינֵיכֶם　and your eyes *will open* (Gen 3:5)

נִפְתְּחוּ הַשָּׁמַיִם　the heavens *opened* (Ezek 1:1)

וְלֹא־נִבְקַע עָנָן　but no cloud *split open* (Job 26:8)

Although it is possible to interpret the same verbs in other contexts as passives (i.e., "to be opened," "to be split open"), they are clearly not passive in the above examples. Whereas an agentive subject is involved in the passive, there is no agent in the middle. The point in the middle verb is not that someone acts on the object (active), nor that the object is acted upon (passive), but that the object acts *on its own* as the subject.

## 3. The Niphal Perfect

### a. Strong Verbs

The original **naqṭal* pattern has been dissimilated to *niqṭal*. The Niphal perfect of the strong root, then, is inflected as follows.

| | | | |
|---|---|---|---|
| *3 ms* | נִקְטַל | *3 cp* | נִקְטְלוּ |
| *3 fs* | נִקְטְלָה | | |
| *2 ms* | נִקְטַ֫לְתָּ | *2 mp* | נִקְטַלְתֶּם |
| *2 fs* | נִקְטַלְתְּ | *2 fp* | נִקְטַלְתֶּן |
| *1 cs* | נִקְטַ֫לְתִּי | *1 cp* | נִקְטַ֫לְנוּ |

### b. I-Guttural Verbs

When the first radical is a guttural, one usually finds the composite *šĕwāʾ* ֱ, instead of the silent ְ. Moreover, the vowel with the prefixed Nûn is influenced by the composite *šĕwāʾ* ֱ, so that it is changed from ִ to ֶ (thus, נֶעֱמַד). The Niphal perfect of עָמַד (to stand), then, is inflected as follows.

| | | | |
|---|---|---|---|
| *3 ms* | נֶעֱמַד | *3 cp* | נֶעֶמְדוּ |
| *3 fs* | נֶעֶמְדָה | | |
| *2 ms* | נֶעֱמַ֫דְתָּ | *2 mp* | נֶעֱמַדְתֶּם |
| *2 fs* | נֶעֱמַדְתְּ | *2 fp* | נֶעֱמַדְתֶּן |
| *1 cs* | נֶעֱמַ֫דְתִּי | *1 cp* | נֶעֱמַ֫דְנוּ |

*Notes*:

i. The 3 fs נֶעֶמְדָה and 3 cp נֶעֶמְדוּ are formed in accordance with XIX.1.d.i.

ii. Some verbs tolerate a silent ◌ְ under the guttural, but the vowel under the Nûn is still ◌ֶ.

נֶחְשַׁב (he reckoned)    נֶחְבָּא (he hid himself)

iii. Occasionally, the original *na-* prefix prevails.

נַחְבֵּאתָ (you hid yourself).

**c.** I-Wāw Verbs

Since the original pattern was **naqṭal*, we understand the Niphal perfect form *nôlaḏ* (from ילד < original *ולד) to have developed as follows: **nawlaḏ* > *nôlaḏ* (IV.2.c.iii.b). The Niphal perfect of יָלַד (to bear), then, is inflected as follows.

| | | | |
|---|---|---|---|
| *3 ms* | נוֹלַד | *3 cp* | נוֹלְדוּ |
| *3 fs* | נוֹלְדָה | | |
| *2 ms* | נוֹלַדְתָּ | *2 mp* | נוֹלַדְתֶּם |
| *2 fs* | נוֹלַדְתְּ | *2 fp* | נוֹלַדְתֶּן |
| *1 cs* | נוֹלַדְתִּי | *1 cp* | נוֹלַדְנוּ |

**d.** II-Wāw/Yōḏ Verbs

II-Wāw and II-Yōḏ verbs are not distinguished from one another in the Niphal perfect. The Niphal perfect of כּוּן (to prepare) is inflected as follows.

| | | | |
|---|---|---|---|
| *3 ms* | נָכוֹן | *3 cp* | נָכוֹנוּ |
| *3 fs* | נָכוֹנָה | | |
| *2 ms* | נְכוּנוֹתָ | *2 mp* | נְכוּנוֹתֶם |
| *2 fs* | נְכוּנוֹת | *2 fp* | נְכוּנוֹתֶן |
| *1 cs* | נְכוּנוֹתִי | *1 cp* | נְכוּנוֹנוּ |

*Note*: An additional *ô* (וֹ) precedes every consonantal afformative, thus opening the syllable and causing the afformative ת to be spirantized (see XVI.10.ii).

Other weak roots are regular for their types (see XIV.2,3).

## 4. The Niphal Imperfect

**a.** Strong Verbs

The characteristic Nûn is infixed and assimilated: **yinqāṭēl* > *yiqqāṭēl*. The Niphal imperfect of the strong verb, then, is inflected as follows.

| | | | |
|---|---|---|---|
| *3 ms* | יִקָּטֵל | *3 mp* | יִקָּטְלוּ |
| *3 fs* | תִּקָּטֵל | *3 fp* | תִּקָּטַ֫לְנָה |
| *2 ms* | תִּקָּטֵל | *2 mp* | תִּקָּטְלוּ |
| *2 fs* | תִּקָּטְלִי | *2 fp* | תִּקָּטַ֫לְנָה |
| *1 cs* | אֶקָּטֵל | *1 cp* | נִקָּטֵל |

**b.** I-Guttural Verbs

Since gutturals and Rêš cannot take the strong *dāgēš*, the *i*-vowel in the preformative is compensatorily lengthened. The Niphal imperfect of עָזַב (to forsake) is as follows.

| | | | |
|---|---|---|---|
| *3 ms* | יֵעָזֵב | *3 mp* | יֵעָזְבוּ |
| *3 fs* | תֵּעָזֵב | *3 fp* | תֵּעָזַ֫בְנָה |
| *2 ms* | תֵּעָזֵב | *2 mp* | תֵּעָזְבוּ |
| *2 fs* | תֵּעָזְבִי | *2 fp* | תֵּעָזַ֫בְנָה |
| *1 cs* | אֵעָזֵב | *1 cp* | נֵעָזֵב |

**c.** I-Wāw Verbs

Since the original first radical (ו) is preceded, it is retained (IV.2.c.ii). The Niphal imperfect of יָלַד (to bear) is inflected as follows.

| | | | |
|---|---|---|---|
| *3 ms* | יִוָּלֵד | *3 mp* | יִוָּֽלְדוּ |
| *3 fs* | תִּוָּלֵד | *3 fp* | תִּוָּלַ֫דְנָה |
| *2 ms* | תִּוָּלֵד | *2 mp* | תִּוָּֽלְדוּ |
| *2 fs* | תִּוָּֽלְדִי | *2 fp* | תִּוָּלַ֫דְנָה |
| *1 cs* | אֶוָּלֵד | *1 cp* | נִוָּלֵד |

**d.** II-Wāw/Yōḏ Verbs

II-Wāw and II-Yōḏ verbs are not distinguished from one another. The Niphal imperfect of כּוּן (prepare) is inflected as follows.

| | | | |
|---|---|---|---|
| *3 ms* | יִכּוֹן | *3 mp* | יִכּ֫וֹנוּ |
| *3 fs* | תִּכּוֹן | *3 fp* | –not attested– |
| *2 ms* | תִּכּוֹן | *2 mp* | תִּכּ֫וֹנוּ |
| *2 fs* | תִּכּ֫וֹנִי | *2 fp* | –not attested– |
| *1 cs* | אִכּוֹן | *1 cp* | נִכּוֹן |

Other weak roots are regular for their types (see XIX.2,3).

## 5. The Niphal Imperative

There is an anomalous *hi-* prefix in the Niphal imperative forms, which sometimes causes confusion with the *hi-* prefix in the Hiphil. The difference between the Hiphil imperative and Niphal imperative forms, however, is in the assimilated Nûn in the first radical.

The following is a synopsis of the Niphal imperative forms.

| *Roots* | *ms* | *fs* | *mp* | *fp* |
|---|---|---|---|---|
| שׁמר | הִשָּׁמֵר | הִשָּֽׁמְרִי | הִשָּֽׁמְרוּ | הִשָּׁמַ֫רְנָה |
| עזב | הֵעָזֵב | הֵעָֽזְבִי | הֵעָֽזְבוּ | הֵעָזַ֫בְנָה |
| שׁמע | הִשָּׁמַע | הִשָּֽׁמְעִי | הִשָּֽׁמְעוּ | הִשָּׁמַ֫עְנָה |
| מלא | הִמָּלֵא | הִמָּֽלְאִי | הִמָּֽלְאוּ | הִמָּלֶ֫אנָה |
| גלה | הִגָּלֵה | הִגָּלִי | הִגָּלוּ | הִגָּלֶ֫ינָה |
| נתן | הִנָּתֵן | הִנָּֽתְנִי | הִנָּֽתְנוּ | הִנָּתַ֫נָּה |
| ילד | הִוָּלֵד | הִוָּֽלְדִי | הִוָּֽלְדוּ | הִוָּלַ֫דְנָה |
| כון | הִכּוֹן | הִכּ֫וֹנִי | הִכּ֫וֹנוּ | – |

## 6. The Niphal Infinitives

**a.** There are two forms of the infinitive absolute, one with a prefixed Nûn and the other with an infixed and assimilated Nûn: נִקְטֹל and הִקָּטֹל.

**b.** The infinitive construct is הִקָּטֵל.

The infinitives of weak roots are regular for their types (see XXII.2.b; XXIII.2).

## 7. The Niphal Participle

**a.** The Niphal participle of the strong verb is inflected as follows.

| | | | |
|---|---|---|---|
| *ms* | נִקְטָל | *mp* | נִקְטְלִים |
| *fs* | נִקְטֶ֫לֶת | *fp* | נִקְטְלוֹת |

*Note*: The ms participle נִקְטָל should not to be confused with the perfect 3 ms נִקְטַל; the former has a long *ā*. Since the vowel before III-ʾÁlep̄ is lengthened (*נִמְצַא > נִמְצָא), however, the participle of III-ʾÁlep̄ verbs cannot be distinguished from the perfect 3 ms. The ms participle of II-Wāw/Yōḏ verbs (נָכוֹן) also cannot be distinguished from the perfect 3 ms (נָכוֹן).

**b.** The Niphal participle of the III-Hē verb גָּלָה (to uncover) is inflected as follows.

| | | | |
|---|---|---|---|
| *ms* | נִגְלֶה | *mp* | נִגְלִים |
| *fs* | נִגְלָה | *fp* | נִגְלוֹת |

## 8. Synopsis of Verbs in Niphal

| *Root* | *Perf.* | *Impf.* | *Impv.* | *Inf. Abs.* | *Inf. Cs.* | *Ptc.* |
|---|---|---|---|---|---|---|
| שׁמר | נִשְׁמַר | יִשָּׁמֵר | הִשָּׁמֵר | הִשָּׁמֹר/נִשְׁמֹר | הִשָּׁמֵר | נִשְׁמָר |
| עזב | נֶעֱזַב | יֵעָזֵב | הֵעָזֵב | הֵעָזֹב/נַעֲזֹב | הֵעָזֵב | נֶעֱזָב |
| שׁבע | נִשְׁבַּע | יִשָּׁבַע | הִשָּׁבַע | הִשָּׁבֵעַ/נִשְׁבּוֹעַ | הִשָּׁבַע | נִשְׁבָּע |
| מלא | נִמְלָא | יִמָּלֵא | הִמָּלֵא | הִמָּלֵא/נִמְלֹא | הִמָּלֵא | נִמְלָא |
| גלה | נִגְלָה | יִגָּלֶה | הִגָּלֵה | הִגָּלֵה/נִגְלֹה | הִגָּלוֹת | נִגְלֶה |
| נתן | נִתַּן | יִנָּתֵן | הִנָּתֵן | הִנָּתֵן/נִתּוֹן | הִנָּתֵן | נִתָּן |
| ילד | נוֹלַד | יִוָּלֵד | הִוָּלֵד | –not attested– | הִוָּלֵד | נוֹלָד |
| כון | נָכוֹן | יִכּוֹן | הִכּוֹן | הִכּוֹן/נָכוֹן | הִכּוֹן | נָכוֹן |

## Vocabulary

*Nouns*:

אַרְיֵה (also אֲרִי; pl.: אֲרָיִים) lion

בֶּ֫טֶן (fs; with sfx: בִּטְנוֹ) belly, body

מוֹעֵד meeting-place, assembly

עֵז (fs; fp.: עִזִּים) (she-)goat

*Verbs*:

חָרַם Hi.: to devote to the ban, utterly destroy. *Noun*: חֵ֫רֶם ban

יָנַק to suckle. *Noun*: יוֹנֵק infant

יָתַר to remain; Ni.: to be left

כּוּן Ni.: to be prepared, established, firm; Hi.: to prepare, install, establish. *Noun*: מָכוֹן place, support

לָחַם to do battle; Ni.: to fight

נָבָא Ni.: to prophesy

נָדַח Ni.: to be scattered, go astray; Hi.: to scatter, disperse

סָתַר Ni.: to hide oneself, be hidden; Hi.: to hide

פּוּץ to be dispersed, scattered

פָּלָא Ni.: to be marvelous, extraordinary (fp. ptc: נִפְלָאוֹת wonders). *Noun*: פֶּ֫לֶא wonder

קָרָה to encounter, meet (= II קָרָא; inf. cs. לִקְרַאת to meet)

שָׁמַד Ni.: to be exterminated; Hi.: to exterminate

# Exercise 26

**a.** Write the following forms in Hebrew:

1. Ni. perf. 3 ms of שָׁמַע
2. Ni. ptc. ms of שָׁמַע
3. Ni. perf. 3 fs of אָסַף
4. Ni. perf. 3 cp of אָסַף
5. Ni. inf. cs. of עָזַב
6. Ni. impv. fs of אָסַף
7. Ni. perf. 3 ms of כּוּן
8. Ni. ptc. ms of כּוּן
9. Ni. perf. 3 fs of פּוּץ
10. Ni. ptc. fs of פּוּץ
11. Ni. impf. 3 fp of פּוּץ
12. Ni. impf. 1 cs of פּוּץ
13. Ni. perf. 2 mp of פּוּץ
14. Ni. impf. 3 mp of לָחַם
15. Ni. Perf. 1 cs of לָחַם
16. Ni. Perf. 1 cs of שָׁבַע
17. Ni. impv. mp of שָׁבַע
18. Ni. Perf. 3 ms of מָנָה
19. Ni. inf. cs. of מָנָה
20. Ni. impf. 3 cp of מָנָה
21. Ni. perf. 2 ms of נָבָא
22. Ni. impv. ms of נָבָא
23. Ni. inf. cs. of נָבָא
24. Ni. impf. 3 cp of נָבָא
25. Ni. perf. 3 fs of יָדַע
26. Ni. ptc. ms of יָדַע
27. Ni. inf. cs. of יָדַע
28. Ni. perf. 3 cp of נָטַע

**b.** Translate Genesis 32 with the help of a dictionary.

*Notes*:

v 5: וָאֵחַר < וָאֶאֱחַר*

v 8: וַיֵּצֶר לוֹ and he became anxious.

# Lesson XXVII

## 1. The Hithpael Pattern

The Hithpael verbal pattern is characterized throughout by an infixed *t* and the doubling of the second radical: *hiṯqaṭṭēl.*

## 2. The Meaning of Hithpael Verbs

**a.** *Reflexive.* The Hithpael verb frequently describes action on or for oneself – that is, the subject of the verb is also its object.

הִתְחַבְּאוּ they hid themselves

הִתְקַדְּשׁוּ they sanctified themselves

There are some reflexive verbs, however, where the subject is not the direct object. Indeed, a direct object (something) may be specified.

וַיִּתְפַּשֵּׁט and he stripped (something) from himself

הִתְפָּרְקוּ they tore (something) from themselves

Also subsumed under this category of reflexives are a few verbs that may be regarded as *tolerative*, where the subject allows an action to affect himself or herself.

הִתְמַכֵּר he let himself be sold

**b.** *Reciprocal.* In some instances, the Hithpael verb implies reciprocity.

הִתְקַשְּׁרוּ they conspired with one another

הִתְרָאוּ they looked at one another

**c.** *Iterative.* Often the Hithpael verb suggests repeated activity.

הִתְהַלֵּךְ he walked about

הִתְהַפֵּךְ he turned back and forth

**d.** *Estimative.* Sometimes a Hithpael verb describes how one shows oneself or regards oneself, whether in truth or in pretense.

| | | | |
|---|---|---|---|
| חָלָה | sick | הִתְחַלּוֹת | to pretend to be sick |
| יְהוּדִי | a Jew | מִתְיַהֲדִים | professing to be Jews |

## 3. The Hithpael of the Strong Verb

Apart from the characteristic elements mentioned in section 1 (above), there are no surprises in the inflections of the strong verb.

**a.** Perfect

| | | | |
|---|---|---|---|
| *3 ms* | הִתְקַטֵּל | *3 cp* | הִתְקַטְּלוּ |
| *3 fp* | הִתְקַטְּלָה | | |
| *2 ms* | הִתְקַטַּ֫לְתָּ | *2 mp* | הִתְקַטַּלְתֶּם |
| *2 fs* | הִתְקַטַּלְתְּ | *2 fp* | הִתְקַטַּלְתֶּן |
| *1 cs* | הִתְקַטַּ֫לְתִּי | *1 cp* | הִתְקַטַּ֫לְנוּ |

**b.** Imperfect

| | | | |
|---|---|---|---|
| *3 ms* | יִתְקַטֵּל | *3 mp* | יִתְקַטְּלוּ |
| *3 fs* | תִּתְקַטֵּל | *3 fp* | תִּתְקַטֵּ֫לְנָה |
| *2 ms* | תִּתְקַטֵּל | *2 mp* | תִּתְקַטְּלוּ |
| *2 fs* | תִּתְקַטְּלִי | *2 fp* | תִּתְקַטֵּ֫לְנָה |
| *1 cs* | אֶתְקַטֵּל | *1 cp* | נִתְקַטֵּל |

**c.** Imperative

| | | | |
|---|---|---|---|
| *ms* | הִתְקַטֵּל | *mp* | הִתְקַטְּלוּ |
| *fs* | הִתְקַטְּלִי | *fp* | הִתְקַטֵּ֫לְנָה |

**d.** Infinitive

Absolute: הִתְקַטֵּל    Construct: הִתְקַטֵּל

**e.** Participle

| | | | |
|---|---|---|---|
| *ms* | מִתְקַטֵּל | *mp* | מִתְקַטְּלִים |
| *fs* | מִתְקַטֶּ֫לֶת | *fp* | מִתְקַטְּלוֹת |

## 4. The Metathesis and Assimilation of the Infixed Tāw

In some environments, the infixed *t* undergoes some changes.

**a.** Verbs with one of the sibilants (ס, צ, שׂ, שׁ) as the first radical show a metathesis (transposition) of the infixed *t* and that sibilant in the Hithpael forms.

מִסְתַּתֵּר < מִתְסַתֵּר* one who hides himself

מִשְׂתַּכֵּר < מִתְשַׂכֵּר* one who hires himself out

יִשְׁתַּמֵּר < יִתְשַׁמֵּר* he will be on guard

In addition to the metathesis, the presence of the emphatic sibilant *ṣ* causes the infixed *t* to change to *ṭ*.

נִצְטַדֵּק < נִתְצַדֵּק* we will show ourselves innocent

הִצְטַיַּ֫דְנוּ < הִתְצַיַּ֫דְנוּ* we took provisions

**b.** Verbs with one of the dentals (ד, ט, ת) as the first radical show assimilation of the infixed *t* into that dental.

*מִתְדַּבֵּר < מְדַבֵּר (one) conversing

*הִתְטַהֲרוּ < הִטַּהֲרוּ they purified themselves

*תִּתְתַּמָּם < תִּתַּמָּם you show yourself blameless

Assimilation also occurs sporadically with other radicals, notably Nûn and Kap̄.

*יִתְנַשֵּׂא < יִנַּשֵּׂא he shall exalt himself

*הִתְנַבְּאוּ < הִנַּבְּאוּ they prophesied

*תִּתְכַּסֶּה < תִּכַּסֶּה it will be concealed

## 5. The Hithpael of Weak Verbs

**a.** II-Guttural and II-Rêš Verbs

Since gutturals and Rêš cannot take the strong *dāgēš*, the vowel preceding the second radical is compensatorily lengthened (XV.3).

יִתְבָּרֵךְ he will bless himself

הִתְרָחַ֫צְתִּי I washed myself

There are also a few instances where one finds virtual doubling instead of compensatory lengthening.

הִטַּהָ֫רְנוּ we cleansed ourselves

**b.** I-Wāw Verbs

Since the first radical of the root is preceded by הִתְ–, יִתְ–, or מִתְ–, it is retained (IV.2.c.ii), e.g., אֶתְוַדַּע I will make myself known (Hith. impf. 1 cs of ידע < original *ודע). On the other hand, the original *w* is irregularly changed to *y* in some instances, e.g., יִתְיָעֲצוּ they consult with one another (Hith. impf. 3 mp of יעץ < *ועץ).

## 6. Synopsis of Verbs in Hithpael

| *Root* | *Perf.* | *Impf.* | *Juss.* | *Impv.* | *Inf.* | *Ptc.* |
|---|---|---|---|---|---|---|
| קדשׁ | הִתְקַדֵּשׁ | יִתְקַדֵּשׁ | יִתְקַדֵּשׁ | הִתְקַדֵּשׁ | הִתְקַדֵּשׁ | מִתְקַדֵּשׁ |
| שׁמר | הִשְׁתַּמֵּר | יִשְׁתַּמֵּר | יִשְׁתַּמֵּר | הִשְׁתַּמֵּר | הִשְׁתַּמֵּר | מִשְׁתַּמֵּר |
| ברך | הִתְבָּרֵךְ | יִתְבָּרֵךְ | יִתְבָּרֵךְ | הִתְבָּרֵךְ | הִתְבָּרֵךְ | מִתְבָּרֵךְ |
| גלה | הִתְגַּלָּה | יִתְגַּלֶּה | יִתְגַּל | הִתְגַּלֵּה | הִתְגַּלּוֹת | מִתְגַּלֶּה |

## 7. The Hishtaphel Pattern

There is another reflexive verbal pattern in Hebrew known as Hishtaphel. It is, however, attested only for the root חוה, which occurs only in this pattern, meaning "to bow down, do obeisance, worship." This verb (which occur 170 times) has been analyzed in BDB as a reflexive of the root שָׁחָה, with the metathesis of the infixed *t* and the sibilant (*š*). From external evidence discovered in this century, however, most scholars have concluded that this important verb is traced to the root חוה. There is, to be sure, a root שָׁחָה (to bow down) attested once in Qal and once in Hiphil, but that root appears to have been secondarily derived from הִשְׁתַּחֲוָה.

The following forms of חוה are attested.

**a.** Perfect

| | | | |
|---|---|---|---|
| *3 ms* | הִשְׁתַּחֲוָה | *3 cp* | הִשְׁתַּחֲווּ |
| *2 ms* | הִשְׁתַּחֲוִיתָ | *2 mp* | הִשְׁתַּחֲוִיתֶם |
| *1 cs* | הִשְׁתַּחֲוֵיתִי | | |

**b.** Imperfect

| | | | |
|---|---|---|---|
| *3 ms* | יִשְׁתַּחֲוֶה | *3 mp* | יִשְׁתַּחֲוּוּ |
| *2 ms* | תִּשְׁתַּחֲוֶה | *2 mp* | תִּשְׁתַּחֲוּוּ |
| *1 cs* | אֶשְׁתַּחֲוֶה | *1 cs* | נִשְׁתַּחֲוֶה |

**c.** Imperative

| | | | |
|---|---|---|---|
| | | *mp* | הִשְׁתַּחֲוּוּ |
| *fs* | הִשְׁתַּחֲוִי | | |

**d.** Infinitive Construct: הִשְׁתַּחֲוֹת

**e.** Participle

| | | | |
|---|---|---|---|
| *ms* | מִשְׁתַּחֲוֶה | *mp* | מִשְׁתַּחֲוִים |

**f.** Wāw-consecutive

| | | | |
|---|---|---|---|
| *3 ms* | וַיִּשְׁתַּחוּ | | |
| | | *3 fp* | וַתִּשְׁתַּחֲוֶ֫יןָ |
| *2 ms* | וַתִּשְׁתַּחוּ | | |

*Note*: יִשְׁתַּחוּ and תִּשְׁתַּחוּ are derived from the apocopated forms *יִשְׁתַּחו and *תִּשְׁתַּחו, respectively. They should not be identified as plural forms, which would be יִשְׁתַּחֲוּוּ and תִּשְׁתַּחֲוּוּ.

## 8. Oaths

**a.** An oath may be introduced simply by some form of the verb **נִשְׁבַּע** (i.e., Ni. of the root **שׁבע** to swear).

**i.** If the oath is positive, the substance of the oath is introduced by **כִּי** (surely).

| | |
|---|---|
| נִשְׁבַּע אֲדֹנָי יְהוִה בְּקָדְשׁוֹ כִּי הִנֵּה יָמִים בָּאִים עֲלֵיכֶם | My lord YHWH swears by his holiness: "The days are coming upon you!" (Amos 4:2) |
| נִשְׁבַּעְתָּ בַּיהוָה אֱלֹהֶיךָ לַאֲמָתֶךָ כִּי־שְׁלֹמֹה בְנֵךְ יִמְלֹךְ אַחֲרָי | You swore by YHWH your God to your servant: "Solomon your son shall reign after me!" (1 Kgs 1:17) |

Sometimes instead of **כִּי** one finds **כִּי אִם** or **אִם לֹא**.

| | |
|---|---|
| נִשְׁבַּע יְהוָה צְבָאוֹת בְּנַפְשׁוֹ כִּי אִם־מִלֵּאתִיךְ | YHWH of Hosts swears by himself: "I will fill you" (Jer 51:14) |
| נִשְׁבַּע יְהוָה צְבָאוֹת לֵאמֹר אִם־לֹא כַּאֲשֶׁר דִּמִּיתִי כֵּן הָיָתָה | YHWH of Hosts swears, saying: "As I have intended, so shall it be" (Isa 14:24) |

**ii.** If the oath is negative, **נִשְׁבַּע** is followed by **אִם** instead of **כִּי**.

| | |
|---|---|
| נִשְׁבַּעְתִּי לְבֵית עֵלִי אִם־יִתְכַּפֵּר עֲוֺן בֵּית־עֵלִי | I swear as regards the house of Eli: "The guilt of the house of Eli will not be expiated" (1 Sam 3:14) |

**b.** An oath may also be introduced by one of the following oath formulae, instead of **נִשְׁבַּע**.

| | | | |
|---|---|---|---|
| חַי יְהוָה | As YHWH lives | חַי אָנִי | As I live |
| חַי אֱלֹהִים | As God lives | חֵי נַפְשְׁךָ | By your life |
| חַי אֵל | As God lives | חֵי פַרְעֹה | By Pharaoh's life |

**i.** If the oath is affirmative, the oath formula is followed by **כִּי**.

חַי־אָנִי ... כִּֽי־מוֹאָב כִּסְדֹם תִּהְיֶה

As I live: "Moab shall become like Sodom" (Zeph 2:9)

Sometimes the oath formula is followed by **כִּי אִם** or **אִם לֹא**, instead of **כִּי**.

חַי־יְהוָה כִּי אִם־יְהוָה יִגֳּפֶנּוּ

As YHWH lives: "YHWH will smite him!" (1 Sam 26:10)

חַי־אָנִי ... אִם־לֹא כַּאֲשֶׁר דִּבַּרְתֶּם בְּאָזְנָי כֵּן אֶעֱשֶׂה לָכֶם

As I live: "What you have spoken into my ears I will do!" (Num 14:28)

**ii.** If the oath is negative, the oath formula is followed by **אִם**, instead of **כִּי**.

חֵי פַרְעֹה אִם־תֵּצְאוּ מִזֶּה

By the life of Pharaoh, "You shall not depart from here!" (Gen 42:15)

**c.** A maledictory oath (a curse) may be introduced by one of the following curse formulae.

כֹּה יַעֲשֶׂה יְהוָה וְכֹה יוֹסִיף

Thus YHWH will do and add more!

כֹּה יַעֲשֶׂה אֱלֹהִים וְכֹה יוֹסִיף

Thus will God do and add more!

כֹּה יַעֲשׂוּן אֱלֹהִים וְכֹה יוֹסִיפוּן

Thus the gods will do and add more!

**i.** If the statement is affirmative, the substance of the curse is usually followed by **כִּי**.

כֹּה־יַעֲשֶׂה אֱלֹהִים וְכֹה יוֹסִף כִּי־מוֹת תָּמוּת

Thus God will do and add more: "You will surely die!" (1 Sam 14:44).

Sometimes the substance of the curse is introduced by **אִם לֹא**, instead of **כִּי**.

| | |
|---|---|
| כֹּה יַעֲשֶׂה־לִּי אֱלֹהִים וְכֹה יוֹסִיף אִם־לֹא שַׂר־צָבָא תִּהְיֶה | Thus will God do to me and add more: "You will certainly become the commander of the army" (2 Sam 19:14) |

**ii.** If the statement is negative, the substance of the curse is introduced by **אִם**, instead of **כִּי** or **אִם לֹא**.

| | |
|---|---|
| כֹּה יַעֲשֶׂה־לְּךָ אֱלֹהִים וְכֹה יוֹסִיף אִם־תְּכַחֵד מִמֶּנִּי דָּבָר | Thus God will do to you and add more: "You shall not hide any thing from me" (1 Sam 3:17) |

## Vocabulary

*Nouns*:

**אוֹצָר** (mp: **אוֹצָרוֹת**) treasure, treasury, storehouse

**דֶּלֶת** (fs; fp: **דְּלָתוֹת**) door

**זָכָר** male

**חִטָּה** (pl. **חִטִּים**) wheat

**נֵר** lamp

**קָצִיר** harvest. *Verb*: **קָצַר** to harvest.

**תְּחִלָּה** beginning. *Verb*: **חָלַל** Ni.: to be profaned; Pi.: to profane; Hi.: to begin

*Verbs*:

**חָסָה** to seek refuge

**יָצַב** Hith.: to position onself, stand

**כָּחַד** Ni.: to be hidden, effaced; Pi.: to hide; Hi. to hide

**נָכַר** Ni.: to be recognized; Hi.: to recognize, acknowledge. *Noun*: **נָכְרִי** foreigner

**נָצַב** Ni.: to stand. *Noun*: **מַצֵּבָה** standing stone

[קָלַל] (Qal perf. 3 ms קַל) to be slight, swift; Pi.: to curse. *Noun*: קְלָלָה curse

שָׂבַע to be satisfied, satiated. *Adjective*: שָׂבֵעַ full, satisfied

שָׁבַע Ni.: to swear

*Conjunction*:

יַ֫עַן because, on account of (also יַ֫עַן אֲשֶׁר because [that])

*Adverb*:

מָתַי when? (also עַד־מָתַי until when? how long?)

## Exercise 27

**a.** Write the following forms in Hebrew:

1. Hith. perf. 3 ms of מָכַר
2. Hith. impf. 3 mp of מָכַר
3. Hith. impf. 1 cs of שָׁמַר
4. Hith. perf. 3 cp of בָּקַע
5. Hith. perf. 1 cs of גָּדַל
6. Hith. ptc. ms of דָּבַר
7. Hith. perf. 3 ms of יָדָה
8. Hith. perf. 3 cp of טָהֵר
9. Hith. impf. 3 mp of טָהֵר
10. Hith. ptc. ms of טָהֵר
11. Hith. impv. mp of טָהֵר
12. Hith. ptc. mp of יָדָה
13. Hith. impf. 1 cs of יָדַע
14. Hith. impf. 1 cp of צָדַק
15. Hith. impf. 3 fs of שָׁפַךְ
16. Hith. inf. cs. of גָּלָה
17. Hith. impf. 3 ms of בָּרַךְ
18. Hith. ptc. ms of בָּרַךְ
19. Hisht. perf. 3 ms of חָוָה
20. Hisht. impf. 3 ms of חָוָה
21. Hith. juss. 3 ms of גָּלָה
22. Hisht. impv. ms of חָוָה

**b.** Translate 1 Samuel 3 with the help of a dictionary.

*Notes*:

v 2: הֵחֵלּוּ began.

v 11: תְּצִלֶּינָה (subject) will tingle.

v 12: הָחֵל the beginning.

# Lesson XXVIII

## 1. Geminate Verbs in Qal

Like geminate nouns (V.1), geminate verbs have identical second and third radicals. There are generally two types of geminate verbs in Qal: one corresponding to the *qāṭal-yiqṭōl* (dynamic verb) type in strong roots, and another corresponding to the *qāṭēl-yiqṭal* (stative verb) type (XVIII.2). The following are some important examples of the two types.

| *Type A* | | *Type B* | |
|---|---|---|---|
| סָבַב | to surround | תַּם | to be complete |
| אָרַר | to curse | חַת | to be shattered |
| בָּלַל | to mix | מַר | to be bitter |
| מָדַד | to measure | קַל | to be small, be swift |
| נָדַד | to wander | רַב | to be numerous |
| שָׁדַד | to devastate | רַע | to be bad |

### a. Perfect

In Type A (e.g., סָבַב to surround) the geminate radical is repeated in the third person forms, whereas the other forms indicate gemination only by means of the *dāgēš*. Type B verbs (e.g., the root תמם to be complete, Qal perfect 3 ms תַּם) indicate gemination in all forms by the *dāgēš*. The 3 ms form of this type shows the loss of gemination in a manner similar to the noun עַם (see V.1.a): thus, *tamm > *tam*. The Qal perfect of the geminate roots סָבַב (to surround) and תַּם (to be complete), representing Types A and B, respectively, are as follows.

| | *Type A* | *Type B* |
|---|---|---|
| *3 ms* | סָבַב | תַּם |
| *3 fs* | סָֽבֲבָה | תַּ֫מָּה |
| *2 ms* | סַבּ֫וֹתָ | תַּ֫מּוֹתָ |
| *2 fs* | סַבּוֹת | תַּמּוֹת |
| *1 cs* | סַבּ֫וֹתִי | תַּ֫מּוֹתִי |
| *3 cp* | סָֽבֲבוּ | תַּ֫מּוּ |
| *2 mp* | סַבּוֹתֶם | תַּמּוֹתֶם |
| *2 fp* | סַבּוֹתֶן | תַּמּוֹתֶן |
| *1 cp* | סַבּ֫וֹנוּ | תַּ֫מּוֹנוּ |

*Notes*:

i. Besides forms like סָֽבֲבוּ, we also get מָֽדְדוּ (with the simple vocal *šĕwāʾ*).

ii. Before the consonantal suffix, one again finds the additional וֹ (see XVI.10.ii), although it may occasionally be omitted, e.g., תַּ֫מְנוּ (from earlier *תַּמְּנוּ, see VI.7) for תַּ֫מּוֹנוּ (we are finished).

iii. If the second radical cannot be doubled by a *dāgēš*, one gets compensatory lengthening (e.g., אָר֫וֹתִי I cursed).

iv. There are inconsistencies in the representation of gemination: sometimes the geminate radical is repeated, but sometimes gemination is indicated only by a *dāgēš*. For example, one finds סְבָב֫וּנִי and סַבּ֫וּנִי as alternate forms without any difference in meaning. Moreover, for the 3 ms, we get the form חָנַן, but the forms with suffixes show gemination by the *dāgēš* (e.g., חַנַּ֫נִי he has been gracious to me).

**b.** Imperfect

The proper inflections of the imperfect of סבב and תמם are provided below. Many geminate verbs, however, form all or some of their imperfect forms so that they end up looking like I-Nûn verbs, e.g., יָסֹּב (like יִפֹּל; XIX.4.a) instead of יָסֹב; יִתַּ֫מּוּ instead of יֵתַ֫מּוּ. Most grammars, therefore, present the alternate forms (those that look like I-Nûn imperfects) alongside the regular forms, and one is expected to learn two possible inflections of the imperfect for each verb. It is easier, however, for the student *not* to memorize a second set of imperfect forms for each of the types. Rather, one should simply assume the following inflections as paradigmatic for geminate verbs, and take the alternate forms as secondary. Should a form like יִדֹּם be encountered in reading, one who does not recognize the verb may assume a I-Nûn root נדם; but failing to locate such a root in the dictionary, one may then conjecture that the root is actually דמם (to be silent, with the imperfect formed as if the root were נדם). The Qal imperfect of the verbs סבב (to surround) and תמם (to be complete) are inflected as follows:

| | *Type A* | *Type B* |
|---|---|---|
| *3 ms* | יָסֹב | יֵתַם |
| *3 fs* | תָּסֹב | תֵּתַם |
| *2 ms* | תָּסֹב | תֵּתַם |
| *2 fs* | תָּסֹ֫בִּי | תֵּתַ֫מִּי |
| *1 cs* | אָסֹב | אֵתַם |
| *3 mp* | יָסֹ֫בּוּ | יֵתַ֫מּוּ |
| *3 fp* | תְּסֻבֶּ֫ינָה | תֵּתַמֶּ֫ינָה |
| *2 mp* | תָּסֹ֫בּוּ | תֵּתַ֫מּוּ |
| *2 fp* | תְּסֻבֶּ֫ינָה | תֵּתַמֶּ֫ינָה |
| *1 cp* | נָסֹב | נֵתַם |

*Note*: Gemination (indicated by a *dāgēš*) is evident only in the forms with afformatives; forms without any endings do not show gemination at all. Not surprisingly, too, when an object suffix is added to a form without the afformative, the gemination is, again, indicated by a *dāgēš*. Thus, יָסֹב *he will surround* (Qal impf. 3 ms) but יְסֻבֵּנִי *he will surround me* (Qal impf. 3 ms + 1 cs object suffix).

**c.** Imperative

The imperative forms are, as one would expect (XXI.3), like the corresponding imperfect forms without the preformative: thus, תָּסֹב (imperfect) but סֹב (imperative); תֵּתַם (imperfect) but תַּם (imperative).

| | Type A | Type B |
|---|---|---|
| *ms* | סֹב | תַּם |
| *fs* | סֹבִּי | תַּמִּי |
| *mp* | סֹבּוּ | תַּמּוּ |
| *fp* | סֹבְנָה | תַּמְנָה |

*Notes*:

i. Some forms that are normally stressed on the penultima are anomalously stressed on the ultima. Hence, we get the 2 fs forms חָגִּי *ḥoggî* (celebrate!), רָנִּי *ronnî* (shout!), גָּזִּי *gozzî* (shear!), etc.

ii. When a suffix is appended to the imperative, we get forms like חָנֵּנִי *ḥonnēnî* (be gracious to me!), סָלּוּהָ *sollûhā* (pile it up!).

**d.** Infinitive

| | Type A | Type B |
|---|---|---|
| *Abs.* | סָבוֹב | – |
| *Cs.* | סֹב | תֹּם |
| *Cs. with sfx.* | סֻבִּי | תֻּמִּי |

*Note*: Infinitive construct forms that repeat the geminate radical – that is, the *qĕlōl* type (like נְדֹד "to wander, wandering") – are also attested.

e. Wāw-consecutive

The accent is consistently retracted (from the ultima to the penult) on the Wāw-consecutive form of Type A, but not of Type B (see XX.4). In Type A, the retraction of accent causes the long *ō*-vowel in the ultima to shorten to *o*, e.g., יָסֹב *yāsōḏ* (jussive) but וַיָּ֫סָב *wayyā́soḇ* (Wāw-consecutive). The Wāw-consecutive form of Type B does not typically retract the accent, but forms like וַיֵּ֫צֶר (from צרר "to be pressed") are attested.

| *Type A* | *Type B* |
|---|---|
| וַיָּ֫סָב | וַיֵּתַם |

f. Participle

The participles of Type A geminates are regular (VIII.3.a). Those of Type B, however, are irregular.

| | *Type A* | | *Type B* | |
|---|---|---|---|---|
| *Act.* | סֹבֵב | סֹבְבִים | תַּם | תַּמִּים |
| | סֹבֶ֫בֶת | סֹבְבוֹת | תַּמָּה | תַּמּוֹת |
| *Pass.* | סָבוּב | סְבוּבִים | | |
| | סְבוּבָה | – | | |

## 2. Geminate Verbs in Niphal

The Niphal forms of geminate verbs show the expected prefixed or infixed and assimilated Nûn (see XXVI.1): prefixed in the Perfect and Participle; infixed and assimilated in the Imperfect, Imperative, and Infinitive.

**a.** Perfect

| | | | |
|---|---|---|---|
| *3 ms* | נָסַב | *3 cp* | נָסַ֫בּוּ |
| *3 fs* | נָסַ֫בָּה | | |
| *2 ms* | נְסַבּ֫וֹתָ | *2 mp* | נְסַבּוֹתֶם |
| *2 fs* | נְסַבּוֹת | *2 fp* | נְסַבּוֹתֶן |
| *1 cs* | נְסַבּ֫וֹתִי | *1 cp* | נְסַבּ֫וֹנוּ |

*Notes*:

i. Besides the regular forms (with the *a*-vowel in the second syllable), there are a few verbs with *ē* in the second syllable, e.g., נָמֵס (it melted), נָסֵ֫בָּה (it has turned itself). There are also isolated examples of 3 cp forms with *ō* in the second syllable (e.g., נָגֹ֫לּוּ they were rolled together; נָבֹ֫זּוּ they were plundered).

ii. A few geminate verbs have Niphal perfect forms with the **niqṭal* pattern, such as **ninḥat* > נִחַת (it was shattered) and **ninḥaltā* > נִחַ֫לְתָּ (you were profaned), both with virtual doubling.

**b.** Imperfect

| | | | |
|---|---|---|---|
| *3 ms* | יִסַּב | *3 mp* | יִסַּ֫בּוּ |
| *3 fs* | תִּסַּב | *3 fp* | תִּסַּבֶּ֫ינָה |
| *2 ms* | תִּסַּב | *2 mp* | תִּסַּ֫בּוּ |
| *2 fs* | תִּסַּ֫בִּי | *2 fp* | תִּסַּבֶּ֫ינָה |
| *1 cs* | אֶסַּב | *1 cp* | נִסַּב |

*Notes*:

i. Besides the regular forms (with *a* as the thematic vowel), variants with *ō* as the thematic vowel (like תִּבּוֹז) are also attested.

ii. When the first radical is a guttural or Rêš, there is compensatory lengthening, e.g., **yinḥat* > יֵחַת (it shall be shattered); יֵרֹ֫מּוּ (they shall rise), יֵרֹ֫עַ (he is ill-treated).

c. Imperative

| | | | |
|---|---|---|---|
| *ms* | הִסַּב | *mp* | הִסַּ֫בּוּ |
| *fs* | הִסַּ֫בִּי | *fp* | הִסַּבֶּ֫ינָה |

d. Infinitive

Absolute: הִסּוֹב      Construct: הִסֵּב

*Notes*: When the first radical is a guttural or Rêš, there is compensatory lengthening, e.g., **hinḥill* > הֵחֵל (to be profaned, profaning).

e. Participle

| | | | |
|---|---|---|---|
| *ms* | נָסָב | *mp* | נְסַבִּים |
| *fs* | נְסַבָּה | *fp* | נְסַבּוֹת |

*Note*: We also find the type נָקֵל (with the vowel *ē* in the second syllable), but the fs form is still נְקַלָּה, not *נְקֵלָּה.

## 3. Geminate Verbs in Hiphil

The Hiphil forms of geminate verbs show the expected *h* prefixed in the Perfect, Imperative, and Infinitive forms, but not in the Imperfect and Participle.

**a.** Perfect

| | | | |
|---|---|---|---|
| *3 ms* | הֵסֵב | *3 cp* | הֵסֵ֫בּוּ |
| *3 fs* | הֵסֵ֫בָּה | | |
| *2 ms* | הֲסִבּ֫וֹתָ | *2 mp* | הֲסִבּוֹתֶם |
| *2 fs* | הֲסִבּוֹת | *2 fp* | הֲסִבּוֹתֶן |
| *1 cs* | הֲסִבּ֫וֹתִי | *1 cp* | הֲסִבּ֫וֹנוּ |

*Notes*:

i. An *a*-vowel is sometimes found instead of *ē* in the second syllable, particularly when the geminate radical is a guttural: הֵרַע (he acted wickedly).

ii. When the geminate radical is a guttural or Rêš, the preceding vowel in the second and first person forms is lengthened from *i* to *ē*: הֲרֵע֫וֹתָ (you acted wickedly).

**b.** Imperfect

| | | | |
|---|---|---|---|
| *3 ms* | יָסֵב | *3 mp* | יָסֵ֫בּוּ |
| *3 fs* | תָּסֵב | *3 fs* | תְּסִבֶּ֫ינָה |
| *2 ms* | תָּסֵב | *2 mp* | תָּסֵ֫בּוּ |
| *2 fs* | תָּסֵ֫בִּי | *2 fp* | תְּסִבֶּ֫ינָה |
| *1 cs* | אָסֵב | *1 cp* | נָסֵב |

*Notes*:

i. An *a*-vowel is sometimes found instead of *ē* in the second syllable, particularly when the geminate radical is a guttural: יָרַע (he will act wickedly).

ii. Besides the יָסֵב type, a variant imperfect like יַסֵּב is also attested.

**c.** Imperative

| | | | |
|---|---|---|---|
| *ms* | הָסֵב | *mp* | הָסֵ֫בּוּ |
| *fs* | הָסֵ֫בִּי | *fp* | הֲסִבֶּ֫ינָה |

**d.** Infinitive

Absolute: הָסֵב Construct: הָסֵב

With Suffixes: הֲסִבִּי

*Note*: An *a*-vowel is sometimes found instead of *ē* in the second syllable, particularly when the geminate radical is a guttural: הָרַע (to act wickedly, acting wickedly).

**e.** Participle

| | | | |
|---|---|---|---|
| *ms* | מֵסֵב | *mp* | מְסִבִּים |
| *fs* | מְסִבָּה | *fp* | מְסִבּוֹת |

*Note*: An *a*-vowel is sometimes found instead of *ē* when the second syllable is a guttural: מֵרַע (one who acts wickedly).

**f.** Wāw-consecutive

The Wāw-consecutive forms of geminate roots are sometimes confused with the Hiphil Wāw-consecutive of II-Wāw/Yōḏ verbs, e.g., וַיָּ֫רַע (and) he acted wickedly (root רעע) or (and) he shouted (root רוע).

## 4. Geminate Roots and Other Roots

It is clear that geminate verbs are frequently confused with other weak verb types, especially I-Nûn and II-Wāw/Yōḏ. Consider the following examples.

יָסֹב Qal impf. 3 ms of סבב, not נסב

יָרוֹן Qal impf. 3 ms of רנן, not רון

נָרוֹץ Ni. perf. 3 ms of רצץ, not רוץ

יָשׁוּד Qal impf. 3 ms of שׁדד, not שׁוד

תֵּחֵל Ni. impf. 3 fs of חלל, not יחל

וַיֵּצֶר Qal Wāw-consecutive 3 ms of צרר, not יצר

וַיָּפֶר Hi. Wāw-consecutive 3 ms of פרר, not פור

יֶחֱמוּ Qal impf. 3 mp of חמם, not חמה

It is simplest at this stage in the study of Hebrew *not* to memorize the exceptional or mixed forms. Rather, when an unknown form is encountered, the root should be reconstructed according to the regular paradigms. But when one is unable to locate the root in the dictionary, one should consider a geminate root. Thus, for example, יָשׁוּד is assumed first to be a Qal impf. form of שׁוד, but when it is learned that no such root is attested, one may then try שׁדד. By the same token, one may assume that נָרוֹץ is a Niphal form of רוץ; but when one learns that רוץ never occurs in Niphal, one may try רצץ. Many geminate verbs, it should be noted, have genuine alternate roots (with the same semantic range) that are II-Wāw/Yōḏ or III-Hē. Examples include the following.

הוּם, הָמַם to be in turmoil

צוּר, צָרַר to tie, be in distress

רָבָה, רָבַב to be numerous

שָׁגָה, שָׁגַג to err, go astray, sin inadvertently

## Vocabulary

*Nouns*:

אָתוֹן (fs; fp: אֲתֹנוֹת) (she-)ass

עֵדֶר herd, flock

*Verbs*:

אָרַר to curse

בָּלַל to mix, confound

[דָּמַם] (Qal perf. 3 ms דַּם) to be silent

[חָתַת] (Qal perf. 3 ms חַת) to be shattered, be dismayed

מָדַד to measure. *Noun*: מִדָּה measure, measurement

סָבַב to surround, go around, turn

פָּלַט to escape; Pi., Hi.: to bring to safety. *Nouns*: פָּלִיט fugitive; פְּלֵיטָה escape, what has escaped/survived

פָּרַר Hi.: to break, frustrate

רָנַן to jubilate, shout for joy

[רָעַע] (Qal perf. 3 ms רַע) to be bad, be evil; Hi. to act wickedly, do mischief

שָׁדַד to destroy, devastate

שָׁמַם to be desolate, be appalled

שָׁקָה Hi.: give drink, irrigate

[תָּמַם] (Qal perf. 3 ms תַּם) to be complete, be whole, be finished. *Adjectives*: תָּם, תָּמִים complete, blameless. *Noun*: תֹּם integrity, completeness

*Adverbs*:

אוּלַי perhaps

# Exercise 28

**a.** Write the following forms:

1. Qal perf. 2 mp of סָבַב
2. Qal impf. 3 mp of סָבַב
3. Qal perf. 1 cs of קָלַל
4. Qal perf. 3 cp of קָלַל
5. Hi. perf. 2 ms of סָבַב
6. Ni. impf. 3 mp of קָלַל
7. Qal perf. 3 ms of תָּמַם
8. Ni. ptc. fs of קָלַל
9. Hi. perf. 3 ms of חָלַל
10. Hi. perf. 2 ms of רָעַע
11. Hi. impf. 1 cs of חָלַל
12. Hi. ptc. ms of חָלַל
13. Qal perf. 1 cs of אָרַר
14. Hi. perf. 2 ms of חָלַל
15. Hi. inf. cs of חָלַל
16. Hi. impf. 3 ms of חָלַל
17. Qal impv. mp of אָרַר
18. Qal impf. 3 ms of רָעַע
19. Hi. perf. 2 ms of רָעַע
20. Hi. impf. 3 ms of רָעַע

**b.** Translate Ruth 1 with the help of a dictionary.

# Lesson XXIX

## 1. The Pual Pattern

The Pual verbal pattern is the passive counterpart of the Piel.

| *Piel* | *Pual* |
|---|---|
| חִבֵּר he joined | חֻבַּר it was joined |
| כִּפֶּר he expiated | כֻּפַּר he was expiated |

Like the Piel, the Pual verbal pattern is characterized by the doubling of the second radical, but verbs in the Pual pattern are also marked by an *u*-class vowel with first radical. The *u*-class vowel in the verb, in fact, may be seen as an indicator of the passive – as we have already seen in the Qal passive participle, קָטוּל *qāṭûl*.

**a.** Perfect

| | | | |
|---|---|---|---|
| *3 ms* | קֻטַּל | *3 cp* | קֻטְּלוּ |
| *3 fs* | קֻטְּלָה | | |
| *2 ms* | קֻטַּ֫לְתָּ | *2 mp* | קֻטַּלְתֶּם |
| *2 fs* | קֻטַּלְתְּ | *2 fp* | קֻטַּלְתֶּן |
| *1 cs* | קֻטַּ֫לְתִּי | *1 cp* | קֻטַּ֫לְנוּ |

*Notes*:

i. Before gutturals and ר, we get compensatory lengthening of *u* > ō (e.g., בֹּרַךְ he was blessed; גֹּרְשׁוּ they were driven out) or virtual doubling (רֻחַץ he was washed; רֻחָמָה she was pitied).

ii. Occasionally, *o* (ָ) may be found in the first syllable instead of *u*: as in כָּסּוּ they were covered (from כסה), instead of *כֻּסּוּ.

**b.** Imperfect

| | | | |
|---|---|---|---|
| *3 ms* | יְקֻטַּל | *3 mp* | יְקֻטְּלוּ |
| *3 fs* | תְּקֻטַּל | *3 fp* | תְּקֻטַּ֫לְנָה |
| *2 ms* | תְּקֻטַּל | *2 mp* | תְּקֻטְּלוּ |
| *2 fs* | תְּקֻטְּלִי | *2 fp* | תְּקֻטַּ֫לְנָה |
| *1 cs* | אֲקֻטַּל | *1 cp* | נְקֻטַּל |

*Note*: Before gutturals and ר, we get compensatory lengthening of *u* > ō (e.g., יְבֹרַךְ he will be blessed), or virtual doubling (e.g., יְרֻחַם he will be pitied).

**c.** Participle

| | | | |
|---|---|---|---|
| *ms* | מְקֻטָּל | *mp* | מְקֻטָּלִים |
| *fs* | מְקֻטָּלָה | *fp* | מְקֻטָּלוֹת |

*Notes*:

i. The fs participle of the מְקֻטֶּ֫לֶת pattern is also attested.

ii. Before gutturals and ר, we get compensatory lengthening of *u* > ō (e.g., מְבֹרֶ֫כֶת).

**Synopsis of Verbs in Pual**

| *Root* | *Perf.* | *Impf.* | *Inf. abs.* | *Inf. cs.* | *Ptc.* |
|---|---|---|---|---|---|
| גנב | גֻּנַּב | יְגֻנַּב | גֻּנֹּב | – | מְגֻנָּב |
| ברך | בֹּרַךְ | יְבֹרַךְ | – | – | מְבֹרָךְ |
| מלא | מֻלָּא | יְמֻלָּא | – | – | מְמֻלָּא |
| גלה | גֻּלָּה | יְגֻלֶּה | – | גֻּלּוֹת | מְגֻלֶּה |
| ילד | יֻלַּד | יְיֻלַּד | – | – | מְיֻלָּד |

## 2. The Hophal Pattern

The Hophal verbal pattern is the passive counterpart of the Hiphil:

| *Hiphil* | *Hophal* |
|---|---|
| הִגִּיד he told | הֻגַּד he was told |
| הִכָּה he struck | הֻכָּה he was stricken |

Like the Hiphil, the Hophal verbal pattern is characterized by the prefixed *h* in the perfect and infinitives, but Hophal verbs are also marked by an *u*-class vowel with first radical. This *u*-class vowel may be *o* ( ָ ), *u* ( ֻ ), or *û* (וּ), depending on its environment.

i. Before a strong radical it is usually *o*.

הָמְלַךְ (Ho. Perf. 3 ms of מלך) he was made king

Not infrequently, however, it is *u* instead of *o*.

הֻשְׁלַךְ (Ho. Perf. 3 ms of שׁלך) he was cast out

ii. Before I-Guttural or I-Rēš it is *o*.

הָחְבָּא (Ho. Perf. 3 ms of חבא) he was hidden

הָרְאֵיתָ (Ho. Perf. 2 ms of ראה) you were shown

iii. Before I-Nûn it is *u*.

הֻגַּד (Perf. 3 ms of נגד) he was told

When the Nûn is unassimilated, however, we find *o* instead of *u*.

הָנְחַלְתִּי (Perf. 1 cs of נחל) I was alloted

iv. For I-Wāw/Yōḏ, II-Wāw/Yōḏ, and Geminate verbs it is *û*.

הוּסַד (Perf. 3 ms of יסד) it was founded

הוּמַת (Perf. 3 ms of מות) it was killed

הוּשַׁד (Perf. 3 ms of שׁדד) he was destroyed

**Synopsis of Hophal Verbs**

| *Root* | *Perf.* | *Impf.* | *Inf. abs.* | *Inf. cs.* | *Ptc.* |
|---|---|---|---|---|---|
| שמר | הָשְׁמַר | יָשְׁמַר | הָשְׁמֵר | – | מָשְׁמָר |
| עבד | הָעֳבַד | יָעֳבַד | הָעֳבֵד | – | מָעֳבָד |
| גלה | הָגְלָה | יָגְלֶה | הָגְלֵה | – | מָגְלֶה |
| יסד | הוּסַד | יוּסַד | הוּסָד | – | מוּסָד |
| נגד | הֻגַּד | יֻגַּד | הֻגֵּד | הֻגַּד | מֻגָּד |
| קום | הוּקַם | יוּקַם | הוּקֵם | – | מוּקָם |

## 3. The Qal Passive

A few verbs which are frequently confused with Pual and Hophal are, in fact, vestiges of an old Qal Passive verbal pattern. In general, we know that these verbs are Qal Passives because they correspond to verbs in Qal, not Piel or Hophal. If a form occurs in Qal, but not in Piel or Hiphil, and seems to be the passive of the verb in Qal, then the verb is probably a Qal passive. For example, since we know from context that אֻכַּל means "it was consumed" (not "it was fed," or the like), and the root does not appear in Piel, forms like אֻכַּל are almost certainly Qal passives.

As another example, we note that the verb נתן does not occur at all in Piel or Hiphil, but יֻתַּן (he/it was given) occurs several times. If the verb were Hophal, one would expect to find at least some examples of נתן in Hiphil. Moreover, the meaning of יֻתַּן (derived from contexts) suggests that יֻתַּן is the passive of Qal, not Hiphil.

Analogous to יֻתַּן, we have a form like יֻקַּח (he was taken). Again, the verb does not appear in Piel or Hiphil. The corresponding perfect is לֻקַּח, a form apparently pointed as a Pual, although there is no evidence that the root לקח was formed like the I-Nûn group outside the Qal verbal pattern (so the Niphal 3 ms is נִלְקַח, not *נִקַּח). If יֻקַּח is a Pual imperfect, one would expect *יְלֻקַּח; if it were Hophal, the perfect of the לֻקַּח type (i.e., without the prefixed *h*-) is problematic. Finally, it should be noted that the participle לֻקָּח is attested – without the –מ prefix that one would expect for the Pual or Hophal participles. Thus, it must be concluded that forms like לֻקַּח and יֻקַּח are Qal passives, not Pual or Hophal.

The following are examples of Qal passive forms.:

| *Root* | *Perf.* | *Impf.* | *Ptc.* |
|---|---|---|---|
| אכל | אֻכַּל | יְאֻכַּל | אֻכָּל |
| ילד | יֻלַּד | – | יוּלָּד |
| לקח | לֻקַּח | יֻקַּח | לֻקָּח |
| נתן | – | יֻתַּן | – |

## 4. Conditional Sentences

A conditional sentence consists of two clauses: a first that states the condition or supposition (the "if-clause" or protasis), and a second that states the consequence (the "then-clause" or apodosis).

**a.** Real Conditions

Conditions that are real, realized, or realizable are typically introduced by אִם in the first clause. The second clause may be introduced by ו, but sometimes ו is left out.

| | |
|---|---|
| אִם־תֵּלְכִי עִמִּי וְהָלָכְתִּי וְאִם־לֹא תֵלְכִי עִמִּי לֹא אֵלֵךְ | *If* you will go with me, (*then*) I will go; but *if* not, (*then*) I will not go (Judg 4:8) |
| אִם־תַּעְצְרֵנִי לֹא־אֹכַל בְּלַחְמֶךָ | *If* you detain me, (*then*) I will not eat your food (Judg 13:16) |

Less frequently, a real condition may be introduced by כִּי or הֵן or, rarely, אֲשֶׁר.

כִּֽי־תִמְצָ֨א אִ֜ישׁ לֹ֣א תְבָרְכֶ֗נּוּ
וְכִֽי־יְבָרֶכְךָ֥ אִ֖ישׁ לֹ֣א תַעֲנֶ֑נּוּ

*If* you meet someone, do not salute him; and *if* any one salutes you, do not answer him (2 Kgs 4:29)

הֵ֣ן צַ֭דִּיק בָּאָ֣רֶץ יְשֻׁלָּ֑ם אַ֝֗ף
כִּֽי־רָשָׁ֥ע וְחוֹטֵֽא

*If* the righteous on earth be recompensed, how much more the wicked sinner? (Prov 11:31)

אֲשֶׁר֩ יִשְׁאָל֨וּן בְּנֵיכֶ֤ם...
וְהוֹדַעְתֶּ֖ם אֶת־בְּנֵיכֶ֑ם

*If* your children should ask ... (*then*) you shall let them know (Josh 4:21–22)

**b.** Hypothetical Conditions

Conditions that are not real, realized or realizable are introduced by **לוּ** (also **לֻא**) "if" or **לוּלֵי** (also **לוּלֵא**) "if not" in the first clause.

ל֣וּ חָפֵ֧ץ יְהוָ֛ה לַהֲמִיתֵ֖נוּ לֹֽא־
לָקַ֤ח מִיָּדֵ֙נוּ֙ עֹלָ֣ה וּמִנְחָ֔ה

*If* YHWH had desired to kill us, (*then*) he would not have taken an offering and a gift from our hand (Judg 13:23)

ל֥וּ חָכְמ֖וּ יַשְׂכִּ֣ילוּ זֹ֑את

If they were wise, (*then*) they would understand this (Deut 32:29)

לוּלֵא֙ חֲרַשְׁתֶּ֣ם בְּעֶגְלָתִ֔י
לֹ֥א מְצָאתֶ֖ם חִידָתִֽי

*If* you had not plowed with my heifer, (*then*) you would not have found my riddle (Judg 14:18)

Sometimes a conditional clause may be introduced without any of the particles mentioned above. In such cases, the "if-clause" and the "then-clause" may each be introduced simply by וְ.

וּבֵרֵ֖ךְ וְלֹ֥א אֲשִׁיבֶֽנָּה

*If* he blesses, (*then*) I cannot reverse it (Num 23:20)

וְעָזַ֥ב אֶת־אָבִ֖יו וָמֵֽת

*If* he leaves his father, (*then*) he will die (Gen 44:22)

## Vocabulary

*Nouns*:

גּוֹרָל (mp. גּוֹרָלוֹת) lot

גַּל wave, heap (of stone). *Verb*: גָּלַל to roll

דָּג (also דָּגָה) fish

הֶ֫בֶל idol, futility

יְרֵכָה (with suff. –יַרְכָת; du.: יַרְכָתַ֫יִם) rear, hindmost part

מֵעִים (always pl.) bowels, entrails

קֵץ end

שָׂכָר reward, wages. *Verb*: שָׂכַר to hire

שְׁאוֹל Sheol, the underworld

תְּהוֹם (fs or ms; fp: תְּהוֹמוֹת) deep, ocean, abyss

*Verbs*:

גָּרַשׁ to drive out

חָבַשׁ to bind, gird

נָבַט Hi.: to gaze, look

נָקָה to be free, innocent. *Adjective*: נָקִי or נָקִיא innocent

פָּלַל Hith.: to pray. *Noun*: תְּפִלָּה prayer

רָחַץ to wash

שָׁוַע Pi.: to cry out for help

*Interjection*:

אֲהָהּ Ah! (Also אָנָּא = אָהּ נָא, and אָנָּה)

*Preposition*:

בַּ֫עַד (cs. בְּעַד; with suffix. –בַּעֲד) through, around, on behalf of

# Exercise 29

**a.** Write the following forms:

1. Pu. perf. 3 cp of גֵּרַשׁ
2. Pu. impf. 3 mp of גֵּרַשׁ
3. Pu. perf. 3 cp of כָּסָה
4. Pu. impf. 3 ms of כָּסָה
5. Ho. perf. 3 ms of גָּלָה
6. Ho. perf. 3 ms of נָכָה
7. Ho. impf. 2 mp of נָכָה
8. Ho. perf. 3 cp of נָכָה
9. Ho. perf. 3 ms of שׁוּב
10. Ho. impf. 3 ms of מוּת
11. Ho. ptc. mp of שׁוּב
12. Pu. perf. 2 mp of יָלַד
13. Pu. perf. 3 ms of רָאָה
14. Ho. ptc. ms of רָאָה
15. Ho. juss. 3 ms of נָגַד
16. Ho. perf. 3 cp of חָבָא
17. Pu. perf. 3 cp of חָבָא
18. Pu. perf. 1 cs of שָׁלַח
19. Pu. ptc. ms of שָׁלַח
20. Ho. perf. 3 fs of שָׁלַךְ

**b.** Translate Jonah 1–2 with the help of a dictionary.

*Note*: v 7: בְּשֶׁלְּמִי = בַּאֲשֶׁר לְמִי (see dictionary under –שֶׁ).

# Lesson XXX

## 1. Polel, Polal, Hithpolel

These verbal patterns are characterized by the presence of a long vowel (*ô*) after the first radical, the absence of the second radical, and the duplication of the third: *qôlēl*, *qôlal*, *hiṯqôlēl*. For II-Wāw/Yōḏ roots, these patterns tend to replace Piel, Pual, and Hithpael, respectively. Hence, although II-Wāw/Yōḏ verbs are attested in Piel, Pual and Hithpael, they are relatively rare; the functions normally met by those verbal patterns are assumed by Polel, Polal, and Hithpolel forms. Geminate verbs, too, are sometimes found in the Polel, Polal, and Hithpolel patterns, rather than Piel, Pual, and Hithpael.

The various forms of the verb קוּם (to arise) are as follows.

**a.** Perfect

| | *Polel* | *Polal* | *Hithpolel* |
|---|---|---|---|
| *3 ms* | קוֹמֵם | קוֹמַם | הִתְקוֹמֵם |
| *3 fs* | קוֹמְמָה | קוֹמְמָה | הִתְקוֹמְמָה |
| *2 ms* | קוֹמַמְתָּ | קוֹמַמְתָּ | הִתְקוֹמַמְתָּ |
| *2 fs* | קוֹמַמְתְּ | קוֹמַמְתְּ | הִתְקוֹמַמְתְּ |
| *1 cs* | קוֹמַמְתִּי | קוֹמַמְתִּי | הִתְקוֹמַמְתִּי |
| *3 cp* | קוֹמְמוּ | קוֹמְמוּ | הִתְקוֹמְמוּ |
| *2 mp* | קוֹמַמְתֶּם | קוֹמַמְתֶּם | הִתְקוֹמַמְתֶּם |
| *2 fp* | קוֹמַמְתֶּן | קוֹמַמְתֶּן | הִתְקוֹמַמְתֶּן |
| *1 cp* | קוֹמַמְנוּ | קוֹמַמְנוּ | הִתְקוֹמַמְנוּ |

*Notes*:

i. Except for the 3 ms, Polel and Polal forms cannot be distinguished from one another (compare XIII.2.i).

ii. We also get forms like כּוֹנֲנוּ (they established) instead of כּוֹנְנוּ and חֹלֲלָה (it has been pierced) instead of חֹלְלָה.

**b.** Imperfect

| | *Polel* | *Polal* | *Hithpolel* |
|---|---|---|---|
| *3 ms* | יְקוֹמֵם | יְקוֹמַם | יִתְקוֹמֵם |
| *3 fs* | תְּקוֹמֵם | תְּקוֹמַם | תִּתְקוֹמֵם |
| *2 ms* | תְּקוֹמֵם | תְּקוֹמַם | תִּתְקוֹמֵם |
| *2 fs* | תְּקוֹמְמִי | תְּקוֹמְמִי | תִּתְקוֹמְמִי |
| *1 cs* | אֲקוֹמֵם | אֲקוֹמַם | אֶתְקוֹמֵם |
| *3 mp* | יְקוֹמְמוּ | יְקוֹמְמוּ | יִתְקוֹמְמוּ |
| *3 fp* | תְּקוֹמֵמְנָה | תְּקוֹמַמְנָה | תִּתְקוֹמֵמְנָה |
| *2 mp* | תְּקוֹמְמוּ | תְּקוֹמְמוּ | תִּתְקוֹמְמוּ |
| *2 fp* | תְּקוֹמֵמְנָה | תְּקוֹמַמְנָה | תִּתְקוֹמֵמְנָה |
| *1 cp* | נְקוֹמֵם | נְקוֹמַם | נִתְקוֹמֵם |

*Notes*:

i. Due to the reduction of the full vowel to *šĕwāʾ*, we cannot distinguish between the active (Polel) and passive (Polal) forms in the 2 fs, 3 mp, and 2 mp.

ii. The frequently attested verb כּוּן (to establish) may show the assimilation of ת in some of the Hithpolel forms (see XXVII.4), e.g., תִּכּוֹנֵן for תִּתְכּוֹנֵן.

**c.** Other Inflections

| | *Polel* | *Polal* | *Hithpolel* |
|---|---|---|---|
| *Impv.* | קוֹמֵם | | הִתְקוֹמֵם |
| *Inf. cs.* | קוֹמֵם | | הִתְקוֹמֵם |
| *Ptc.* | מְקוֹמֵם | מְקוֹמָם | מִתְקוֹמֵם |

## 2. Pilpel, Polpal, Hithpalpel

These verbal patterns are characterized by the repetition of the first and last radicals. Again, they correspond in function roughly to Piel, Pual, and Hithpael, respectively. Verbs in these patterns are mostly geminates, with a few that are II-Wāw/Yōḏ.

| *Root* | *Pilpel* | *Polpal* | *Hithpalpel* | |
|---|---|---|---|---|
| גלל | גִּלְגֵּל | | הִתְגַּלְגֵּל | to roll |
| קלל | קִלְקֵל | | הִתְקַלְקֵל | to shake swiftly |
| כול | כִּלְכֵּל | כָּלְכַּל | | to sustain |

## 3. Minor Patterns

There are a few uncommon patterns.

**a.** Poel, Poal, Hithpoel

These verbal patterns are similar to the Polel, Polal, Hithpolel series, but they are built on triliteral roots: *qôṭēl*, *qôṭal*, *hiṯqôṭēl*.

| | | |
|---|---|---|
| Poel perf. 3 ms | שֹׁרֵשׁ | it has taken root (Isa 40:24) |
| Poal perf. 3 cp | שֹׁרָשׁוּ | they have taken root (Jer 12:2) |
| Hithpoel impf. 3 mp | יִתְגֹּעֲשׁוּ | they surge (Jer 46:8) |

**b.** Palal, Pulal

These verbal patterns retain all three radicals but also repeat the third: *qaṭlal*, *quṭlal*.

| | | |
|---|---|---|
| Palal perf. 3 ms | שַׁאֲנַן | it has been at ease (Jer 48:11) |
| Pulal perf. 3 ms | אֻמְלַל | it has failed (Joel 1:10) |

**c.** Pealal

This verbal pattern retains all three radicals but also repeat the last two: *qĕṭalṭal.*

Pealal perf. 3 ms סְחַרְחַר it palpitates (Ps 38:11)

Finally, there are isolated and sometimes disputed examples of other patterns, including patterns based on four radicals and mixed forms. One should consult a reference grammar when such forms are encountered.

## 4. Uses of כִּי

The particle כִּי is used a variety of ways.

**a.** It may introduce a *causal* clause, and so should be translated as "because" or "for."

כִּי עָשִׂיתָ זֹּאת אָרוּר אַתָּה — *because* you have done this, you are cursed (Gen 3:14)

חָנֵּנִי יְהוָה כִּי אֻמְלַל אָנִי — Be gracious to me, YHWH, *for* I am languishing (Ps 6:3)

**b.** It may introduce an *object* clause after verbs of perception (to see, hear, know, understand, etc.). In such cases, כִּי may be translated as "that" or it may not be translated at all.

עַתָּה יָדַעְתִּי כִּי־יְרֵא אֱלֹהִים אַתָּה — now I know (*that*) you are a fearer of God (Gen 22:12)

**c.** It may introduce a clause stating the *result* of an action, and so should be translated as "(so) that."

מָה רָאִיתָ כִּי עָשִׂיתָ אֶת־הַדָּבָר הַזֶּה — What were you thinking *that* you were doing this thing? (Gen 20:10)

**d.** After a negative, it may be a strong *adversative* meaning "but."

לֹא־תִקְרָא אֶת־שְׁמָהּ
שָׂרָי כִּי שָׂרָה שְׁמָהּ

You shall not call her "Sarai," *but* (rather) "Sarah" shall be her name (Gen 17:15)

לֹא כִּי צָחָקְתְּ

No, *but* you did laugh! (Gen 18:15)

This usage is related to **כִּי אִם** (but rather, except):

לֹא יַעֲקֹב יֵאָמֵר עוֹד
שִׁמְךָ כִּי אִם־יִשְׂרָאֵל

Your name will no longer be called "Jacob," but rather "Israel" (Gen 32:29)

**e.** In *temporal* clauses (see XX.5), **כִּי** may be translated as "when."

וַיְהִי כִּי־זָקֵן יִצְחָק

*When* Isaac was old ... (Gen 27:1)

**f.** In conditional clauses (see XXIX.4), it states a *real condition*, and is translated as "if."

כִּי־תִמְצָא אִישׁ לֹא תְבָרְכֶנּוּ
וְכִי־יְבָרֶכְךָ אִישׁ לֹא תַעֲנֶנּוּ

*If* you meet someone, do not salute him; and if any one salutes you, do not answer him (2 Kgs 4:29)

**g.** In some cases, it has an *asseverative* (emphatic) force, and may be translated as "indeed," "surely," "truly," or the like.

כִּי־לֶאֱוִיל יַהֲרָג־כָּעַשׂ

*Indeed*, vexation kills the fool! (Job 5:2)

Thus, too, **כִּי** introduces affirmative statements in oaths (see XXVII.8).

**h.** Sometimes it has a *concessive* force, meaning "though."

כִּי נָפַלְתִּי קָמְתִּי

*though* I have fallen, I will rise again (Mic 7:8)

**j.** Sometimes it introduces *direct speech* and is, therefore, not translated.

וַיֹּאמֶר כִּי־אֶהְיֶה עִמָּךְ

He said: "I will be with you" (Exod 3:12)

## Vocabulary

*Nouns*:

הָדָר (also הֲדָרָה) splendor, grandeur, adornment

זָמִיר (pl. זְמִרוֹת) song. Also מִזְמֹור psalm. *Verb*: זָמַר Pi. to make melody

יַ֫עַר forest

עוֹף bird, fowl. *Verb*: עוּף to fly

צוּר rock (mountain)

צַר adversary

תֵּ֫בֵל world

*Verbs*:

אוֹר to become bright; Hi.: to illumine, shine

בָּחַן to test, try

בָּשַׂר Pi.: to make known, bring news

גִּיל to be joyful, rejoice

כָּרַע to bend the knee

נוּעַ to shake, tremble

נָסָה Pi.: to test

רוּעַ Hi.: to shout. *Noun*: תְּרוּעָה alarm, shout

תָּעָה to wander about, be confused

*Adverbs*:

בַּל not. Also בְּלִי without

## Exercise 30

**a.** Translate Isaiah 6.

**b.** Translate Num 6:24–26.

## 1. Strong Verbs

| | | *Qal* | *Niphal* | *Piel* | *Pual* | *Hithpael* | *Hiphil* | *Hophal* | |
|---|---|---|---|---|---|---|---|---|---|
| Perf. | *3 ms* | קָטַל | נִקְטַל | קִטֵּל | קֻטַּל | הִתְקַטֵּל | הִקְטִיל | הָקְטַל | *3 ms* |
| | *3 fs* | קָֽטְלָה | נִקְטְלָה | קִטְּלָה | קֻטְּלָה | הִתְקַטְּלָה | הִקְטִ֫ילָה | הָקְטְלָה | *3 fs* |
| | *2 ms* | קָטַ֫לְתָּ | נִקְטַ֫לְתָּ | קִטַּ֫לְתָּ | קֻטַּ֫לְתָּ | הִתְקַטַּ֫לְתָּ | הִקְטַ֫לְתָּ | הָקְטַ֫לְתָּ | *2 ms* |
| | *2 fs* | קָטַלְתְּ | נִקְטַלְתְּ | קִטַּלְתְּ | קֻטַּלְתְּ | הִתְקַטַּלְתְּ | הִקְטַלְתְּ | הָקְטַלְתְּ | *2 fs* |
| | *1 cs* | קָטַ֫לְתִּי | נִקְטַ֫לְתִּי | קִטַּ֫לְתִּי | קֻטַּ֫לְתִּי | הִתְקַטַּ֫לְתִּי | הִקְטַ֫לְתִּי | הָקְטַ֫לְתִּי | *1 cs* |
| | *3 cp* | קָֽטְלוּ | נִקְטְלוּ | קִטְּלוּ | קֻטְּלוּ | הִתְקַטְּלוּ | הִקְטִ֫ילוּ | הָקְטְלוּ | *3 cp* |
| | *2 mp* | קְטַלְתֶּם | נִקְטַלְתֶּם | קִטַּלְתֶּם | קֻטַּלְתֶּם | הִתְקַטַּלְתֶּם | הִקְטַלְתֶּם | הָקְטַלְתֶּם | *2 mp* |
| | *2 fp* | קְטַלְתֶּן | נִקְטַלְתֶּן | קִטַּלְתֶּן | קֻטַּלְתֶּן | הִתְקַטַּלְתֶּן | הִקְטַלְתֶּן | הָקְטַלְתֶּן | *2 fp* |
| | *1 cp* | קָטַ֫לְנוּ | נִקְטַ֫לְנוּ | קִטַּ֫לְנוּ | קֻטַּ֫לְנוּ | הִתְקַטַּ֫לְנוּ | הִקְטַ֫לְנוּ | הָקְטַ֫לְנוּ | *1 cp* |
| Impf. | *3 ms* | יִקְטֹל | יִקָּטֵל | יְקַטֵּל | יְקֻטַּל | יִתְקַטֵּל | יַקְטִיל | יָקְטַל | *3 ms* |
| | *3 fs* | תִּקְטֹל | תִּקָּטֵל | תְּקַטֵּל | תְּקֻטַּל | תִּתְקַטֵּל | תַּקְטִיל | תָּקְטַל | *3 fs* |
| | *2 ms* | תִּקְטֹל | תִּקָּטֵל | תְּקַטֵּל | תְּקֻטַּל | תִּתְקַטֵּל | תַּקְטִיל | תָּקְטַל | *2 ms* |
| | *2 fs* | תִּקְטְלִי | תִּקָּֽטְלִי | תְּקַטְּלִי | תְּקֻטְּלִי | תִּתְקַטְּלִי | תַּקְטִ֫ילִי | תָּקְטְלִי | *2 fs* |
| | *1 cs* | אֶקְטֹל | אֶקָּטֵל | אֲקַטֵּל | אֲקֻטַּל | אֶתְקַטֵּל | אַקְטִיל | אָקְטַל | *1 cs* |
| | *3 mp* | יִקְטְלוּ | יִקָּֽטְלוּ | יְקַטְּלוּ | יְקֻטְּלוּ | יִתְקַטְּלוּ | יַקְטִ֫ילוּ | יָקְטְלוּ | *3 mp* |

| | | | | | | | | | |
|---|---|---|---|---|---|---|---|---|---|
| | *3 fp* | תִּקְטֹלְנָה | תִּקָּטַלְנָה | תְּקַטֵּלְנָה | תְּקֻטַּלְנָה | תִּתְקַטֵּלְנָה | תַּקְטֵלְנָה | תָּקְטַלְנָה | *3 fp* |
| | *2 mp* | תִּקְטְלוּ | תִּקָּטְלוּ | תְּקַטְּלוּ | תְּקֻטְּלוּ | תִּתְקַטְּלוּ | תַּקְטִילוּ | תָּקְטְלוּ | *2 mp* |
| | *2 fp* | תִּקְטֹלְנָה | תִּקָּטַלְנָה | תְּקַטֵּלְנָה | תְּקֻטַּלְנָה | תִּתְקַטֵּלְנָה | תַּקְטֵלְנָה | תָּקְטַלְנָה | *2 fp* |
| | *1 cp* | נִקְטֹל | נִקָּטֵל | נְקַטֵּל | נְקֻטַּל | נִתְקַטֵּל | נַקְטִיל | נָקְטַל | *1 cp* |
| Impv. | *2 ms* | קְטֹל | הִקָּטֵל | קַטֵּל | | הִתְקַטֵּל | הַקְטֵל | | *2 ms* |
| | *2 fs* | קִטְלִי | הִקָּטְלִי | קַטְּלִי | | הִתְקַטְּלִי | הַקְטִילִי | | *2 fs* |
| | *2 mp* | קִטְלוּ | הִקָּטְלוּ | קַטְּלוּ | | הִתְקַטְּלוּ | הַקְטִילוּ | | *2 mp* |
| | *2 fp* | קְטֹלְנָה | הִקָּטַלְנָה | קַטֵּלְנָה | | הִתְקַטֵּלְנָה | הַקְטֵלְנָה | | *2 fp* |
| Inf. | *Abs.* | קָטוֹל | הִקָּטֹל | קַטֹּל | קֻטֹּל | הִתְקַטֵּל | הַקְטֵל | הָקְטֵל | *Abs.* |
| | | | נִקְטֹל | קַטֵּל | | | | | |
| | *Cs.* | קְטֹל | הִקָּטֵל | קַטֵּל | | הִתְקַטֵּל | הַקְטִיל | | *Cs.* |
| Ptc. | *Act.* | קֹטֵל | | מְקַטֵּל | | מִתְקַטֵּל | מַקְטִיל | | *Act.* |
| | *Pass.* | קָטוּל | נִקְטָל | | מְקֻטָּל | | | מָקְטָל | *Pass.* |
| *wyqtl* | | וַיִּקְטֹל | וַיִּקָּטֵל | וַיְקַטֵּל | וַיְקֻטַּל | וַיִּתְקַטֵּל | וַיַּקְטֵל | וַיָּקְטַל | |
| Juss. | | יִקְטֹל | יִקָּטֵל | יְקַטֵּל | יְקֻטַּל | יִתְקַטֵּל | יַקְטֵל | יָקְטַל | |

## 2. I-Guttural Verbs

| | | *Qal* | | | *Niphal* | *Hiphil* | *Hophal* | |
|---|---|---|---|---|---|---|---|---|
| Perf. | *3 ms* | עָמַד | חָזַק | אָכַל | נֶעֱזַב | הֶעֱמִיד | הָעֳמַד | *3 ms* |
| | *3 fs* | עָֽמְדָה | חָֽזְקָה | אָֽכְלָה | נֶֽעֶזְבָה | הֶעֱמִ֫ידָה | הָֽעָמְדָה | *3 fs* |
| | *2 ms* | עָמַ֫דְתָּ | חָזַ֫קְתָּ | אָכַ֫לְתָּ | נֶעֱזַ֫בְתָּ | הֶעֱמַ֫דְתָּ | הָעֳמַ֫דְתָּ | *2 ms* |
| | *2 fs* | עָמַדְתְּ | חָזַקְתְּ | אָכַלְתְּ | נֶעֱזַבְתְּ | הֶעֱמַדְתְּ | הָעֳמַדְתְּ | *2 fs* |
| | *1 cs* | עָמַ֫דְתִּי | חָזַ֫קְתִּי | אָכַ֫לְתִּי | נֶעֱזַ֫בְתִּי | הֶעֱמַ֫דְתִּי | הָעֳמַ֫דְתִּי | *1 cs* |
| | *3 cp* | עָֽמְדוּ | חָֽזְקוּ | אָֽכְלוּ | נֶֽעֶזְבוּ | הֶעֱמִ֫ידוּ | הָֽעָמְדוּ | *3 cp* |
| | *2 mp* | עֲמַדְתֶּם | חֲזַקְתֶּם | אֲכַלְתֶּם | נֶעֱזַבְתֶּם | הֶעֱמַדְתֶּם | הָעֳמַדְתֶּם | *2 mp* |
| | *2 fp* | עֲמַדְתֶּן | חֲזַקְתֶּן | אֲכַלְתֶּן | נֶעֱזַבְתֶּן | הֶעֱמַדְתֶּן | הָעֳמַדְתֶּן | *2 fp* |
| | *1 cp* | עָמַ֫דְנוּ | חָזַ֫קְנוּ | אָכַ֫לְנוּ | נֶעֱזַ֫בְנוּ | הֶעֱמַ֫דְנוּ | הָעֳמַ֫דְנוּ | *1 cp* |
| Impf. | *3 ms* | יַֽעֲמֹד | יֶֽחֱזַק | יֹאכַל | יֵעָזֵב | יַֽעֲמִיד | יָֽעֳמַד | *3 ms* |
| | *3 fs* | תַּֽעֲמֹד | תֶּֽחֱזַק | תֹּאכַל | תֵּעָזֵב | תַּֽעֲמִיד | תָּֽעֳמַד | *3 fs* |
| | *2 ms* | תַּֽעֲמֹד | תֶּֽחֱזַק | תֹּאכַל | תֵּעָזֵב | תַּֽעֲמִיד | תָּֽעֳמַד | *2 ms* |
| | *2 fs* | תַּֽעַמְדִי | תֶּֽחֶזְקִי | תֹּאכְלִי | תֵּעָֽזְבִי | תַּֽעֲמִ֫ידִי | תָּֽעָמְדִי | *2 fs* |
| | *1 cs* | אֶֽעֱמֹד | אֶֽחֱזַק | אֹכַל | אֵעָזֵב | אַֽעֲמִיד | אָֽעֳמַד | *1 cs* |
| | *3 mp* | יַֽעַמְדוּ | יֶֽחֶזְקוּ | יֹאכְלוּ | יֵעָֽזְבוּ | יַֽעֲמִ֫ידוּ | יָֽעָמְדוּ | *3 mp* |

| | | | | | | | | |
|---|---|---|---|---|---|---|---|---|
| | 3 fp | תַּעֲמֹ֫דְנָה | תֶּחֱזַ֫קְנָה | תֹּאכַ֫לְנָה | תֵּעָזַ֫בְנָה | תַּעֲמֵ֫דְנָה | תָּעֳמַ֫דְנָה | 3 fp |
| | 2 mp | תַּעַמְדוּ | תֶּחֶזְקוּ | תֹּאכְלוּ | תֵּעָזְבוּ | תַּעֲמִ֫ידוּ | תָּעָמְדוּ | 2 mp |
| | 2 fp | תַּעֲמֹ֫דְנָה | תֶּחֱזַ֫קְנָה | תֹּאכַ֫לְנָה | תֵּעָזַ֫בְנָה | תַּעֲמֵ֫דְנָה | תָּעֳמַ֫דְנָה | 2 fp |
| | 1 cp | נַעֲמֹד | נֶחֱזַק | נֹאכַל | נֵעָזֵב | נַעֲמִיד | נָעֳמַד | 1 cp |
| Impv. | 2 ms | עֲמֹד | חֲזַק | אֱכֹל | הֵעָזֵב | הַעֲמֵד | | 2 ms |
| | 2 fs | עִמְדִי | חִזְקִי | אִכְלִי | הֵעָזְבִי | הַעֲמִ֫ידִי | | 2 fs |
| | 2 mp | עִמְדוּ | חִזְקוּ | אִכְלוּ | הֵעָזְבוּ | הַעֲמִ֫ידוּ | | 2 mp |
| | 2 fp | עֲמֹ֫דְנָה | חֲזַ֫קְנָה | אֱכֹ֫לְנָה | הֵעָזַ֫בְנָה | הַעֲמֵ֫דְנָה | | 2 fp |
| Inf. | Abs. | עָמוֹד | | אָכוֹל | נַעֲזוֹב<br>הֵאָכֹל | הַעֲמֵד | הָעֳמֵד | Abs. |
| | Cs. | עֲמֹד | | אֱכֹל | הֵעָזֵב | הַעֲמִיד | | Cs. |
| Ptc. | Act. | עֹמֵד | | אֹכֵל | | מַעֲמִיד | | Act. |
| | Pass. | עָמוּד | | אָכוּל | נֶעֱזָב | | מָעֳמָד | Pass. |
| *wyqtl* | | וַיַּעֲמֹד | וַיֶּחֱזַק | וַיֹּאכַל | וַיֵּעָזֵב | וַיַּעֲמֵד | | |
| Juss. | | יַעֲמֹד | יֶחֱזַק | יֹאכַל | יֵעָזֵב | יַעֲמֵד | | |

## 3. II-Guttural Verbs

| | | *Qal* | *Niphal* | *Piel* | | *Pual* | *Hithpael* | |
|---|---|---|---|---|---|---|---|---|
| Perf. | *3 ms* | בָּחַר | נִבְחַר | מֵאֵן | מִהֵר | בֹּרַךְ | הִתְבָּרֵךְ | *3 ms* |
| | *3 fs* | בָּֽחֲרָה | נִבְחֲרָה | מֵֽאֲנָה | מִֽהֲרָה | בֹּֽרְכָה | הִתְבָּֽרֲכָה | *3 fs* |
| | *2 ms* | בָּחַ֫רְתָּ | נִבְחַ֫רְתָּ | מֵאַ֫נְתָּ | מִהַ֫רְתָּ | בֹּרַ֫כְתָּ | הִתְבָּרַ֫כְתָּ | *2 ms* |
| | *2 fs* | בָּחַרְתְּ | נִבְחַרְתְּ | מֵאַנְתְּ | מִהַרְתְּ | בֹּרַכְתְּ | הִתְבָּרַכְתְּ | *2 fs* |
| | *1 cs* | בָּחַ֫רְתִּי | נִבְחַ֫רְתִּי | מֵאַ֫נְתִּי | מִהַ֫רְתִּי | בֹּרַ֫כְתִּי | הִתְבָּרַ֫כְתִּי | *1 cs* |
| | *3 cp* | בָּֽחֲרוּ | נִבְחֲרוּ | מֵאֲנוּ | מִהֲרוּ | בֹּרְכוּ | הִתְבָּֽרֲכוּ | *3 cp* |
| | *2 mp* | בְּחַרְתֶּם | נִבְחַרְתֶּם | מֵאַנְתֶּם | מִהַרְתֶּם | בֹּרַכְתֶּם | הִתְבָּרַכְתֶּם | *2 mp* |
| | *2 fp* | בְּחַרְתֶּן | נִבְחַרְתֶּן | מֵאַנְתֶּן | מִהַרְתֶּן | בֹּרַכְתֶּן | הִתְבָּרַכְתֶּן | *2 fp* |
| | *1 cp* | בָּחַ֫רְנוּ | נִבְחַ֫רְנוּ | מֵאַ֫נּוּ | מִהַ֫רְנוּ | בֹּרַ֫כְנוּ | הִתְבָּרַ֫כְנוּ | *1 cp* |
| Impf. | *3 ms* | יִבְחַר | יִבָּחֵר | יְמָאֵן | יְמַהֵר | יְבֹרַךְ | יִתְבָּרֵךְ | *3 ms* |
| | *3 fs* | תִּבְחַר | תִּבָּחֵר | תְּמָאֵן | תְּמַהֵר | תְּבֹרַךְ | תִּתְבָּרֵךְ | *3 fs* |
| | *2 ms* | תִּבְחַר | תִּבָּחֵר | תְּמָאֵן | תְּמַהֵר | תְּבֹרַךְ | תִּתְבָּרֵךְ | *2 ms* |
| | *2 fs* | תִּבְחֲרִי | תִּבָּֽחֲרִי | תְּמָֽאֲנִי | תְּמַהֲרִי | תְּבֹרְכִי | תִּתְבָּֽרֲכִי | *2 fs* |
| | *1 cs* | אֶבְחַר | אֶבָּחֵר | אֲמָאֵן | אֲמַהֵר | אֲבֹרַךְ | אֶתְבָּרֵךְ | *1 cs* |
| | *3 mp* | יִבְחֲרוּ | יִבָּֽחֲרוּ | יְמָֽאֲנוּ | יְמַהֲרוּ | יְבֹרְכוּ | יִתְבָּֽרֲכוּ | *3 mp* |

| | | | | | | | | |
|---|---|---|---|---|---|---|---|---|
| | *3 fp* | תִּבְחַ֫רְנָה | תִּבָּחַ֫רְנָה | תְּמָאֵ֫נָּה | תְּמַהֵ֫רְנָה | תְּבֹרַ֫כְנָה | תִּתְבָּרֵ֫כְנָה | *3 fp* |
| | *2 mp* | תִּבְחֲרוּ | תִּבָּחֲרוּ | תְּמָאֲנוּ | תְּמַהֲרוּ | תְּבֹרְכוּ | תִּתְבָּרֲכוּ | *2 mp* |
| | *2 fp* | תִּבְחַ֫רְנָה | תִּבָּחַ֫רְנָה | תְּמָאֵ֫נָּה | תְּמַהֵ֫רְנָה | תְּבֹרַ֫כְנָה | תִּתְבָּרֵ֫כְנָה | *2 fp* |
| | *1 cp* | נִבְחַר | נִבָּחֵר | נְמָאֵן | נְמַהֵר | נְבֹרַךְ | נִתְבָּרֵךְ | *1 cp* |
| Impv. | *2 ms* | בְּחַר | הִבָּחֵר | מָאֵן | מַהֵר | | הִתְבָּרֵךְ | *2 ms* |
| | *2 fs* | בַּחֲרִי | הִבָּחֲרִי | מָאֲנִי | מַהֲרִי | | הִתְבָּרֲכִי | *2 fs* |
| | *2 mp* | בַּחֲרוּ | הִבָּחֲרוּ | מָאֲנוּ | מַהֲרוּ | | הִתְבָּרֲכוּ | *2 mp* |
| | *2 fp* | בְּחַ֫רְנָה | הִבָּחַ֫רְנָה | מָאֵ֫נָּה | מַהֵ֫רְנָה | | הִתְבָּרֵ֫כְנָה | *2 fp* |
| Inf. | *Abs.* | בָּחוֹר | נִבְחוֹר | מָאֵן | מַהֵר | | הִתְבָּרֵךְ | *Abs.* |
| | *Cs.* | בְּחֹר | הִבָּחֵר | מָאֵן | מַהֵר | | הִתְבָּרֵךְ | *Cs.* |
| Ptc. | *Act.* | בֹּחֵר | | מְמָאֵן | מְמַהֵר | | מִתְבָּרֵךְ | *Act.* |
| | *Pass.* | בָּחוּר | נִבְחָר | | | מְבֹרָךְ | | *Pass.* |
| *wyqtl* | | וַיִּבְחַר | וַיִּבָּחֵר | וַיְמָאֵן | וַיְמַהֵר | | וַיִּתְבָּרֵךְ | |
| Juss. | | יִבְחַר | יִבָּחֵר | יְמָאֵן | יְמַהֵר | | יִתְבָּרֵךְ | |

## 4. III-Guttural Verbs

| | | *Qal* | *Niphal* | *Piel* | *Pual* | *Hithpael* | *Hiphil* | *Hophal* | |
|---|---|---|---|---|---|---|---|---|---|
| Perf. | *3 ms* | שָׁלַח | נִשְׁלַח | שִׁלַּח | שֻׁלַּח | הִשְׁתַּלַּח | הִשְׁלִיחַ | הָשְׁלַח | *3 ms* |
| | *3 fs* | שָֽׁלְחָה | נִשְׁלְחָה | שִׁלְּחָה | שֻׁלְּחָה | הִשְׁתַּלְּחָה | הִשְׁלִ֫יחָה | הָשְׁלְחָה | *3 fs* |
| | *2 ms* | שָׁלַ֫חְתָּ | נִשְׁלַ֫חְתָּ | שִׁלַּ֫חְתָּ | שֻׁלַּ֫חְתָּ | הִשְׁתַּלַּ֫חְתָּ | הִשְׁלַ֫חְתָּ | הָשְׁלַ֫חְתָּ | *2 ms* |
| | *2 fs* | שָׁלַ֫חַתְּ | נִשְׁלַ֫חַתְּ | שִׁלַּ֫חַתְּ | שֻׁלַּ֫חַתְּ | הִשְׁתַּלַּ֫חַתְּ | הִשְׁלַ֫חַתְּ | הָשְׁלַ֫חַתְּ | *2 fs* |
| | *1 cs* | שָׁלַ֫חְתִּי | נִשְׁלַ֫חְתִּי | שִׁלַּ֫חְתִּי | שֻׁלַּ֫חְתִּי | הִשְׁתַּלַּ֫חְתִּי | הִשְׁלַ֫חְתִּי | הָשְׁלַ֫חְתִּי | *1 cs* |
| | *3 cp* | שָֽׁלְחוּ | נִשְׁלְחוּ | שִׁלְּחוּ | שֻׁלְּחוּ | הִשְׁתַּלְּחוּ | הִשְׁלִ֫יחוּ | הָשְׁלְחוּ | *3 cp* |
| | *2 mp* | שְׁלַחְתֶּם | נִשְׁלַחְתֶּם | שִׁלַּחְתֶּם | שֻׁלַּחְתֶּם | הִשְׁתַּלַּחְתֶּם | הִשְׁלַחְתֶּם | הָשְׁלַחְתֶּם | *2 mp* |
| | *2 fp* | שְׁלַחְתֶּן | נִשְׁלַחְתֶּן | שִׁלַּחְתֶּן | שֻׁלַּחְתֶּן | הִשְׁתַּלַּחְתֶּן | הִשְׁלַחְתֶּן | הָשְׁלַחְתֶּן | *2 fp* |
| | *1 cp* | שָׁלַ֫חְנוּ | נִשְׁלַ֫חְנוּ | שִׁלַּ֫חְנוּ | שֻׁלַּ֫חְנוּ | הִשְׁתַּלַּ֫חְנוּ | הִשְׁלַ֫חְנוּ | הָשְׁלַ֫חְנוּ | *1 cp* |
| Impf. | *3 ms* | יִשְׁלַח | יִשָּׁלַח | יְשַׁלַּח | יְשֻׁלַּח | יִשְׁתַּלַּח | יַשְׁלִיחַ | יָשְׁלַח | *3 ms* |
| | *3 fs* | תִּשְׁלַח | תִּשָּׁלַח | תְּשַׁלַּח | תְּשֻׁלַּח | תִּשְׁתַּלַּח | תַּשְׁלִיחַ | תָּשְׁלַח | *3 fs* |
| | *2 ms* | תִּשְׁלַח | תִּשָּׁלַח | תְּשַׁלַּח | תְּשֻׁלַּח | תִּשְׁתַּלַּח | תַּשְׁלִיחַ | תָּשְׁלַח | *2 ms* |
| | *2 fs* | תִּשְׁלְחִי | תִּשָּֽׁלְחִי | תְּשַׁלְּחִי | תְּשֻׁלְּחִי | תִּשְׁתַּלְּחִי | תַּשְׁלִ֫יחִי | תָּשְׁלְחִי | *2 fs* |
| | *1 cs* | אֶשְׁלַח | אֶשָּׁלַח | אֲשַׁלַּח | אֲשֻׁלַּח | אֶשְׁתַּלַּח | אַשְׁלִיחַ | אָשְׁלַח | *1 cs* |
| | *3 mp* | יִשְׁלְחוּ | יִשָּֽׁלְחוּ | יְשַׁלְּחוּ | יְשֻׁלְּחוּ | יִשְׁתַּלְּחוּ | יַשְׁלִ֫יחוּ | יָשְׁלְחוּ | *3 mp* |

| | | | | | | | | | |
|---|---|---|---|---|---|---|---|---|---|
| | *3 fp* | תִּשְׁלַחְנָה | תִּשָּׁלַחְנָה | תְּשַׁלַּחְנָה | תְּשֻׁלַּחְנָה | תִּשְׁתַּלַּחְנָה | תַּשְׁלַחְנָה | תָּשְׁלַחְנָה | *3 fp* |
| | *2 mp* | תִּשְׁלְחוּ | תִּשָּׁלְחוּ | תְּשַׁלְּחוּ | תְּשֻׁלְּחוּ | תִּשְׁתַּלְּחוּ | תַּשְׁלִיחוּ | תָּשְׁלְחוּ | *2 mp* |
| | *2 fp* | תִּשְׁלַחְנָה | תִּשָּׁלַחְנָה | תְּשַׁלַּחְנָה | תְּשֻׁלַּחְנָה | תִּשְׁתַּלַּחְנָה | תַּשְׁלַחְנָה | תָּשְׁלַחְנָה | *2 fp* |
| | *1 cp* | נִשְׁלַח | נִשָּׁלַח | נְשַׁלַּח | נְשֻׁלַּח | נִשְׁתַּלַּח | נַשְׁלִיחַ | נָשְׁלַח | *1 cp* |
| Impv. | *2 ms* | שְׁלַח | הִשָּׁלַח | שַׁלַּח | | הִשְׁתַּלַּח | הַשְׁלַח | | *2 ms* |
| | *2 fs* | שִׁלְחִי | הִשָּׁלְחִי | שַׁלְּחִי | | הִשְׁתַּלְּחִי | הַשְׁלִיחִי | | *2 fs* |
| | *2 mp* | שִׁלְחוּ | הִשָּׁלְחוּ | שַׁלְּחוּ | | הִשְׁתַּלְּחוּ | הַשְׁלִיחוּ | | *2 mp* |
| | *2 fp* | שְׁלַחְנָה | הִשָּׁלַחְנָה | שַׁלַּחְנָה | | הִשְׁתַּלַּחְנָה | הַשְׁלַחְנָה | | *2 fp* |
| Inf. | *Abs.* | שָׁלוֹחַ | נִשְׁלוֹחַ<br>הִשָּׁלֵחַ | שַׁלֵּחַ | | הִשְׁתַּלֵּחַ | הַשְׁלֵחַ | | *Abs.* |
| | *Cs.* | שְׁלֹחַ | הִשָּׁלַח | שַׁלַּח | | הִשְׁתַּלַּח | הַשְׁלִיחַ | | *Cs.* |
| Ptc. | *Act.* | שֹׁלֵחַ | | מְשַׁלֵּחַ | | מִשְׁתַּלֵּחַ | מַשְׁלִיחַ | | *Act.* |
| | *Pass.* | שָׁלוּחַ | נִשְׁלָח | | מְשֻׁלָּח | | | מָשְׁלָח | *Pass.* |
| *wyqtl* | | וַיִּשְׁלַח | וַיִּשָּׁלַח | וַיְשַׁלַּח | וַיְשֻׁלַּח | וַיִּשְׁתַּלַּח | וַיַּשְׁלַח | וַיָּשְׁלַח | |
| Juss. | | יִשְׁלַח | יִשָּׁלַח | יְשַׁלַּח | יְשֻׁלַּח | יִשְׁתַּלַּח | יַשְׁלַח | יָשְׁלַח | |

## 5. III-ʾÁlep̄ Verbs

| | | *Qal* | *Niphal* | *Piel* | *Pual* | *Hithpael* | *Hiphil* | *Hophal* | |
|---|---|---|---|---|---|---|---|---|---|
| Perf. | *3 ms* | מָצָא | נִמְצָא | מִצֵּא | מֻצָּא | הִתְמַצֵּא | הִמְצִיא | הֻמְצָא | *3 ms* |
| | *3 fs* | מָֽצְאָה | נִמְצְאָה | מִצְּאָה | מֻצְּאָה | הִתְמַצְּאָה | הִמְצִיאָה | הֻמְצְאָה | *3 fs* |
| | *2 ms* | מָצָאתָ | נִמְצֵאתָ | מִצֵּאתָ | מֻצָּאתָ | הִתְמַצֵּאתָ | הִמְצֵאתָ | הֻמְצָאתָ | *2 ms* |
| | *2 fs* | מָצָאת | נִמְצֵאת | מִצֵּאת | מֻצָּאת | הִתְמַצֵּאת | הִמְצֵאת | הֻמְצָאת | *2 fs* |
| | *1 cs* | מָצָאתִי | נִמְצֵאתִי | מִצֵּאתִי | מֻצָּאתִי | הִתְמַצֵּאתִי | הִמְצֵאתִי | הֻמְצָאתִי | *1 cs* |
| | *3 cp* | מָֽצְאוּ | נִמְצְאוּ | מִצְּאוּ | מֻצְּאוּ | הִתְמַצְּאוּ | הִמְצִיאוּ | הֻמְצְאוּ | *3 cp* |
| | *2 mp* | מְצָאתֶם | נִמְצֵאתֶם | מִצֵּאתֶם | מֻצָּאתֶם | הִתְמַצֵּאתֶם | הִמְצֵאתֶם | הֻמְצָאתֶם | *2 mp* |
| | *2 fp* | מְצָאתֶן | נִמְצֵאתֶן | מִצֵּאתֶן | מֻצָּאתֶן | הִתְמַצֵּאתֶן | הִמְצֵאתֶן | הֻמְצָאתֶן | *2 fp* |
| | *1 cp* | מָצָאנוּ | נִמְצֵאנוּ | מִצֵּאנוּ | מֻצָּאנוּ | הִתְמַצֵּאנוּ | הִמְצֵאנוּ | הֻמְצָאנוּ | *1 cp* |
| Impf. | *3 ms* | יִמְצָא | יִמָּצֵא | יְמַצֵּא | יְמֻצָּא | יִתְמַצֵּא | יַמְצִיא | יֻמְצָא | *3 ms* |
| | *3 fs* | תִּמְצָא | תִּמָּצֵא | תְּמַצֵּא | תְּמֻצָּא | תִּתְמַצֵּא | תַּמְצִיא | תֻּמְצָא | *3 fs* |
| | *2 ms* | תִּמְצָא | תִּמָּצֵא | תְּמַצֵּא | תְּמֻצָּא | תִּתְמַצֵּא | תַּמְצִיא | תֻּמְצָא | *2 ms* |
| | *2 fs* | תִּמְצְאִי | תִּמָּֽצְאִי | תְּמַצְּאִי | תְּמֻצְּאִי | תִּתְמַצְּאִי | תַּמְצִיאִי | תֻּמְצְאִי | *2 fs* |
| | *1 cs* | אֶמְצָא | אֶמָּצֵא | אֲמַצֵּא | אֲמֻצָּא | אֶתְמַצֵּא | אַמְצִיא | אֻמְצָא | *1 cs* |
| | *3 mp* | יִמְצְאוּ | יִמָּֽצְאוּ | יְמַצְּאוּ | יְמֻצְּאוּ | יִתְמַצְּאוּ | יַמְצִיאוּ | יֻמְצְאוּ | *3 mp* |

| | | | | | | | | | |
|---|---|---|---|---|---|---|---|---|---|
| | *3 fp* | תִּמְצֶאנָה | תִּמָּצֶאנָה | תְּמַצֶּאנָה | תְּמֻצֶּאנָה | תִּתְמַצֶּאנָה | תַּמְצֶאנָה | תֻּמְצֶאנָה | *3 fp* |
| | *2 mp* | תִּמְצְאוּ | תִּמָּצְאוּ | תְּמַצְּאוּ | תְּמֻצְּאוּ | תִּתְמַצְּאוּ | תַּמְצִיאוּ | תֻּמְצְאוּ | *2 mp* |
| | *2 fp* | תִּמְצֶאנָה | תִּמָּצֶאנָה | תְּמַצֶּאנָה | תְּמֻצֶּאנָה | תִּתְמַצֶּאנָה | תַּמְצֶאנָה | תֻּמְצֶאנָה | *2 fp* |
| | *1 cp* | נִמְצָא | נִמָּצֵא | נְמַצֵּא | נְמֻצָּא | נִתְמַצֵּא | נַמְצִיא | נֻמְצָא | *1 cp* |
| Impv. | *2 ms* | מְצָא | הִמָּצֵא | מַצֵּא | | הִתְמַצֵּא | הַמְצֵא | | *2 ms* |
| | *2 fs* | מִצְאִי | הִמָּצְאִי | מַצְּאִי | | הִתְמַצְּאִי | הַמְצִיאִי | | *2 fs* |
| | *2 mp* | מִצְאוּ | הִמָּצְאוּ | מַצְּאוּ | | הִתְמַצְּאוּ | הַמְצִיאוּ | | *2 mp* |
| | *2 fp* | מְצֶאנָה | הִמָּצֶאנָה | מַצֶּאנָה | | הִתְמַצֶּאנָה | הַמְצֶאנָה | | *2 fp* |
| Inf. | *Abs.* | מָצוֹא | נִמְצֹא | מַצֹּא | | הִתְמַצֵּא | הַמְצֵא | | *Abs.* |
| | *Cs.* | מְצֹא | הִמָּצֵא | מַצֵּא | | הִתְמַצֵּא | הַמְצִיא | | *Cs.* |
| Ptc. | *Act.* | מֹצֵא | | מְמַצֵּא | | מִתְמַצֵּא | מַמְצִיא | | *Act.* |
| | *Pass.* | מָצוּא | נִמְצָא | | מְמֻצָּא | | | מֻמְצָא | *Pass.* |
| *wyqtl* | | וַיִּמְצָא | וַיִּמָּצֵא | וַיְמַצֵּא | וַיְמֻצָּא | וַיִּתְמַצֵּא | וַיַּמְצֵא | וַיֻּמְצָא | |
| Juss. | | יִמְצָא | יִמָּצֵא | יְמַצֵּא | יְמֻצָּא | יִתְמַצֵּא | יַמְצֵא | | |

## 6. III-Hē Verbs

| | | *Qal* | *Niphal* | *Piel* | *Pual* | *Hithpael* | *Hiphil* | *Hophal* | |
|---|---|---|---|---|---|---|---|---|---|
| Perf. | *3 ms* | גָּלָה | נִגְלָה | גִּלָּה | גֻּלָּה | הִתְגַּלָּה | הִגְלָה | הָגְלָה | *3 ms* |
| | *3 fs* | גָּֽלְתָה | נִגְלְתָה | גִּלְּתָה | גֻּלְּתָה | הִתְגַּלְּתָה | הִגְלְתָה | הָגְלְתָה | *3 fs* |
| | *2 ms* | גָּלִ֫יתָ | נִגְלֵ֫יתָ | גִּלִּ֫יתָ | גֻּלֵּ֫יתָ | הִתְגַּלִּ֫יתָ | הִגְלִ֫יתָ | הָגְלֵ֫יתָ | *2 ms* |
| | *2 fs* | גָּלִית | נִגְלֵית | גִּלִּית | גֻּלֵּית | הִתְגַּלִּית | הִגְלִית | הָגְלֵית | *2 fs* |
| | *1 cs* | גָּלִ֫יתִי | נִגְלֵ֫יתִי | גִּלִּ֫יתִי | גֻּלֵּ֫יתִי | הִתְגַּלִּ֫יתִי | הִגְלִ֫יתִי | הָגְלֵ֫יתִי | *1 cs* |
| | *3 cp* | גָּלוּ | נִגְלוּ | גִּלּוּ | גֻּלּוּ | הִתְגַּלּוּ | הִגְלוּ | הָגְלוּ | *3 cp* |
| | *2 mp* | גְּלִיתֶם | נִגְלֵיתֶם | גִּלִּיתֶם | גֻּלֵּיתֶם | הִתְגַּלִּיתֶם | הִגְלִיתֶם | הָגְלֵיתֶם | *2 mp* |
| | *2 fp* | גְּלִיתֶן | נִגְלֵיתֶן | גִּלִּיתֶן | גֻּלֵּיתֶן | הִתְגַּלִּיתֶן | הִגְלִיתֶן | הָגְלֵיתֶן | *2 fp* |
| | *1 cp* | גָּלִ֫ינוּ | נִגְלֵ֫ינוּ | גִּלִּ֫ינוּ | גֻּלֵּ֫ינוּ | הִתְגַּלִּ֫ינוּ | הִגְלִ֫ינוּ | הָגְלֵ֫ינוּ | *1 cp* |
| Impf. | *3 ms* | יִגְלֶה | יִגָּלֶה | יְגַלֶּה | יְגֻלֶּה | יִתְגַּלֶּה | יַגְלֶה | יָגְלֶה | *3 ms* |
| | *3 fs* | תִּגְלֶה | תִּגָּלֶה | תְּגַלֶּה | תְּגֻלֶּה | תִּתְגַּלֶּה | תַּגְלֶה | תָּגְלֶה | *3 fs* |
| | *2 ms* | תִּגְלֶה | תִּגָּלֶה | תְּגַלֶּה | תְּגֻלֶּה | תִּתְגַּלֶּה | תַּגְלֶה | תָּגְלֶה | *2 ms* |
| | *2 fs* | תִּגְלִי | תִּגָּלִי | תְּגַלִּי | תְּגֻלִּי | תִּתְגַּלִּי | תַּגְלִי | תָּגְלִי | *2 fs* |
| | *1 cs* | אֶגְלֶה | אֶגָּלֶה | אֲגַלֶּה | אֲגֻלֶּה | אֶתְגַּלֶּה | אַגְלֶה | אָגְלֶה | *1 cs* |
| | *3 mp* | יִגְלוּ | יִגָּלוּ | יְגַלּוּ | יְגֻלּוּ | יִתְגַּלּוּ | יַגְלוּ | יָגְלוּ | *3 mp* |

| | | | | | | | | | |
|---|---|---|---|---|---|---|---|---|---|
| | 3 fp | תִּגְלֶינָה | תִּגָּלֶינָה | תְּגַלֶּינָה | תְּגֻלֶּינָה | תִּתְגַּלֶּינָה | תַּגְלֶינָה | תָּגְלֶינָה | 3 fp |
| | 2 mp | תִּגְלוּ | תִּגָּלוּ | תְּגַלּוּ | תְּגֻלּוּ | תִּתְגַּלּוּ | תַּגְלוּ | תָּגְלוּ | 2 mp |
| | 2 fp | תִּגְלֶינָה | תִּגָּלֶינָה | תְּגַלֶּינָה | תְּגֻלֶּינָה | תִּתְגַּלֶּינָה | תַּגְלֶינָה | תָּגְלֶינָה | 2 fp |
| | 1 cp | נִגְלֶה | נִגָּלֶה | נְגַלֶּה | נְגֻלֶּה | נִתְגַּלֶּה | נַגְלֶה | נָגְלֶה | 1 cp |
| Impv. | 2 ms | גְּלֵה | הִגָּלֵה | גַּלֵּה | | הִתְגַּלֵּה | הַגְלֵה | | 2 ms |
| | 2 fs | גְּלִי | הִגָּלִי | גַּלִּי | | הִתְגַּלִּי | הַגְלִי | | 2 fs |
| | 2 mp | גְּלוּ | הִגָּלוּ | גַּלּוּ | | הִתְגַּלּוּ | הַגְלוּ | | 2 mp |
| | 2 fp | גְּלֶינָה | הִגָּלֶינָה | גַּלֶּינָה | | הִתְגַּלֶּינָה | הַגְלֶינָה | | 2 fp |
| Inf. | *Abs.* | גָּלוֹה | נִגְלֹה | גַּלֵּה | | | הַגְלֵה | הָגְלֵה | *Abs.* |
| | | | הִגָּלֵה | גַּלֹּה | | | | | |
| | *Cs.* | גְּלוֹת | הִגָּלוֹת | גַּלּוֹת | גֻּלּוֹת | הִתְגַּלּוֹת | הַגְלוֹת | | *Cs.* |
| Ptc. | *Act.* | גֹּלֶה | | מְגַלֶּה | | מִתְגַּלֶּה | מַגְלֶה | | *Act.* |
| | *Pass.* | גָּלוּי | נִגְלֶה | | מְגֻלֶּה | | | מָגְלֶה | *Pass.* |
| *wyqṭl* | | וַיִּגֶל | וַיִּגָּל | וַיְגַל | וַיְגֻל | וַיִּתְגַּל | וַיֶּגֶל | | |
| Juss. | | יִגֶל | יִגָּל | יְגַל | יְגֻל | יִתְגַּל | יֶגֶל | | |

# 7. I-Nûn Verbs

| | | Qal | | | Niphal | Hiphil | Hophal | |
|---|---|---|---|---|---|---|---|---|
| Perf. | 3 ms | נָפַל | נָגַע | נָתַן | נִצַּל | הִצִּיל | הֻצַּל | 3 ms |
| | 3 fs | נָֽפְלָה | נָֽגְעָה | נָֽתְנָה | נִצְּלָה | הִצִּ֫ילָה | הֻצְּלָה | 3 fs |
| | 2 ms | נָפַ֫לְתָּ | נָגַ֫עְתָּ | נָתַ֫תָּ | נִצַּ֫לְתָּ | הִצַּ֫לְתָּ | הֻצַּ֫לְתָּ | 2 ms |
| | 2 fs | נָפַלְתְּ | נָגַ֫עַתְּ | נָתַתְּ | נִצַּלְתְּ | הִצַּלְתְּ | הֻצַּלְתְּ | 2 fs |
| | 1 cs | נָפַ֫לְתִּי | נָגַ֫עְתִּי | נָתַ֫תִּי | נִצַּ֫לְתִּי | הִצַּ֫לְתִּי | הֻצַּ֫לְתִּי | 1 cs |
| | 3 cp | נָֽפְלוּ | נָֽגְעוּ | נָֽתְנוּ | נִצְּלוּ | הִצִּ֫ילוּ | הֻצְּלוּ | 3 cp |
| | 2 mp | נְפַלְתֶּם | נְגַעְתֶּם | נְתַתֶּם | נִצַּלְתֶּם | הִצַּלְתֶּם | הֻצַּלְתֶּם | 2 mp |
| | 2 fp | נְפַלְתֶּן | נְגַעְתֶּן | נְתַתֶּן | נִצַּלְתֶּן | הִצַּלְתֶּן | הֻצַּלְתֶּן | 2 fp |
| | 1 cp | נָפַ֫לְנוּ | נָגַ֫עְנוּ | נָתַ֫נּוּ | נִצַּ֫לְנוּ | הִצַּ֫לְנוּ | הֻצַּ֫לְנוּ | 1 cp |
| Impf. | 3 ms | יִפֹּל | יִגַּע | יִתֵּן | יִנָּצֵל | יַצִּיל | יֻצַּל | 3 ms |
| | 3 fs | תִּפֹּל | תִּגַּע | תִּתֵּן | תִּנָּצֵל | תַּצִּיל | תֻּצַּל | 3 fs |
| | 2 ms | תִּפֹּל | תִּגַּע | תִּתֵּן | תִּנָּצֵל | תַּצִּיל | תֻּצַּל | 2 ms |
| | 2 fs | תִּפְּלִי | תִּגְּעִי | תִּתְּנִי | תִּנָּֽצְלִי | תַּצִּ֫ילִי | תֻּצְּלִי | 2 fs |
| | 1 cs | אֶפֹּל | אֶגַּע | אֶתֵּן | אֶנָּצֵל | אַצִּיל | אֻצַּל | 1 cs |
| | 3 mp | יִפְּלוּ | יִגְּעוּ | יִתְּנוּ | יִנָּֽצְלוּ | יַצִּ֫ילוּ | יֻצְּלוּ | 3 mp |

| | | | | | | | | |
|---|---|---|---|---|---|---|---|---|
| | *3 fp* | תִּפֹּ֫לְנָה | תִּגַּ֫עְנָה | תִּתֵּ֫נָּה | תִּנָּצַ֫לְנָה | תַּצֵּ֫לְנָה | תֻּצַּ֫לְנָה | *3 fp* |
| | *2 mp* | תִּפְּלוּ | תִּגְּעוּ | תִּתְּנוּ | תִּנָּצְלוּ | תַּצִּ֫ילוּ | תֻּצְּלוּ | *2 mp* |
| | *2 fp* | תִּפֹּ֫לְנָה | תִּגַּ֫עְנָה | תִּתֵּ֫נָּה | תִּנָּצַ֫לְנָה | תַּצֵּ֫לְנָה | תֻּצַּ֫לְנָה | *2 fp* |
| | *1 cp* | נִפֹּל | נִגַּע | נִתֵּן | נִנָּצֵל | נַצִּיל | נֻצַּל | *1 cp* |
| Impv. | *2 ms* | נְפֹל | גַּע | תֵּן | הִנָּצֵל | הַצֵּל | | *2 ms* |
| | *2 fs* | נִפְלִי | גְּעִי | תְּנִי | הִנָּצְלִי | הַצִּ֫ילִי | | *2 fs* |
| | *2 mp* | נִפְלוּ | גְּעוּ | תְּנוּ | הִנָּצְלוּ | הַצִּ֫ילוּ | | *2 mp* |
| | *2 fp* | נְפֹ֫לְנָה | גַּ֫עְנָה | תֵּ֫נָּה | הִנָּצַ֫לְנָה | הַצֵּ֫לְנָה | | *2 fp* |
| Inf. | *Abs.* | נָפוֹל | נָגוֹעַ | נָתוֹן | הִנָּצֵל | הַצֵּל | הֻצֵּל | *Abs.* |
| | *Cs.* | נְפֹל | גַּ֫עַת | תֵּת | הִנָּצֵל | הַצִּיל | הֻצַּל | *Cs.* |
| | | | נְגֹעַ | נְתֹן | | | | |
| Ptc. | *Act.* | נֹפֵל | נֹגֵעַ | נֹתֵן | | מַצִּיל | | *Act.* |
| | *Pass.* | נָפוּל | נָגוּעַ | נָתוּן | נִצָּל | | מֻצָּל | *Pass.* |
| *wyqṭl* | | וַיִּפֹּל | וַיִּגַּע | וַיִּתֵּן | וַיִּנָּצֵל | וַיַּצֵּל | וַיֻּצַּל | |
| Juss. | | יִפֹּל | יִגַּע | יִתֵּן | יִנָּצֵל | יַצֵּל | | |

## 8. I-Wāw/Yōḏ Verbs

| | | Qal | Niphal | Hiphil | Hophal | Qal | Hiphil | |
|---|---|---|---|---|---|---|---|---|
| Perf. | *3 ms* | יָשַׁב | נוֹשַׁב | הוֹשִׁיב | הוּשַׁב | | הֵיטִיב | *3 ms* |
| | *3 fs* | יָֽשְׁבָה | נוֹשְׁבָה | הוֹשִׁ֫יבָה | הוּשְׁבָה | | הֵיטִ֫יבָה | *3 fs* |
| | *2 ms* | יָשַׁ֫בְתָּ | נוֹשַׁ֫בְתָּ | הוֹשַׁ֫בְתָּ | הוּשַׁ֫בְתָּ | | הֵיטַ֫בְתָּ | *2 ms* |
| | *2 fs* | יָשַׁבְתְּ | נוֹשַׁבְתְּ | הוֹשַׁבְתְּ | הוּשַׁבְתְּ | | הֵיטַבְתְּ | *2 fs* |
| | *1 cs* | יָשַׁ֫בְתִּי | נוֹשַׁ֫בְתִּי | הוֹשַׁ֫בְתִּי | הוּשַׁ֫בְתִּי | | הֵיטַ֫בְתִּי | *1 cs* |
| | *3 cp* | יָֽשְׁבוּ | נוֹשְׁבוּ | הוֹשִׁ֫יבוּ | הוּשְׁבוּ | | הֵיטִ֫יבוּ | *3 cp* |
| | *2 mp* | יְשַׁבְתֶּם | נוֹשַׁבְתֶּם | הוֹשַׁבְתֶּם | הוּשַׁבְתֶּם | | הֵיטַבְתֶּם | *2 mp* |
| | *2 fp* | יְשַׁבְתֶּן | נוֹשַׁבְתֶּן | הוֹשַׁבְתֶּן | הוּשַׁבְתֶּן | | הֵיטַבְתֶּן | *2 fp* |
| | *1 cp* | יָשַׁ֫בְנוּ | נוֹשַׁ֫בְנוּ | הוֹשַׁ֫בְנוּ | הוּשַׁ֫בְנוּ | | הֵיטַ֫בְנוּ | *1 cp* |
| Impf. | *3 ms* | יֵשֵׁב | יִוָּשֵׁב | יוֹשִׁיב | יוּשַׁב | יִיטַב | יֵיטִיב | *3 ms* |
| | *3 fs* | תֵּשֵׁב | תִּוָּשֵׁב | תּוֹשִׁיב | תּוּשַׁב | תִּיטַב | תֵּיטִיב | *3 fs* |
| | *2 ms* | תֵּשֵׁב | תִּוָּשֵׁב | תּוֹשִׁיב | תּוּשַׁב | תִּיטַב | תֵּיטִיב | *2 ms* |
| | *2 fs* | תֵּֽשְׁבִי | תִּוָּֽשְׁבִי | תּוֹשִׁ֫יבִי | תּוּשְׁבִי | תִּיטְבִי | תֵּיטִ֫יבִי | *2 fs* |
| | *1 cs* | אֵשֵׁב | אִוָּשֵׁב | אוֹשִׁיב | אוּשַׁב | אִיטַב | אֵיטִיב | *1 cs* |
| | *3 mp* | יֵֽשְׁבוּ | יִוָּֽשְׁבוּ | יוֹשִׁ֫יבוּ | יוּשְׁבוּ | יִיטְבוּ | יֵיטִ֫יבוּ | *3 mp* |

| | | | | | | | | |
|---|---|---|---|---|---|---|---|---|
| | *3 fp* | תֵּשַׁ֫בְנָה | תִּוָּשַׁ֫בְנָה | תּוֹשֵׁ֫בְנָה | תּוּשַׁ֫בְנָה | תִּיטַ֫בְנָה | תֵּיטֵ֫בְנָה | *3 fp* |
| | *2 mp* | תֵּשְׁבוּ | תִּוָּשְׁבוּ | תּוֹשִׁ֫יבוּ | תּוּשְׁבוּ | תִּיטְבוּ | תֵּיטִ֫יבוּ | *2 mp* |
| | *2 fp* | תֵּשַׁ֫בְנָה | תִּוָּשַׁ֫בְנָה | תּוֹשֵׁ֫בְנָה | תּוּשַׁ֫בְנָה | תִּיטַ֫בְנָה | תֵּיטֵ֫בְנָה | *2 fp* |
| | *1 cp* | נֵשֵׁב | נִוָּשֵׁב | נוֹשִׁיב | נוּשַׁב | נִיטַב | נֵיטִיב | *1 cp* |
| Impv. | *2 ms* | שֵׁב | הִוָּשֵׁב | הוֹשֵׁב | | | הֵיטֵב | *2 ms* |
| | *2 fs* | שְׁבִי | הִוָּשְׁבִי | הוֹשִׁ֫יבִי | | | הֵיטִ֫יבִי | *2 fs* |
| | *2 mp* | שְׁבוּ | הִוָּשְׁבוּ | הוֹשִׁ֫יבוּ | | | הֵיטִ֫יבוּ | *2 mp* |
| | *2 fp* | שֵׁ֫בְנָה | הִוָּשַׁ֫בְנָה | הוֹשֵׁ֫בְנָה | | | הֵיטֵ֫בְנָה | *2 fp* |
| Inf. | *Abs.* | יָשׁוֹב | הִוָּשֵׁב | הוֹשֵׁב | | | הֵיטֵב | *Abs.* |
| | *Cs.* | שֶׁ֫בֶת | הִוָּשֵׁב | הוֹשִׁיב | הוּשַׁב | | הֵיטִיב | *Cs.* |
| Ptc. | *Act.* | יֹשֵׁב | | מוֹשִׁיב | | יֹטֵב | מֵיטִיב | *Act.* |
| | *Pass.* | יָשׁוּב | נוֹשָׁב | | מוּשָׁב | | | *Pass.* |
| *wyqṭl* | | וַיֵּ֫שֶׁב | וַיִּוָּשֵׁב | וַיּ֫וֹשֶׁב | וַיּוּשַׁב | וַיִּיטַב | וַיֵּ֫יטֶב | |
| Juss. | | יֵ֫שֶׁב | יִוָּשֵׁב | יוֹשֵׁב | יוּשַׁב | יִיטַב | יֵיטֶב | |

## 9. II-Wāw Verbs

| | | *Qal* | *Niphal* | *Polel* | *Polal* | *Hiphil* | *Hophal* | |
|---|---|---|---|---|---|---|---|---|
| Perf. | *3 ms* | קָם | נָכוֹן | קוֹמֵם | קוֹמַם | הֵקִים | הוּקַם | *3 ms* |
| | *3 fs* | קָ֫מָה | נָכ֫וֹנָה | קוֹמְמָה | קוֹמְמָה | הֵקִ֫ימָה | הוּקְמָה | *3 fs* |
| | *2 ms* | קַ֫מְתָּ | נְכוּנ֫וֹתָ | קוֹמַ֫מְתָּ | קוֹמַ֫מְתָּ | הֲקִימ֫וֹתָ | הוּקַ֫מְתָּ | *2 ms* |
| | *2 fs* | קַמְתְּ | נְכוּנוֹת | קוֹמַמְתְּ | קוֹמַמְתְּ | הֲקִימוֹת | הוּקַמְתְּ | *2 fs* |
| | *1 cs* | קַ֫מְתִּי | נְכוּנ֫וֹתִי | קוֹמַ֫מְתִּי | קוֹמַ֫מְתִּי | הֲקִימ֫וֹתִי | הוּקַ֫מְתִּי | *1 cs* |
| | *3 cp* | קָ֫מוּ | נָכ֫וֹנוּ | קוֹמְמוּ | קוֹמְמוּ | הֵקִ֫ימוּ | הוּקְמוּ | *3 cp* |
| | *2 mp* | קַמְתֶּם | נְכוּנוֹתֶם | קוֹמַמְתֶּם | קוֹמַמְתֶּם | הֲקִימוֹתֶם | הוּקַמְתֶּם | *2 mp* |
| | *2 fp* | קַמְתֶּן | נְכוּנוֹתֶן | קוֹמַמְתֶּן | קוֹמַמְתֶּן | הֲקִימוֹתֶן | הוּקַמְתֶּן | *2 fp* |
| | *1 cp* | קַ֫מְנוּ | נְכוּנ֫וֹנוּ | קוֹמַ֫מְנוּ | קוֹמַ֫מְנוּ | הֲקִימ֫וֹנוּ | הוּקַ֫מְנוּ | *1 cp* |
| Impf. | *3 ms* | יָקוּם | יִכּוֹן | יְקוֹמֵם | יְקוֹמַם | יָקִים | יוּקַם | *3 ms* |
| | *3 fs* | תָּקוּם | תִּכּוֹן | תְּקוֹמֵם | תְּקוֹמַם | תָּקִים | תּוּקַם | *3 fs* |
| | *2 ms* | תָּקוּם | תִּכּוֹן | תְּקוֹמֵם | תְּקוֹמַם | תָּקִים | תּוּקַם | *2 ms* |
| | *2 fs* | תָּק֫וּמִי | תִּכּ֫וֹנִי | תְּקוֹמְמִי | תְּקוֹמְמִי | תָּקִ֫ימִי | תּוּקְמִי | *2 fs* |
| | *1 cs* | אָקוּם | אֶכּוֹן | אֲקוֹמֵם | אֲקוֹמַם | אָקִים | אוּקַם | *1 cs* |
| | *3 mp* | יָק֫וּמוּ | יִכּ֫וֹנוּ | יְקוֹמְמוּ | יְקוֹמְמוּ | יָקִ֫ימוּ | יוּקְמוּ | *3 mp* |

| | | | | | | | | |
|---|---|---|---|---|---|---|---|---|
| | *3 fp* | תְּקוּמֶ֫ינָה | תִּכּ֫וֹנָּה | תְּקוֹמֵ֫מְנָה | תְּקוֹמַ֫מְנָה | תְּקִמֶ֫ינָה | תּוּקַ֫מְנָה | *3 fp* |
| | *2 mp* | תָּק֫וּמוּ | תִּכּ֫וֹנוּ | תְּקוֹמְמוּ | תְּקוֹמְמוּ | תָּקִ֫ימוּ | תּוּקְמוּ | *2 mp* |
| | *2 fp* | תְּקוּמֶ֫ינָה | תִּכּ֫וֹנָּה | תְּקוֹמֵ֫מְנָה | תְּקוֹמַ֫מְנָה | תְּקִמֶ֫ינָה | תּוּקַ֫מְנָה | *2 fp* |
| | *1 cp* | נָקוּם | נִכּוֹן | נְקוֹמֵם | נְקוֹמַם | נָקִים | נוּקַם | *1 cp* |
| Impv. | *2 ms* | קוּם | הִכּוֹן | קוֹמֵם | | הָקֵם | | *2 ms* |
| | *2 fs* | ק֫וּמִי | הִכּ֫וֹנִי | קוֹמְמִי | | הָקִ֫ימִי | | *2 fs* |
| | *2 mp* | ק֫וּמוּ | הִכּ֫וֹנוּ | קוֹמְמוּ | | הָקִ֫ימוּ | | *2 mp* |
| | *2 fp* | קֹ֫מְנָה | הִכּ֫וֹנָּה | קוֹמֵ֫מְנָה | | הָקֵ֫מְנָה | | *2 fp* |
| Inf. | *Abs.* | קוֹם | הִכּוֹן | | | הָקֵם | | *Abs.* |
| | *Cs.* | קוּם | הִכּוֹן | קוֹמֵם | | הָקִים | הוּקַם | *Cs.* |
| Ptc. | *Act.* | קָם | | מְקוֹמֵם | | מֵקִים | | *Act.* |
| | *Pass.* | קוּם | נָכוֹן | | מְקוֹמָם | | מוּקָם | *Pass.* |
| *wyqṭl* | | וַיָּ֫קָם | וַיִּכּוֹן | וַיְקוֹמֵם | וַיְקוֹמַם | וַיָּ֫קֶם | וַיּוּקַם | |
| Juss. | | יָקֹם | יִכּוֹן | יְקוֹמֵם | יְקוֹמַם | יָקֵם | יוּקַם | |

## 10. Geminate Verbs

| | | *Qal* | | *Niphal* | *Hiphil* | *Hophal* | |
|---|---|---|---|---|---|---|---|
| Perf. | *3 ms* | סָבַב | תַּם | נָסַב | הֵסֵב | הוּסַב | *3 ms* |
| | *3 fs* | סָֽבֲבָה | תַּ֫מָּה | נָסַ֫בָּה | הֵסֵ֫בָּה | הוּסַ֫בָּה | *3 fs* |
| | *2 ms* | סַבּ֫וֹתָ | תַּ֫מּוֹתָ | נְסַבּ֫וֹתָ | הֲסִבּ֫וֹתָ | הוּסַבּ֫וֹתָ | *2 ms* |
| | *2 fs* | סַבּוֹת | תַּמּוֹת | נְסַבּוֹת | הֲסִבּוֹת | הוּסַבּוֹת | *2 fs* |
| | *1 cs* | סַבּ֫וֹתִי | תַּ֫מּוֹתִי | נְסַבּ֫וֹתִי | הֲסִבּ֫וֹתִי | הוּסַבּ֫וֹתִי | *1 cs* |
| | *3 cp* | סָֽבֲבוּ | תַּ֫מּוּ | נָסַ֫בּוּ | הֵסֵ֫בּוּ | הוּסַ֫בּוּ | *3 cp* |
| | *2 mp* | סַבּוֹתֶם | תַּמּוֹתֶם | נְסַבּוֹתֶם | הֲסִבּוֹתֶם | הוּסַבּוֹתֶם | *2 mp* |
| | *2 fp* | סַבּוֹתֶן | תַּמּוֹתֶן | נְסַבּוֹתֶן | הֲסִבּוֹתֶן | הוּסַבּוֹתֶן | *2 fp* |
| | *1 cp* | סַבּ֫וֹנוּ | תַּ֫מּוֹנוּ | נְסַבּ֫וֹנוּ | הֲסִבּ֫וֹנוּ | הוּסַבּ֫וֹנוּ | *1 cp* |
| Impf. | *3 ms* | יָסֹב | יֵתַם | יִסַּב | יָסֵב | יוּסַב | *3 ms* |
| | *3 fs* | תָּסֹב | תֵּתַם | תִּסַּב | תָּסֵב | תּוּסַב | *3 fs* |
| | *2 ms* | תָּסֹב | תֵּתַם | תִּסַּב | תָּסֵב | תּוּסַב | *2 ms* |
| | *2 fs* | תָּסֹ֫בִּי | תֵּתַ֫מִּי | תִּסַּ֫בִּי | תָּסֵ֫בִּי | תּוּסַ֫בִּי | *2 fs* |
| | *1 cs* | אָסֹב | אֵתַם | אֶסַּב | אָסֵב | אוּסַב | *1 cs* |
| | *3 mp* | יָסֹ֫בּוּ | יֵתַ֫מּוּ | יִסַּ֫בּוּ | יָסֵ֫בּוּ | יוּסַ֫בּוּ | *3 mp* |

| | | | | | | | |
|---|---|---|---|---|---|---|---|
| | *3 fp* | תְּסֻבֶּ֫ינָה | תְּתַמֶּ֫ינָה | תִּסַּבֶּ֫ינָה | תְּסִבֶּ֫ינָה | תּוּסַבֶּ֫ינָה | *3 fp* |
| | *2 mp* | תָּסֹ֫בּוּ | תֵּתַ֫מּוּ | תִּסַּ֫בּוּ | תָּסֵ֫בּוּ | תּוּסַ֫בּוּ | *2 mp* |
| | *2 fp* | תְּסֻבֶּ֫ינָה | תְּתַמֶּ֫ינָה | תִּסַּבֶּ֫ינָה | תְּסִבֶּ֫ינָה | תּוּסַבֶּ֫ינָה | *2 fp* |
| | *1 cp* | נָסֹב | נֵתַם | נִסַּב | נָסֵב | נוּסַב | *1 cp* |
| Impv. | *2 ms* | סֹב | תַּם | הִסַּב | הָסֵב | | *2 ms* |
| | *2 fs* | סֹ֫בִּי | תַּ֫מִּי | הִסַּ֫בִּי | הָסֵ֫בִּי | | *2 fs* |
| | *2 mp* | סֹ֫בּוּ | תַּ֫מּוּ | הִסַּ֫בּוּ | הָסֵ֫בּוּ | | *2 mp* |
| | *2 fp* | סֹ֫בְנָה | תַּ֫מְנָה | הִסַּבֶּ֫ינָה | הֲסִבֶּ֫ינָה | | *2 fp* |
| Inf. | *Abs.* | סָבוֹב | | הִסֹּב | הָסֵב | | *Abs.* |
| | *Cs.* | סֹב | תֹּם | הִסֵּב | הֵסֵב | | *Cs.* |
| Ptc. | *Act.* | סֹבֵב | תַּם | נָסָב | מֵסֵב | | *Act.* |
| | *Pass.* | סָבוּב | | | | מוּסָב | *Pass.* |
| *wyqṭl* | | וַיָּ֫סָב | וַיִּ֫תַּם | וַיִּסַּב | וַיָּ֫סֶב | וַיּוּסַב | |
| Juss. | | יָסֹב | יֵתַם | יִסַּב | יָסֵב | יוּסַב | |

# English-Hebrew Glossary*

be able יָכֹל (XIX)
be afraid יָרֵא (XIII)
after אַחֲרֵי, אַחַר (VI)
angel מַלְאָךְ (IV)
announce הִגִּיד (XVI)
anoint מָשַׁח (XIII)
another אַחֵר (VII)
answer עָנָה (XVII)
be ashamed בּוֹשׁ (XIV)
ask שָׁאַל (VIII)

battle מִלְחָמָה (IV)
be הָיָה (XIV)
bear (beget) יָלַד (VIII)
bless בֵּרַךְ (XV)
brother אָח (V)
build בָּנָה (VIII)
burnt offering עוֹלָה (IV)

camp חָנָה (XII)
cast out הִשְׁלִיךְ (XVI)
city עִיר (V)
charge צִוָּה (XV)
choose בָּחַר (XIV)
cloud עָנָן (XII)
come בּוֹא (VIII)
command צִוָּה (XV)

complete (verb) כִּלָּה (XV)
consecrate קִדֵּשׁ (XV)
consume אָכַל (VIII)
count סִפֵּר (XV)
covenant בְּרִית (II)
criminal (adj.) רָשָׁע (VII)

Daniel דָּנִאֵל (IX)
darkness חֹשֶׁךְ (II)
daughter בַּת (V)
David דָּוִד (VI)
day יוֹם (V)
deed מַעֲשֶׂה (V)
die מוּת (XIV)
do עָשָׂה (V)
drink שָׁתָה (XVI)

ear אֹזֶן (III)
earth אֶרֶץ (III)
eat אָכַל (VIII)
enter בּוֹא (VIII)
evil רַע (VII)
eye עַיִן (III)

face פָּנִים (III)
famine רָעָב (VII)
fast צוֹם (XX)
father אָב (V)

* This glossary is intended to assist students in doing the English-Hebrew exercises and does not represent a complete list of words in the book. The verbs are given according to the pertinent verbal pattern, and the lesson in which the word appears in the Vocabulary is given in parentheses.

field שָׂדֶה (IX)
fill מִלֵּא (XIV)
fire אֵשׁ (IX)
flee נוּס (XIX)
food לֶ֫חֶם (IV)
forget שָׁכַח (XVII)
forsake עָזַב (XIII)
from מִן (VI)
fruit פְּרִי (IV)

garment בֶּ֫גֶד (XI)
give נָתַן (VIII)
go הָלַךְ (VIII)
go forth יָצָא (VIII)
good גָּדוֹל (VII)
govern מָשַׁל בְּ- (X)

hand יָד (III)
hasten מִהַר (XV)
hate שָׂנֵא (XVII)
head רֹאשׁ (V)
heaven שָׁמַ֫יִם (III)
heavy כָּבֵד (VII)
holy קָדוֹשׁ (II)
hurry מִהַר (XV)

important כָּבֵד (VII)
in בְּ- (VI)
iniquity עָוֹן (IV)
inquire דָּרַשׁ (XVI)
instead תַּ֫חַת (VI)
Israel יִשְׂרָאֵל (X)

Jerusalem יְרוּשָׁלַ֫ם (VI)
Judah יְהוּדָה (VI)

judge (noun) שֹׁפֵט (III)
judgment מִשְׁפָּט (III)

keep שָׁמַר (VIII)
kill הָרַג (XVI)
kingdom מַמְלָכָה (II)
know יָדַע (VIII)

lad נַ֫עַר (X)
leave עָזַב (XIII)
lie (recline) שָׁכַב (X)
live (verb) חָיָה (XIV)
life חַיִּים (VII)
lift נָשָׂא (XIV)
light אוֹר (IV)
like (as) כְּ- (VI)
listen שָׁמַע (VIII)
little קָטֹן (VII)
love (verb) אָהַב (VIII)

make עָשָׂה (V)
many רַב (VII)
master אָדוֹן (IV)
matter דָּבָר (II)
messenger מַלְאָךְ (IV)
minister (serve) שֵׁרֵת (XV)
mother אֵם (III)
mountain הַר (VI)
mouth פֶּה (III)

name שֵׁם (IX)
nation גּוֹי (II)
new חָדָשׁ (II)
night לַ֫יְלָה (VI)
nose אַף (XII)

old, be old זָקֵן (VII; XIII)

palace הֵיכָל (IV)
people עַם (V)
perform פָּעַל (XV)
place מָקוֹם (IV)
plant נָטַע (XVI)
possess יָרַשׁ (XIX)
praise הִלֵּל (XV)
precious יָקָר (VII)
prevail חָזַק (VII)
priest כֹּהֵן (III)
prince שַׂר (V)
prophet נָבִיא (II)

ram אַיִל (IV)
record (write) כָּתַב (VIII)
recount סִפֵּר (XV)
register (write) כָּתַב (VIII)
reject מָאַס (XX)
remember זָכַר (XIII)
reside יָשַׁב (VIII)
righteous צַדִּיק (II)
run רוּץ (XIX)

sacrifice זָבַח (IX)
save הוֹשִׁיעַ (XVI)
say אָמַר (VIII)
see רָאָה (VIII)
seed זֶרַע (IX)
seek בִּקֵּשׁ (XV)
send שָׁלַח (IX)
set שִׂים (XIV)
sign אוֹת (X)
sin offering חַטָּאת (VI)
sit יָשַׁב (VIII)
snatch (XVI) הִצִּיל
sojourn (XIV) גּוּר
spirit (IV) רוּחַ
staff (VIII) מַטֶּה
stand (VIII) עָמַד
stone (IV) אֶבֶן
strength (XII) עֹז
stretch out נָטָה (VIII); שָׁלַח (IX)
strike הִכָּה (XVI)
sword חֶרֶב (III)

take לָקַח (XIII)
tent אֹהֶל (V)
this זֶה, זֹאת (X)
touch נָגַע (XX)

very מְאֹד (VII)
vessel כְּלִי (V)

where? אַיֵּה (X)
who? מִי (X)
whoever מִי (X)
wicked רָשָׁע (VII)
wife אִשָּׁה (V)
be willing אָבָה (XIII)
wisdom חָכְמָה (II)
woman אִשָּׁה (V)
word דָּבָר (II)
write כָּתַב (VIII)

# Scripture Index

(not including texts in the Exercises)

# Subject Index